1-2-3® for Windows™ QuickStart

Greg Harvey

1-2-3® for Windows QuickStart™

Copyright © 1991 by Que Corporation

Library of Congress Catalog Number: 91-062306

ISBN 0-88022-723-0

94   93   92   91   4   3   2   1

Interpretation of the printing code: the rightmost double-digit number is the year of the book's printing; the rightmost single-digit number is the number of the book's printing. For example, a printing code of 91-4 shows that the fourth printing of the book occurred in 1991.

Screens reproduced in this book were created using Collage Plus from Inner Media, Inc., Hollis, NH.

1-2-3 for Windows QuickStart covers 1-2-3 for Windows Version 1.0.

Publisher: Lloyd J. Short

Associate Publisher: Karen A. Bluestein

Acquisitions Editor: Tim Ryan

Product Development Manager: Mary Bednarek

Managing Editor: Paul Boger

Designer: Scott Cook

Production Team: Jill Bomaster, Scott Boucher, Brad Chinn, Denny Hager, Phil Kitchell, Anne Owen, Julie Pavey, Tad Ringo, Bruce Steed, Lisa Wilson

About the Author

Greg Harvey is a well-known computer consultant and author of training manuals and user guides. He has taught 1-2-3 to users of all levels for the past four years. Besides 1-2-3, Harvey has written books on popular PC software packages such as WordPerfect and WordStar, and Macintosh packages such as HyperCard and PageMaker.

Product Directors
Kathie-Jo Arnoff
Joyce Nielsen

Production Editor
Cheryl Robinson

Editors
Jo Anna Arnott
Pamela Wampler
Laura Wirthlin

Technical Editors
Jerry Ellis
Rick Winter

*Composed in Garamond and Macmillan
by Que Corporation*

Trademark Acknowledgments

Contents at a Glance

Table of Contents

Introduction

If you are new to Lotus 1-2-3 for Windows or are upgrading from an earlier DOS version (such as Release 2.2 or 3.1) this book is for you. *1-2-3 for Windows QuickStart* allows you to grasp the basics of using 1-2-3 for Windows—enabling you to begin creating your own worksheets (or modify existing worksheets created by others) with a minimum of effort. You don't even need to be familiar with Windows or mice—all the basics are covered, as well as how to install 1-2-3 if it is not already installed on your computer.

1-2-3 for Windows QuickStart uses a tutorial approach that takes you through important concepts step-by-step, describing all the fundamentals you need to know about the program. The text supplies essential information and provides comments on what you see. Many illustrations help guide you through procedures and clarify new concepts.

Learning any new program can be an intimidating experience. *1-2-3 for Windows QuickStart* is designed to help shorten your learning curve by enabling you to learn basic concepts quickly. Whether you are completely new to 1-2-3 or are already a user of an earlier DOS-based version, you will find *1-2-3 for Windows QuickStart* an efficient method for learning the fundamentals of this new, graphical 1-2-3.

What does this book contain?

Who should use this book?

What do you need to run 1-2-3 for Windows?

What is new in 1-2-3 for Windows?

Conventions used in this book

What Does This Book Contain?

The chapters in *1-2-3 for Windows QuickStart* are organized to take you from basic information to more sophisticated tasks, including creating macros and customizing the Icon palette.

Chapter 1, "An Overview of 1-2-3," shows you the wide range of 1-2-3's capabilities and gives you valuable information on the benefits of using 1-2-3 under the graphical user interface offered by Windows. In this chapter you learn how 1-2-3 functions as a spreadsheet, and you learn about its charting, database, and macro capabilities, as well as its compatibility with other versions of 1-2-3.

Chapter 2, "Introducing Worksheet Fundamentals," introduces you to the parts of the 1-2-3 window and worksheet windows, using the mouse and keyboard, and accessing 1-2-3's on-line Help window.

Chapter 3, "Getting Started," teaches you how to start 1-2-3 for Windows and open worksheet files. You also learn how to navigate the Worksheet window, select 1-2-3 commands in pull-down menus and dialog boxes, save your worksheet files, exit 1-2-3 for Windows, and switch between 1-2-3 and other programs that you run under Windows.

Chapters 4, 5, and 6 cover all the basic tasks you need to begin creating your own spreadsheets. Chapter 4, "Entering and Formatting Data," teaches how to enter, edit, and enhance all types of data (including labels, values, and formulas) in your worksheet. Chapter 5, "Working with Ranges," shows you how to select and name a cell range. It also shows you how to cut and paste and search for strings in ranges of data in a worksheet. And Chapter 6, "Managing the Worksheet Environment," explains how to modify your worksheet by changing column widths and row heights, freezing titles, and splitting the Worksheet window into separate panes. It also teaches you how to modify the display of the 1-2-3 window as well as control when and how a worksheet is recalculated and protect a worksheet model from further changes.

Chapter 7, "Using Functions," introduces you to 1-2-3's built-in functions for performing a variety of calculations. Among the built-in functions illustrated are those for performing mathematical, financial, statistical, and logical calculations.

Chapter 8, "Printing Reports," shows you how to select a printer, preview the printout, and print your data in simple reports. You also learn how to enhance your reports by hiding columns and rows, adding headers and footers, changing the page layout, and inserting page breaks.

Chapter 9, "Managing Files," describes how to use passwords to protect your worksheets, work with multiple files in memory, and link different files with formulas. This chapter also explains how to save parts of worksheets in separate files and how to import files into 1-2-3.

Chapter 10, "Creating Graphs," teaches you how to create graphs with 1-2-3. This chapter takes you from creating a new graph in its own Graph window to selecting a new graph type and enriching the basic graph with headings, legends, and other enhancements. In addition, the chapter teaches you to place graphs in worksheets where they can be printed.

Chapter 11, "Managing Data," explains how to use 1-2-3 for database management. You learn to create and modify a database, as well as to sort and search for specific records.

Chapter 12, "Using Macros," gives you an introduction to the concept of simple keystroke macros. The chapter teaches you to plan, position, create, name, and edit simple macros. The chapter includes macros you can use to start your own macro library.

Chapter 13, "Customizing the Icon Palette," teaches you how to modify the Icon palette supplied with 1-2-3 for Windows. Here, you learn how to modify the icons on the palette and create your own icons and assign macros that you've created to them.

The book concludes with an appendix, which shows you how to install 1-2-3 Release 3.1.

Who Should Use This Book?

1-2-3 for Windows QuickStart is designed as an introductory guide for new 1-2-3 users. Whether you are sitting down with 1-2-3 for Windows for the first time or are upgrading from an earlier version of 1-2-3, *1-2-3 for Windows QuickStart* contains just enough information to get you going quickly. The book highlights important concepts and takes you through important information by providing steps and explanations interwoven with numerous examples and illustrations.

What You Need To Run 1-2-3 for Windows

There are no prerequisites to using this book, or, for that matter, to using 1-2-3 for Windows. This text assumes, of course, that you have the program, Windows 3.0, sufficient hardware, and a desire to learn to use the program.

The system requirements for running 1-2-3 for Windows include the following:

- At least an IBM AT or compatible computer with an 80286, 80386, 80386SX, or 80486 microprocessor.
- A hard disk drive with at least 8M available disk space.
- DOS version 3.0 or later.
- Microsoft Windows version 3.0 or later.
- At least 3M of available RAM.
- An EGA, VGA, high resolution CGA or Hercules graphics adapter for Windows 3.0.
- Optional: A printer installed in Windows 3.0.
- Optional (but highly recommended!): A mouse to use 1-2-3 for Windows more efficiently and easily.

What Is New in 1-2-3 for Windows

Although 1-2-3 for Windows offers essentially the same nucleus of features as version 3.1 of 1-2-3 for DOS, it also contains several new features, many of which are the direct result of the graphical user interface provided by Windows.

This graphical version of 1-2-3 has the following additional features:

- Fully compliant Windows application, which means that 1-2-3 supports standard pull-down menus, dialog boxes, full mouse control, inter-application communication via the Clipboard, multiple applications in memory, and links with other applications.
- Preconfigured Icon palette for the Worksheet and Graph window, which contains SmartIcons that perform the most commonly used tasks at the click of the mouse button.
- Fully customizable suite of SmartIcons that can be grouped in new libraries to create a different palette or attached to your macros. 1-2-3 for Windows also enables you to create new custom SmartIcons that can perform macro functions.

- 1-2-3 Classic window that allows you to access the program using the / (slash) command menu supported by all previous versions of 1-2-3 for DOS. You also can access Wysiwyg commands in the 1-2-3 Classic window by typing a : (colon). The program also runs all 1-2-3 for DOS macros without modification.

- Graph gallery that enables you to select a new chart type by clicking an icon representing its graphic presentation. All charting in 1-2-3 for Windows takes place in a special Graph window with its own pull-down menus and Icon palette.

- Named styles that can assign complex formatting (such as a new font, attribute, color, borders, and shading) to a selected range in a single operation.

- Transcript window that records all your keystrokes, which can be used to create keystroke macros in a worksheet.

- Backsolver, a goal-seeking tool, that allows you to achieve a desired result for a single variable.

- Solver, a utility that performs goal-seeking problems for single or multiple variables, providing you with a range of answers that fall within your parameters.

- Adobe Type Manager (ATM), which is a utility designed to improve the quality of display fonts especially at larger point sizes.

This book introduces you to all of these new features in 1-2-3 for Windows with the exception of Solver and Backsolver. For detailed information on how to use these specialized features, refer to Que's *Using 1-2-3 for Windows*.

Learning More about 1-2-3 for Windows

After you learn the fundamentals presented in this book, you may want to learn more advanced applications of 1-2-3. Que Corporation has several 1-2-3 for Windows books you can use. Among these are the following books:

- *Using 1-2-3 for Windows* is a reference book that provides comprehensive coverage of all aspects of using 1-2-3 for Windows. A quick command reference and tear-out command chart are included with this book.

- *1-2-3 for Windows Quick Reference* is an affordable, compact reference to the most commonly used 1-2-3 for Windows commands and functions. This is a handy book to keep near your computer when you need to quickly find the purpose of a command and the steps for using it.

Both of these books can be found in better bookstores worldwide. In the
United States, you can call Que Corporation at 1-800-428-5331 to order books
or obtain further information.

Where To Find More Help

You can use 1-2-3's context-sensitive Help feature to answer some of your
questions as you work with 1-2-3 for Windows. Using Help is explained and
illustrated in Chapter 2. You also can refer to the appropriate sections of the
Lotus documentation provided with the 1-2-3 for Windows program.

Should all else fail, contact your computer dealer or Lotus Customer Support
at 1-800-223-1662. In Canada, contact Lotus Customer Support at 1-800-668-
8236.

For more information on how to use Windows 3.0, new computer users can
benefit from reading Que's *Windows 3 QuickStart*.

Conventions Used in This Book

A number of conventions are used in *1-2-3 for Windows QuickStart* to help
you learn the program. This section provides examples of these conventions
to help you distinguish among the different elements in 1-2-3 for Windows.

References to keys are as they appear on the keyboard of the IBM Personal
Computer and most compatibles. The function keys, F1 through F10, perform
particular commands in 1-2-3. In the text, the function key name and the
corresponding function key number are usually listed together, such as
Calc (F9).

Direct quotations of words that appear on the screen are spelled as they
appear on the screen and are printed in a `special typeface`. Information
you are asked to type is printed in **boldface blue** type.

The menu letter that you can type after pressing the Alt key to activate a menu
or select a menu or dialog box option is boldfaced and blue as in File Save As
or Worksheet Column Width.

Elements printed in uppercase include functions (SUM) and cell references (A1..G5 and B:C4).

When two keys appear together separated by a + (plus) as in Ctrl + Ins, you press and hold down the first key as you also press the second key. When two keys appear together without a plus sign between them, such as End Home, the first key is pressed and released before the second key is pressed.

An Overview of 1-2-3

Before you pick up that mouse and start using 1-2-3 for Windows, you need to know the range of capabilities offered by this new graphical version of 1-2-3. Both beginning and experienced 1-2-3 users will profit from the general information found in this chapter—information about how 1-2-3 makes use of the Windows environment and the benefits of using this industry-standard spreadsheet program under the graphical user interface provided by Windows.

Unlike previous versions of Lotus 1-2-3 that ran under Windows without supporting the Windows environment, you will find that 1-2-3 for Windows provides you with a 100-percent Windows-compliant application that marries the best of the Windows user interface to the most advanced generation of 1-2-3 technology. Better yet, 1-2-3 for Windows provides complete compatibility with earlier DOS-based versions.

In this chapter, you glimpse how 1-2-3 for Windows operates under Windows at the same time that you learn what it can do for you.

1

Key Terms in This Chapter

GUI — (Graphical User Interface, pronounced "Gooey") Refers to operating environments (such as Windows and OS/2 on IBM-compatible computers or System 7 on the Macintosh) that rely more on the manipulation of symbolic graphic elements than on typed commands and that provide a standard menu structure.

Windows — A Graphical User Interface (GUI) built on the DOS operating system that provides a Common User Access (CUA) to all the applications that run under it.

CUA — (Common User Access) Refers to the common menu structure, keystroke shortcuts, and methods of working offered by the Windows graphical user interface.

Windows program — A program such as 1-2-3 for Windows that does not run without Windows and that makes full use of the GUI environment provided by Windows.

Non-windows program — A program that can run with or without Windows and that is not necessarily CUA-compliant.

Icons — Symbols whose graphics suggest their function. 1-2-3 for Windows widely uses a special set of icons, called SmartIcons, as shortcuts for selecting commands.

Mouse — A hand-held device used to select data, menu commands, and options in Windows programs.

Whether you are an experienced computer user who is new to the 1-2-3 program or you are using a computer for the first time, you quickly can grasp the fundamentals of 1-2-3 for Windows. If you start by learning the most basic concepts of 1-2-3 and gradually build on your knowledge and experience, you will be amazed by how easily you learn this program.

1

You will find that this book uses an easy, step-by-step approach to teach you the fundamental tasks you will perform with 1-2-3 for Windows. Bear in mind that many of the techniques you use in 1-2-3 for Windows are common to all Windows applications; most of the fundamentals you learn while mastering 1-2-3 for Windows will carry over to other Windows programs you use.

The Benefits of Using 1-2-3 for Windows

In order to understand the benefits you derive from using 1-2-3 for Windows, you need to understand the general advantages of operating a computer program under a graphical user interface (GUI). Understanding the advantages of a graphical user interface is all the more important if you are using 1-2-3 for Windows and others you work with are using versions of 1-2-3 for DOS. You may be asking, "Should we *all* be using 1-2-3 for Windows?"

Windows was developed by Microsoft Corporation, an industry leader both in developing operating systems and in developing application programs for the IBM and Macintosh computers. According to Microsoft, a true GUI environment meets a number of specific criteria. The following are among the most important of these criteria:

- The computer screen displays a true representation of how the computer will print the information.

- The user interface is graphically oriented and makes extensive use of *icons* (symbols that graphically represent a document, program, or command).

- The user interface provides standard elements in all applications, including menus, dialog boxes, and windows. For example, after you learn to print with the File Print command in 1-2-3 for Windows, you know how to print with every other Windows program.

- The user interface permits direct manipulation of the screen. For example, you can move a window containing a 1-2-3 spreadsheet across the screen by dragging the window in that direction with the mouse.

- The user interface uses the *object-action* model, meaning that you select the object you want to affect before you select the command you want to apply to the object.

- The user can customize the application.

- The user interface supports the immediate use of multiple applications.

11

1

- The user interface supports inter-application communication.
- The user interface is easy to install and to use!

You will find that 1-2-3 for Windows supports all these GUI criteria. As such, it gives you freedom to work the way you want to work while providing you with a standardized user interface that is intuitive and fun to use.

Because 1-2-3 for Windows is significantly easier to learn and use than its non-Windows counterparts, you can learn faster and, consequently, be more productive with the program. With the common user access supported by 1-2-3 for Windows, you also will find it easier to learn and to use other Windows programs. In no time at all—even if you have never used a computer program before—you will find it quite natural to work with several programs at one time and to transfer information back and forth between the programs at will.

Using Icons

By now, you surely have the impression that graphics are important in Windows programs such as 1-2-3. You will encounter several standard graphic elements in 1-2-3 for Windows, and, indeed, in all Windows programs.

One of the most basic graphic elements is the *icon*. Icons are small symbols whose graphics suggest their function. Some icons are better at representing their function than others. Icons representing simple actions fare better than those depicting more complex operations. For example, the Edit Cut SmartIcon is the 1-2-3 for Windows icon for cutting data. The scissors immediately suggests this function. On the other hand, the Edit Undo SmartIcon is the icon for undoing the last action you performed in 1-2-3. The function of this SmartIcon is much less obvious. Only after you know the purpose of this icon does the graphic with the arrow turning back (retracing your path) make sense.

Windows also represents application programs by icons (at least until you open them). For example, the File Manager program included in Windows has a filing cabinet icon to suggest its function as the file management program in Windows. The 1-2-3 for Windows program has the traditional logo of 1-2-3 (a spreadsheet-graphics-database program with macros is too complex an idea to be rendered adequately by a single symbol).

Much like Alice in *Alice in Wonderland*, program icons change size in Windows quickly and often. When you position the mouse pointer on the 1-2-3 icon and rapidly click the left mouse button twice (a technique known as *double-clicking*), the 1-2-3 for Windows program starts.

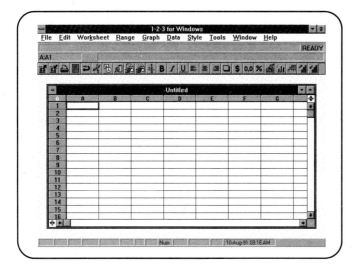

When the program finishes loading, 1-2-3 for Windows opens in a full-screen window.

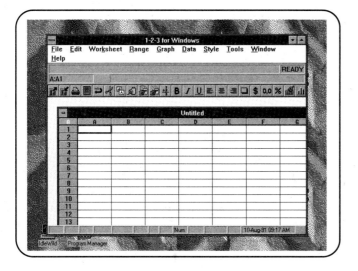

With the click of a button, you can reduce this full-screen program window to a somewhat smaller version on the Windows desktop.

1

By clicking a different button, you can reduce a program to its program icon— even while the program is running.

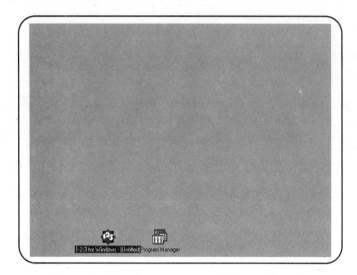

In addition to icons, 1-2-3 for Windows uses several other important GUI elements. Before you meet all of these elements in the next chapter, however, you need to learn more about one other element: the *pointer*, or, more precisely, the *mouse pointer*.

Using the Mouse

The *pointer* is a free-floating cursor that indicates your current position on-screen; its usual shape is an arrowhead (pointing toward the left). The pointer changes shape, however, to indicate a change in function. For example, when you position the pointer over the area in the 1-2-3 worksheet window where you can edit the contents of a cell, the arrowhead changes to an I-beam shape. This shape indicates that you can select the text you want to edit or insert the cursor (now called the *insertion point*) at some place in the text.

You move the pointer with the *mouse*, a hand-held device whose movements on your desk correlate with the movement of the pointer on-screen. The mouse may be the most difficult aspect of 1-2-3 for Windows for you to master. Many users initially find working with the mouse more difficult than anticipated and more tiring than using the keyboard. Although the *point-and-click*, *drag*, and *double-click* techniques used by 1-2-3 for Windows do require some time and effort to master, with a little perseverance, you will find using the mouse to be as natural as typing with the keyboard.

Note: The best way to become expert with the mouse is to play Solitaire, which is the card game included with Windows. In this game, you learn to point-and-click, drag, and double-click as you are entertained.

Although you can use 1-2-3 for Windows without a mouse, you have very little incentive to do so. Because the Windows environment is set up for direct manipulation of the screen, you will find that the mouse provides, if not the ideal tool, at least a much better tool than the keyboard for performing many of 1-2-3's routine tasks. After you master the techniques for selecting pull-down menu commands and dialog box options with the mouse, you will use the same techniques throughout the program. This consistent way to access program features is especially helpful because it enables you to give your full attention to the new 1-2-3 command or procedure you are learning.

The advantages of using the mouse do not mean that the keyboard has no place in 1-2-3 for Windows. Windows programs such as 1-2-3 always enable the user to select commands and dialog box options with an Alt+letter key combination. Whenever possible, the designers of 1-2-3 have assigned mnemonic combinations that use the first letter of each command, such as Alt+FP to choose the File Print command. Be aware, however, that such combinations are not always possible. For example, The Edit menu has four options that begin with the letter C: Cut, Copy, Clear, and Clear Special. You press Alt+EC to copy data, Alt+ET to cut data, Alt+EE to erase data, and Alt+ER to erase just the data or its formatting.

If you feel more comfortable using the keyboard to accomplish a particular operation in 1-2-3, you have no reason not to do so. As you become more experienced with 1-2-3 for Windows, you will start mixing keyboard and mouse techniques, depending on the task and your degree of familiarity with the procedure.

The Object-Action Model

Before you start looking at the major functions of the 1-2-3 program in more detail, you should examine one more aspect of working with a Windows program such as 1-2-3. Recall that earlier, in recounting the major features of a true GUI, the *object-action* model was mentioned as one of the important aspects of the user interface. Windows programs as a whole (including 1-2-3 for Windows) consistently follow this pattern, in which you select the things you want a command to affect before you choose the command itself.

Put simply, in terms of 1-2-3 for Windows, you routinely select the cell or group of cells (the objects) before you choose the command you want to apply to them (the action). This method is the direct opposite of the way 1-2-3 versions operate under DOS. For example, under DOS you select the command, such as /Range Erase (the action), and then you select the cells you want to erase (the objects). In 1-2-3 for Windows, you do the opposite—you select the cells you want to erase (preferably with the mouse), then press the Del key to erase them.

If you have experience with DOS programs, you may find this way of working somewhat backwards at the outset. In time, however, you undoubtedly will find this way of working in a graphical environment to be quite natural. You also will benefit from the fact that all Windows programs work the same way. Even if you don't know which menu in a new Windows program contains a particular command, you will know enough to select the text or data that you want the command to affect before you look for the command.

If you use the Icon palette (accessible only with the mouse) to perform routine tasks, you can realize an extra benefit from the object-action model: you can perform a whole series of actions on a single group of cells without selecting the cells again and again. For example, to format a series of numbers in bold and italics using the Currency format (which adds the dollar signs and commas), you select the cells, then click the Bold SmartIcon and you're done!

The 1-2-3 Electronic Spreadsheet

The heart and soul of 1-2-3 for Windows, and any of the other versions, is its *electronic spreadsheet*. Sometimes known as a ledger sheet or accountant's green sheet, a spreadsheet is a specialized piece of paper on which information is recorded in columns and rows. The 1-2-3 program's multiple worksheet and file capabilities extend this analogy further—providing multiple accounting worksheets that you can use simultaneously. Spreadsheets usually contain a mix of descriptive text and accompanying numbers and calculations. Typical business applications include balance sheets, income statements, inventory status reports, sales reports, and consolidations that use multiple worksheets.

Although you may be unfamiliar with business applications for spreadsheets, you already use a rudimentary spreadsheet if you keep a checkbook. Similar to an accountant's pad, a checkbook register is a paper grid divided by lines into rows and columns. Within this grid, you record the check numbers, the dates, the transaction descriptions, the check amounts, any deposits, and the running balance.

1

NUMBER	DATE	DESCRIPTION OF TRANSACTION	PAYMENT/DEBT (–)	√	FEE (IF ANY) (–)	DEPOSIT/CREDIT (+)	BALANCE $1000 00
1001	9/3/89	Department Store Credit	51 03				948 97
1002	9/13/89	Electric	95 12				853 85
1003	9/14/89	Grocery	74 25				779 60
1004	9/15/89	Class Supplies	354 57				425 03
	9/16/89	Deposit				250 00	675 03
1005	9/21/89	Telephone	49 43				625 60

A manual checkbook register.

What happens if you make an invalid entry in your checkbook register or if you have to void an entry? Such procedures are messy because you must erase or cross out entries, rewrite them, and recalculate everything. The limitations of manual spreadsheets are apparent even with this simple example of a checkbook register.

For complex business applications, the dynamic quality of an electronic spreadsheet such as 1-2-3 is indispensable. You can change one number and recalculate the entire spreadsheet in an instant. Entering new values is nearly effortless. Performing calculations on a column or row of numbers is accomplished with formulas—usually the same type of formulas that calculators use.

Compare the manual checkbook register to the electronic one that follows. Notice that the electronic checkbook register appears in its own window and has columns and rows. Columns are marked by letters across the top of the worksheet; rows are numbered along the side. Each transaction is recorded in a row, the same way you record data in a manual checkbook.

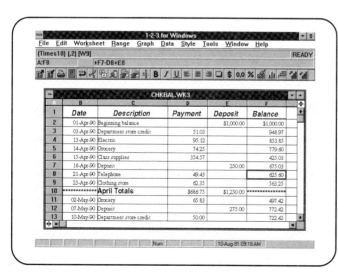

An "electronic" checkbook register.

1

Assigning column letters, row numbers, and worksheet letters lends itself well to creating formulas. The formula

+F7–D8+E8

in the upper left corner of the electronic checkbook translates to

Previous BALANCE minus PAYMENT plus DEPOSIT

As you can see from this simple example, formulas enable you to establish mathematical relationships between values stored in certain places on your spreadsheet. As a result, you can make changes to a spreadsheet and quickly see the results. In the electronic checkbook, if you delete an entire transaction (row), the spreadsheet automatically recalculates. You also can change an amount without worrying about recalculating your figures, because the electronic spreadsheet automatically updates all balances.

If you forget to record a check or deposit with 1-2-3, you can insert a new row at the appropriate location for the omitted transaction and enter the information. 1-2-3 moves subsequent entries down one row and automatically calculates the new balance. Inserting a new column is just as easy. Indicate where you want the new column to go, and 1-2-3 inserts a blank column at that point and moves existing information to the right of the new column.

This simple checkbook example demonstrates how valuable an electronic spreadsheet is for maintaining financial data. Although you may not decide to use 1-2-3 to balance your personal checkbook, an electronic spreadsheet is an indispensable tool in a modern office.

1-2-3 for Windows has a number of capabilities, but the foundation of the program is the electronic spreadsheet (more commonly called the *worksheet*). The database-management elements of the program share the framework provided by the worksheet. Also, you easily can generate sophisticated business graphs from your worksheet data.

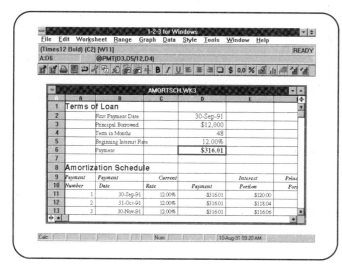

1-2-3's integrated electronic spreadsheet replaces traditional financial modeling tools, reducing the time and effort needed to perform even sophisticated accounting tasks.

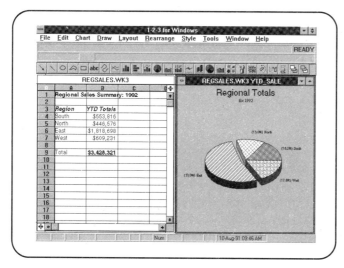

1-2-3's graphics capabilities make it easy to create sophisticated presentations and enable you to see worksheets and charts together on-screen.

1

1-2-3's database management capabilities help you track and maintain impor- tant information.

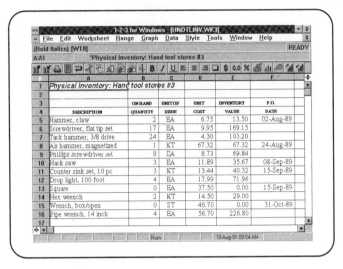

With 1-2-3 for Windows, you can have several worksheets open at one time and freely transfer information among them.

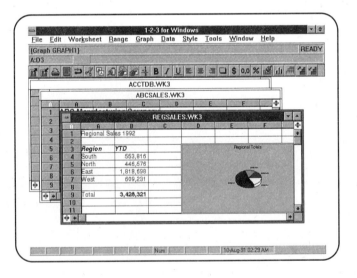

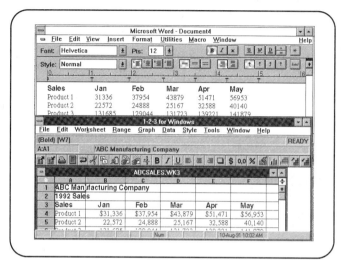

With 1-2-3 for Windows, you also can have several different programs running at one time and freely transfer information between them.

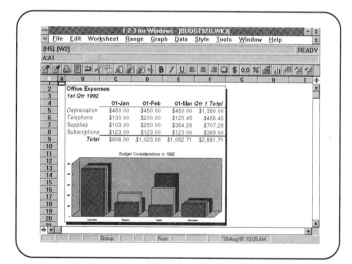

With 1-2-3 for Windows graphics capabilities, you can generate professional-looking worksheets in no time at all.

1

1-2-3 Graphics

1-2-3 for Windows makes generating professional-looking graphs from your worksheet data easy. The program supports eleven basic graph types: line, area, bar, pie, XY (scatter), HLCO (high-low-close-open), Mixed (bar and line), 3-D line, 3-D area, 3-D bar, and 3-D pie.

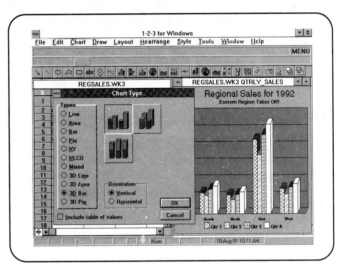

The graph gallery enables you to select from several variations for each graph type.

To select a new graph type, you simply click its icon in the Graph Gallery.

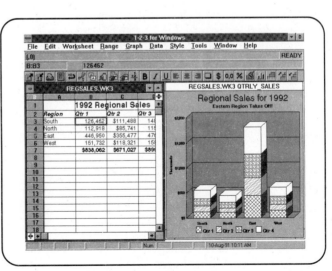

The graphs you create in 1-2-3 are dynamically linked to the worksheet data.

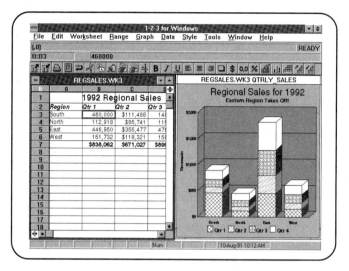

If you change worksheet values you used in the graph, 1-2-3 automatically updates the graph.

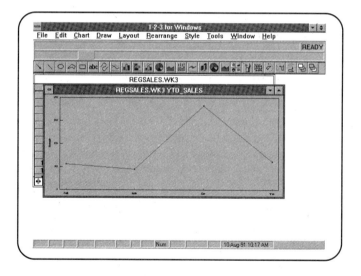

When you create a new graph in 1-2-3 for Windows, the program opens a new window that presents your data as a line graph.

You can use the commands in the Graph window menu and its Icon palette to enhance the graph.

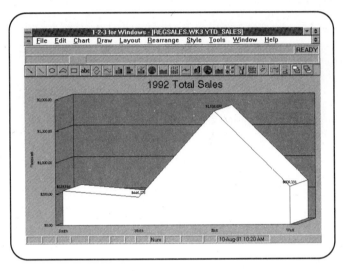

After you are satisfied with the chart, you can place it in the worksheet, where you can print the chart alone or with its supporting data.

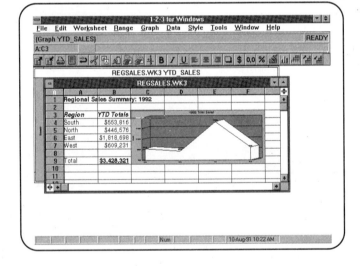

1-2-3 Database Management

The third major function of 1-2-3 for Windows is database management. The program enables you to use its worksheet structure to set up database tables that track and retrieve large amounts of information. When you use 1-2-3's true database-management commands and functions, you can sort, search, copy, or perform statistical analyses on data in up to 8,191 records (with up to 256 fields of information).

1-2-3 has sophisticated facilities for performing sort and search operations. You can sort the database on any number of items and by numerous criteria, and you can find a particular record with a few simple keystrokes.

Macros and SmartIcons

1-2-3 for Windows includes two other features that help you to work in 1-2-3 for Windows the way you want to work: macros and SmartIcons. You can use 1-2-3's macros and SmartIcons to automate and customize 1-2-3 for your particular applications.

Macros enable you to play back command sequences exactly as you recorded them. By using 1-2-3 macros, you can reduce multiple keystrokes to a two-keystroke operation. Simply press the two keys, and 1-2-3 does the rest— whether you are formatting a range, creating a graph, or printing a worksheet.

If you click a SmartIcon with the mouse, 1-2-3 performs the operation assigned to that icon. In addition to using the Icon palette as Lotus ships it with the program, you can customize the palette to contain the icons you use most often. Moreover, you can create your own icons, attach macros to the icons, and then add these custom icons to the Icon palette.

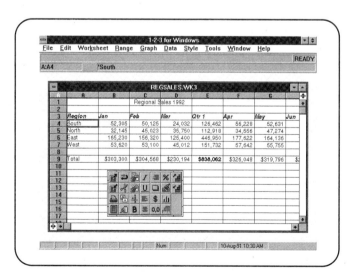

1-2-3 for Windows assigns the most common worksheet tasks to the icons on the SmartIcons palette.

1

Compatibility with Other Versions of 1-2-3

If you have been using 1-2-3 for some time, you will be happy to learn that 1-2-3 for Windows responds appropriately to all the / (slash) commands. When you press the / key, 1-2-3 for Windows opens a special window (called the *1-2-3 Classic window*) that contains all the familiar menus and menu options. You can always rely on the 1-2-3 Classic window while you are learning the new standard pull-down menus (to see you through when you need to get things done quickly).

1-2-3 for Windows supports two sets of menus: the 1-2-3 Classic menu (called by pressing /) and the standard Windows pull-down menus.

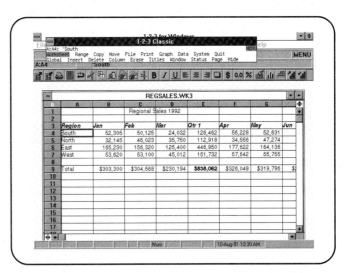

Thanks to the 1-2-3 Classic menu, all the macros you created in previous versions of 1-2-3 run flawlessly without any modification. This feature gives you time to convert existing macros to the new interface without depriving you of their use in the interim.

1-2-3 for Windows uses the same WK3 and FM3 files as 1-2-3 Release 3.0 and 3.1, assuring complete compatibility between 1-2-3 for Windows and these DOS versions. 1-2-3 for Windows also can read worksheets created with any earlier version of 1-2-3, such as Release 2.01, Release 2.2, or Release 2.3. You also can import graph files created with these versions and saved in PIC files directly into the 1-2-3 for Windows worksheet (where you can print them).

Summary

In this overview of 1-2-3 for Windows, you were introduced to the general capabilities of 1-2-3 for Windows. You also learned something about how 1-2-3 for Windows uses the Windows graphical environment to provide a program that is easy to learn and to use. You also were introduced to the basic functions of 1-2-3 and how they can help you to get your work done.

Specifically, you learned the following key information about 1-2-3 and the Windows environment:

- 1-2-3 for Windows is a 100-percent Window-compliant program that offers you all the benefits of a graphical user interface.

- 1-2-3 for Windows enables you to use the mouse or the keyboard to select commands.

- The 1-2-3 spreadsheet is the core of the 1-2-3 program, enabling you to set up models that perform complex calculations.

- 1-2-3 for Windows offers you sophisticated charting capabilities for presenting your worksheet data in graphic form.

- You can use a 1-2-3 database to store and retrieve large amounts of information.

- You can use macros to customize the way you work in 1-2-3 by playing command sequences at the touch of two keys. You also can attach your macros to SmartIcons and add these icons to the Icon palette.

- 1-2-3 for Windows is completely compatible with 1-2-3 Release 3.0 and 3.1. You even can access and use the familiar / command menus (used by these and earlier versions of the program) in a special window called the 1-2-3 Classic window.

Now you can proceed from the general principles about 1-2-3 for Windows to specific features and commands. The only way to convince you that 1-2-3 for Windows is easy to learn and to use is to do just that. In the next chapter, you begin your mastery of 1-2-3 by learning your way around the 1-2-3 Window, the place where you do all your work.

Introducing Worksheet Fundamentals

2

This chapter introduces you to the basic components of 1-2-3 under Windows. This chapter also introduces you to the graphical user interface provided by Windows 3.0 as it is used by 1-2-3. In addition to learning the basic components of the 1-2-3 window, you learn how to use the mouse and the keyboard and how to obtain on-line help at any time when using the program.

If you already have used Windows 3.0 programs and are anxious to get started using 1-2-3, you may want to simply scan the sections on the 1-2-3 window before jumping ahead to the next chapter. In the next chapter you learn how to start the program and how to use the 1-2-3 commands.

Understanding the 1-2-3 window

Understanding the parts of a worksheet window

Using the mouse

Learning the keyboard

Using on-line help

2

Key Terms in This Chapter

1-2-3 window   The on-screen work area that consists of the program Title bar, 1-2-3 Menu bar, Control line, all Worksheet and graph windows you open, Icon palette, and Status line.

Menu bar   The second line of the 1-2-3 window. Contains the 1-2-3 command menus. Activated by pressing F10 or the Alt key, or by clicking the mouse on a command.

Title bar   The top line of the 1-2-3 window and all Worksheet windows. Contains the Control menu box and displays the name of the program or worksheet file.

Control line   The fourth line of the 1-2-3 window. Shows the address of the current cell and is used to enter and edit data in cells of the current worksheet.

Worksheet window   The framed area in the 1-2-3 window. Contains a single worksheet file. Each Worksheet window has its own Title bar along with the worksheet grid and scroll bars.

Worksheet   The on-screen grid of columns and rows. Contains the data and formulas of the spreadsheet. Each worksheet file can contain up to 256 worksheets. Note that *worksheet* is also used to refer to the actual data and formulas entered into the worksheet grid.

Cell   The intersection of each column and row in a worksheet.

Cell address   The worksheet letter (A-IV), column letter (A-IV), and row number (1-8192) of the cell. The worksheet letter is separated from the column letter and row number with a colon, as in A:B30 or C:A100.

Mouse pointer   The indicator that you move with the mouse. The pointer assumes the shape of an arrowhead when it is used to select cells or 1-2-3 commands, or when it is used to scroll the worksheet. The pointer assumes the shape of an I-beam when it is used to edit text on the Control line. The pointer assumes the shape of a double-headed arrow when it is used to select and widen columns or rows or to split the Worksheet window into panes.

Scroll bars	Vertical and horizontal bars at the right and bottom edges of each Worksheet window. These scroll bars enable you to display new parts of the spreadsheet. Each scroll bar has a split box, two scroll arrows, and a scroll box.

Understanding the 1-2-3 Window

Before you begin using 1-2-3, you need to know how 1-2-3 for Windows presents information on the screen. To familiarize yourself with on-screen information, look at the *1-2-3 window*, which is the name given to the program window that contains your work. The window includes the 1-2-3 command menus and dialog boxes, as well as the worksheet and graph windows that contain electronic spreadsheets and charts you create with the program.

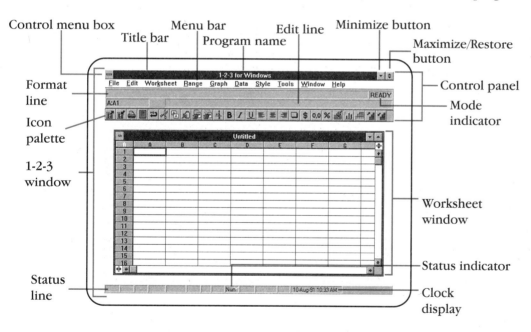

When you first start 1-2-3, you see the Control panel consisting of the Title bar, Menu bar, Format line, and Edit line at the top of the 1-2-3 window.

Below the Control panel, you see a new Worksheet window called Untitled (1-2-3 automatically opens a new Worksheet window whenever you start the program). At the bottom of the window, you see the Status line.

31

2

The Control Panel

The top part of the 1-2-3 window is the Control panel. The Control panel consists of four lines: the Title bar, Menu bar, Format line, and Edit line. The Control panel provides a great deal of information. It indicates the location of the cell pointer in a worksheet, the contents and formatting of the current cell, and the general state, or mode, of 1-2-3 for Windows.

The Title Bar

The 1-2-3 window Title bar occupies the first line of the Control panel. The following components make up the Title bar:

- **The program Control menu box.** Click this box (or press Alt+space bar) to display the program Control menu. You can use this menu to move or resize the 1-2-3 window, access the Windows 3.0 program, or close the 1-2-3 window and exit the 1-2-3 program.

- **The program name (1-2-3 for Windows).** When you select a 1-2-3 command from the Menu bar, a description of the command temporarily replaces the program name. When you enlarge the current Worksheet window to full size, the file name is displayed in square brackets following the program name.

- **The Minimize button.** Click the Minimize button (the box with the downward-pointing arrow) to shrink the entire 1-2-3 window (including all open worksheets and graphs) to a program icon at the bottom of the Windows desktop.

- **The Maximize or Restore button.** Click the Maximize button (the box with the upward-pointing arrow) to expand the 1-2-3 window so that it fills the entire screen. When you use the Maximize button to enlarge the 1-2-3 window, the Maximize button changes to the Restore button (the box with the two-pointed arrow). Click the Restore button to return the full-screen 1-2-3 window to its previous size on the screen.

The Menu Bar

The Menu bar appears on the second line of the Control panel. The Menu bar contains the 1-2-3 menus and the command options you select to perform various operations as you build a worksheet or a graph with the program. The actual menus that appear in the Menu bar vary according to the type of window that is currently active in the 1-2-3 window.

1-2-3 for Windows supports a variety of windows:

- **Worksheet window.** This window contains the 1-2-3 electronic spreadsheet file. Each worksheet file can consist of multiple sheets that contain the values, formulas, and text required by your spreadsheet.

- **Graph window.** This window contains the graph you create from spreadsheet data.

- **Help window.** This window displays on-line information about using 1-2-3 for Windows. You can keep the Help window open as you create a spreadsheet in a Worksheet window. When you keep the Help window open, you can refer to its topics as you work with new 1-2-3 commands.

- **1-2-3 Classic window.** This window contains the Lotus 1-2-3 Release 3.1 menus. You can use these menus to select commands instead of the 1-2-3 for Windows Menu bar. If you press the / (slash) key, the program displays the 1-2-3 command menus. If you press the : (colon) key, the program displays the Wysiwyg menus.

- **Print Preview window.** This window shows how your worksheet report will look when it is printed.

- **Transcript window.** This window contains a running log of up to the last 512 keystrokes you made in 1-2-3 for Windows. You can cut and paste these keystrokes when creating 1-2-3 macros.

- **Macro Trace window.** This window shows you the current location and instructions of a macro as it runs. You can use this window to debug macros that are not yet working properly.

When you first start 1-2-3, the program automatically opens a new Worksheet window called Untitled.

When a Worksheet window, such as Untitled, is the current window, 1-2-3 displays the Worksheet menu with the menus File through Help.

33

2

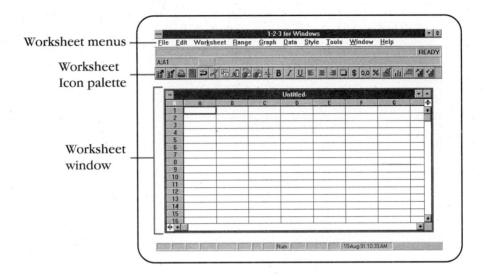

Worksheet menus ⟶

Worksheet
Icon palette ⟶

Worksheet
window ⟶

If you build a worksheet and create a new graph using the worksheet data,
1-2-3 for Windows displays the data in a graph window.

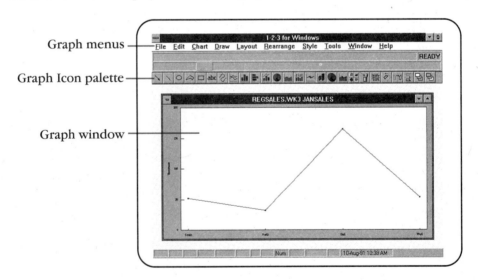

Graph menus ⟶

Graph Icon palette ⟶

Graph window ⟶

The Menu bar changes and displays the Graph menu. The Icon palette in
the 1-2-3 window also changes. The Icon palette contains a selection of
SmartIcons that enable you to quickly select various graph commands.
Each menu in the Menu bar contains a list of several related subcommands,

or options, that appear when you select the menu. To select a 1-2-3 command from the Menu bar, you first choose the menu that contains the command and then select the correct option from that menu. For example, to save a worksheet, choose the File menu and then select the Save option from that menu.

The Format Line

The third line of the Control panel is the Format line. The first part of this line contains an abbreviation that describes the formatting assigned to the current cell (see Chapter 5, "Working with Ranges," for more information on the formatting description). The second part of the Format line contains the Mode indicator. The Mode indicator informs you of the general state of the program.

A Mode indicator always appears in the upper right corner of the third line of the 1-2-3 window. The indicator reflects the program's current condition. For example, READY is displayed whenever data can be entered into the worksheet or a command can be selected from a menu. VALUE is displayed when you enter numbers or formulas, and LABEL is displayed when you enter letters for a worksheet title or heading.

Table 2.1 summarizes the name and purpose of each Mode indicator in 1-2-3 for Windows.

Table 2.1
Mode Indicators

Indicator	Description
EDIT	You pressed the Edit (F2) key or clicked a cell entry in the Contents box of the Control line to make changes to the entry.
ERROR	You tried to get 1-2-3 to do something it can't do; you need to press the Esc or Enter key to get back to READY mode.
FIND	You selected Data Query Find, and 1-2-3 has selected a record that matches the search criteria.
GROUP	You selected Worksheet Global Settings Group to group together the worksheets in the active Worksheet window.

continued

2

Table 2.1 *(continued)*

Indicator	Description
LABEL	You are entering a label in the Contents box of the Control line.
MENU	You pressed the Alt key, the Menu (F10) key, or clicked on the Main menu and are in the process of selecting a 1-2-3 command.
POINT	You selected a range to build a formula.
READY	1-2-3 is waiting for a command or cell entry.
VALUE	You are entering a value in the Contents box of the Control line.
WAIT	1-2-3 is busy processing, and you must wait before choosing a command or making a cell entry.

The Edit Line

The fourth line of the Control panel window is the Edit line. The first part of the Edit line contains the Address box that displays the address of the current cell. The second part (to the right) of the Edit line contains the Contents box. The Contents box is the area in which you type the entry that you want to place in the current cell.

Cancel box —— —— Confirm box   Contents box

Address box ——

Edit line

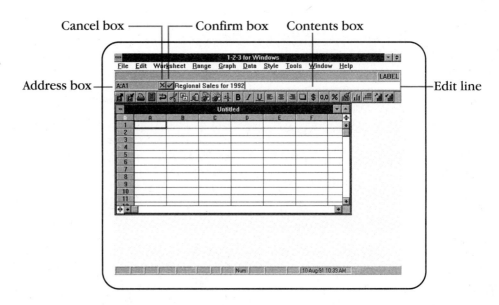

As you type a cell entry, the Contents box displays the characters. A Confirm button and Cancel button appear between the Address box and the Contents box.

The Work Area

The work area appears beneath the Control line of the 1-2-3 window. This area displays all open 1-2-3 windows, such as worksheet or graph windows containing the spreadsheets and graphs you're building. The work area of the 1-2-3 window also displays all dialog or message boxes that request additional information or ask for confirmation when you use certain commands. You can size and arrange all open 1-2-3 windows displayed in the work area. You also can move any dialog or message boxes that the program displays.

The Icon Palette

At the top of the work area in the 1-2-3 window, the program displays the Icon palette. The Icon palette contains a series of SmartIcons that you can use to perform certain 1-2-3 worksheet tasks quickly. The following SmartIcons are available when you start the program:

Table 2.2
The Icon Palette

SmartIcon	Operation Performed
	Opens an existing file.
	Saves the current file.
	Prints a range.
	Previews the print range.
	Undoes last command or action.
	Cuts to the Clipboard.
	Copies to the Clipboard.
	Pastes from the Clipboard.
	Selects the range to copy to.
	Selects the range to move to.

continued

2

Table 2.2 *(continued)*

SmartIcon	Operation Performed
	Sums the nearest adjacent range.
	Applies bold.
	Applies italics.
	Applies underlining.
	Aligns left.
	Aligns center.
	Aligns right.
	Applies Currency format.
	Applies Comma format.
	Applies Percent format.
	Selects range to apply current formatting to.
	Creates a new graph.
	Turns on Perspective view.
	Goes to the next window.
	Goes to the previous window.

When you install the program, 1-2-3 automatically places the Icon palette at the top of the screen. You can change the location of the Icon palette, however, as you work. To change the position of the Icon palette, follow these steps:

1. From the Tools menu, select the SmartIcons option.

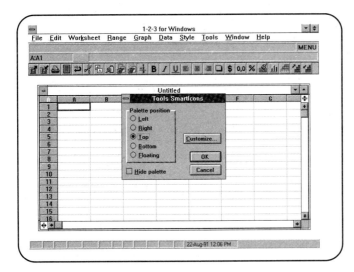

1-2-3 displays the
Tools SmartIcons
dialog box.

2. Select the desired option under Palette position.

   Choose the **L**eft option to display the palette so that it runs vertically down the left edge of the 1-2-3 window.

   Choose the **R**ight option to display the palette so that it runs vertically down the right side of the 1-2-3 window.

   Choose the **T**op option to display the palette at the top of the 1-2-3 window underneath the Control line.

   Choose the **B**ottom option to display the palette at the bottom of the 1-2-3 window.

   Choose the **F**loating option to display the palette in its own window so that you can move it.

   Select the **H**ide palette option to hide the display of the Icon palette in the 1-2-3 window.

3. Select the OK button.

When you use the **F**loating option to display the Icon palette in its own window, you can move the palette and change its shape.

Here, you see
the floating Icon
palette positioned
within the current
Worksheet
window.

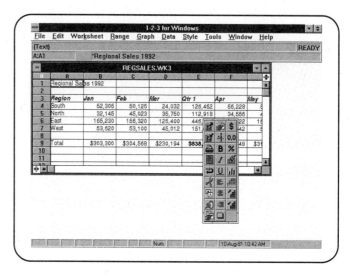

Note: 1-2-3 for Windows enables you to customize the icons in the Icon palette. See Chapter 13 for information on how to make such changes. To review the function of a SmartIcon in the Icon palette, click the SmartIcon with the right mouse button.

The Status Line

The last line of the 1-2-3 window contains the Status line. This line contains the Status indicators, lock key indicators (Cap, Num, and Scroll), and the clock display that shows the current date and time.

Status indicators report on the general state of the current window. The Status indicators include general message indicators, such as Calc or End, as well as warnings, such as Mem or Circ. The indicators disappear as soon as you make changes in the active window to rectify the reported condition. Table 2.3 shows you the Status indicators used by 1-2-3 for Windows.

2

Table 2.3
The Status Indicators

Indicator	Description
Calc	Manual recalculation has been turned on in the active worksheet file, and the worksheet needs to be recalculated. Press the Calc key, F9.
Caps	You pressed the Caps Lock key to type all letters in uppercase without having to press the Shift key.
Circ	One or more formulas in the worksheets on the desktop contains circular references. Select the **About 1-2-3** option on the Help menu to identify the location of the circular reference(s).
Cmd	1-2-3 is running a macro.
End	You pressed the End key, and 1-2-3 is waiting for you to press a direction key.
File	You pressed the File key combination (Ctrl+End) to move between worksheet files you have open.
Group	You turned on GROUP mode in the current file to apply the same formatting to all worksheets in the current file.
Mem	Computer memory needed to store data is low. To continue working, you need to save the worksheet before taking steps to free memory.
Num	You pressed the Num Lock key to enter numbers from the numeric keypad.
Ro	The active worksheet file has read-only status. Changes made to the worksheet can't be saved under the same file name.
Scroll	You pressed the Scroll Lock key so that the arrow keys move the worksheet as well as the cell pointer.

continued

Table 2.3 *(continued)*

Indicator	Description
Sst	1-2-3 is in the process of running a macro in STEP mode.
Step	You activated STEP mode to execute a macro one step at a time.
Zoom	You pressed the Zoom key combination (Alt+F6) after splitting the Worksheet window into separate panes or turning on Perspective view.

By default, the program displays the current date and time in the lower right corner of the Status line. If you want, you can change the way the clock displays the date and time or eliminate the clock display altogether by choosing the Tools menu and selecting the User Setup option.

1-2-3 displays the Tools User Setup dialog box.

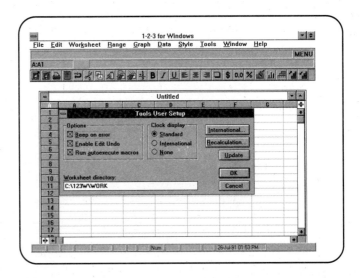

To change to the International display for dates and times (such as 02/15/92 13:15 or May 15, 1993 1:15 PM), select the International option under Clock display. To eliminate the clock altogether, select the None option. To make your changes to the clock display permanent, select the Update button before selecting the OK button.

2

Note: If the date and time are not correct in the clock display on the Status line, you can change them. First, return to the Windows 3.0 desktop (press [Alt]+[Esc]), and then select the Control Panel icon in the Main Group window. Select the Date/Time icon in the Control Panel dialog box and make any required changes to the date or time in the Date or Time text boxes. When the date and time are correct, select the OK option, close the Control Panel dialog box, and return to 1-2-3 for Windows. The clock display in the Status line will now display correctly.

Understanding the Worksheet Window

As mentioned earlier, when you first start 1-2-3, the program automatically opens a new Worksheet window in the work area. You then can use this worksheet to create a new model, such as a budget or product cost analysis spreadsheet.

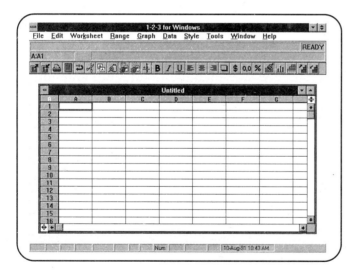

A Worksheet window has its own Control menu box, Title bar, and Maximize and Minimize button just like the 1-2-3 window.

In addition, the Worksheet window contains scroll bars that you can use to view new parts of the worksheet in the window. Beneath the Title bar, you see part of the worksheet grid, with most monitors displaying at least columns A through G and rows 1 through 17.

2

The Worksheet Frame

The first column and row at the top left of the Worksheet window display the letter and number designations for columns and rows. This area is the *worksheet frame*. The worksheet frame shows you the letter of the worksheet as well as its column letters and row numbers. The worksheet letter designation is located in the upper left corner of the frame, at the intersection of the row that shows the column letters and the column that shows the row numbers.

Worksheets and columns in a Worksheet window are indicated by letters of the alphabet, while the rows are numbered. To identify worksheets or columns beyond the 26th, 1-2-3 begins doubling the letters so that the 27th worksheet in your file is AA and its 28th column is AB.

When you first open a new worksheet file, 1-2-3 places the worksheet in a small window in which you can see only the first 6 columns (A through F) and 11 rows. If you click the Maximize button to make the Worksheet window full size, you can see the first 8 columns (A through H) and 20 rows of the worksheet. The entire worksheet grid, however, is huge: it consists of a total of 256 columns and 8,192 rows. Moreover, a Worksheet window (or file) can contain up to 256 individual worksheets, all with 256 columns and 8,192 rows of their own. In terms of letter designations, the 256th sheet of a worksheet file as well as the 256th column carries the letter designation IV.

The Worksheet Cell

The intersection of each column and row of a worksheet is a cell. The grid lines that divide the columns and rows in the worksheet effectively form the borders of each cell. Each cell in a worksheet has a cell address that is derived from the cell's worksheet, column, and row location. Each cell address, therefore, has three parts: the cell's worksheet letter followed by the cell's column letter and row number. To keep from confusing the sheet designation with that of the column, a colon is placed between the worksheet and column letter, as in cell A:A1 or B:C50.

The address of the selected cell (the cell that contains the cell pointer) is always listed in the Address box of the Control line of the 1-2-3 window. As you move the cell pointer to new cells in the same worksheet or in a different worksheet, the cell address is updated in the Control line, keeping you constantly apprised of your present location in the Worksheet window.

The Scroll Bars

As noted earlier, you can see at one time only a very small part of any worksheet in a Worksheet window. 1-2-3 offers several methods for viewing new parts of the worksheet in the window. One of the easiest ways to view new parts of a worksheet is with the scroll bars located on the right and bottom of each Worksheet window.

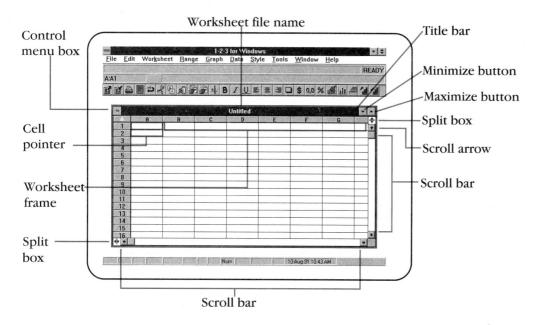

Worksheet file name

Title bar

Control menu box

Minimize button

Maximize button

Cell pointer

Split box

Scroll arrow

Worksheet frame

Scroll bar

Split box

Scroll bar

Both the vertical and horizontal scroll bars have two scroll arrows and a scroll box each.

You can click the scroll arrows to scroll the worksheet in small increments, or you can drag the scroll box to scroll the worksheet in large moves. Each scroll bar also contains a split box that you can use to split the Worksheet window into vertical or horizontal panes.

The following scrolling techniques are available when you use the scroll bars:

To scroll the worksheet up or down a row at a time, click the up or down scroll arrow in the vertical scroll bar.

To scroll the worksheet left or right a column at a time, click the left or right scroll arrow in the horizontal scroll bar.

To scroll the worksheet up or down one window at a time, click the scroll bar once above or below the scroll box on the vertical scroll bar.

2

To scroll the worksheet left or right one window at a time, click the scroll bar once above or below the scroll box on the horizontal scroll bar.

To scroll the worksheet continuously, click the appropriate scroll arrow and hold the mouse button down until the part of the worksheet you want to see comes into view, and then release the mouse button.

To scroll to a particular position in the worksheet, drag the scroll box to the approximate position on the vertical or horizontal scroll bar before you release the mouse button. For example, to horizontally scroll to the middle of the worksheet, drag the scroll box to the middle of the horizontal scroll bar.

Using the Mouse

The mouse provides the most natural way to select menu options and manipulate elements in a 1-2-3 Worksheet window. Even the most diehard keyboard enthusiasts may prefer the mouse to select ranges of cells as well as to select, move, and size Worksheet windows and graphics in 1-2-3. Although some users at the outset (especially users with some experience using 1-2-3 under DOS) may choose 1-2-3 menu options with Alt+letter key combinations, many users may find themselves using the mouse to make menu selections as manipulating worksheets with the mouse becomes more routine.

1-2-3 for Windows supports either a two-button mouse (like the Microsoft mouse) or a three-button mouse (like the Logitech mouse).

You need to master three basic mouse-button techniques in 1-2-3 for Windows. These techniques include:

Clicking	Press and then immediately release the left mouse button.
Double-clicking	Click the left mouse button twice in rapid succession. The timing of the clicks is crucial in double-clicking. If you wait too long between clicks, 1-2-3 interprets your action as two clicks instead of one double-click.
Dragging	Click and hold the left mouse button as you move the mouse.

Note: You can adjust the double-click and mouse tracking speed of your mouse in Windows. Select the Main group window, double-click on the Control panel icon to open the Control panel window, and then double-click the Mouse icon to open the Mouse window.

Selecting a Menu Option

The 1-2-3 command menus are always displayed in the Menu bar at the top of the 1-2-3 window. Each menu contains various options that appear as soon as you select the menu in the Menu bar. In addition to these 1-2-3 menus, you also can access the Control menu, a standard Windows menu. The Control menu options enable you to switch between programs and minimize or restore the 1-2-3 desktop. To access this menu, click the Control menu box (the box with the line in its center, located in the upper left corner of the 1-2-3 window). When selecting the Control menu, be careful not to double-click the Control menu box; this action closes the 1-2-3 desktop instead of displaying the Control menu options.

To select a 1-2-3 menu on the Menu bar, position the mouse pointer on the menu's name and click the left mouse button.

2

As soon as you click the left mouse button, all of the options available on that menu are displayed.

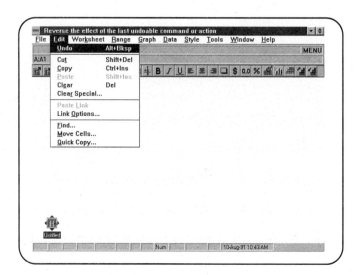

If you forget which menu contains the particular option you want, you can locate the menu by dragging the mouse across the options on the Menu bar. As you drag the mouse over each menu name, the program displays the menu's options in turn.

To choose an option from a selected menu, click on the option's name. If you already know which menu contains the option you want to use and you want to select it quickly, you can save time by dragging to that menu and then continuing to drag down until the option is selected (indicated by highlighting on the option) before you release the left mouse button.

If a menu option appears dimmed, the option is not currently available for selection. If a check mark appears before an option, the option can be toggled on and off. If a key combination follows an option, the combination represents a keyboard shortcut you can use to select the command, without accessing the menus.

If a menu option is followed by ellipses (three dots) as in the case of the Save As... option on the File menu, a dialog box that contains more options appears as soon as you select the menu option. If an option is followed by a triangle (▶) as is the case with the Import From and Administration options on the File menu, a cascade menu that contains more options appears to the option's right as soon as you click the option or drag to it.

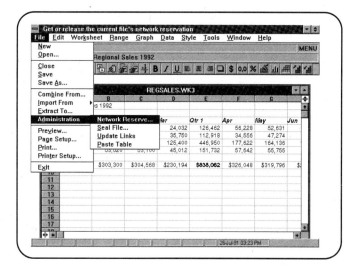

After a cascade menu is displayed, such as the Administration cascade menu, you can choose options just as you would any other menu options.

Selecting a Cell

To select a cell with the mouse, position the pointer somewhere on the cell and click the left mouse button. As soon as you do, 1-2-3 places the cell pointer (indicated by the heavy outline around the borders of the cell) in the cell, and the cell address in the Address box of the Control line is updated to show the cell pointer's new location. Also, if the cell you select contains any data, the data is displayed in the Contents box on this line.

Selecting a cell with the mouse is often a lot less work than selecting a cell with the direction keys. With the mouse, you simply point to the desired cell in the window and click it. With arrow keys, you must press them until you have moved the cell pointer all the way from its current location to its desired location.

2

Selecting Text in a Cell

After you have entered data in a cell, the only way to edit the data is within the Contents box on the Control line of the 1-2-3 window. To edit the contents of a cell, you often have to select the text you want to replace or erase. 1-2-3 displays the text you select by highlighting the text (that is, showing the text in inverse video).

Whenever you move the pointer over text in the Contents box, the pointer changes from an arrowhead to an I-beam shape. To select text with the mouse, position the I-beam immediately in front of the first character to be included and then drag the mouse until all of the remaining text is highlighted. To select several words on a single line of text, drag to the right until all the words are highlighted.

Selecting a Worksheet Window

1-2-3 for Windows enables you to have multiple worksheet files open at one time, each within its own Worksheet window. All Worksheet windows that you have open are considered active; however, only one Worksheet window can be current at any one time, and only the worksheet in the current window can be edited.

To select a window and make it current, position the pointer somewhere on the window and click the left mouse button. 1-2-3 immediately places the selected Worksheet window on top of the work area. You also will notice that the Title bar in the Worksheet window becomes highlighted (it changes color on a color monitor) as soon as you select its window.

If you are working on a worksheet within a full-size window (a window that takes up the entire screen), you have to resize the active window before you can select another Worksheet window with the mouse. If the Worksheet window you want to select is no longer visible on the screen, you may have to rearrange or resize the windows on the screen.

Note: Rather than using the mouse, you can use the Next Window key combination (Ctrl + F6) to cycle through the active windows when working with full-size Worksheet windows.

Sizing and Moving a Worksheet Window

The Title bar of the 1-2-3 window and that of each open Worksheet window contain two size buttons located in the upper right corner: a Minimize button (the downward-pointing arrow) followed by a Maximize button (the upward-pointing arrow).

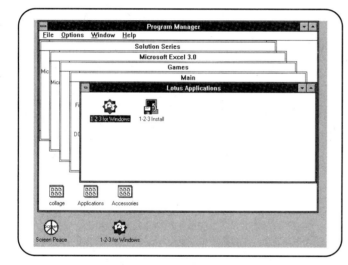

Click the Minimize button on the Title bar of the 1-2-3 window to reduce the window to the 1-2-3 for Windows program icon shown at the bottom of the Windows File Manager screen.

To restore the 1-2-3 window to its previous size, double-click the 1-2-3 for Windows program icon.

Note: If you lose track of the 1-2-3 program icon, press Ctrl + Esc to bring the icon back.

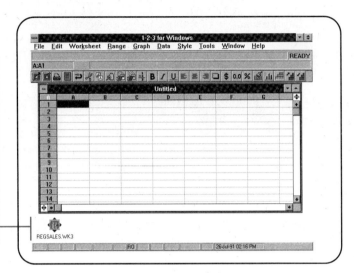

Click the Mini-
mize button on
the Title bar of
the current
Worksheet
window to reduce
the window to
the worksheet
icon shown at the
bottom of the
work area of the
1-2-3 window.

To restore the Worksheet window to its previous size, double-click the worksheet icon.

To enlarge the 1-2-3 window so that it takes up the entire screen, click the
Maximize button in the upper right corner of the screen. To enlarge a
Worksheet window so that it takes up the entire work area of the 1-2-3 window, click the Maximize button in the upper right corner of the Worksheet
window. Note that when you maximize a Worksheet window, the window
loses its Title bar and the program places the file name in the Title bar of the
1-2-3 window in brackets, as in

```
1-2-3 for Windows - [REGSALES.WK3]
```

If you use the Maximize button to enlarge the 1-2-3 window or a Worksheet
window, a Restore button appears. To restore the window to its previous size
and position on the screen, click the Restore button. The icon for this button
contains two arrows: one pointing up and the other pointing down. The
Restore button for the 1-2-3 window replaces the Maximize button in the
upper right corner of the screen. The Restore button for the full-size
Worksheet window is located on the second line of the 1-2-3 window right
underneath the 1-2-3 window Maximize or Restore button.

To modify the size of the 1-2-3 window or a Worksheet window that is neither
enlarged to full-size nor reduced to an icon, position the pointer on the frame
of the window and hold down the left mouse button until the pointer changes

2

to a double-headed arrow. Then drag the mouse until the window is the size and shape you want before you release the left mouse button. When resizing a window with the mouse, you can use the following techniques:

To make a window shorter from the bottom, click the bottom frame. When the pointer changes to the double-headed arrow pointing up and down, drag the mouse upward. To make the window taller, click the same side and drag the mouse downward.

To make the window wider from the right, click the right frame. When the pointer changes to the double-headed arrow pointing left and right, drag the mouse to the right. To make the window narrower, click the same side and drag the mouse to the left.

To make the window smaller by shortening it from the bottom and narrowing it from the right, click the lower right corner. When the pointer changes to the double-headed arrow pointing diagonally up to the left and down to the right, drag up toward the left. To make the window larger, click the same corner and drag the mouse down toward the right.

Note: You also can resize a window in a single direction by clicking and dragging the top or left frame. You can resize a window in two directions by dragging from any of the other three corners.

Moving the 1-2-3 window in the Windows 3.0 desktop or a Worksheet window in the work area is a snap with the mouse. You simply position the pointer anywhere within the window's Title bar and then drag the mouse in the direction you want to move the window. When the window is positioned where you want it on the screen, release the left mouse button.

Learning the Keyboard

1-2-3 for Windows uses the following areas of the keyboard:

- The alphanumeric or "typing" keys located in the center of the keyboard. This area includes special keys, such as Esc, Ctrl, Alt, Shift, Backspace, and Enter.
- The numeric keypad containing number and direction keys on the right side of the keyboard.

2

The enhanced keyboard includes a dedicated direction-key keypad in addition to the numeric keypad.

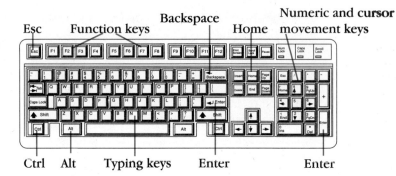

In the original keyboard design, the number and direction-key functions are combined in the single numeric keypad.

- The function keys labeled F1 to F10 (1-2-3 doesn't use F11 or F12) located at the top of the enhanced keyboard.

These keys sometimes are labeled F1 to F10 and located on the left side of the Personal Computer AT keyboard.

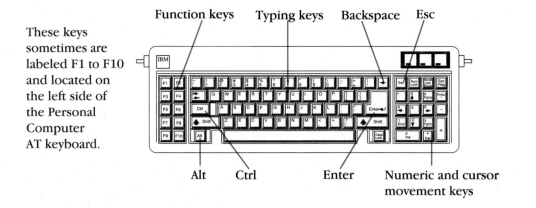

Alphanumeric Keys

Most of the alphanumeric keys on the keyboard perform the same actions as those on a typewriter. In addition to the number, letter, and punctuation keys in the standard QWERTY arrangement, the alphanumeric keys include keys that have special functions in 1-2-3. Some of these keys are the / (slash), : (colon), Tab, Back Tab, Backspace, Enter, Shift, Ctrl (Control), Alt (Alternate), Caps Lock, Num Lock, and Scroll Lock keys.

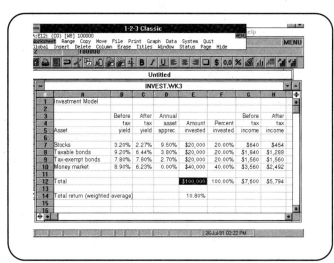

The / (slash) key is used to display the 1-2-3 Classic Window with the Lotus 1-2-3 Release 3.1 command menus. The : (colon) key is used to display the same window with the Release 3.1 Wysiwyg menus.

The Tab key is used to pan the worksheet in the active window one window to the right; you also can use Ctrl+right arrow. The Tab key works as it does in a word processor only when you are editing a cell entry in the Contents box on the Control line. The Tab key advances the insertion point (or cursor) five spaces to the right in the text. You also can use the Tab key in a dialog box to move to the next set of options.

On the IBM keyboard, the combination Shift+Tab works as a back tab. You use back tab in a 1-2-3 worksheet to pan the worksheet to the left one window; you also can use Ctrl+left arrow. When editing a cell entry in the Contents box on the Control line, the back tab moves the cursor five spaces to the left in the text. In a dialog box, the back tab takes you to a previous set of options.

The Backspace key (marked with a left arrow and abbreviated in Windows programs as BkSp) is used only when editing a cell entry in the Contents box on the Control line. There, the Backspace key deletes the character immediately to the left of the cursor. Don't confuse this key with the left-arrow key located on the direction-key or numeric keypad, which is marked identically. The left-arrow key is nondestructive; it simply moves the cursor one character to the left in the text in the Contents box.

The Enter key is used to confirm selections you make with 1-2-3 menus or options you choose in dialog boxes. The Enter key is also used to enter data in a cell.

The Shift key is used to create uppercase letters or to access the shifted character on keys that combine two different characters (such as the @ symbol on the 2 key and the ? on the / key). Note that pressing the Caps Lock key produces only uppercase letters; this key does not access the shifted character on such keys.

The Shift, Ctrl, and Alt keys are used in combination with special keys, such as the Insert and Delete keys as well as certain function keys to access particular 1-2-3 commands. In addition to the Menu (F10) key, you also can press the Alt key to access the 1-2-3 Menu bar if you don't want to use a mouse. If you know which menu you want to use, you can press Alt plus the letter that is underlined in the menu name. For example, to display the options on the File menu, you can press (Alt)+(F). After a 1-2-3 pull-down menu is displayed, you can select an option by typing the letter that is underlined in the option's name. If you know the menu letter assigned to the menu you want to choose, you can accelerate the selection process even more. Press the Alt key and then type the menu and option letters. For instance, to save under the same file name the changes you have made to a worksheet, press (Alt)+(F)(S) to select the Save option on the File menu.

The IBM keyboard contains three special lock keys: Caps Lock, Num Lock, and Scroll Lock. All three of these lock keys act like a toggle switch. Each time you press the key, it switches to its opposite state: from off to on or from on to off. Caps Lock is used to type only capital letters from the QWERTY keys, Num Lock to enter just numbers with the numeric keypad, and Scroll Lock to freeze the cell pointer in the worksheet when you scroll new parts of a worksheet with the direction keys.

Enhanced keyboards have individual LEDs (light emitting diodes) that remain lit when a particular lock key is engaged. 1-2-3 shows that a particular lock key is engaged by displaying an abbreviation of the key's name in the lower right corner of the last line of the 1-2-3 window, immediately to the left of the clock display. 1-2-3 displays Caps for Caps Lock, Num for Num Lock, and Scroll for Scroll Lock.

The Numeric Keypad and Direction Keys

The numeric keypad on the keyboard contains both direction keys and number keys. To use the direction keys to move the cell pointer to a new location in a worksheet, make sure that the Num Lock key is disengaged. To disengage Num Lock so that you can move the cell pointer instead of enter numbers, press the Num Lock key in the upper left corner of the numeric pad.

If you have an enhanced keyboard, you can use the separate direction-key keypad to the immediate left of the numeric keypad to move the cell pointer even when Num Lock is engaged. With an enhanced keyboard, you can enter numerical data using the numeric keypad and still move the cell pointer using the direction-key keypad.

If your keyboard follows the original IBM keyboard design so that it has only a single numeric keypad, you must leave the Num Lock key disengaged to move the cell pointer in the worksheet. To enter numbers in the cell, you can either use the number keys on the top row of the QWERTY keys or hold down the Shift key as you enter numbers from the numeric keypad. Because the Shift key only engages Num Lock temporarily, you then can move the cell pointer to a new cell by releasing the Shift key before you press the appropriate direction key on the numeric keypad.

The Function and Accelerator Keys

1-2-3 for Windows assigns to special function keys and accelerator keys a number of commonly used operations. While most of these keys simply provide shortcuts for selecting commands from the 1-2-3 menus, a few function keys perform operations that are not duplicated in the 1-2-3 menus.

If you are familiar with the function keys in earlier releases of 1-2-3 for DOS, you can see that most of the functions used in the Windows version are the same (or very similar). Accelerator keys use the Shift, Ctrl, and Alt keys in combination with special keys, such as the Delete and Insert keys. Many of the functions these keys perform, such as cutting and pasting text and closing windows, are common to all Windows programs. Table 2.4 lists all the function and accelerator keys in 1-2-3 for Windows. Note that some of the function keys only work in particular modes. When a function key works only in a mode other than READY, this mode is noted in the table in parentheses.

Table 2.4
The Function and Accelerator Keys

Key(s)	Name	Function
Del	Delete	Deletes the selected data without copying it to the Clipboard (use Undo, Alt+Backspace, to restore).
F1	Help	Displays 1-2-3's Help window to give you on-line help.

continued

57

2

Table 2.4 *(continued)*

Key(s)	Name	Function
F2	Edit	Switches to EDIT mode and places the insertion point (cursor) at the end of the contents of the current cell in the Contents box for editing.
F3	Name	Displays a dialog box that lists all the available names from which you can choose. When entering a formula, type one of the operators and then press F3 to list all named ranges (VALUE mode). When entering a function, type @ and then press F3 to list the functions (VALUE mode). When specifying a range for a 1-2-3 command, select the command and then press F3 to list all named ranges (POINT mode).
F4	Abs	Anchors the cell pointer on the current cell (READY mode). Cycles a range or cell reference between a relative, absolute, and mixed reference (EDIT or POINT mode).
F5	Goto	Displays the Range Goto dialog box where you designate the cell address or the name of the range you want to move the cell pointer to.
F6	Pane	Moves the cell pointer between panes set up in a worksheet with the Worksheet Split Horizontal, Vertical, or Perspective option or with the split boxes on the scroll bars.
F7	Query	Repeats the most recent Data Query Find or Data Query Extract command. During a Data Query Find operation, this key switches the program between FIND and READY mode.

Key(s)	Name	Function
F8	Table	Repeats the last Data What-if Table command.
F9	Calc	Recalculates all formulas that require updating in the current worksheet file.
F10	Menu	Selects the 1-2-3 Menu bar.
⇧Shift + Del	Cut	Moves selected data to the Clipboard.
⇧Shift + Ins	Paste	Copies data from the Clipboard to the location of the cell pointer or insertion point.
Ctrl + Esc	Task Manager	Switches from the 1-2-3 window to the Windows Task Manager where you can switch to another running program.
Ctrl + Break	Break	Cancels the 1-2-3 command or operation you are selecting and returns you immediately to READY mode.
Ctrl + Ins	Copy	Copies the selected data to the Clipboard.
Ctrl + F4	Close Window	Closes the current window.
Ctrl + F6	Next Window	Activates the next open window in the 1-2-3 window.
Alt + ←Backspace	Undo	Cancels the most recent action made in the current worksheet or graph window.
Alt + Tab↹	Switch Program	Selects the next program that is running under windows.

continued

2

59

2

Table 2.4 *(continued)*

Key(s)	Name	Function
Alt + -	Control Menu	Opens the Control menu for the current worksheet or graph window (same as clicking on the Control menu box with the mouse).
Alt + F1	Compose	Enables you to enter in a worksheet special symbols and characters that are not on the keyboard.
Alt + F3	Run	Displays a list of macros to run.
Alt + F4	Close Desktop	Closes the 1-2-3 window and exits 1-2-3, thereby returning you to the Windows 3.0 desktop.
Alt + F7	Add-In 1	Activates add-in programs that are loaded with the **Tools** Add-in **Load** command.
Alt + F8	Add-In 2	Activates add-in programs that are loaded with the **Tools** Add-in **Load** command.
Alt + F9	Add-In 3	Activates add-in programs that are loaded with the **Tools** Add-in **Load** command.

Using On-Line Help

1-2-3 for Windows offers extensive on-line help in a special 1-2-3 for Windows Help window you can access at any time while using the program. Once the 1-2-3 Help menu is displayed, you can keep the window displayed in the work area of the 1-2-3 window while you continue to work on your spreadsheets and graphs in their own windows. That way, you can get help on a particular procedure and keep those instructions displayed on-screen as you perform the procedure in a nearby worksheet or graph window.

To get context-sensitive help that is directly related to the action you are performing, press the Help (F1) key. You can use the Help key in the following situations:

If you select a menu or menu option or open a dialog box and then press the Help key, the program displays information on that command or dialog box in the 1-2-3 Help window.

If 1-2-3 displays a message in an alert box and you then press the Help key, the program displays information about that message in the 1-2-3 Help window.

If you type @ in the Contents box and then press the Help key, the program displays the Function Index in the 1-2-3 Help window.

If you type @ plus the name of a function followed by an open parenthesis as in @SUM(, the program displays information on that function in the 1-2-3 Help window.

If you type { in the Contents box and then press the Help key, the program displays the Macro Command Index in the 1-2-3 Help window.

If you type { plus the name of a macro command keyword as in {LAUNCH, the program displays information on that macro command in the 1-2-3 Help window.

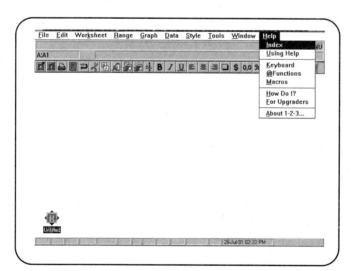

You also can get help by choosing the Help menu and selecting one of the Help options.

2

The Help pull-down menu contains the following Help options:

Table 2.5
Help Options

Option	Function
Index	Displays a list of all help topics. To get information about a particular topic, select the appropriate cross-reference.
Using Help	Gives you information about using 1-2-3's on-line help.
Keyboard	Gives you information about the 1-2-3 function keys, accelerator keys, and navigation keys.
@Functions	Gives you general information about using @functions as well as specific information on each @function.
Macros	Gives you general information about creating and using macros as well as specific information on each macro command.
How Do I?	Displays an alphabetical list of common tasks with cross-references to the appropriate 1-2-3 for Windows commands.
For Upgraders	Displays information showing the 1-2-3 Release 3.1 equivalent for each 1-2-3 for Windows command.
About 1-2-3	Displays the About 1-2-3 dialog box containing the version number of the program, copyright notice, and 1-2-3 status information. The information indicates the location of any circular reference in the current worksheet.

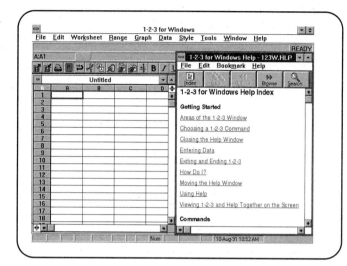

2

Most help topics contain cross-references indicated by an underlined keyword or phrase in the help text (and shown in green on a color monitor).

Each cross-reference leads to related help topics that can give you more information.

To select a cross-reference and display a related help topic with the mouse, follow these steps:

1. Position the mouse pointer somewhere on the cross-reference.

   The pointer changes shape, assuming the shape of the hand icon.

2. Click the left mouse button.

You also can select a cross-reference with the keyboard. Simply press the Tab÷ key until the appropriate cross-reference is highlighted and then press ↵Enter to display the related help text.

Using the Help Menus

The 1-2-3 Help window has its own Menu bar that contains the File, Edit, Bookmark, and Help menus. When this window is displayed, you can choose any of these Help menus just as you would choose a worksheet or graph menu in the 1-2-3 window.

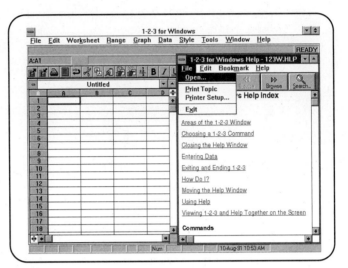

You select the File menu as you do any 1-2-3 worksheet command.

The File menu enables you to open other help files (the 123.HLP is the main help file used by the program) with the **O**pen option, print the currently displayed help topic with the **P**rint Topic option, select your printer with the **P**rinter Setup option, or close the 1-2-3 **H**elp menu with the **E**xit option.

Note: 1-2-3 for Windows on-line help contains information about the program that is not found in the printed documentation. This exclusive information includes a glossary, an error message index, and function and macro command descriptions. If you want to print this information, select the help topic from the Help Index and then select the **P**rint Topic option on the **F**ile menu in the 1-2-3 Help window.

The **E**dit menu in the 1-2-3 Help window contains two options: **C**opy (Ctrl + Ins) and **A**nnotate. You can use the **E**dit **C**opy command to copy to the Clipboard the text of the currently selected help topic. Once you have copied the help information to the Clipboard, you can paste the information into a worksheet. To paste the information, select the Worksheet window and then choose the **E**dit **P**aste command from the Menu bar in the 1-2-3 window (or press ⇧Shift + Ins).

2

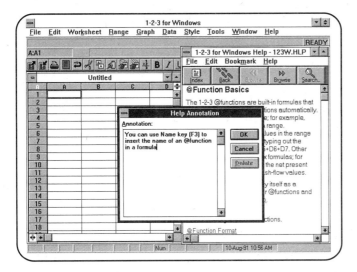

You can use the Annotate option to add your own comments and notes to a particular help topic.

Select the topic you want to annotate and then choose the **A**nnotate option on the **E**dit menu of the 1-2-3 Help window. 1-2-3 displays the Help Annotation dialog box. Type your comments in the **A**nnotation list box and then select the OK button. When the program closes the dialog box, a paper clip appears to the left of the help topic heading to remind you that a note has been attached to that topic. To display your comments in the Help Annotation box, you simply click the mouse on the paper clip.

The Book**m**ark menu contains a single option, **D**efine. You use the Book**m**ark **D**efine command to mark your place in the help topics you refer to frequently. You then can return to them quickly.

To mark a help topic for speedy retrieval, select the topic with the Help Index or select one of the options on the 1-2-3 **H**elp menu. Then, choose the **D**efine option on the Book**m**ark menu in the 1-2-3 Help window.

2

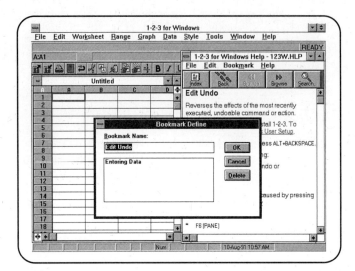

1-2-3 displays the
Bookmark Define
dialog box.

The program places the name of the currently selected help topic in the
Bookmark Name text box. If you want to name the bookmark something else,
type the new name in this box. Otherwise, select the OK button. 1-2-3 will
number the bookmark name you assign and add it to the Bookmark menu. To
return to a help topic, simply select the Bookmark name from this menu (click
it with the mouse or type its number with the keyboard).

The Help menu in the 1-2-3 Help window has two options: Using Help F1 and
About. Select the Using Help F1 option to obtain general information about
the Microsoft Help system (which 1-2-3 for Windows uses along with all other
Windows programs). Select the About option to display a dialog box showing
the version and copyright notice for Microsoft Help.

Using the Help Command Buttons

In addition to the pull-down menus, the 1-2-3 Help window contains five
command buttons that you can use to navigate through help topics. These
Help command buttons perform the following tasks:

Table 2.6
Help Command Buttons

Help Button	Function
Index	Displays a list of all help topics (the same as selecting the Index option on the Help menu in the 1-2-3 window).
Back	Displays the most recent help topic you selected. You can continue to move back through the topics you have reviewed one at a time. When you reach the first topic you looked at, this button becomes dimmed.
Browse	Displays the previous topic in a series of cross-referenced topics. When you reach the first topic in the series, this button becomes dimmed.
Browse	Displays the next topic in a series of cross-referenced topics. When you reach the last topic in the series, this button becomes dimmed.
Search	Enables you to search for specific help topics that contain keywords.

Searching for a Help Topic

The Search command button in the 1-2-3 for Windows Help window enables you to select a keyword and then search for all help topics that contain that keyword. Once you have located all the topics that contain the keyword, you then can select one and display its help information in the Help window.

To search for a help topic using keywords, follow these steps:

1. Click the Search button with the mouse, or press S.

2

1-2-3 displays the
Search dialog
box.

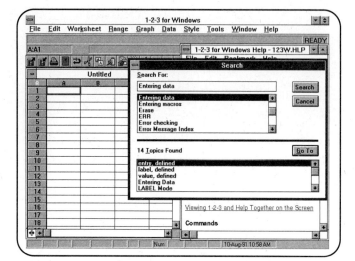

2. Type the first few letters of the keyword you want to use until the word is selected in the list of keywords in the **S**earch For list box, or scroll through this list until you highlight the desired keyword.

3. Click the Search command button, or press ⏎Enter to search the help topics.

    1-2-3 will indicate the number of topics found and display them in the **T**opics Found list box.

4. Select the help topic you want to view in the **T**opics Found list box, and then select the **G**o To button either by clicking it with the mouse or pressing **G**. If you decide that you don't want to review any of the help topics, select the Cancel button to return to the 1-2-3 Help window.

Displaying a Definition or Example

In addition to cross-references, some 1-2-3 help topics contain keywords that have definitions or examples attached to them. Such keywords appear in the text with a dotted underline (and in green on a color monitor).

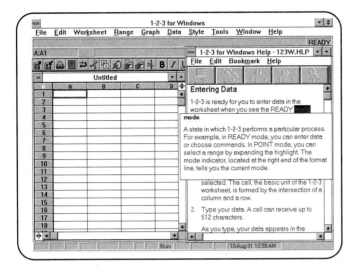

The definition or example related to a keyword appears in a pop-up box.

To display the pop-up box associated with a keyword, position the mouse pointer on the term until the pointer changes to the hand icon and then hold down the left mouse button. The pop-up box remains displayed as long as you hold down the mouse button. As soon as you release the mouse button, the box disappears.

Note: To display a definition or example with the keyboard, press ⎆Tab⎆ until the keyword marked with the dotted underline is highlighted, then hold down ⎆Enter⎆. To remove the pop-up box, simply release ⎆Enter⎆.

Exiting Help

To exit Help, you need to close the Help window. To close the Help window, choose the File menu and select the Exit option in the 1-2-3 Help window Menu bar or simply double-click the Control menu box in the 1-2-3 for Windows Help window. Note that you can't close the 1-2-3 Help window by pressing the Esc key.

Summary

In this chapter, you learned how 1-2-3 for Windows presents information on the screen and how to identify the various parts of the 1-2-3 window that contains all of your work. You also learned about the components of the

2

Worksheet window, how the program uses the mouse and keyboard, as well as how to obtain on-line information.

Specifically, you learned the following key information about 1-2-3 for Windows:

■ The 1-2-3 window consists of several components: the Control panel, made up of the Title bar, Menu bar, Format line, and Edit line; the Icon palette; the work area; and the Status line. Remember that the work area of the 1-2-3 window actually contains the worksheet and graph windows as well as any other special 1-2-3 windows, such as the Help window. The work area also displays any dialog or alert message boxes.

■ 1-2-3 for Windows presents the worksheet in the window as a blank grid of columns and rows that form individual cells.

■ 1-2-3 addresses each cell in the worksheet by the worksheet and column letter and row as shown by the Worksheet window frame or the Address box in the Control line.

■ 1-2-3 keeps you informed of the current state of the program with Mode indicators and the state of the current Worksheet window with Status indicators.

■ You can use the mouse to select cells, menu options, text in cells, and other windows open in the work area by clicking, double-clicking, and dragging.

■ You can also use the keyboard to select cells and commands in 1-2-3. The program uses the various parts of the keyboard, including the alphanumeric keys, direction keys, and function keys.

■ You can obtain on-line, context-sensitive help information about 1-2-3 by pressing the Help (F1) key after selecting a command or after a dialog or message box appears on-screen.

■ You can search for specific help information by selecting the appropriate option on the Help menu or by using the Search button in the 1-2-3 for Windows Help window.

Getting Started

This chapter introduces the fundamentals of starting and using Lotus 1-2-3 for Windows. In this chapter, you become acquainted with the operation of 1-2-3 in the Windows 3.0 operating environment and learn fundamental worksheet skills, including how to start the program, move the cell pointer, make menu selections, start new worksheets, save your work, and exit the program.

This chapter also gives you information about how to use 1-2-3 for Windows with other programs. You learn how to switch between 1-2-3 and the other programs you are running under Windows. You also learn how to use the Clipboard to move information to and from 1-2-3 and other programs that you run under Windows.

Opening a worksheet file

Moving the cell pointer

Choosing 1-2-3 commands

Canceling command selections

Saving a worksheet

Exiting 1-2-3 for Windows

Using 1-2-3 in the Windows environment

Copying and pasting text through the clipboard

3

Key Terms in This Chapter

Cell pointer

The indicator that tells you which cell in the worksheet is selected (current) and is ready to accept data. 1-2-3 for Windows displays the cell pointer by shading the cell or by using a different color on a color monitor.

Worksheet file

A disk copy of all the worksheet data contained in a Worksheet window. You need to save a copy of the data on disk because all data in a window is held in the RAM memory of the computer and disappears as soon as you exit 1-2-3 or turn off your computer. After you save data in a worksheet file, you can retrieve this information into a Worksheet window for subsequent work sessions.

File name

A descriptive name that you give a worksheet when you save its data in a worksheet file. 1-2-3 for Windows always displays the file name in the Title bar of the Worksheet window.

Default file name

A numbered file name that 1-2-3 automatically assigns to an untitled worksheet when you first save the file. The first default file name is FILE0001.WK3, the second is FILE0002.WK3, and so on.

Clipboard

A special area of memory that holds text or graphics that you cut or copy.

Starting 1-2-3 for Windows

Windows 3.0 provides several methods for starting 1-2-3. This section assumes that you have successfully installed the program onto your hard disk. If you have not installed the program, refer to the Appendix for complete instructions on installing 1-2-3 for Windows before you continue.

Starting 1-2-3 from the Program Manager

At the C> prompt, you type **win** and press ⏎Enter. You are placed in the Program Manager. The easiest way to start 1-2-3 from the Program Manager is to select the Lotus Applications Group window, and then choose the 1-2-3 program icon as follows:

1. If you can't see the Lotus Applications window in the Program Manager, choose the Window menu, and then select the Cascade (⟨⬆Shift⟩+⟨F5⟩) or the Tile (⟨⬆Shift⟩+⟨F4⟩) command.

2. Select the 1-2-3 for Windows program icon in the Lotus Applications window.

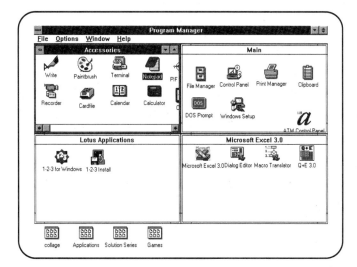

The Lotus Applications window is displayed.

3. Position the mouse pointer on the 1-2-3 for Windows program icon and double-click the mouse or click the icon and press ⟨⬏Enter⟩. You also can choose the File menu, and then select the Open command.

Windows 3.0 also provides an alternative method for starting 1-2-3 for Windows in the Program Manager. This method doesn't require you to have the Windows Applications Group window open at all. It does, however, require you to type the 1-2-3 start-up command in a dialog box.

To use the alternative method, follow these steps:

1. At the C> prompt, type **win**

2. From the File menu, select the Run command.

3. Type the following 1-2-3 for Windows start-up command in the Command Line text box of the Run dialog box:

    123w.exe

If you haven't added the location of the 1-2-3 for Windows program files to the PATH command in your AUTOEXEC.BAT file, you must precede the start-up command with the path name that indicates the disk drive and directory path:

c:\123w\123w.exe

3

4. Position the pointer on the OK button, and then click the left mouse button or press ⏎Enter to start 1-2-3. If you want the Program Manager to shrink to an icon as soon as 1-2-3 for Windows starts, select the Run Minimized check box before you click the OK button.

If you make an error as you enter the 1-2-3 start-up command, Windows displays an alert box with the following message:

```
Cannot find file; check to ensure the
path and filename are correct
```

If Windows displays this message, click the OK button (or press ⏎Enter), and edit the command line in the Run dialog text box before you select the OK button again.

To open a particular worksheet file at the same time you start 1-2-3 for Windows, enter the 1-2-3 start-up command in the text box of the Run dialog box, press the space bar, and then type the path and file name of the worksheet you want to use.

To open the worksheet file REGSALES.WK3 in the 123W directory WORK, enter the start-up command shown in the text box before you select the OK button.

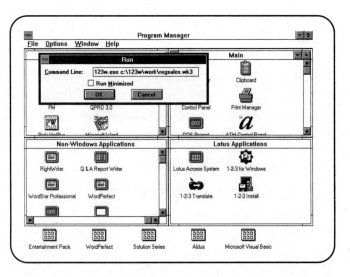

Starting 1-2-3 from the File Manager

In Windows 3.0, you also can start 1-2-3 for Windows from the File Manager. To start the File Manager from the Program Manager, select the Main Group window, then double-click the File Manager icon (the two-drawer filing cabinet) or click the icon and press ↵Enter).

After you start the File Manager, you can start 1-2-3 by following these steps:

1. Locate the 123W folder in the Directory Tree window.

2. To open the file, double-click the file name or click the file name and press ↵Enter). For example, double-click the 123.EXE file icon or click this file icon and then press ↵Enter).

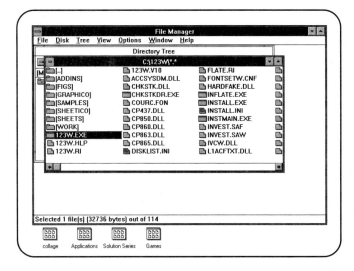

Select the 123.EXE file in the C:\123W*.* document window.

To open a particular 1-2-3 worksheet file at the same time you start 1-2-3 in the File Manager, follow these steps:

1. In the Directory Tree window, locate the folder that holds the worksheet you want to open.

2. To open the folder, double-click the folder icon or click the folder icon and press ↵Enter).

3. Locate the worksheet file icon in the Document window, and then double-click the icon or click the icon and press ↵Enter).

3

To open the
REGSALES.WK3
folder when you
start 1-2-3 for
Windows, double-
click the file icon
or click the icon
and press ⏎Enter.

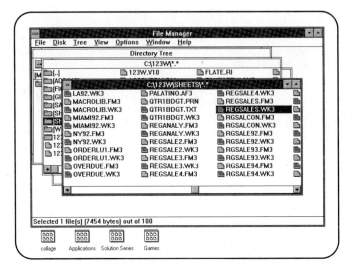

1-2-3 opens the selected worksheet file as soon as 1-2-3 for Windows is
loaded into memory. In the example, the worksheet file REGSALES.WK3
opens as soon as 1-2-3 for Windows starts.

Note: Remember that if you launched 1-2-3 for Windows from the File Manager, you return to the File Manager when you exit 1-2-3 for Windows. To
return to the Program Manager, quit the File Manager by choosing the File
menu and then selecting the Exit option. When the Exit File Manager dialog
box appears, click the OK button or press ⏎Enter.

Opening a Worksheet File

If you start 1-2-3 without designating a worksheet file that you want to open at
the same time, the program opens a new Worksheet window, called Untitled,
in the work area of the 1-2-3 window. You can immediately begin building a
new spreadsheet in the Untitled Worksheet window.

If you use the File Save command to save your work, 1-2-3 assigns a default
file name (such as FILE0001.WK3) to the Untitled window. If you already have
numbered files such as FILE0001.WK3 and FILE0002.WK3 in the current
directory, 1-2-3 for Windows assigns the next available number to the file
name (such as FILE0003.WK3). To save your worksheet under a more descriptive file name, choose the File Save As command and assign a new file name
before you save your changes with File Save (see "Saving a Worksheet" later in
this chapter for more information on this topic).

Note: If you close the Untitled Worksheet window when no other Worksheet window is open, 1-2-3 for Windows creates another Untitled window to replace the window you closed. To get rid of the Untitled window, you must specify a file to open when you start 1-2-3 for Windows or open an existing file before you close the Untitled window.

To use a worksheet file that you created and saved on disk, follow these steps:

3

1. From the File menu, select the Open command.

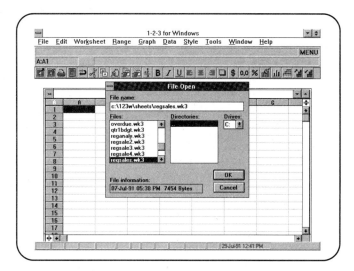

1-2-3 displays the File Open dialog box, which shows all of the worksheet files located in the current directory in its Files list box.

2. If the worksheet file you want to use is not located on the current drive, select the Drives drop-down list box, or click its drop-down box, and then select the letter of the drive that holds the file.

3. If the worksheet file you want to use is not located in the current directory, select the appropriate directory in the Directories list box. If the directory you want is located at a higher level in the file hierarchy, double-click the .. (double period) to go to the next higher level. If the directory you want is located at a lower level beneath a displayed directory, double-click that directory to open it.

4. Select the worksheet file you want to open in the Files list box.

   1-2-3 displays the entire path name of that worksheet file in the File name text box. In the File information box, 1-2-3 displays the date and time of the file's last revision and the file's size in bytes.

5. Select the OK button to open the file.

   1-2-3 places the worksheet file you selected in a new window, positions that window in front of any other open windows, and makes that window the current window. As soon as the program finishes loading the selected worksheet file in the new window, you can begin working on the file.

Note: If you use the mouse in 1-2-3 for Windows, you can select the File Open dialog box simply by clicking the the SmartIcon in the Icon palette.

Opening More Than One Worksheet File

Many times you will want to open more than one worksheet file in the 1-2-3 window. You open more than one worksheet file, for example, when you copy data from an existing worksheet file into a new worksheet you are building.

To open additional worksheet files, you use the File Open command just as you do to open a single worksheet file. Each time you retrieve a new worksheet file with File Open, 1-2-3 places it in a new window, positions that window in front of any other open windows, and makes that window the current window.

1-2-3 cascades each additional Worksheet window to the right so that you can see each worksheet's Title bar.

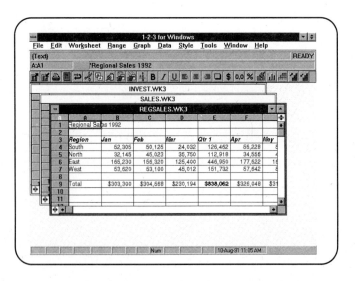

You can use the File Open command to open many different worksheet files at one time, provided that your computer has sufficient memory to hold them all. Because only one Worksheet window can be selected at any one time, however, you can work on only one worksheet file at a time regardless of how many worksheets you have open in the 1-2-3 window. For more information on working with more than one worksheet file, see "Working with Multiple Files" in Chapter 9.

Opening a New Worksheet File

To start a new worksheet file, you use the File New command. The File New command opens an additional Worksheet window that contains a single blank worksheet. As soon as you open a new Worksheet window, the new window becomes the current window and is placed on the top of any other open windows so that you can begin building a new spreadsheet.

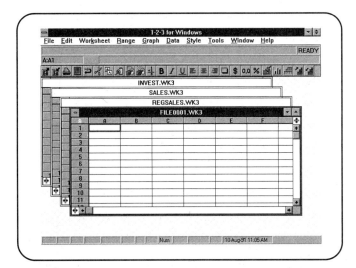

When you use the File New command, 1-2-3 assigns the window a default file name such as FILE002.WK3 (or the next available number).

If you use the File Save command to save your work, 1-2-3 assigns this default file name to the file (use File Save As to give the file a different name).

Closing a Worksheet File

To keep the work area as uncluttered as possible as well as to free computer memory, close any worksheet files that you are no longer using. To close a worksheet file, choose the File Close command or use the WorkSheet Control menu box.

3

To close a Worksheet window using the Worksheet Control menu box, double-click the box or click the box and then select Close. You also can close the window by pressing the accelerator keys Ctrl + F4.

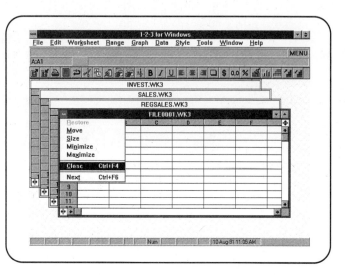

If you make changes to a worksheet that you have not saved and you select the Close command from the 1-2-3 File menu (Close) or from the Worksheet window's Control menu (Close), 1-2-3 displays the File Close dialog box and asks whether you want to save the file.

To save changes, select the Yes option (by pressing ↵Enter) or typing Y). To close the file without saving it, select the No option. To save your work under a different file name, select the Cancel option, and use the File Save As command.

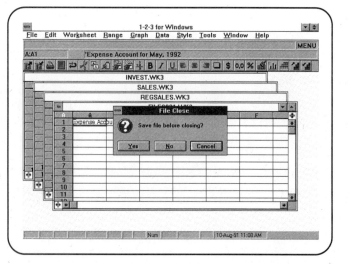

Moving the Cell Pointer

The cell pointer indicates your current position in the worksheet file; its location determines where you can add new worksheet data or which existing data you can edit. To add data to a cell or to make changes to data in a cell, you first must position the cell pointer in that cell. The worksheet cell that contains the cell pointer is called the selected or current cell.

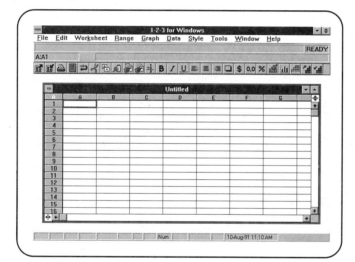

The cell pointer appears as an outline on a color monitor. When you open a new worksheet, the cell pointer appears in the first cell, A1.

When you save a worksheet, the position of the cell pointer also is saved. If you have more work to do on a worksheet, position the pointer at the place at which you want to continue working before you save the file (so that you can begin work there as soon as you open the file again). You can move the cell pointer to another cell in a worksheet with the mouse or with the keyboard.

Moving the Cell Pointer with the Mouse

You can use the mouse to move the cell pointer to any currently visible cell in any open Worksheet window in the 1-2-3 window. Position the mouse pointer somewhere inside the cell and click the left mouse button. When you click the mouse button, 1-2-3 shifts the location of the cell pointer to that cell, making it the active cell. This move is confirmed in the control panel by the appearance of the new cell address in the Address box and the contents of the current cell (if any) in the contents box.

If the cell you want to use is not visible in the Worksheet window, use the horizontal and vertical scroll bars to scroll the window until you can see the cell (see "The Scroll Bars" in Chapter 2 for more information).

To move the cell pointer to a cell in another worksheet file, a Worksheet window containing that file must be open in the work area of the 1-2-3 window. If that Worksheet window (the window containing the cell you want to use) is not visible in the work area, resize and move the current window to reveal the Worksheet window you need.

When you click a cell in another Worksheet window, you not only select that cell, but also make that Worksheet window the current window. 1-2-3 places that Worksheet window on the top of the work area and highlights its Title bar.

Moving the Cell Pointer with the Keyboard

1-2-3 offers a host of keyboard commands that you can use to move the cell pointer. Most of these keyboard commands use the direction keys (the four arrow keys and the Home, End, PgUp, and PgDn keys) alone or in combination with the Ctrl key. 1-2-3 also enables you to move to a specific cell address with the GoTo function key, F5.

Unlike moving the cell pointer with the mouse, many of these keyboard commands not only move the cell pointer, but also scroll a new part of the worksheet into view. Table 3.1 summarizes the keys you can use to move the cell pointer. These keys are divided into three types: pointer-movement keys, used to move the cell pointer in a single worksheet; worksheet navigation keys, used to move the pointer between different worksheets in a single file; and file navigation keys, used to move the pointer between open worksheet files. The next few sections explain their use in more detail.

Table 3.1
Moving the Cell Pointer with the Keyboard

Key	Name	Function
Pointer-Movement Keys		
←	Left	Moves the cell pointer left one column.
→	Right	Moves the cell pointer right one column
↑	Up	Moves the cell pointer up one row.
↓	Down	Moves the cell pointer down one row.

Key	Name	Function
Ctrl + ←, ⇧Shift + Tab⇥	Big Left	Moves the cell pointer left by one window-width.
Ctrl + → or Tab⇥	Big Right	Moves the cell pointer right by one window-width.
PgUp	Page Up	Moves the cell pointer up by one window-length.
PgDn	Page Down	Moves the cell pointer down by one window-length.
End + ←, End + →, End + ↑, End + ↓	End Left, End Right, End Up, End Down	If the cell pointer is on a cell that contains data, it moves in the direction of the arrow key to the last occupied cell followed by a blank cell. If the cell pointer is on a blank cell, it moves in the direction of the arrow to the next occupied cell.
Home	Home	Moves the cell pointer to cell A1 of the active worksheet.
End Home	End Home	Moves the cell pointer to the lower right corner of the active area in the current worksheet (the rectangular area beginning with cell A1 and extending to the rightmost and lowest occupied cells in that worksheet).

Worksheet Navigation Keys

Key	Name	Function
Ctrl + PgUp	Next Sheet	Moves the cell pointer to next worksheet in the current file.
Ctrl + PgDn	Previous Sheet	Moves the cell pointer to preceding worksheet in the current file.
Ctrl + Home	First Cell	Moves the cell pointer to the first cell of the first worksheet in the current file (cell A:A1).
End Ctrl + Home	Last Cell	Moves the cell pointer to the lower right corner of the active area in the worksheet file (the three-dimensional area extending from cell A:A1 to the rightmost and lowest occupied cells of the last worksheet that contains data in that file).

continued

3

83

3

Table 3.1 *(continued)*

Key	Name	Function
End Ctrl + PgUp	End Next Sheet	Moves the cell pointer to the last worksheet containing data in the current file.
End Ctrl + PgDn	End Prev Sheet	Moves the cell pointer to the first worksheet containing data in the current file.
File Navigation Keys		
Ctrl + End Ctrl + PgUp	Next File	Moves the cell pointer to the cell you last selected in the next active file.
Ctrl + End Ctrl + PgDn	Previous	Moves the cell pointer to the cell you last selected in the preceding active file.
Ctrl + End + Home	First File	Moves the cell pointer to the cell you last selected in the first active file.
Ctrl + End End	Last File	Moves the cell pointer to the cell you last selected in the last active file.

Moving a Cell at a Time

To move the cell pointer in the worksheet one cell at a time, press one of the four arrow keys on the numeric keypad (with Num Lock disengaged) or on the dedicated cursor-movement keypad. To move one column left or right from the cell pointer's current position, press ← or →, respectively. To move one row up or down from the cell pointer's current position, press ↑ or ↓, respectively.

If the cell pointer is in a cell that is in the last column or row visible in the window, moving the pointer with one of the arrow keys also shifts the view of the worksheet so that a new column or row comes into view.

Moving a Window at a Time

You also can use a key combination to scroll the worksheet and move the cell pointer horizontally by one window. Press Tab↹ or Ctrl + → (called Big Right) to move to the right. Press ⇧Shift + Tab↹ or Ctrl + ← (called Big Left) to move to the left.

To scroll the worksheet and move the cell pointer vertically by one window (20 rows at a time when the window is full size), press PgUp or PgDn on the numeric keypad or dedicated direction-key keypad.

Using the Home Key

Press Home to move the cell pointer to the first cell (A1) of the active worksheet. If you are working with a file that has more than one worksheet, pressing the Home key moves the cell pointer to cell A1 of the current worksheet. For example, if you are working in worksheet C, pressing Home moves the pointer to cell C:A1 from anywhere in worksheet C. To move the cell pointer to the first cell of the first worksheet in the file (cell A:A1) from anywhere in the file, press Ctrl + Home (called the First Cell key combination).

Using the End Key

You always use the End key with another direction key. When you press End alone, 1-2-3 displays an End indicator in the Status line at the bottom of the 1-2-3 Window. This indicator tells you that 1-2-3 is waiting for you to press an arrow key, the Home key, or another direction key combination (such as Ctrl+PgUp).

Note: Always press the End key independently of the direction key you want to use. For example, to move the cell pointer to the last row of a table, press and release End before you press and release ↓. This combination is unlike a key combination such as Ctrl + Home (indicated by the plus sign), for which you hold the Ctrl key as you press and release the Home key.

When you press the End key followed by one of the arrow keys, 1-2-3 moves the cell pointer in one of two ways. If the cell pointer is in a cell that contains data, the cell pointer moves in the direction of the arrow to the last cell containing data. This technique is very useful when you want to move directly to the end of a column or row in a table that contains no blank cells. You can use this technique not only to move to the last cell in a column or row, but also to select all the cells.

If the cell pointer is in an empty cell, the cell pointer moves in the direction of the arrow to the next cell containing data. This technique is useful when you want to make sure that there are no cells containing data in a particular part of a worksheet. For example, if the cell pointer is located in cell L50 and you want to determine that there are no more cells containing data in row 50 between column L and the right end of the worksheet, press End and →. If all the cells are blank, the cell pointer moves to cell IV50. Otherwise, the cell pointer stops in the next cell containing data that exists in row 50.

Using the End and Home Keys

When you press the Home key after pressing End, 1-2-3 moves the cell pointer to the last cell of the active area of the current worksheet. The active area is the rectangular area that extends from cell A1 to the cell in the lowest row and rightmost column containing data. The size of the active area affects the amount of memory used by 1-2-3. Note that the last cell of the active area may itself be blank.

To move to the last cell of the active area of the current worksheet, press End Home.

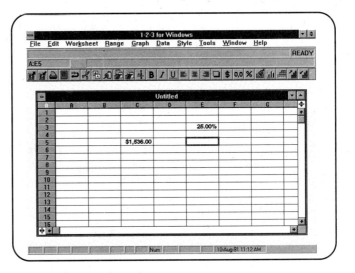

Assume that cells E3 and C5 are the only cells in the worksheet that contain data. The active area extends from column A to column E (the rightmost column containing data because of the entry in cell E3) and from row 1 to row 5 (the lowest row containing data because of the entry in cell C5); that is, the active area extends from cell A1 to cell E5. Although cell E5 is blank, 1-2-3 moves the cell pointer to cell E5 if you press End Home (because E5 is the last cell of the active area).

If you are working on a file that contains several worksheets, you can move the cell pointer to the last cell of the active area of the entire file by pressing End and then Ctrl+Home (called the Last Cell key combination). When you work with multiple worksheets, the active area is a three-dimensional area that extends from cell A:A1 to the rightmost column with a cell containing data, the lowest row with a cell containing data, and the last worksheet containing data. As with a single worksheet, the last cell of the active area may be blank.

3

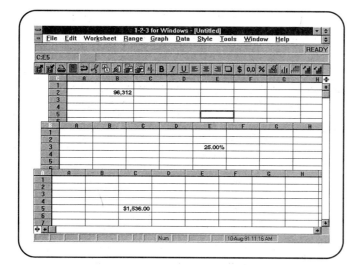

To move to the last cell of the active area of a file that contains more than one worksheet, press End Ctrl+ Home.

For example, consider a worksheet file containing three worksheets, A through C, in which only cells A:C5, B:E3, and C:B2 contain data. The active area extends from cell A:A1 through cell C:E5 (which is blank). The rightmost column of the active area is column E because of the entry in cell B:E3, the lowest row of the active area is row 5 because of the entry in cell A:C5, and the last worksheet of the active area is C because of the entry in cell C:B2. If you press End and then Ctrl+Home, the cell pointer moves to cell C:E5.

Moving a Worksheet at a Time

If you work with a file that contains several worksheets, you can press Ctrl+PgUp (called Next Sheet) or Ctrl+PgDn (called Previous Sheet) to move through the file one worksheet at a time. With Next Sheet key combination, you progress up to the last worksheet in the file (from worksheet A to B, B to C, and so on). With Previous Sheet key combination, you progress toward the first worksheet in the file (from worksheet D to C, C to B, and so on). Note that the cell pointer stays in the same column and row as you move through the worksheets; if the pointer is in cell A:A2 when you press Ctrl+PgUp, it moves to cell B:A2, and if the pointer is in cell C:F15 when you press Ctrl+PgDn, it moves to cell B:F15.

Note: The easiest way to visualize and associate Ctrl+PgUp with moving to the Next worksheet and Ctrl+PgDn with moving to the Previous worksheet in a file is to turn on perspective view with the **W**indow **S**plit **P**erspective command or by clicking the Perspective view SmartIcon on the Icon palette.

3

In perspective view, 1-2-3 shows you part of three consecutive worksheets which cascade up and back toward the right. When you press the Next Sheet key combination, you see the cell pointer move up and back to the next worksheet and when you press the Previous Sheet key combination, you see the cell pointer move down and forward to the previous worksheet in the current window.

If you press the Next Sheet key combination and your computer responds by beeping, the file contains no more worksheets after the current one. Likewise, if you press the Previous Sheet key combination and the computer beeps, the file contains no more worksheets before the current one.

Note: If you are using a mouse, you can move to the next and previous worksheet by simply clicking the Go to the next worksheet SmartIcon.

You also can use the End key with Ctrl+PgUp or Ctrl+PgDn to move the cell pointer to the current file's next or preceding worksheet that contains data. When you press Ctrl+PgUp after you press End, 1-2-3 moves the cell pointer up toward the end of the file to the next worksheet that contains data. If you press Ctrl+PgDn after pressing the End key, the program moves the cell pointer down toward the beginning of the file to the preceding worksheet that contains data.

Moving a File at a Time

If you are working with multiple-worksheet files, you can press Ctrl + End (called the File key combination) with other direction keys to move between files. Press Ctrl + End Home to move to the cell you last selected in the first active file (the one you first opened). Press Ctrl + End End to move to the cell you last selected in the last active file (the one you last opened).

You also can use the File key combination with Ctrl+PgUp and Ctrl+PgDn to move through the active worksheet files in the 1-2-3 window. Press Ctrl + End Ctrl + PgUp to move to the cell you last selected in the next active file. Press Ctrl + End Ctrl + PgDn to move to the cell you last selected in the previous active file.

Note: You always can press the Next Window key combination (Ctrl + F6) to make the next open worksheet or graph window current.

Using the GoTo Key

You can use the Goto function key (F5) or the Range Go To command to move the cell pointer to and select a specific cell in the current worksheet, current worksheet file, or any open worksheet file in the work area of 1-2-3 Windows.

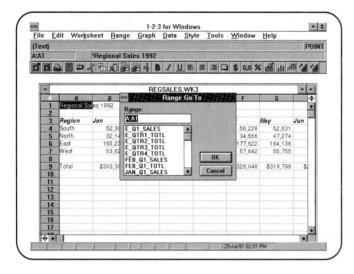

To move directly to a new cell, press F5 or choose the **Range** menu and select the **Go** To option, and 1-2-3 displays the Range Go To dialog box.

In the **Range** text box, you see the address of the current cell. To move the pointer to a new cell, enter the address of the cell to which you want to move. If you assigned a range name to the cell or range to which you want to move, select the name in the **Range** list box. After entering the cell address or selecting the range name, select the OK button or press ↵Enter to move the cell pointer.

To indicate the cell to which you want to move in the **Range** text box of the Range Go To dialog box, do one of the following techniques:

- To move the cell pointer to a cell in the current worksheet, type the column letter and row number of the cell address (such as B10). For example, if you enter **B10** when worksheet D is selected, the pointer moves to cell D:B10. If the cell is in view in the Worksheet window, 1-2-3 moves the pointer without scrolling the worksheet. If the cell is not in view, 1-2-3 scrolls the worksheet so that the cell (D:B10 in this example) is the first cell visible in the window.

- To move the cell pointer to a cell in a different worksheet in the current file, type the worksheet letter followed by a colon, then the column letter and row number of the cell address (such as **C:K15** when the cell pointer is in A:A1).

- To move the cell pointer to cell A1 of a worksheet in the current file, type the letter of the worksheet followed by a colon (such as **C:** to move to C:A1 when the cell pointer is in cell A:A1).

- To move the cell pointer to the top left cell in a range, type the name that you assigned to the range (such as **QTR1_SALES**) or select the name in the Range list box.

To move the cell pointer to the first cell in open EMPLOYEE.WK3 worksheet file, type **<<EMPLOYEE>>** or select <<EMPLOYEE.WK3>> in the Range list box.

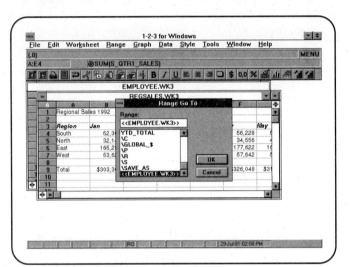

To move the cell pointer to a different worksheet file that is open in a 1-2-3 window, type the file name enclosed in double-angle brackets (such as **<<EMPLOYEE>>**) or select the file name in the Range list box (where it appears as <<EMPLOYEE.WK3>>). When you select the OK button or press ⏎Enter, 1-2-3 moves the cell pointer to the first cell in this file.

To move the pointer to a specific cell in that file, enter the cell address after selecting the file name (such as <<EMPLOYEE.WK3>>C5 to move to cell C5). To move to the first cell of a named range in the new file, type the range name after selecting the file (such as <<EMPLOYEE.WK3>>deptnum).

Choosing 1-2-3 Commands

In 1-2-3 for Windows, you usually select commands by using the menus on the Menu bar of the 1-2-3 window. (Remember that the menus change according to whether a worksheet or graph window is current.) You also can select some commands by pressing a function key (refer to table 2.3 in Chapter 2). For some of the more complex 1-2-3 commands, selecting the command involves using a dialog box that contains additional options.

Choosing Menu Options

To select commands from the 1-2-3 menus, you can use the mouse or the keyboard. To select a menu with the mouse, move the pointer to the menu's name and click the left mouse button to open the menu and view its options. To select an option from the open menu, click the option. To select a menu option quickly, drag through the appropriate menu until you reach the option, then release the mouse button.

To choose an option from a 1-2-3 menu with the keyboard, press Alt or F10 to select the Menu bar, then press ← or →, to select the menu you want to open. When the appropriate menu is highlighted, press the ↓ or ↵Enter to open the menu and view its options. To select an option from the menu, press ↓ until the option is highlighted and then press ↵Enter.

If a triangle (▶) appears to the right of a menu option, that option leads to a cascade menu, which contains a list of further options. To open the cascade menu, highlight the option with the triangle and press ↵Enter or →. To select an option on the cascade menu, press ↓ to highlight that option and press ↵Enter.

Instead of using the direction keys to select menus and menu options, you also can type the underlined letter in the menu or option name (which appear in this book in boldfaced blue type). For example, to open the File menu, you press Alt + F. Then, to select the New option on the File menu, you press N. After you learn the menu letters of the commands, you can shorten this procedure by typing the entire sequence. For example, to open a new worksheet file with the File New command, press Alt, then press F and N in succession.

If the menu option has a keyboard shortcut, the accelerator keys appear in the menu to the right of the option name. To use the accelerator keys to select a 1-2-3 command, press the key combination without opening the menu. For example, to use the accelerator keys to undo the effects of your last 1-2-3 command, press Alt + ◆Backspace. This technique is much faster than using the keyboard or the mouse to access the Edit menu and then select the Undo option.

Selecting Options in Dialog Boxes

When you select a menu or a menu option followed by an ellipsis (...), 1-2-3 displays a dialog box of additional options. In addition to using dialog boxes to request additional information from you about a menu choice, 1-2-3 also uses dialog boxes to display warnings and program messages that tell you the status of a command or why 1-2-3 was unable to execute the command.

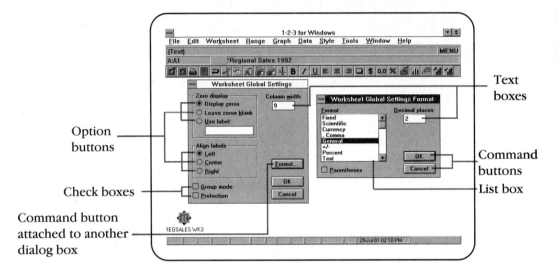

The Worksheet Global Settings and Worksheet Global Settings Format dialog boxes show text and check boxes and option and command buttons.

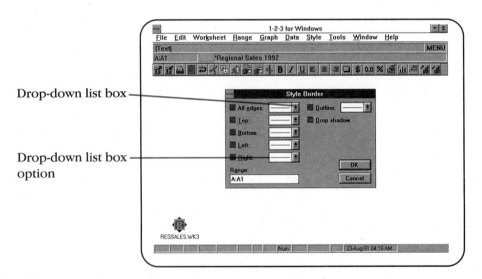

The Style Border dialog box shows drop-down list boxes.

Dialog boxes enable you to select multiple command options without accessing several menus on different levels. Because they present your choices in one place, dialog boxes usually make it easier to specify the necessary information for complex commands.

Moving and Making Selections in a Dialog Box

3

Dialog boxes can contain several types of boxes and buttons. You need to be familiar with each type of dialog box item because 1-2-3 for Windows uses every type of box and button offered by Windows 3.0. These dialog box items include the following items:

- A **Text box** provides a data-entry area for you to enter information. You can edit the entry in a text box by clicking the mouse pointer in the text at the point you want to enter text, or you can press Tab↹ to highlight all the text and then type the new entry.

- A **List box** displays all available choices for that item. If a list box contains more choices than it can display at one time, use the list box's Scroll bar to display more selections. To select a different option, click that option or press ↑ or ↓ to highlight the option and then press ↵Enter.

- A **Drop-down list box** displays the current or default selection. This type of box contains a drop-down button to the right of the current choice. To select a different option with the mouse, click the drop-down button to list the available choices, then click the option you want. To select a new option with the keyboard, press ↑ or ↓ until the option you want appears in the box.

- A **Check box** displays a list of options that you can toggle on or off. A check box can be in one of three states: selected which is indicated by an X in the box, unselected which is indicated by an empty box, or unknown which is indicated by grey shading in the check box. To select a check box option, click its box to put an X in it. You also can select a box by pressing Tab↹ until the item is selected (indicated by a dotted rectangle around the item name) and then press the space bar. To deselect a check box option, click its box or press the space bar to remove the X. To deselect a check box option when its state is unknown by 1-2-3 (indicated by grey shading), click its box twice or select the item and press the space bar twice, once to put an X in the box and a second time to remove it.

93

- An **Option button** displays a list of mutually exclusive options for an item. When an option button is selected, it contains a black dot. You can select only one option in the list at one time. To choose a new option, click a new option button, press an arrow key to move it, or type the underlined letter.

- A **Command button** executes a particular action as soon as it is selected. Command buttons are large rectangular buttons that display the name of the command they initiate. If the name of the command is followed by an ellipsis (...), a new dialog box of choices appears when you click on that command button.

Many times you need to move around a dialog box to choose several options before you select the OK button to execute the command. If you are using a mouse, click the current selection or the button or box that accompanies the selection you want to change.

If you are using the keyboard, press Tab⇄ to move to the next option (from left to right and top to bottom) or ⇧Shift + Tab⇄ to move in the opposite direction. To move to another selection within a group of options (such as a group of option buttons), press the direction keys. 1-2-3 indicates which dialog box option is currently selected by highlighting the current value or by placing a dotted rectangle around the option name (or by doing both).

You can select a dialog box option quickly by typing the underlined letter in the option name (just as you can select menu options). In this book, the underlined letters appear in boldfaced blue type.

To change an entry in a text box with the mouse, highlight its text with the I-beam pointer, then type the new entry. To change only part of the entry, select just the characters you want to change, then type the new ones. To delete part of the entry, select the characters you want to delete and press Del or ◆Backspace. If you choose the text box with the Tab⇄ key, 1-2-3 selects the entire entry.

If you select a list box with the Tab key, use the direction keys to move to the option you want to use and press ↵Enter. If you select a check box, press the space bar to toggle on or off the option. If you select an option button or command button, press ↵Enter to activate the button.

After you indicate all of your changes in the dialog box, choose the OK command button to make your changes and return to your document. To leave the dialog box without making any changes, select the Cancel button instead.

Each dialog box contains a default command button, which is indicated by a heavy outline around the button. This button is activated when you press the Enter key. Although the OK button is usually the default command button, this may not always be the case. The program always chooses the safest command button as the default. In dialog boxes that change 1-2-3 for Windows default settings, an Update command button appears above the OK and Cancel buttons. If you want your dialog box settings to become the new program defaults, select the Update button instead of OK .

3

Canceling Command Selections

The easiest way to cancel a command selection from an open 1-2-3 menu is to position the pointer somewhere outside the menu and click the left mouse button. To back out of the pull-down menus one level at a time, you also can press Esc. To close all the menus and return to READY mode, you can press Ctrl + Break (the Break key is often marked Pause on top and Break on its side).

If you open a dialog box, but want to leave it without changing any options, you can't close the box simply by clicking somewhere outside its boundary— you must choose the Cancel option or press Esc. If the dialog box doesn't contain a Cancel command button, you close the box with the mouse by double-clicking its Control menu box or by selecting the Close option from its Control menu (you also can select this option by pressing the accelerator keys Alt + F4).

Saving a Worksheet

The worksheet you build in the Worksheet window exists only in the computer's (RAM) memory. Because this memory is erased as soon as you exit 1-2-3, you must save a copy of the worksheet as a disk file if you want to have a permanent copy of this work. As you work on your worksheet, save your changes routinely (to avoid redoing your work if someone in your office turns off your computer or the computer loses power).

As mentioned earlier, 1-2-3 for Windows assigns default file names such as FILE0001.WK3 to any untitled worksheet file you save with the File Save command. To give your worksheet a descriptive file name that can help you identify its contents and locate it in a directory listing, use the File Save As command instead when you save your worksheet for the first time. Then, after assigning your own file name to the worksheet with File Save As, you can use the File Save command regularly to save all changes that you make to the file.

3

You must specify the file path as well as the file name when you save a file with File Save As. The file path consists of the drive and directory in which the file is located. For example, in the file specification

C:\123W\BUDGET92.WK3

C:\123W is the file path and BUDGET92.WK3 is the file name. The path identifies C: as the drive and 123W as the directory in which you want to save the BUDGET92.WK3 file. Most often, you will want to separate your worksheet files from the program files in the 123W directory. To do so, create a subdirectory one level below the 123W directory. For example, in the file specification

C:\123W\WORK\BUDGET92.WK3

WORK is a subdirectory in the 123W directory. Notice that a \ (backslash) must separate each part of the file specification, including the drive, directory, subdirectory, and file name. Keeping your worksheet files in their own subdirectories makes it easier to back up your work on floppy disks.

Note: When you save a file with the File Save As command, the path name includes the default worksheet directory as part of the file name. If you save an untitled worksheet with the File Save command, the program saves the file with a default file name in this worksheet default directory. If you install 1-2-3 for Windows on drive C of your hard disk, the worksheet default directory is C:\123W\SAMPLES. To change the default directory, you use the Tools User Setup Worksheet directory command (see Chapter 9 for more information on changing the default directory).

Every file in a particular directory or subdirectory must have a unique file name. File names in 1-2-3 for Windows include the three-character file extension WK3 separated from the main file name with a period. 1-2-3 adds this extension to the file name you specify—you don't have to enter it yourself.

To save and name your worksheet with the File Save As command, follow these steps:

1. Select the window that contains the worksheet you want to save. With the mouse, click anywhere in that Worksheet window. With the keyboard, repeatedly press Ctrl + F6 (the Next Window key combination) until you highlight that Worksheet window's Title bar.

2. From the File menu, select the Save As command.

    1-2-3 opens the File Save As dialog box.

    The program lists the current drive and directory and the default file name in the File name text box.

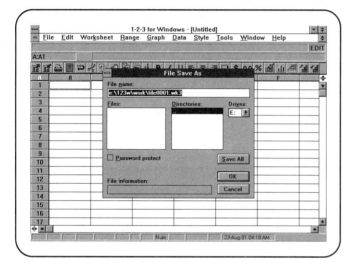

In the File Save As dialog box, 1-2-3 lists the current drive, directory, and the default file name in the File name text box.

3. To save the file on a different drive, select the Drives drop-down list box and select the letter of the drive that you want to hold the file.

4. If you want to save the worksheet file in a different directory, select the appropriate directory in the Directories list box. If the directory you want is on a higher level in the file hierarchy, double-click the .. (double period) to go to the next higher level. If the directory you want is located on a lower level beneath a specific directory, double-click that directory to open it.

5. To change the default file name to your own descriptive file name, use the I-beam pointer to select the part of the file name you want to replace.

3

To change the file name, highlight the part of the name (such as file0001) that you want to replace.

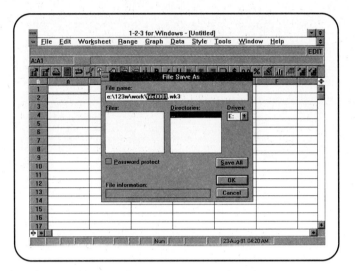

6. After selecting the part of the name you want to replace, type your own descriptive name (up to eight characters in length).

Type the new file name (such as **budget92**).

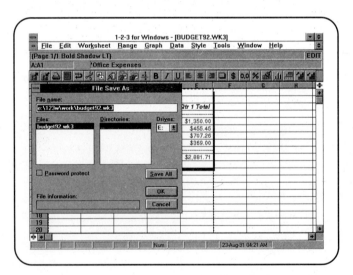

7. Select the OK button.

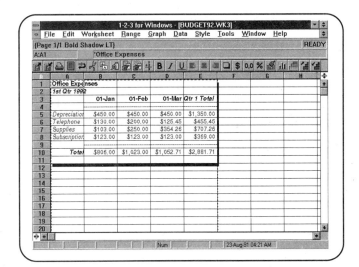

1-2-3 saves the file, and the new file name appears in the Title bar.

If you specified a file name that already exists in that directory, 1-2-3 displays a dialog box that asks you to confirm replacement of the existing file.

After you name and save a worksheet file with the File Save As command, you can save subsequent changes to the file using the File Save command. You should save frequently to avoid losing work. When working with more than one worksheet file in the 1-2-3 window, make sure that you select the appropriate Worksheet window before you choose File Save.

Note: If you use the mouse in 1-2-3 for Windows, you can select the File Save command simply by clicking the second icon in the Icon palette.

Naming Worksheet Files

Choose a name that describes its function and that helps you identify its contents. 1-2-3 for Windows restricts file names to eight characters and does not accept spaces. Substitute dashes (-) or underscores (_) for spaces (as in QTR1_EXP.WK3) in the file name.

Although 1-2-3 appends the file extension WK3 to any main file name that you enter in the File name text box, you can add your own file extension at the time you enter the worksheet file name. Your extension can include up to three characters that you separate from the main file name with a period(.).

3

When choosing the file name and extension, you should avoid the following symbols:

> * ? : ; , \ / &

Be aware that 1-2-3 for Windows is set to search for files that use WK and one other character (WK*), such as WK1 or WK3. If you add an extension that doesn't follow this pattern, 1-2-3 does not display that worksheet's file name in list boxes that show the current directory's worksheet files. (These list boxes appear when you select 1-2-3 commands such as File Open or File Combine From.)

In addition, both 1-2-3 for Windows and Windows 3.0 use certain extensions to differentiate types of program and document files that they use. Table 3.2 lists the most common 1-2-3 and Windows extensions. To avoid confusing your 1-2-3 worksheet files with other types of files, do not use these extensions for worksheet files.

Table 3.2
File Name Extensions Used by 1-2-3 and Windows

Extension	Meaning
AF3	A font library file created when you replace the font settings.
AL3	A page setup file created when you save the page format settings used to print worksheet reports.
BAK	A 1-2-3 Release 2.2, 2.3, 3.0, or 3.1 backup file.
ENC	A 1-2-3 for Windows or Release 3.0 or 3.1 encoded file.
EXE	A program or executable file.
INI	A Windows initial settings file.
FM#	A 1-2-3 for Windows or 1-2-3 Rel. 3.1 format file.
PIF	A Windows program initiation file.
TMP	A 1-2-3 for Windows temporary file which 1-2-3 deletes when you exit 1-2-3 for Windows.
WG1	A 1-2-3/G (for OS/2) worksheet file.
WKS	A 1-2-3 Release 1A worksheet file.
WK1	A 1-2-3 Release 2.2 or 2.3 worksheet file.
WK3	A 1-2-3 for Windows, Release 3.0, or 3.1 worksheet file.
WR1	A Symphony worksheet file.

Saving All Active Worksheet Files

As you work with more than one worksheet file in the 1-2-3 window, you don't have to save the updates to each file individually. Instead, you can save your changes to all the worksheet files by following these steps:

1. From the File menu, select the Save As command.

   1-2-3 displays the File Save As dialog box.

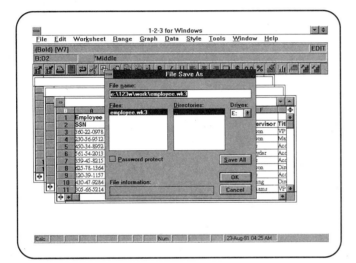

To update all active files, select the Save All command button in the File Save As dialog box.

2. Select the Save All command button rather than the OK button.

   1-2-3 saves each file that has been changed.

Exiting 1-2-3 for Windows

When you finish with 1-2-3 and are ready to quit the program, choose the File menu and select the Exit option. If you saved all the worksheet files you have open, the program closes the 1-2-3 window and returns you to the Windows operating environment. If you selected the Minimize on Use option when you started 1-2-3 for Windows, the Program Manager or File Manager (depending on which you used to start 1-2-3) appears as a program icon in the Windows desktop. To restore the icon to a window, click the icon and select the Restore or Maximize option or double-click the icon. After you restore the Program Manager or File Manager window, you can launch another program or return to DOS by selecting the File Exit Windows command.

3

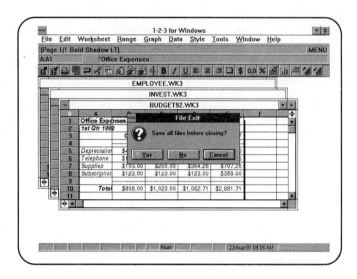

If you made any unsaved changes, 1-2-3 displays the File Exit dialog box.

If you do not save your changes to any of the open worksheet files when you select the File Exit command, 1-2-3 displays the File Exit dialog box. This dialog box asks whether you want to save all files before exiting the program. Select the Yes option to save all files. Select the No option in the rare situation where you want to abandon your changes.

Using 1-2-3 in the Windows Environment

1-2-3 for Windows, unlike its DOS-based predecessors, enables you to run multiple programs and transfer information among them. The Windows environment makes transferring information so easy that in no time at all you will find yourself routinely shuttling information to and from 1-2-3 and other programs—even if 1-2-3 is the only computer program you ordinarily use. For example, you can copy a table of data stored in a Word for Windows document into a 1-2-3 for Windows worksheet or bring a graph created in 1-2-3 for Windows into CorelDRAW! or another graphics program.

Returning to Windows without Exiting 1-2-3

To start another program while 1-2-3 is running, you first need to return to the Program Manager in the Windows operating environment. Click the Minimize button in the 1-2-3 window to reduce 1-2-3 to the program icon. You also can press Ctrl+Esc or select the Switch To option on the Control menu to return to the Program Manager.

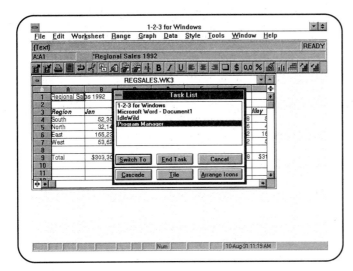

To return to the Program Manager, display the Task List window by pressing Ctrl + Esc or by selecting the Switch To option on the Control menu.

In the Task List window, select Program Manager in the list box and click the Switch To command button or double-click Program Manager.

In the Program Manager, you can start a new program (provided that your computer has sufficient memory) by double-clicking the appropriate program icon or by accessing the File menu, selecting the Run option, typing the correct start-up command, and then selecting the OK option.

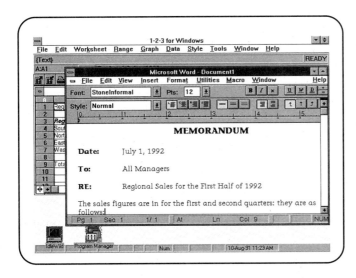

In this example, you see Word for Windows in the active window with 1-2-3 for Windows in the background.

3

Switching Between 1-2-3 and Other Programs

When you have more than one program in memory, you can switch between them as often as needed.

The windows containing 1-2-3 and Word are positioned one above the other; the 1-2-3 window is active, and Word for Windows is in the background.

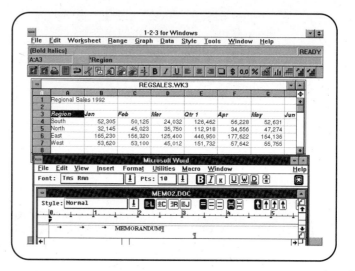

To switch to a different program, activate the program by clicking anywhere in its window. To make it easier to switch back and forth between programs, resize and reposition the program windows so that they barely overlap.

If you are running a program in a full-screen window and don't want to move and resize it or are unable to do this (for example, if you are running a non-Windows program such as dBASE IV on an 80286 computer), you can switch to a new program via the Task List window.

Copying and Pasting Text with the Clipboard

1-2-3's Cut, Copy, and Paste commands on the Edit menu make it simple to move or copy information to new places in the same worksheet file or to other open worksheet files. As one of the major benefits of using a Windows' program, you can cut and paste data between files created by other programs (such as between a 1-2-3 for Windows worksheet and a Word for Windows document).

1-2-3, like all other Windows programs, performs its cut, copy, and paste techniques with the use of the *Clipboard*. The Clipboard is a reserved area of computer memory that stores any text or graphics you select with the Cut or Copy commands. You can retrieve the text or graphics stored in the Clipboard at any time by selecting the **P**aste command. Because the information stored in the Clipboard stays there until you turn off your computer or replace it with other text or graphics, you can copy between any open documents in open or running programs.

Suppose that you create a memorandum in Word for Windows congratulating your sales managers on their brilliant first and second quarter sales in 1992. To emphasize your praise, you want to include in the memo the sales numbers for each region that are stored in a 1-2-3 for Windows worksheet. To bring the sales figures in the 1-2-3 worksheet into your Word for Windows document, follow these steps:

1. Start 1-2-3 for Windows. Switch to the Program Manager using the Task List and start the other program to which you want to copy worksheet data.

   In this example, you start Word for Windows. You then enter the text for the memo up to the point at which you want to insert the worksheet data from 1-2-3. To format the worksheet data, set up a table in Word for Windows that contains the same number of columns and rows as used in the worksheet.

2. Activate the 1-2-3 Window by clicking it or using the Task List, and then open the worksheet file that contains the data you want to copy.

   In this example, you switch to 1-2-3 for Windows and open the regional sales worksheet that contains the first and second quarter sales figures you want to copy to your Word for Windows memo.

3. Select the range of cells in the worksheet that you want to copy to a different program.

   You start by highlighting the cells in the regional sales worksheet that contain the first quarter sales figures in this example.

4. On the 1-2-3 Menu bar, choose the **E**dit menu and select the **C**opy command (or press Ctrl + Ins) to copy the selected data to the Clipboard.

3

Copy the first quarter sales table to the Clipboard by highlighting the cells that contain the data and then choose Edit Copy.

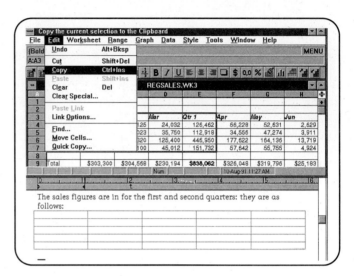

5. Activate the program that contains the document to which you want to copy the worksheet data by clicking its window or using the Task List.

   In this example, select the document window in Word for Windows that contains the sales memo.

6. Position the cursor at the place in the document at which you want the worksheet data copied.

   In this example, select all of the cells in the Word for Windows table in the sales memorandum document rather than just placing the cursor at the beginning of the table. This procedure ensures that worksheet data you transfer from the Clipboard will be properly copied into each cell of the table.

7. From the Edit menu, select Paste or press ⇧Shift + Ins. Be careful that you don't select Edit on the 1-2-3 menu bar by mistake.

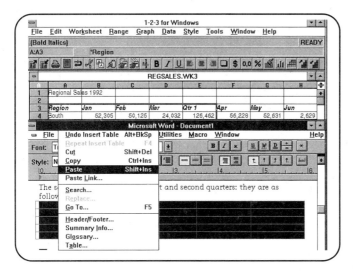

Copy the first quarter sales data from the Clipboard into the table in the Word for Windows sales memorandum by choosing **E**dit **P**aste.

3

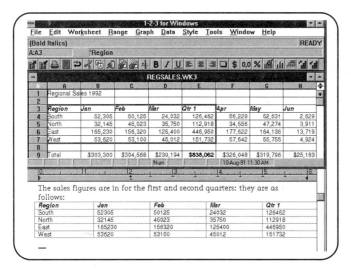

The sales figures are pasted into the Word for Windows table.

Summary

In this chapter, you first learned how to start 1-2-3 from the Windows 3.0 Program Manager or File Manager. Remember that when you start 1-2-3, the program opens a new Worksheet window called Untitled in the 1-2-3 window (where you can begin work on a new spreadsheet). If you want to work on a worksheet you previously saved rather than starting a new worksheet, you use the File Open command, then select the Untitled Worksheet window and close it with the File Close command. If you want to open additional Worksheet windows, you repeat the File Open command.

Specifically, you learned the following key information about 1-2-3 for Windows:

■ To start 1-2-3 for Windows in the Windows Program Manager, locate the 1-2-3 program icon in the Lotus Applications group window and double-click the icon or select it and press ⏎Enter.

■ You also can start 1-2-3 in the Program Manager by choosing the File Run command then entering the startup command **123w.exe** in the Command line text box. To open a worksheet file at the same time you start 1-2-3, enter the complete file name (including path name) after the 1-2-3 startup command. Remember to separate the startup command and file name by a space in the Command line text box.

■ To start 1-2-3 for Windows in the Windows File Manager, open the 123W folder in the Directory tree, and double-click the 123W.EXE file. Or you can select it and press ⏎Enter. To open a worksheet file at the same time you start 1-2-3, open the folder containing the worksheet file, double-click its name or select the file name, and press ⏎Enter.

■ If you don't select a worksheet to open at the time you start 1-2-3 for Windows, the program automatically opens a blank Worksheet window called Untitled so that you can start a new worksheet.

■ To open an existing worksheet file, choose the File Open command. You can use this command repeatedly to open several different files at one time, each in its own Worksheet window.

■ To start a new worksheet during a work session, choose the File New command. The program opens a new Worksheet window to which it assigns a default file name.

■ To close a Worksheet window that contains a worksheet file you are no longer using, choose the File Close command. You also can close the window by double-clicking the Worksheet window's control menu box or pressing Ctrl + F4.

■ You can move the cell pointer in the worksheet by selecting the new cell with the mouse or by pressing specific pointer-movement keys. If you use a mouse, you must scroll the portion of the worksheet containing the new cell into view before you can select it. If you use the keyboard, 1-2-3 scrolls the worksheet as well as selects a new cell.

■ To move the cell pointer to a specific cell in the worksheet, press the Goto key (F5) or choose the Range Go To command. Enter the cell address to go to, or select the range name to move to the first cell in that range.

■ You can select commands from the 1-2-3 for Windows menu bars using the mouse or keyboard.

■ To save a worksheet the first time, choose the File Save As command and enter a descriptive file name.

■ To save changes to a worksheet file under the same file name, choose the File Save command.

■ To save all worksheet files open in 1-2-3 for Windows, choose the File Save As command and select the Save All command button.

■ To exit 1-2-3 for Windows, choose the File Exit command. If you made changes to any open worksheets since you last saved them, the program displays the File Exit dialog box. Select the Yes command button to save all changes.

■ To open other programs, switch to the Program Manager using the Task List and start the new application. You can switch between 1-2-3 for Windows and another program by clicking the program window or using the Task List.

■ To transfer data between 1-2-3 for Windows and other Windows programs that are running, copy and paste the data with the Clipboard.

In the next chapter, you learn the skills needed to build worksheets. As part of this process, you learn how to enter, edit, and format data in a worksheet.

Entering and Formatting Data

4

This chapter teaches the basic techniques you need to know to build your own worksheets in 1-2-3. This chapter teaches you how to enter, edit, and format various types of data in your worksheet, including text, numbers, and formulas.

As you will see, 1-2-3 for Windows gives you a great deal of control over the appearance of the data in your worksheet. You can format numbers with a specific number format or change the alignment of text in cells. You can specify a different font or font attribute for your data. You can even change the colors of cells or add borders and shading to emphasize data. Moreover, to simplify applying complex formatting to worksheet data, 1-2-3 for Windows enables you to assign a name to the formatting in a cell. This procedure creates a style. You can use that style to apply the same type of formatting to other cells in the worksheet.

Key Terms in This Chapter

Label	A text entry that can't be used in an arithmetic calculation. All labels begin with a label prefix that determines how the text is aligned in its cell.
Value	A numeric entry or a formula that can be used in another arithmetic calculation.
Formula	A special entry that performs a calculation and returns some kind of result in the cell where it is entered.
Formatting	The process of changing the way cells display their data in the worksheet. Formatting is most often accomplished with the options on the Style menu.
Cursor (Insertion point)	The flashing, vertical marker that indicates where a character will be inserted in the Contents box of the Edit line when you type a cell entry. To move the cursor, click the I-beam pointer to position the cursor before a new character, or press the direction keys.
I-beam pointer	The shape that the mouse pointer assumes when you position the pointer in the Contents box of the Edit line.

Understanding the Worksheet Defaults

When you start a new worksheet, 1-2-3 uses global default settings (built-in settings) that determine how the entries you make are formatted and displayed in the cells of each new worksheet and graph you create. The program also employs defaults that determine some of the ways 1-2-3 for Windows operates. As you use 1-2-3, you change the default settings to suit the particular worksheet or graph you are creating and the way you like to work.

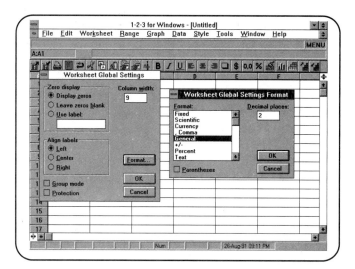

This screen shows the Worksheet Global Settings and Worksheet Global Settings Format dialog boxes.

4

By default, all columns in the worksheet are nine characters wide, labels are aligned with the left border of their cells, zeros are displayed, and General is the global format for displaying values.

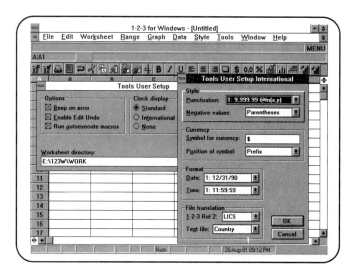

This screen shows the Tools User Setup and Tools User Setup International dialog boxes.

By default in the Tools User Setup dialog box, the program beeps when you make an error, the Undo feature is enabled, the clock is displayed at the bottom of the 1-2-3 window, and the 123W subdirectory called WORK is the default worksheet directory (where all files are automatically saved unless you change the path name).

The Tools User Setup International dialog box controls the default punctuation, currency symbol, and the way the international date and time formats are displayed. This dialog box tells you that the comma (,) is the default character used to separate thousands in numbers and arguments in functions and the period (.) denotes decimal fractions. The dollar sign ($) is the default currency symbol, and it is used as a prefix so that it always precedes the values it modifies. The international date format uses slashes (/) to separate the month, day, and year, and the international time format uses the colon (:) to separate the hour, minutes, and seconds.

Guidelines for Entering Data

When entering data in a worksheet, you must first select the cell where you want the data to appear. To select a cell, position the cell pointer in the cell before you begin typing the entry.

As you type the entry, 1-2-3 displays each character in the Contents box of the Edit line in the Control panel.

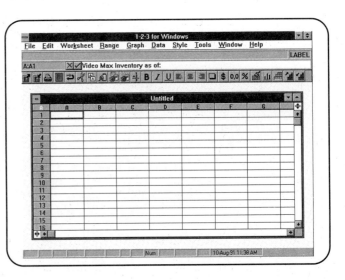

The entry is not displayed in the selected cell until you press the Enter key or one of the arrow keys, or click the Confirm icon (the check mark that appears between the Address box and Contents box when you start an entry). If you make a mistake while typing the entry, press Backspace to delete the incorrect characters.

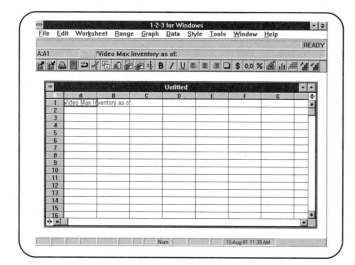

If you press ↵Enter or click the Confirm icon on the Edit line, 1-2-3 enters the data in the current cell without moving the cell pointer.

To speed up data entry when entering a series of headings or numbers in the worksheet, you can use the arrow keys to enter the data and move to the next cell at the same time.

If you find that you are about to enter the data in the wrong cell and want to suspend the operation, click the Cancel icon or press Esc to clear the Contents box.

1-2-3 discriminates between two types of data entry: a label that is a text entry and a value that is a number or formula. The program always tries to anticipate which type of entry you are making by the first character you type. If you begin an entry with a number from 0 to 9 or any of these symbols

+ – ($ @ # . (period)

1-2-3 assumes you are entering a value in the selected cell, and the Value mode indicator appears in the desktop Title bar. If you begin an entry with any other character, 1-2-3 assumes you are entering a label and displays the Label mode indicator.

115

Entering Labels

All labels in a worksheet are preceded by a label prefix that not only identifies the entry as a label but also determines how the text is aligned in the cell. 1-2-3 uses the following label prefixes:

- ' (apostrophe) for a left-aligned label
- " (quotation mark) for a right-aligned label
- ^ (circumflex) for a centered label
- \ (backslash) for a repeating label
- | (vertical bar) for a nonprinting label

When the following conditions are true, you don't have to type a label prefix: the label will be left-aligned in the cell and the entry doesn't begin with a character, such as a number or arithmetic operator, that 1-2-3 associates with a value. To enter the heading First Quarter in a cell, for example, simply type the words and press Enter or one of the arrow keys. 1-2-3 automatically adds the ' (apostrophe) label prefix to your text so that the label is left-aligned in the cell and the cell contents in the Edit line becomes `'First Quarter`.

If, however, you want to enter the heading as 1st Quarter in the cell, you must begin the entry with a label prefix, such as ' (apostrophe). Without a label prefix, 1-2-3 enters into VALUE mode as soon as you type the **1** in the word *1st*. 1-2-3 will beep at you and go into EDIT mode as soon as you press Enter or an arrow key to insert the value called 1st Quarter in the selected cell. At that point, you must edit the entry in the Contents box. Add a label prefix in front of the first character so that 1-2-3 will accept the entry.

Note: Remember that all labels that begin with a number, such as street addresses like 120 Pine Street, must be prefaced with a label prefix, as in '120 Pine Street. If you know ahead of time that you want to center or right-align a label in its cell, you can type the appropriate label prefix as part of the entry, as in "120 Pine Street. You can, however, always change the alignment of labels after you have entered them with the **Style Alignment** command.

Long Labels

Some titles and headings you enter in a worksheet will be longer than the current width of the column. The display of a long label spills over to neighboring cells to the right of the selected cell as long as the neighboring cells remain empty.

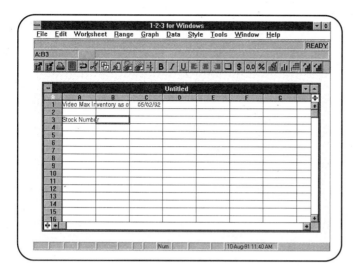

In this example, you see that the letters *er* in Number entered in cell A3 spill over into cell B3.

4

As soon as you enter data in a neighboring cell that displays some of the characters that spill over a long label, the new entry cuts off the display of that part of the long label.

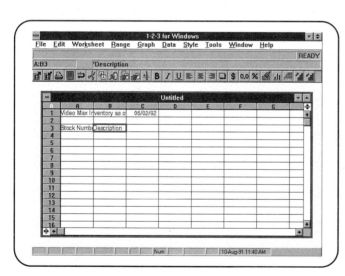

The display of the letter *r* in cell B3 in the word Number is cut off when you enter Description in cell B3.

117

When a long label is truncated by an entry to the right, widen the column that contains the cell with the long label to redisplay all of the text.

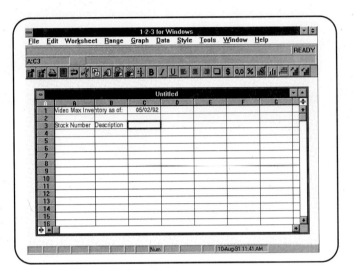

The easiest way to widen a column is to position the pointer on the edge of the frame of the column and drag the border to the right with the mouse. Drag until the column is wide enough to accommodate the display of the entire label. (You learn about widening columns in Chapter 6.)

Changing the Label Prefix Globally

If you find that most of the labels in the worksheet you are building need to be centered or right-aligned in their cells, you can change the label prefix globally so that, by default, all labels you enter are centered or right-aligned in their cells. That way, you don't have to continually add the correct label prefix as you enter the titles and headings for the worksheet.

To change the global label prefix, follow these steps:

1. From the Worksheet menu, select the Global Settings option.

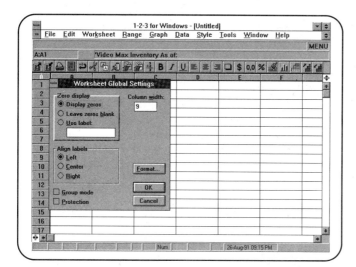

1-2-3 displays the Worksheet Global Settings dialog box.

2. Select the Center option under Align labels to change the global label prefix to ^ (circumflex), or select the Right option to change the global label prefix to " (quotation mark). Select the Left option to return to the global default.

3. Select the OK button to put the new global label prefix into effect and return to the worksheet.

Repeating Labels

You can repeat any character or sequence of characters by prefacing the character(s) with \ (backslash), the repeating label prefix. To repeat a string of asterisks (******) in a cell, for example, type * as the entry in the Contents box of the Edit line. To repeat a string of asterisks and hyphens (*-*-*-) in a cell, type *- as the entry.

Always use this label prefix to repeat characters in a cell instead of typing them. Should you later change the width of the column that contains the repeating characters, 1-2-3 will automatically increase or decrease the number of repeated characters accordingly so that the repeating entry always fills the entire cell.

119

You can use the repeating label prefix with the hyphen (\-) to place a string of underscores across the entire width of a cell.

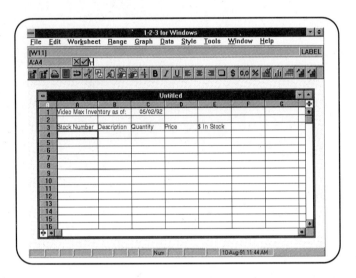

You can copy this label across several columns in a row to separate one part of the table from another.

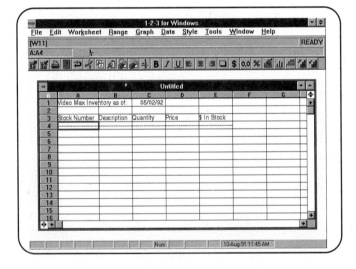

This technique is often used to create a line of single-underscores beneath columns of summed numbers. The line separates the columns from the numbers above. This technique also is used to create a line of double-underscores beneath cells with grand totals to emphasize the bottom line.

Note: You can use the **Style Border** command to underline or double under-line cells that contain special values rather than using repeating labels. See "Adding Cell Borders" later in this chapter for details.

120

Entering Numbers

Entering numbers in a worksheet is a straightforward process. With few exceptions, you simply type the numbers in the Contents box of the Edit line as you would write them out long hand.

1-2-3 does not always store the number in the cell exactly as you enter it. Keep in mind the following points when entering numbers in a worksheet:

- Positive numbers do not require a plus sign. If you type the plus sign as part of the number, as in +50, 1-2-3 drops the plus sign and stores the number 50 when you complete the entry.

- Negative numbers can be entered with a minus sign (hyphen), as in −45, or enclosed in parentheses, as in (45). If you use parentheses, 1-2-3 changes them to a minus sign as soon as you enter the negative number.

- If you enter trailing zeros for the decimal part of a number, as in 23.400, 1-2-3 drops the zeros and stores the number 23.4.

- If you enter commas to separate thousands, as in 340,500, 1-2-3 drops the commas and stores the number 340500.

- If you are entering financial figures and type the dollar sign ($) as part of the number, as in $500.45, 1-2-3 drops the dollar sign and stores the number 500.45.

- If you are entering a percentage and type the percent sign as part of the number, as in 14%, 1-2-3 drops the percent sign, divides the number by 100, and stores the result as 0.14. Numbers with more digits than can be displayed in the current cell width are automatically converted to scientific notation when you complete the entry.

- The appearance of a number in the worksheet depends on several factors specific to the cell in which you enter it, including the number's format, the cell's font, and column width. By default, 1-2-3 uses a global format called General that applies to all numbers entered into a new worksheet. Because the General number format stores only significant digits of the number, all formatting characters, such as parentheses, commas, dollar signs, percent signs, and the like, are dropped from the entry.

4

In this example, the price in D5 was entered as $450.35. With General as the global format, however, 1-2-3 drops the dollar sign and places only 450.35 in the cell.

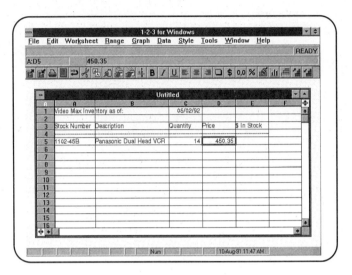

To retain formatting characters, such as dollar signs and commas, in data entry, change the worksheet global format from General to Automatic with the Worksheet Global Settings Format command.

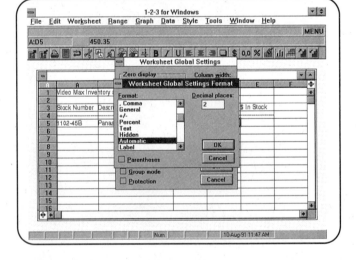

After making Automatic the global format, numbers retain the format you give them during entry.

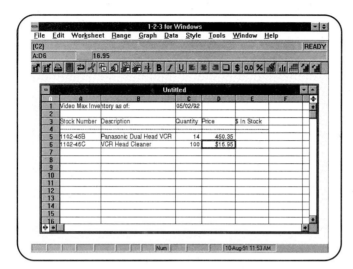

Now that Automatic is the global format, the dollar sign in the entry $16.95 in cell D6 is retained in the cell display, and the Currency format is assigned to the cell.

4

When the global format is Automatic, 1-2-3 assigns a format to the number according to the way you enter it. When the global format is set to General, you must select the values after they have been entered and format them in groups with the **R**ange **F**ormat command. See "Formatting Values" later in this chapter for more information.

When 1-2-3 can't display the value in the cell given the current number format, font size, and column width, the program displays a string of asterisks across the cell (*****).

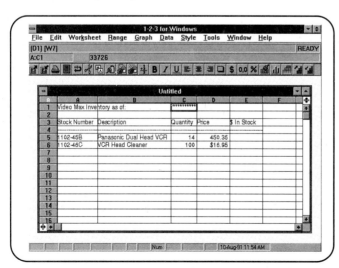

In this example, you see a string of asterisks in cell C1 because the new format selected for the date requires too many characters to be displayed in the current column width.

123

To display such a value in the worksheet, increase the width of the column until the formatted value once again replaces the asterisks in the worksheet.

4

After widening the column, the date in cell C1 is displayed once again in the worksheet.

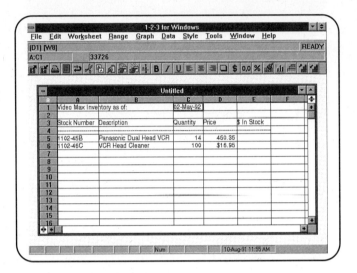

As an alternative to widening the column, you can try using a smaller font in the cell to see whether 1-2-3 can then display the value in its column. See "Selecting Fonts" later in this chapter for specific information on choosing new fonts.

Entering Dates and Times

Dates and times are stored as values rather than labels in a worksheet. A date is stored in the worksheet as a serial number. The serial number represents the number of days that have elapsed before or after the date you enter and December 31, 1899. According to this system, January 1, 1900, is stored as the serial number 1 while January 1, 1992, is stored as 33604. A time is stored in the worksheet as a time fraction that represents the decimal equivalent of the time entered on a 24-hour clock. The time 9:00 AM, therefore, is stored as the fraction 0.375 while 9:00 PM is stored as the fraction 0.875.

Fortunately, you don't have to know the equivalent serial number or time fraction when entering a date or time in your worksheet. All you have to do is enter the date or time in a format that 1-2-3 recognizes. For example, you can enter the date January 11, 1992, either as

1/11/92

124

or

> **11-Jan-92**

1-2-3 enters the correct serial number, 33614, in the cell. Suppose, however, that you enter this date following the common format:

> **1-11-92**

The program instead enters the value –102 in the cell because this method of entering the date does not correspond to a recognized date format. As a result, 1-2-3 misinterprets the entry as a formula in which 1 is added to –11 and –92, yielding the result –102.

When entering a time in the worksheet, simply follow the common practice of separating the hour from the minutes with a colon. To enter the correct time fraction for 8:25 AM in a cell, you type **8:25** and then press **Enter**. When entering a time after noon, append the designation **pm** onto the time or convert the time into a 24-hour clock equivalent. To enter, for instance, the time fraction for 8:25 PM, you can enter in the cell either **8:25 pm** or **20:25**.

You must enter dates and times as serial numbers and time fractions so that you can use them in formulas that calculate elapsed days and hours. You also must make sure that these serial numbers and time fractions are displayed in a discernible manner in the worksheet. If the global format is still set to the default of General, 1-2-3 will display dates and times as serial numbers and time fractions in the worksheet regardless of how you enter them. To have the program display dates and times in the worksheet just as you enter them, change the worksheet global format from General to Automatic. Otherwise, you have to select the dates and times in groups and format them with the **Range Format** command to avoid seeing the serial numbers and time fractions.

Entering Formulas

A *formula* is a special entry that performs a calculation and returns some kind of result in the cell where it's entered. The real power of 1-2-3 lies in its capability to store formulas that use numbers you have entered in other cells to perform computations. Once the formulas are in place, 1-2-3 then automatically recalculates formula results whenever you change any of the numbers the formulas depend on.

In 1-2-3, you can create simple formulas that perform straightforward operations, such as addition, subtraction, multiplication, or division, as well as more complex formulas that perform intricate operations, such as finding the average of a group of numbers, the square root of a number, or the future value of an investment.

Using Mathematical Operators in Formulas

Most simple formulas you create consist of a combination of cell references and constant numbers separated by one or more mathematical operators. Table 4.1 shows you the mathematical operators and the operation each performs.

Table 4.1
Mathematical Operators

Operator	Operation
+	Addition
–	Subtraction
*	Multiplication
/	Division
^	Exponentiation

To add 50 to the quantity stored in cell D15, for example, create the following mathematical formula in the cell in which you want the new result to appear:

50+D15

If cell D15 currently contains the number 50 when you enter the formula 50+D15 in cell D16, 1-2-3 will calculate the result 100 and display the result in this cell of the worksheet.

When the first element of the formula you are creating is a cell reference, you must begin the formula with one of the characters that places 1-2-3 into Value mode. Most of the time, you use the plus sign (+) because it doesn't affect the value in the cell. You can, however, use the minus sign (–) when you want to use the negative of the cell's contents or the open parenthesis (() when you want to group the cell in the formula. If you don't add one of these characters, 1-2-3 will misinterpret the letter of the worksheet or column in the cell reference as denoting a label and will enter the formula as a label.

For example, to build a formula in cell E5 that multiplies the quantity stored in cell C5 by the price stored in D5, enter in this cell +C5*D5.

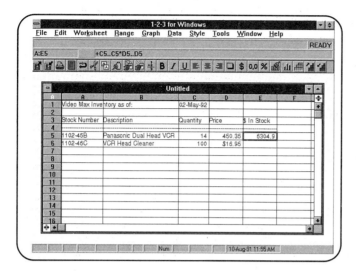

Although the result 6304.9 is displayed in the cell in the worksheet, the contents of cell E5 appear in the Contents box of the Edit line as the formula +C5..C5*D5..D5.

4

Because the cell contains a formula that uses cell references instead of numbers (+C5*D5 as opposed to 14*450.35), 1-2-3 can recalculate the result in E5 whenever you enter either a new quantity or price in cell C5 or D5, respectively.

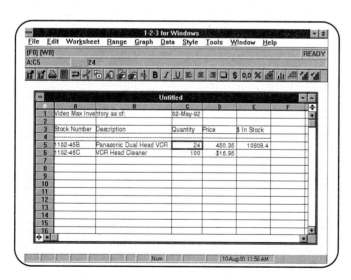

In this example, you see that the result in cell E5 has changed from 6304.9 to 10808.4 when the quantity in cell C5 was increased from 14 to 24.

4

Other Types of Formulas

Although you most often use mathematical formulas in your worksheets, you can use other types of formulas supported by 1-2-3. In addition to mathematical formulas, the program supports logical formulas, which compare two values or labels and produce a true or false result, and string formulas, which perform operations only on labels.

Logical formulas set up a condition that compares two values or labels in the worksheet with the use of the logical operators shown in table 4.2. A logical formula always produces either one of two results: 1 when the condition in the formula is true or 0 when the condition is false.

Table 4.2
Logical Operators

Operator	Function
=	Equal to
<	Less than
>	Greater than
<=	Less than or equal to
=	Greater than or equal to
<>	Not equal to
#AND#	Logical AND, both conditions must be true
#OR#	Logical OR, either condition can be true
#NOT#	Logical NOT, first condition must not be true

For example, suppose that you build the following formula in cell C2:

    +A2>B2

1-2-3 will calculate the result 1 in this cell when cell A2 contains a value that is larger than the one in B2 and will calculate the result 0 when the value in A2 is smaller than B2.

Suppose that you build this formula in cell C3:

    +A3=B3

The program will calculate the result 1 for true when the value or label in cell A3 is the same as the one in cell B3. Otherwise, the formula will calculate the result 0 for false.

128

String formulas use only one operator, the string operator & (ampersand). The string operator is used to *concatenate*, or join, labels. Suppose, for example, that you create the following formula in cell C3 and A4 contains the label Boston and B4 contains the label Massachusetts:

    +A4&B4

The formula will return the following result in cell C3:

    Boston Massachusetts

To add a space between Boston and Massachusetts in the new label in C3, you join a single space to the two other labels in the string formula as follows:

    +A4&" "&B4

This formula will return the following result in the cell in which it's entered:

    Boston Massachusetts

Using Functions in Formulas

Many of the formulas you create in 1-2-3 rely on functions rather than the use of mathematical, logical, or string operators. A *function* is a built-in formula that performs a particular type of calculation. Each function begins with the @ (at) symbol followed by the function name, as in @SUM, which totals a range of numbers, or @PI, which returns the value of the mathematical constant pi.

As you will learn in Chapter 7, the functions included in 1-2-3 fall into various categories. You need to know what information, if any, the function requires to perform its particular type of calculation.

Note: 1-2-3 goes into VALUE mode whenever you type the @ symbol as the first character in an entry because 1-2-3 is anticipating a formula that uses a function. You must, therefore, use a label prefix to enter any worksheet heading or title that begins with the @ symbol.

Correcting Errors in Formulas

1-2-3 does not allow you to enter an invalid formula in a cell. If you enter a formula in the Contents box that 1-2-3 can't evaluate, the program goes into EDIT mode and positions the cursor at the first place in the formula that 1-2-3 can't process. You then can correct the formula so that the formula can be entered into the cell.

129

Common errors in formulas include extra or missing parentheses in a formula, misspelled function names, and missing or the wrong type of information in functions. If your formula uses a function and you can't immediately figure out what is wrong, press the Help (F1) key to look up the function and check its syntax. After you have identified the error, edit the formula (see "Editing Data" later in this chapter for more about editing the contents of a cell) and then press ↵Enter.

Sometimes when 1-2-3 calculates a formula, it displays ERR as the result in the cell instead of the expected answer. ERR stands for *error value*. This value is returned whenever you enter a valid formula in a cell that 1-2-3 can't calculate. One of the most common causes of ERR is division by zero. If, for example, you enter the formula +C4/D4 in cell E4 and cell D4 is empty or contains 0, 1-2-3 will place ERR in E4.

Another common cause of ERR is the deletion of a column, row, or worksheet that contains a cell referenced in the formula. If, for example, you enter the formula +C5-D5 in E5 and then delete column C, the formula will be adjusted to cell D5 where the cell will return ERR, and its contents will become +ERR-C5.

If a formula returns ERR and the formula's answer is subsequently referenced to in other formulas in the worksheet, those formulas also return ERR. To get rid of ERR values, you first must find the formula that is the source of the error value. If, when you locate this formula, you find that the ERR value is caused by division by zero, you can remedy the situation simply by entering a number in the cell that is used as the divisor. If, on the other hand, the error value is caused by the deletion of one or more cells referenced in the formula, you will have to recreate the formula in order to remove the ERR value.

Changing the Order in which Formulas Are Evaluated

When 1-2-3 calculates a formula that you build in a cell, 1-2-3 evaluates every element in the formula from left to right in a prescribed order called the *order of precedence* (shown in table 4.3).

Table 4.3
Order of Precedence for Operators

Operators	Operation	Precedence
^	Exponentiation	1
−+	Negative, positive value	2

130

Operators	Operation	Precedence
* /	Multiplication, division	3
+ −	Addition, subtraction	4
= <>	Equal to, not equal to	5
< >	Less than, greater than	5
<=	Less than or equal to	5
=>	Greater than or equal to	5
#NOT#	Logical NOT	6
#AND# #OR#	Logical AND, logical OR	7
&	string concatenation	7

4

The program always performs the series of operations according to the order of precedence unless you override the order with the use of parentheses. For example, consider the following formula:

  3+5*4

Because multiplication ranks higher in the order of precedence than addition (3 for multiplication as opposed to 4 for addition), 1-2-3 performs the multiplication operation before it performs the addition, resulting in the answer of 23 (5*4=20 and 20+3=23).

If you want to alter the order of precedence in this formula so that the program performs the addition before the multiplication, you can do so with parentheses as follows:

  (3+5)*4

With the addition of the parentheses to this formula, 1-2-3 performs the addition before the multiplication despite its natural precedence, resulting in an answer of 32 (3+5=8 and 8*4=32).

If you use more than one pair of parentheses to group operations and change the order in which the formula is evaluated, 1-2-3 always performs the operation in the inmost pair of parentheses first. Then, 1-2-3 works its way outward to each succeeding pair of parentheses. To see how this process works, first consider this formula:

4

4*(5–2)+5

1-2-3 first performs the subtraction of 5–2 in the parentheses, and then multiplies the result of 3 by 4. Next, 1-2-3 adds the product of 12 to 5, resulting in a final answer of 17.

Now consider what happens to the same formula when you then add a second pair of parentheses as follows:

4*((5–2)+5)

1-2-3 still performs the subtraction of 5–2 first because 5–2 is in the inmost parentheses. Next, however, the program then adds 5 to the result of the difference, 3, because of the grouping of the second pair of parentheses. Only then does 1-2-3 multiply the sum of 8 by 4, giving you a new answer of 32.

Designating Cell References in Formulas by Pointing

With 1-2-3, you can point to the cells you want to use in a formula rather than type the addresses as you build the formula on the Edit line. Pointing is the safest and most efficient method for including cell references in a formula. If you type a cell reference, you may enter the wrong cell reference in a formula as the result of a simple typographical error that you don't catch. 1-2-3 will then use the incorrect cell reference as it calculates the formula (provided that you have entered a legitimate cell reference), and then you have to detect the error based on the result alone. If, however, you have to physically select the cell in order to include the cell in a formula (as you do in pointing), you are less likely to choose the wrong cell, causing the formula to return an incorrect result.

When pointing to cells you want to use in a formula, you can select the cells either with the mouse or with the arrow keys. Before 1-2-3 will enable you to point to cells, however, the program must be in VALUE mode. If the first element in your formula will be a cell reference, remember to type the + (plus sign) to put the program into VALUE mode before you start pointing.

To see how pointing works, read these steps for creating the simple formula +C5*D5 in cell E5 with the mouse:

1. Select cell E5 by clicking it.
2. Type $\boxed{+}$ (plus sign) to put 1-2-3 in VALUE mode.
3. Click cell C5.
4. Type $\boxed{*}$ (asterisk) to indicate the operation of multiplication.

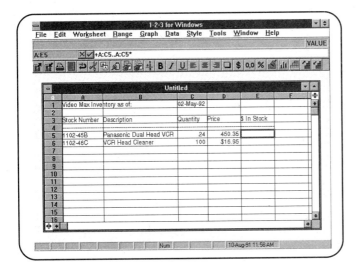

The formula in the Contents box now reads +A:C5..A:C5*.

4

5. Click cell D5.

The cell pointer returns to cell E5, with the complete formula in the Contents box.

The Contents box on the Edit line now reads +A:C5..A:C5*A:D5..A:D5.

6. Click the Confirm icon to enter this formula in cell E5.

133

1-2-3 displays the calculated result 10808.4 in cell E5 in the worksheet and the formula +C5..C5*D5..D5 in the Contents box on the Edit line.

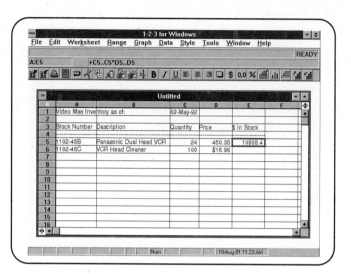

If you prefer, you can point to the cells you want to include in the formula with the arrow keys instead of the mouse. Here are the steps for creating the previous formula with the keyboard:

1. Move the cell pointer to cell E5 with the arrow keys.

2. Type ⊕ (plus sign) to put 1-2-3 in VALUE mode.

3. Press ← twice to move the cell pointer to cell C5.

   The program goes into POINT mode, and the Contents box on the Edit line contains +A:C5.

4. Type ✳ (asterisk) to indicate the operation of multiplication.

   The cell pointer returns to cell E5, and the formula in the Contents box becomes +A:C5*.

5. Press ← once to move the cell pointer to cell D5.

   The Contents box now reads +A:C5*A:D5.

6. Press ⏎Enter to enter the formula in cell E5.

1-2-3 displays the calculated result 10808.4 in cell E5 in the worksheet and the formula +C5*D5 in the Contents box on the Edit line.

Enhancing the Appearance of Data

After you enter the text, numbers, and formulas, you can enhance the appearance of the data. 1-2-3 for Windows provides powerful and easy-to-use tools for making your worksheet data easier to read. You can select new fonts, font attributes, number formats, or alignment for your data as well as assign borders, colors, or shading to the cells that contain the data.

4

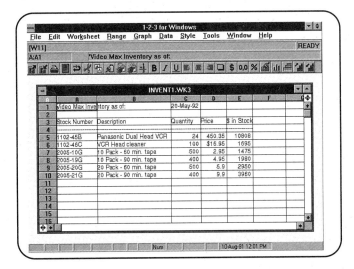

This worksheet is an example of an unformatted worksheet.

135

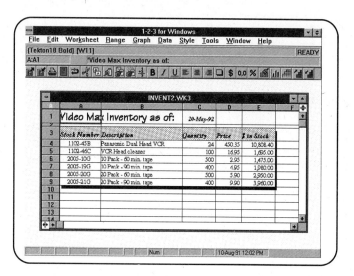

Here is the same worksheet after a variety of formatting techniques have been applied.

In 1-2-3 for Windows, the most efficient method for building a worksheet is to enter all headings, numbers, and formulas then go back and format each group of cells as required. You can, however, assign a format to cells before you even enter data. If you assign a format first, data entered in the cells takes on the formatting as soon as you complete the entry.

Note: Keep in mind that the formatting you assign to cells is transferred along with the labels or values when you copy or move the data to new locations in the worksheet file.

Formatting Values

You can use the Worksheet Global Settings Format and the Range Format commands to change the way values are displayed in the worksheet. Commonly used 1-2-3 number formats include fixed decimal place, scientific notation, comma, currency, percentage, dates, and times. The global format setting affects all values in the entire worksheet file. Range format settings override the global format for whatever cells are selected.

To change the way a group of values is displayed in the worksheet with the Range Format command, follow these steps:

1. Select the cells you want to format.

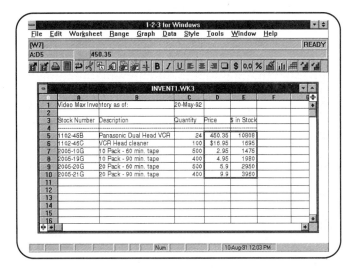

If you are using the mouse, drag the pointer to select the cells. If you are using the keyboard, position the cell pointer in the first cell and press F4. Then use the cursor keys to extend the cell pointer's outline so that it encloses the cells you want selected.

4

2. From the Range menu, select the Format option.

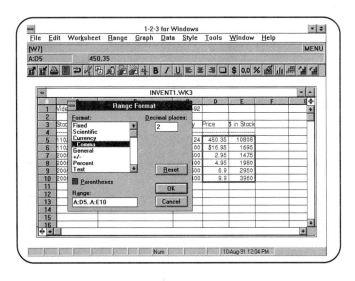

1-2-3 displays the Range Format dialog box.

3. Locate the name of the format you want to use (refer to table 4.4) in the Format list box and select the format.

4. If the format you selected in the Format list box displays decimal places (as do the Fixed, Currency, Comma, and Percent formats) and you want to use a number other than 2, select the Decimal places text box and enter a value between 0 and 15.

5. If you want negative values displayed in parentheses rather than with a minus sign and the format you selected in the **F**ormat list box doesn't automatically do so (as is the case with the Fixed format), select the **P**arentheses check box.

6. Select the OK command button.

1-2-3 applies to the selected cells the format you chose.

4

In this example, the cells are formatted with Comma format with 2 decimal places. Notice that the abbreviation for this format (,2) now appears at the beginning of the Format line of the Control panel.

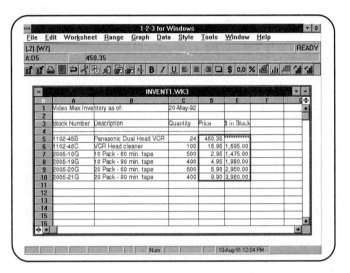

Number formats apply only to values in the range. If the cells you selected contain labels and you choose one of these number formats, 1-2-3 does not affect the appearance of the cells. However, if you later replace their contents with values of some kind, the program then displays these values in the format you assigned earlier.

If you find after using the **R**ange **F**ormat command that you want to restore the global format to the cells you changed, select the cells, choose the **R**ange **F**ormat command again, and this time select the **R**eset command button in the Range Format dialog box.

Note: Although selecting cells before you format them is usually the easiest method, you can select the **R**ange **F**ormat command first, select the desired format, and then designate the cell range in the **R**ange text box (see Chapter 5 for more information on cell ranges).

Table 4.4 explains the function of each format in the **F**ormat list box in the Range Format dialog box. The table also shows examples of how entries are displayed in the worksheet when a particular format is selected. Note that the

Format Indicator column in this table shows you the abbreviation for the format that you apply to the cell. This indicator appears in the Format line of the Control panel when you position the cell pointer in a cell that uses the format. Also, the Cell Display examples in this table all use the default of two decimal places for those formats which display decimal places.

Table 4.4
1-2-3 Range and Worksheet Global Formats

Format	Description	Cell Entry	Format Indicator	Cell Display
Fixed	Displays values in the range with a fixed number of decimal places (up to 15); uses a minus sign for negative values and a leading zero for decimal values.	3456.456 –3456.456 0	(F2) (F2) (F2)	33456.46 –3456.46 0.00
Scientific	Displays values in the range in scientific notation, powers of 10 with an exponent between –99 and 99.	3456.456 –3456.456 0	(S2) (S2) (S2)	3.46E+03 –3.46E+03 0.00E+00
Currency	Displays values in the range with currency symbol, thousands separators, and leading zero for decimal values. Negative values are enclosed in parentheses.	3456.456 –3456.456 0	(C2) (C2) (C2)	3,456.46 ($3,456.46) 0.00

continued

4

139

Table 4.4 *(continued)*

Format	*Description*	*Cell Entry*	*Format Indicator*	*Cell Display*
Comma	Displays values in the range with thousands separators and leading zero for decimal values. Negative values are enclosed in parentheses.	3456.456 −3456.456 0	(,2) (,2) (,2)	3,456.46 (3,456.46) 0.00
General	Displays values in the range without thousands separators or trailing zeros to the right of the decimal point. The minus sign is used to display negative values.	3456.456 −3456.456 0	(G) (G) (G)	3456.456 −3456.456 0
+/−	Displays values in the range (rounded to the nearest whole number) as a series of plus (+) or minus (−) signs. Positive values are represented by plus signs, negative values by minus signs, and a value between −1 and +1 by a period (.)	3 −4 (+)	(+) (+) 0	+++ − − − (+)

Format	Description	Cell Entry	Format Indicator	Cell Display
Percent	Displays values in the range as percentages by multiplying them by 100 and adding the percent sign.	.34 −.23 0	(P2) (P2) (P2)	34.00% −23.00% 0.00%
Text	Displays numbers in the range in General format. Displays the contents of formulas in the range instead of their calculated result.	3,456.456 −3456.456 +D32+D33	(T) (T) (T)	3,456.56 −3456/56 +D32+D33
Hidden	Suppresses the display of all entries in the range without disturbing the contents of any cell. The entries appear in the Control line when each cell is selected unless the range is protected (see "Protecting a Worksheet" in Chapter 6).	3456.456 −3456.456 0	(H) (H) (H)	

4

continued

4

Table 4.4 *(continued)*

Format	Description	Cell Entry	Format Indicator	Cell Display
Automatic	Displays existing values in the range in General format. Assigns formats to new number entries according to the format used when entering them. If a new entry in the range starts with a value but mixes text and numbers, 1-2-3 stores it as a label. If an invalid formula is entered in the range, the program stores it as a label as well.	.45% Feb-15-92 $1,200.34 –6,700.12	(P2) (D1) (C2) (,2)	0.45% 15-Feb-92 $1,200.34 (6,700.12)
Label	Displays existing values in the range in General format. Adds label prefix to all new entries made in the range.	3456.456 –3456.456 0	(L) (L) (L)	3456.456 –3456.456 0
1: 31-Dec-90	Day-Month-Year	33689	(D1)	26-Mar-92
2: 31-Dec	Day-Month	33689	(D2)	26-Mar
3: Dec-90	Month-Year	33689	(D3)	Mar-92
4: Long Intl Date	Month/Day/Year (Long International)	33689	(D4)	03/26/92
5: Short Intl Date	Month/Day (Short International)	33689	(D5)	03/26
6: 11:59:59 AM	Hour:Minutes: Seconds	0.97482639	(D6)	11:23:45 PM
7: 11:59 AM	Hour:Minutes	0.97482639	(D7)	11:23 PM

Format	Description	Cell Entry	Format Indicator	Cell Display
8: Long Intl Time	Hour:Minutes: Seconds (Long International using 24-hour clock)	0.97482639	(D8)	23:23:45
9: Short Intl Time	Hour:Minutes (Short International using 24-hour clock)	0.97482639	(D9)	23:23

Note: If you use the mouse, you can quickly format cells with the Comma format with 0 decimal places. Select the cells and then click the SmartIcon. To format with the Currency format and 0 decimal places, click the SmartIcon. To format with the Percent format and 0 decimal places, click the SmartIcon. To return the selected values to their original formatting, simply click the same SmartIcon a second time with the cell highlighted.

Changing the International Settings

1-2-3 enables you to change the display of the Long and Short International date and time formats and Currency and Comma number formats in the worksheet. By modifying the international user settings, you can specify a currency symbol other than the dollar sign; or you can use the period as the thousands separator and the comma as the decimal point in the style of many European countries. You also can modify the order in which the International date formats display the month, day, and year information; choose between a 12- and 24-hour clock for time formats; and change the character used to separate date and time information.

To change any of the international user settings, follow these steps:

1. From the Tools menu, select the User Setup option.

   1-2-3 displays the Tools User Setup dialog box.

2. Click the International command button to display the Tools User Setup International dialog box.

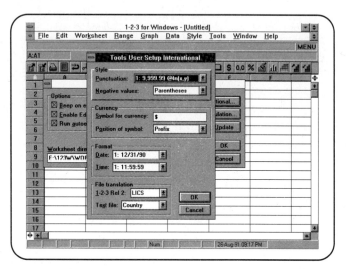

1-2-3 displays the
Tools User Setup
International
dialog box.

4

3. Select the appropriate drop-down list boxes in the User Setup International dialog box and choose the new setting as follows:

   Select the Punctuation option under Style to modify the separator used by the Comma format and in functions.

   Select the Negative values option to modify the way negative numbers are displayed when you format values with the Comma or Currency formats. By default, the Parentheses option is selected so that negative values are enclosed in parentheses as in ($45.00). Select the Sign option to have the negative sign placed before the negative value.

   Select the Symbol for Currency and Position of Symbol options under Currency to modify the Currency format. To change the currency symbol, enter the new symbol in the Symbol for Currency text box.

   Choose the Date option under Format to modify the display of the Long and Short International date formats.

   Select the Time option to modify the way the Long and Short International Time formats are displayed.

4. Select the OK button to put your changes in effect in the current worksheet file.

Note: To enter a new currency symbol that uses a special character not found on the keyboard, such as the Pound or Yen symbol, use the Compose key (Alt+F1) and the compose sequence to enter the appropriate LMBCS character.

Aligning Labels in Cells

By default, 1-2-3 aligns all labels with the left margin of cells and all values with the right margin. In 1-2-3 for Windows, you can change the alignment of labels to centered or right-aligned; values always remain right-aligned in their cells.

To change the alignment of labels in their cells, follow these steps:

1. Select the cells whose alignment you want to change.
2. From the Style menu, select the Alignment option.

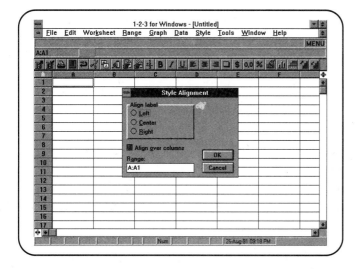

1-2-3 displays the Style Alignment dialog box.

3. To center the labels in their cells, select the Center option button under Align label. To right-align the labels in their cells, select the Right option button. To return to left-align, select the Left option button.
4. Select the OK button in the Style Alignment dialog box.

Note: Remember that you can always change the alignment of labels by adding the correct label prefix (' to left-align, ^ to center, and " to right-align) to the beginning of the label.

Aligning a Label Over Columns

1-2-3 for Windows not only enables you to align labels in their cells but also align labels over several columns. Using this feature, you can easily center a worksheet title over the table of data it describes. Gone are the days when you had to pad a title with extra spaces to center it over a table in the worksheet.

When aligning a label over several columns, 1-2-3 for Windows gives you four alignment options: **Left**, **Right**, **Center**, or **Even**. The **Even** option is used to expand the label over the columns by adding extra space between the words and letters the label contains. This option has no effect, however, if the label ends with a period (.), colon (:), question mark (?), or exclamation point (!).

To align a label over several columns, follow these steps:

1. Select cells in all the columns you want to align a label over.

In this example, cells A1 through F1 are selected. The title of the worksheet will be centered between columns A and F.

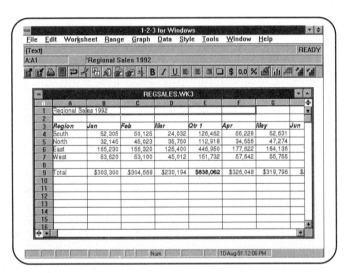

2. From the **S**tyle menu, select the **A**lignment option.

    1-2-3 displays the Style Alignment dialog box.

3. Select the Align **o**ver columns option and place a check mark in the check box.

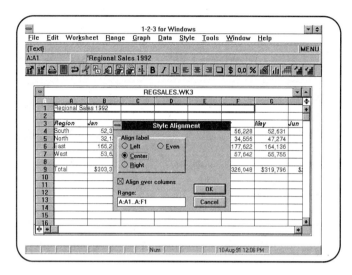

The options under Align labels change to include a fourth option, Even.

4

4. Select the appropriate option button under Align label:

   Left to align the label with the first selected column.

   Center to center the label between the selected columns.

   Right to align the label with the last selected column.

   Even to stretch the label between the selected columns.

5. Select the OK button in the Style Alignment dialog box.

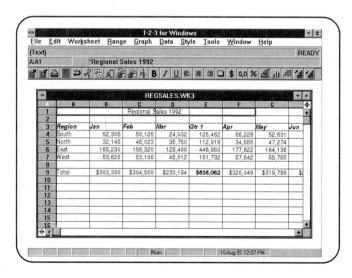

You see the result of using the Center option with the Align over columns option.

147

The worksheet title is now centered between columns A and F. Note that the title remains centered between these columns even if you change the size of the title's font.

Selecting Fonts

1-2-3 for Windows, unlike its DOS predecessors, always displays the text in your worksheet as it will appear printed on paper. The program enables you to use up to 8 different fonts in any worksheet you create. A font is defined as a particular size of a typeface, such as 10-point Arial or 12-point Times New Roman. In addition to the 8 fonts, you can use up to 3 different font attributes: bold, italics, and underlining.

In this example, you see samples of 3 different fonts: Arial 14 point, Times New Roman 12 point, and Symbol 12 point (Greek characters).

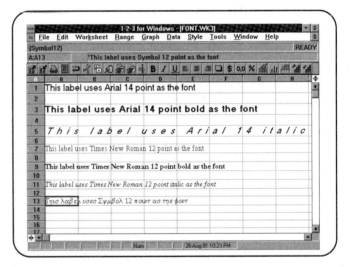

The Helvetica and Times font samples also include labels using the bold and italic font attributes.

The default font set created by Lotus for your printer determines which 8 fonts are available when you begin work on a new worksheet (see Chapter 8 for more information on choosing a printer). The first font listed in the default font set becomes the default font. This font is automatically used whenever you enter data in a new worksheet. If, for example, you're using a laser printer, such as an HP LaserJet Series II or an Apple LaserWriter II/NT, the first font in the default font set is 10-point Arial; this is the default font that is applied to all new entries in the worksheet.

With 1-2-3 for Windows, you easily can assign a new font to cells in your worksheet. If you select a font size for a cell that is taller than the height of its row, 1-2-3 automatically adjusts the row height to accommodate the new size (see Chapter 6 for information on manually adjusting the height of the row). To select a new font for the worksheet, follow these steps:

1. Select the cells that will use the new font.

2. From the Style menu, select the Font option.

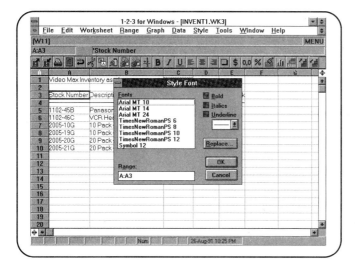

1-2-3 displays the Style Font dialog box.

3. Select the new font in the Fonts list box.

4. If you want to add attributes, such as bold or underlining, to the font, place a check mark in the appropriate check boxes (Bold, Italics, or Underline). If you mark the Underline check box, you can also select a new thickness for the underlining. Select the thickness from the drop-down list box below the check box.

   Remember that you can assign more than one font attribute at a time, if you like.

5. Select the OK button to apply the new font to the range of cells shown in the Range text box.

Note: If you use the mouse, you can assign the bold, italics, or underlining attribute to selected cells directly from the Icon palette. To select bold, click the Bold SmartIcon; to select italics, click the Italics SmartIcon; to select underlining, click the Underline SmartIcon. If you later want to eliminate the attributes from the cells, simply select the cell again and click the same SmartIcon.

149

Replacing Fonts in the Font Set

1-2-3 for Windows enables you to create your own font library of the font sets made up of the typefaces and font sizes you want to group together. Although you are limited to eight fonts per font set, you can add as many font sets to your font library as you like.

Once you create a font set, you can retrieve it and use it in the worksheet you're building. If you want, you can even replace the default font set with one of your own creation.

To create a font set, follow these steps:

1. From the Style menu, select the Font option.

2. Select the Replace command button in the Style Font dialog box.

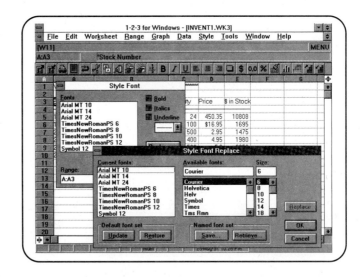

1-2-3 displays the Style Font Replace dialog box.

3. Select the font you want to replace in the Current fonts list box.

4. Select the typeface you want to substitute in the Available fonts list box.

5. Select the point size you want to use in the Size list box.

6. Select the Replace command button.

   1-2-3 replaces the font you selected in the Current fonts list box with the one you designated in the Available fonts and Size list boxes.

7. Repeat steps 3 through 6 for each font that you want to replace in the

Current fonts list box.

When you are finished replacing fonts, you can save them in their own named font set.

8. Select the **S**ave command button under Named font set.

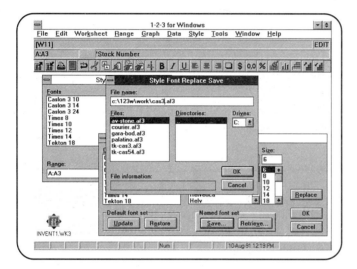

1-2-3 displays the Style Font Replace Save dialog box in which you assign a name to your new font set.

9. Edit the path name as required and enter a file name in the File name list box for the font set you are saving. 1-2-3 automatically appends the extension AF3 to the file name you designate.

10. Select the OK button in the Style Font Replace Save dialog box.

1-2-3 returns you to the Style Font Replace dialog box.

11. Select the OK button in the Style Font Replace dialog box.

1-2-3 returns you to the Style Font dialog box.

12. To apply one of your new fonts to the cells that are currently selected, select the font in the Fonts list box and then select the OK button. Otherwise, just select the OK button to return to your worksheet.

If you changed the default font in your new font set, 1-2-3 automatically applies that font to all cells in the worksheet that use the default font as soon as the program closes the Style Font dialog box. The program does not, however, change any cells you specifically formatted with the **S**tyle **F**ont command.

If you want, you can replace the default font set that Lotus has chosen for your printer with a font set of your own making. To replace the default font, create

151

and save the font set as described previously. Then select the Update command button under Default font set in the Style Font Replace dialog box.

To use one of your font sets in a new worksheet without making it the default font set, follow these steps:

1. From the Style menu, select the Font option.
2. Select the Replace command button in the Style Font dialog box.
3. Select the Retrieve command button under Named font set.

   1-2-3 displays the Font Replace Save dialog box.

4. Select the named font file you want to use in the File name list box of the Style Font Replace Save dialog box.

5. Select the OK button to return to the Style Font Replace dialog box.

   1-2-3 returns you to the Style Font Replace dialog box. The Fonts list box displays all of the fonts in the set you just selected.

6. At this point, you can make any necessary changes to the fonts in the set you retrieved. Otherwise, select the OK button to return to the Style Font Replace dialog box.

7. To apply one of the fonts in the new set to the cells that are currently selected, select the font in the Fonts list box and then select the OK button. Otherwise, just select the OK button to return to your worksheet.

As you are working on a worksheet, you can return to the default font set created by Lotus (as long as you haven't replaced it with one of your own with Update) and use one of its fonts. To use a default font set, select the Restore command button under Default font set in the Style Font Replace dialog box.

Choosing Colors

1-2-3 for Windows enables you to select different colors for the text and background of cells with the Style Color command. If you have a color monitor, colors assigned to cell ranges with this command are displayed on the screen. If you are using a color printer, the colors are printed. Colors are displayed in shades of gray on a monochrome monitor; colors are printed in black and white on a black-and-white printer.

You can use the Style Color command to assign different colors to different types of data. For example, you can format a table of data in a worksheet so that its headings are displayed in blue on a white background, positive values are displayed in regular black text, and negative numbers are displayed in red.

To assign a new color to cells in your worksheet, follow these steps:

1. Select the cells you want to assign the new color to.

2. From the Style menu, select the Color option.

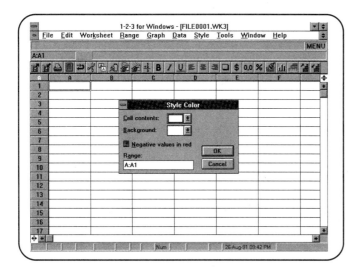

1-2-3 displays the Style Color dialog box.

3. Choose the color you want for the data in the Cell contents drop-down list box.

4. Choose the color you want for the background of the cells in the Background drop-down list box.

5. If you want negative values in the selected cells to be displayed in red (using whatever background color you selected), select the Negative values in red check box.

6. Select the OK button to return to the worksheet where you will now see your new color combination (provided you have a color monitor).

Note: You can change the colors for all cells in the worksheet that contain negative values, and you can change the colors used to display other parts of the worksheet, such as the color of the foreground and background of the worksheet frame or that of the grid lines. To make these changes, use the Window Display Options command (see Chapter 6 for more information on changing the colors in the 1-2-3 window).

Adding Cell Borders

In 1-2-3 for Windows, you can draw attention to different types of data in the worksheet by assigning borders to the cells. The program enables you to draw thin, double, or thick lines around all or any part of the cells' borders with the Style Border command. You can use this command to outline the entire block of cells you selected or to create a drop shadow effect for the block. (1-2-3 creates a shadow effect by drawing a thick line on the bottom and right edge of the block, making it appear as though it were casting a shadow).

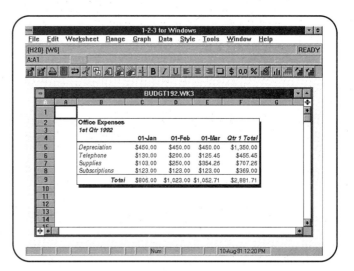

In this example, an outline border and drop shadow have been applied to the table of office expenses.

To separate areas of the table, a heavy border line was drawn on the bottom of cells B4 through F4, and a light line was drawn at the top of cells B9 through F9.

To assign borders to the cells you have selected, follow these steps:

1. Select the block of cells you want to assign borders to.
2. From the Style menu, select the Border option.

154

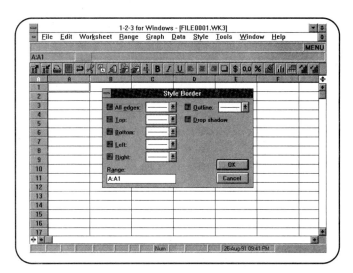

1-2-3 displays the
Style Border
dialog box.

3. Place a check mark in the check boxes for all of the border options you want to use:

   All edges to draw lines around the edges of every cell you have selected.

   Top to draw lines on the top edges of the selected cells.

   Bottom to draw lines on the bottom edges of the selected cells.

   Left to draw lines on the left edges of the selected cells.

   Right to draw lines on the right edges of the selected cells.

   Outline to draw lines on the outside edges of the block of cells.

   Drop shadow to draw thick lines on the right and bottom outside edges of the block of cells.

4. By default, 1-2-3 draws a thin, single line for all the borders you select. To switch to either a double line or thick line for the border options you have selected, choose the drop-down list boxes for the options and select the type of line you want.

5. Select the OK command button to return to the worksheet and have the program draw the borders you specified.

Note: To better see the borders you have assigned with the Style Border command, you can suppress the display of the worksheet grid. Choose the Window Display Options command. Then deselect the Grid lines check box under options and select OK.

155

To eliminate the borders that you assign to cells, select the cells again, choose the **S**tyle **B**order command, and remove the check mark from the check box of each border option you no longer want to use.

Shading Cells

1-2-3 for Windows gives you three types of shading that you can apply to cells in your worksheet. You can use shading to call attention to cells that contain important data in a worksheet. You can also use shading in long tables; you can shade column headings and every other row to make printed reports easier to read.

To use shading in the worksheet, follow these steps:

1. Select the block of cells you want to shade.

2. From the **S**tyle menu, select the **S**hading option.

1-2-3 displays the
Style Shading
dialog box.

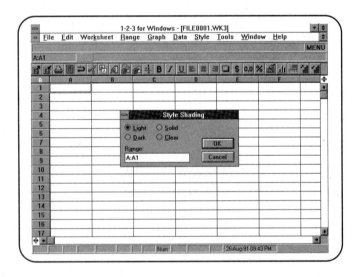

3. Select the option button for the type of shading you want to use:

   Light for light dot-patterned shading.

   Dark for dark dot-patterned shading.

   Solid for solid black shading in the selected cells (don't use this option in cells that contain data).

4. Select the OK command button to return to the worksheet and have the program shade the cells you have selected.

To remove shading from cells, select them. Then choose the Style Shading command and select the Clear option.

Naming Styles

1-2-3 for Windows makes formatting large worksheets a great deal easier with the use of named styles. The program enables you to define up to eight named styles in any worksheet file. A named style can indicate the font, font attributes, colors, borders, and type of shading you want to use in the worksheet.

Note: A named style can't include alignment information selected with the Style Alignment command or format information selected with the Range Format command.

All named styles in 1-2-3 for Windows are defined by example. When you define by example, you manually format a prototype cell using the desired Style menu commands, and then 1-2-3 incorporates its formatting into that style. After you have defined a style in this way, the style's name is displayed on the Style pull-down menu under the Name option. To assign the formatting placed in a style to other cells in the worksheet, simply select the cells and then choose the named style from the Style pull-down menu.

To understand how named styles are created and used, examine the following example. A number of named styles are defined from prototype cells and then applied to the other cells that require the same type of formatting in the worksheet.

Before you begin defining the styles you will use to format your worksheet, define a default style. You can use this style to restore text to just the default font without any other attributes.

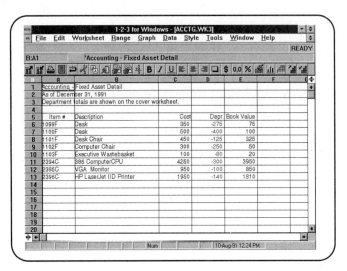

You see a simple fixed asset table. All of its entries use the default font (10-point Helvetica).

4

To create such a style in this example, follow these steps:

1. Select a cell that contains an entry formatted only with the default font (cell A1 in this example).

2. From the **S**tyle menu, select the **N**ame option.

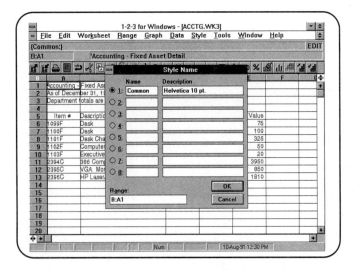

1-2-3 displays the Style Name dialog box.

3. Select the number of the style you want to define between 1 and 8.

4. Select the Name text box and enter a name for your style. You can use up to six characters. (Normal is used in this example.)

5. Select the Description text box (you can press Tab↹) and enter a description for the style. You can use up to 24 characters.

   Whenever you highlight the style in the Style pull-down menu, the description you give to your style appears in the Title bar of the 1-2-3 window.

6. Make sure that the cell address listed in the Range text box includes an example that contains only the formatting you want included in the style you're creating. If this is not the case, change the cell address listed in the Range box to one that exemplifies the style you want to create.

7. Select the OK button to create your style.

1-2-3 adds the style name to the appropriate option number in the Style pull-down menu.

After defining a default style, you are ready to format the prototype cells required to create the other named styles.

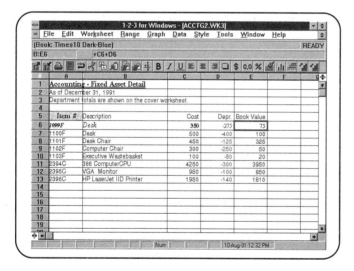

You see a version of the fixed asset worksheet, showing the formatting of the various prototype cells that will be used to create the rest of the required named styles.

Cell A1 is formatted for the Title style used to format the worksheet titles; cell A5 is formatted for the Column style used to format the column headings; A6 is formatted for the Item# style used to format the item numbers; B6 is formatted for the Desc style used to format the item descriptions; C6 is formatted for the Cost style used to format the numbers showing the original cost of each item; D6 is formatted for the Depr style used to format the numbers showing the accumulated depreciation for each item; and E6 is formatted for the Book style to be used to format the numbers showing the current book value of each item.

After manually formatting prototype cells with the commands on the **Style** menu, use the same steps outlined for creating the default style to define all of these styles.

4

You see all of the names and descriptions in the Style Name dialog box for the styles required to format the fixed asset table.

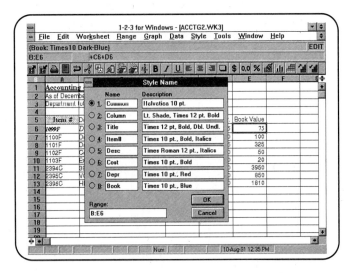

After you create your named styles in the Style Name dialog box, they are ready to use directly from the Style pull-down menu.

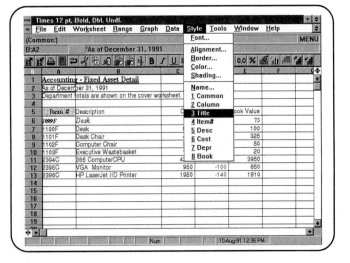

160

To apply a named style to cells, follow these steps:

1. Select the cells you want to format with the style.

2. From the Style menu, select the style from the pull-down menu. You can select a style either by dragging to the style name with the mouse or by typing the style's number.

Note: If you haven't selected more than one cell when you choose the style, 1-2-3 displays a Style dialog box that shows the number of the style in the Title bar and the address of the single-cell range in the Range text box. To apply the style to a group of cells, highlight them with the mouse or direction keys before you select OK.

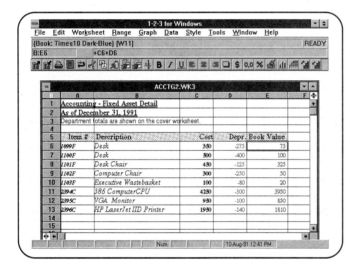

A worksheet formatted entirely with named styles.

Editing Data

When you need to change the data you have entered in a cell of the worksheet, you can choose between two methods: either replace the entire entry in the cell or edit only the parts of the entry that need modification.

To replace the contents of the cell, follow these steps:

1. Select the cell you want to change either by clicking the cell with the mouse or using the arrow keys on the keyboard to move the cell pointer to the cell.

2. Type the new contents for the cell in the Contents box on the Edit line.

3. Click the Confirm icon on the Edit line, or press ⏎Enter to replace the existing cell entry with the new entry you just typed.

If the contents of the cell only require slight changes, you do not need to replace the cell's entire contents as described above. Instead, you can put the program in EDIT mode by pressing the Edit (F2) key.

4

Once in EDIT mode, 1-2-3 positions the cursor (insertion point) at the end of the entry in the Contents box, and the Confirm and Cancel icons reappear on the Edit line.

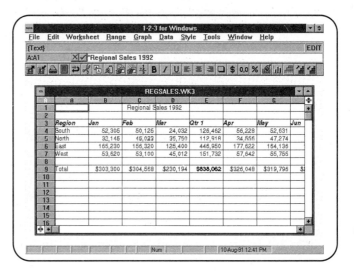

You can also put 1-2-3 into EDIT mode simply by double clicking the cell that contains the entry you want to edit.

As soon as the program is in EDIT mode, you can move the cursor to the place in the entry that needs modifications. You can use the direction keys to move the cursor through the text, or click the I-beam pointer to reposition the cursor between characters.

To delete characters, you can either position the cursor immediately after the last character to be erased and press the Backspace key, or select the characters with the I-beam pointer and press the Delete key. To insert new text, position the cursor between the two characters where you want the new text to appear and then begin typing. 1-2-3 is always in Insert mode and will not type over existing text.

Table 4.5 shows you the keys you can use to move the cursor and make changes to the contents of a cell when 1-2-3 is in EDIT mode.

Table 4.5
Keys Used in Edit Mode

Key	Function
→	Moves the cursor one character to the right.
←	Moves the cursor one character to the left.
↑	Completes the edit and moves the cell pointer up one row.
↓	Completes the edit and moves the cell pointer down one row.
◆Backspace	Deletes the character to the left of the cursor.
Ctrl →	Moves the cursor to the beginning of the next word to the right.
Ctrl ←	Moves the cursor to the beginning of the previous word to the left.
Home	Moves the cursor to the beginning of the entry.
End	Moves the cursor to the end of the entry.
Del	Deletes all selected text or the character to the right of the cursor if no text is selected.
↵Enter	Completes the edit by updating the cell display and returning the program to READY mode.
Esc	Clears the entire entry from the Contents box.
Esc Esc	Returns 1-2-3 to READY mode without changing the entry in the selected cell.

Using Undo

1-2-3 for Windows includes a powerful Undo feature that enables you to reverse the effect of the last change you made to the worksheet. If, for example, you accidentally delete part of a cell entry, you can restore it by choosing the Edit menu and selecting the Undo option, or by pressing the Undo key combination, Alt + ◆Backspace.

The Undo feature not only restores deleted data but can also cancel the last issued 1-2-3 command. For example, if you move data to a new place in the worksheet and then decide that you should have left the data in its original position, you can use the Undo feature to cancel the move.

Note: If you use the mouse, you can choose the Edit Undo command simply by clicking the SmartIcon in the Icon palette.

What Undo Can't Do

4

The Undo feature, unfortunately, cannot undo everything that you can do in 1-2-3 for Windows. Undo is powerless to reverse the effect of most File commands, such as File Save and Save As, File Print, File Combine From, File Import From, and File Extract To.

Turning Off Undo

Undo works by creating a temporary backup copy of your entire worksheet each time you select a new 1-2-3 command or create or edit a cell entry. This backup copy is stored in the temporary memory of the computer (RAM). As your worksheet grows, you may not have sufficient memory available to hold both the temporary backup and the original worksheet. To free needed memory and complete your worksheet, you may need to turn off the Undo feature.

To deactivate the Undo feature, follow these steps:

1. From the Tools menu, select the User Setup option.

   1-2-3 displays the Tools User Setup dialog box.

2. Select the Enable Edit Undo check box under Options and remove the check mark from the check box (click it with the mouse or press the space bar).

3. Select the OK button.

After you complete and save your worksheet, you can close its window and then turn on the Undo feature again. To do this, repeat the steps above, this time making sure that you place a check mark in the Enable Undo check box before selecting the OK option.

Summary

In this chapter, you learned the basic skills required to build a new worksheet. First, you learned the fundamental techniques for entering data in the worksheet. Remember that 1-2-3 differentiates between two basic types of data: labels or text and values. Values include constant numbers as well as formulas. Recall that dates and times are entered in the worksheet as special values rather than as labels. By storing a date as a serial number and a time as a fractional number, you can then create formulas that calculate elapsed time. As part of data entry, you learned how to construct elementary formulas. While most of your formulas will perform arithmetic calculations with the mathematical operators, remember that 1-2-3 also supports the use of logical and string formulas, too.

After learning how to enter data, you then learned how to modify the display of the data in a worksheet to make the data appear exactly as you want. You also learned how to format values with range format and enhance all types of worksheet entries with 1-2-3's many Style menu commands.

Finally, you learned how to edit the data you have entered in a worksheet. If an entry requires radical editing, you can simply replace it by reentering it. However, if the entry only requires slight changes, you can save time by changing the program to Edit mode and then making the necessary modifications to the contents on the Control line rather than retyping the entire entry.

Specifically, you learned the following key information:

- To enter data in a cell, you select the cell with the mouse or keyboard, type the entry in the Contents box of the Edit line, then click the Confirm button, press a direction key, or press ↵Enter to place it in the cell.

- 1-2-3 for Windows accepts only two types of entries: a label or a value. Labels represent text that can't be calculated mathematically (even when the text consists solely of numbers) and are always preceded by a label prefix (', ^, ", \, or |). Values represent numbers or formulas that can be included in mathematic calculations.

- By default, labels are left-aligned in their cells. If the label contains more characters than fit in the width of the cell, the display of those characters spills over to neighboring cells to the right provided that these neighboring cells contain no data of their own.

4

■ You can change the alignment of labels in their cells by editing the label prefix character (' for left-aligned, ^ for center, or " for right-aligned) or using the Style Alignment command.

■ By default, values are right-aligned in cells. You cannot change their alignment.

■ You enter dates and times in the worksheet following one of 1-2-3's recognized date or time formats such as 1/13/93 or 11:45 pm. When you do, 1-2-3 enters a serial date number or time fraction in the cell, which can be used in formulas that perform arithmetic calculations.

■ Formulas represent special values that perform some type of calculation. Formulas can contain numbers, special built-in functions, or references to cells that contain values or other formulas.

■ When you create a formula that uses cell references, 1-2-3 recalculates the formula's result if you change the values in any of the cells referred to.

■ To edit data in a cell, select the cell and then replace the entry or press the Edit key (F2) and edit the part of the entry that needs to be changed.

■ After you enter data in a worksheet, you can enhance its appearance by using the Range Format options or the commands on the Style menu. Use Range Format to format values in the worksheet. Use the Style menu commands to assign shading or borders to your data or to change the fonts, colors, or alignment of the data.

■ 1-2-3 for Windows enables you to create and save up to eight different named styles that facilitate assigning complex formatting to cells in the worksheet. Each named style is created by formatting a cell with all of the attributes to be included in the style and then defining the style from that example.

■ Use the Edit Undo command or the Undo key combination (Alt + ◆Backspace)) to reverse the effect of the last action you took in 1-2-3 for Windows.

In the chapter ahead, you will learn more about working with groups, or ranges, of cells. As part of this process, you will learn how to cut and paste different types of data in the worksheet.

Working with Ranges

Some tasks associated with building a worksheet are more efficient when applied to a group of cells rather than individual cells. In this chapter, you learn how to work with ranges and use more of the 1-2-3 commands that typically work with ranges rather than individual cells.

To initiate this process, you first learn the different methods for defining a range in 1-2-3 for Windows. With this knowledge, you are ready to learn specific commands on the Range and Edit menus that work with ranges. These menus include the commands for naming ranges, erasing their contents, copying and moving ranges to new locations in the worksheet, transposing (exchanging) columns and rows, and searching and replacing data.

Key Terms in This Chapter

Range	A rectangular block of cells in which all cells are contiguous (touching). In 1-2-3 for Windows, you can specify either two-dimensional ranges in the same worksheet or three-dimensional ranges that span more than one worksheet.
Range address	The address defined by two opposite cells, usually the upper left and lower right corners of the range, separated by two periods (A2..C20).
Range name	A descriptive name assigned to a cell range that can then be used in formulas or commands in place of the cell address of the range.
Relative reference	A cell address in a formula that, when the formula is copied, is adjusted to reflect its new location in the worksheet. By default, all cell addresses in a formula you create are relative.
Absolute reference	A cell address in a formula that, when the formula is copied, remains the same. 1-2-3 uses the dollar sign ($) to designate absolute references ($A:$C$3).

Understanding Cell Ranges

A range is a rectangular block of adjacent cells. In 1-2-3, the smallest possible range consists of a single cell and the largest possible range consists of all cells in all the worksheets in the file. Most of the ranges you work with are somewhere in between.

Most of the ranges you work with are two-dimensional: they form various size blocks on one worksheet.

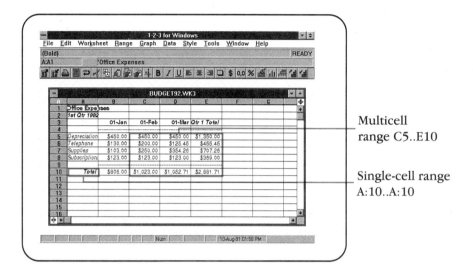

Multicell
range C5..E10

Single-cell range
A:10..A:10

5

But ranges in 1-2-3 for Windows also can be three-dimensional; that is,
a 3-D block of cells spans more than one worksheet.

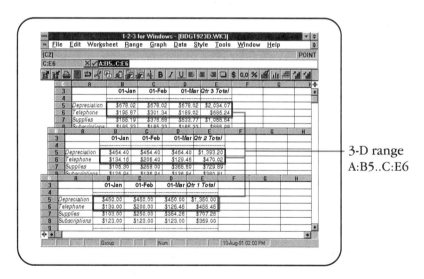

3-D range
A:B5..C:E6

169

A wide variety of 1-2-3 commands and operations require you to designate the range, including all the commands on the Range worksheet menu.

You also designate ranges when formatting, erasing, and moving or copying cells as well as when building formulas for your worksheet.

Designating a Range

As a cell is designated in a worksheet by its cell address, a range is designated by its *range address*. The range address is given by indicating the cell address of any two corners of the range that are diagonally opposite each other. To indicate that the two cell addresses belong to the same range, they are separated by two periods—B3..D10, for example.

1-2-3 supports three methods for designating the range:

- Point to the cells in the range by extending the cell pointer's outline so that it encloses them. When you point to a range, 1-2-3 for Windows enters the range address for you in the selected text box as you point out the range.
- Type the range address in the text box of the dialog box.
- Type the range name assigned to the range in a text box or select it from a list of ranges in a list box.

Preselecting a Range

In Windows programs, such as 1-2-3, it is customary to designate the range before you select the command that uses it. Preselecting the range enables you to select multiple 1-2-3 commands in succession and apply their operations to the same range. By preselecting a range of numbers, for example, you can format them with the Currency format using the **Range Format** command, change their font to 12-point Times Roman Bold using the **Style Font** command, and, finally, shade them with the **Style Shading** command. If you do not preselect the range, you must designate it each time you select any one of these three formatting commands.

Note, however, that the only way you can preselect a range in 1-2-3 for Windows is by highlighting the range with the mouse or keyboard. You can designate a range by typing the range address or using the range name only after you have selected the 1-2-3 command that works with it.

5

Pointing out a Range

More often than not, you will find it easier to designate a range by pointing. As long as the range is on a single worksheet, you can use either the mouse or the keyboard to select the range.

Follow these steps for preselecting the range B5..E8 using the mouse:

1. Click the mouse pointer in cell B5 to select it, and then hold down the left mouse button.

2. Drag the mouse pointer three columns to the right and down to select all the cells in rows 5 through 8 in columns B through E.

   As you drag the mouse, 1-2-3 remains in POINT mode. When you release the mouse button after selectng the range B5..E8, the program returns to READY mode.

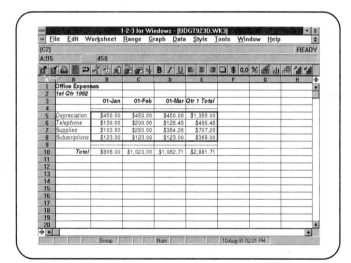

You have selected the cell range B5..E8.

Follow these steps for preselecting the range B5..E8 using the keyboard:

1. Press the direction keys to move the cell pointer to cell B5.

2. Press F4 to anchor the range on cell B5.

   Cell B5 is known as the *anchor cell* because the cell pointer now extends the range in any direction from cell B5. Note that the program goes into POINT mode as soon as you press F4 to anchor the range.

3. Press → three times to extend the range from the single-cell range B5..B5 to the multicell range B5..E5.

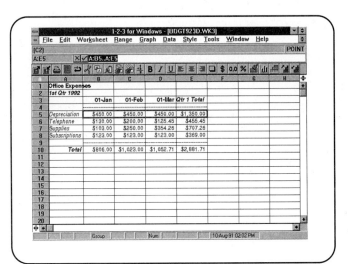

1-2-3 extends the range B5..E5 in the worksheet.

4. Press ⬇ three times to expand the range from B5..E5 to B5..E8.

The range now includes B5..E8 in the worksheet.

Cell E8 is known as the *free cell* of the range because it is not anchored. If you need to make the range larger or smaller, you do so by moving the free cell.

Note: While preselecting a range in 1-2-3 for Windows, the Address box of the Edit line does not display the range address. It only displays the address of the free cell as you extend the cell range.

Highlighting a Three-Dimensional Range

Any range that spans more than a single worksheet is known as a three-dimensional or *3-D range*. To highlight a 3-D range, you first point out the range in two dimensions in a single worksheet, and then you expand that two-dimensional range to other worksheets in the file, making it three-dimensional.

As you point out the range in two dimensions in a single worksheet, you can use either the mouse or the keyboard to select the cells. When expanding the range to other worksheets, however, you must use the keyboard.

If you are working with three-dimensional ranges, you will find it helpful to turn on perspective view in the Worksheet window. Perspective view shows a small part of three adjacent worksheets, cascading up to the right. By default, as you scroll to new parts of the current worksheet, 1-2-3 scrolls the other worksheets in unison.

To get a feel for how you go about highlighting a three-dimensional range, follow these steps for preselecting the 3-D range A:B5..C:E8, the range that extends from B5 to E8 in worksheets A, B, and C:

1. If necessary, click the Maximize button in the 1-2-3 window or press Alt + - and select the Maximize option to increase the current Worksheet window to full size.

2. From the Window menu, select the Split option.

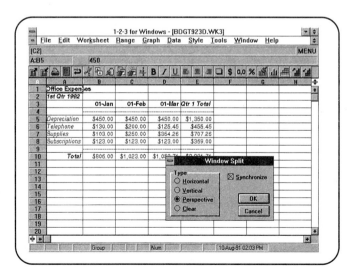

1-2-3 displays the Window Split dialog box.

5

3. Select the **Perspective** option button.

4. Click OK.

   1-2-3 displays the first few rows of worksheets A through C.

5. Click the vertical scroll bar to scroll the worksheet up until you can see rows 1 through 5 in all three worksheets.

6. Select cell A:B5.

7. Highlight the two-dimensional range B5..E8 in worksheet A.

The range B5..E8 is in worksheet A.

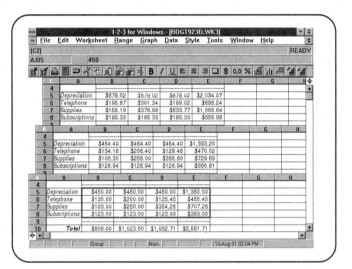

8. Press the Next Sheet key combination, Ctrl + PgUp, to expand the range to the same block of cells in worksheet B (range A:B5..B:E8).

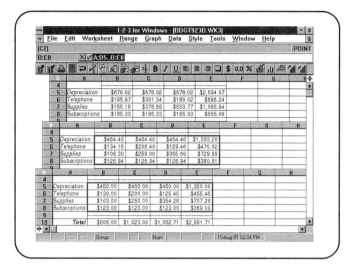

The range
A:B5..B:E8 is
selected in
worksheet B.

9. Press the Next Sheet key combination, Ctrl + PgUp, to expand the
range to the same block of cells in worksheet C (range A:B5..C:E8).

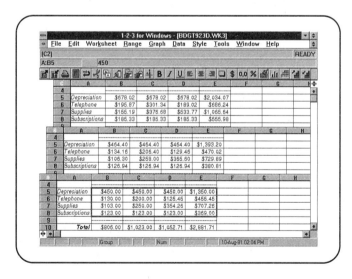

The range
A:B5..C:E8 is
highlighted in
worksheet C.

Note: To enlarge the current worksheet temporarily so that it takes up the entire Worksheet window, press the Zoom key combination, Alt + F6. To switch to perspective view, press the Zoom key again (it acts as a toggle). To restore the view in the current worksheet file to a single worksheet, choose the Window Split command and select the Clear option button before selecting OK.

Modifying a Range

You can change the size of a range after you have selected it. If you're designating the range with the mouse, you can change the size of the outline border with the mouse pointer any time up to the moment you release the left mouse button. Just move the mouse to modify the highlighted area's shape and size.

If you designate the range with the keyboard, you can change the size of the range by using the appropriate cursor-movement keys. If the range is two-dimensional, you use the cursor-movement keys. If the range is three-dimensional, you may have to use a combination of the Next Sheet (Ctrl + PgUp), Prev Sheet (Ctrl + PgDn), and cursor-movement keys.

If you select the wrong range, you can cancel your selection, and then designate the range again. The method for canceling a range depends on whether you highlighted the range with the mouse or keyboard:

- If you pointed out the range with the mouse, click the first cell of the correct range (clicking any cell in the worksheet automatically deselects the highlighted range).

- If you used the keyboard, press the Esc key. 1-2-3 immediately deselects all but the anchor cell of the range.

Typing the Range Address

If you are typing a range address, you must specify the address of the cell in the upper left and lower right corner of the range separated by two periods— F3..G24, for example.

If you are designating a three-dimensional range, you first enter the address of the cell in the upper left corner of the first worksheet and then the address of the cell in the lower right corner of the last worksheet—A:F3..C:G24, for example.

You can type the range address in any dialog box that contains a Range text box. To replace the existing range address (showing the range that is currently selected), highlight the text with the mouse using the I-beam pointer or press Tab⇒ until the Range text box is selected.

Using Range Names

5

You can use the Range Name command to assign descriptive names to the ranges in your worksheet. You then can use the range name instead of cell addresses when you perform any operation that uses ranges.

Range names are useful tools for documenting the function of formulas in your spreadsheet. Range names also are easier to remember and understand than cell addresses. Naming a cell that contains year-to-date totals as YTD_Total, for example, is much more descriptive and easier to recall than the cell address B:C54.

Range names are useful for several reasons:

- 1-2-3 accepts range names in place of the range address in any function that works with ranges or in any dialog box that contains a Range text box. After you create a range name for a range that has been used in formulas in the worksheet, 1-2-3 automatically replaces the range address with the range name throughout the file.

- You can use the range name with the Range Go To command (or the GoTo key, F5) to move the cell pointer to a new place in the worksheet file. Note that when you use the Range GoTo command to move to a multicell range, 1-2-3 always positions the cell pointer in the upper left cell of the range.

- You can designate ranges of cells to be moved, copied, or printed by using their range names, making it easy to change the print range when you need to print different parts of a large spreadsheet.

Range names can contain up to 15 characters. Although you should make your range names as descriptive as possible, don't use spaces in them. You cannot use a range name with spaces in formulas.

In this example, the range name S_Qtr1_Sales is assigned to cell range B4..D4 that contains the first quarter sales figures for the southern region.

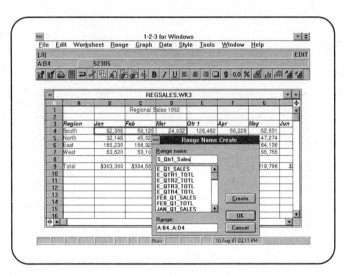

After the range name is defined, it can be used in the @SUM formula that totals the first quarter sales in the southern region.

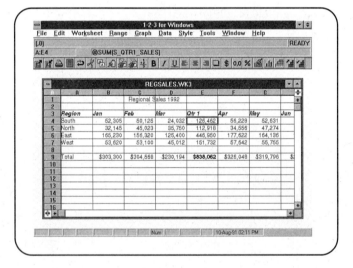

5

178

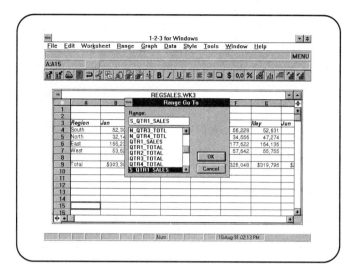

You also can use the range name with the **R**ange **G**oTo command to move the cell pointer directly to the first cell in the range.

Naming a Group of Cells

To assign a name to a range, follow these steps:

1. Select the range of cells you want named.

   If you are naming a single cell, just select that cell or position the cell pointer in it.

2. Choose **R**ange **N**ame.

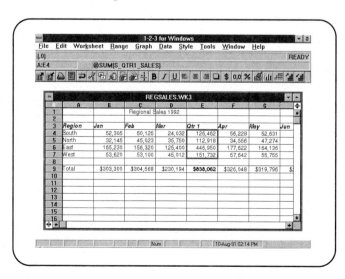

The range of cells to be named is B:E4..E7 in this example.

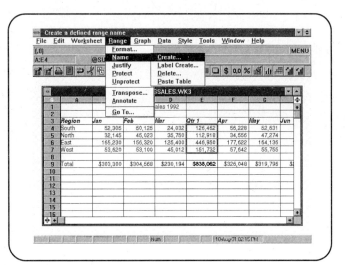

1-2-3 displays the
Range Name
cascade menu.

3. Select the Create option.

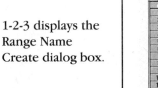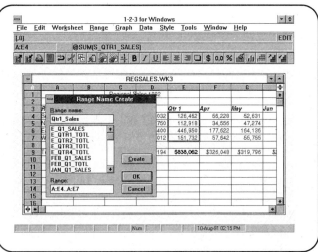

1-2-3 displays the
Range Name
Create dialog box.

4. Type the range name in the text box in the Range Name Create dialog box.

5. Check the range address in the Range text box to make sure that it is correct (remember that you can move the Range Name Create dialog box if you need to).

6. Select the **C**reate command button.

    1-2-3 names the range.

7. Select OK.

    1-2-3 returns you to the worksheet.

Naming Ranges with Adjacent Labels

To assign range names to a series of one-cell entries with adjacent labels or to a series of columns or rows with headings, you can use the **R**ange **N**ame **L**abel Create command. This command enables you to name cells with labels in the adjacent cells, all in a single operation. The names must be text entries (labels); you cannot use numeric entries or blank cells to name adjacent cells with the **R**ange **N**ame **L**abel Create command.

To use **R**ange **N**ame **L**abel Create to assign names to single-cell entries, follow these steps:

1. Select the range of cells containing the labels you want to assign as range names. Remember that you can use this command on only adjacent cells.

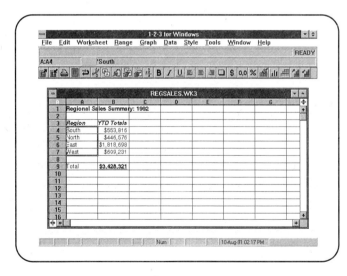

The names in the range A4..A7 are selected so that they can be assigned as range names to the year-to-date totals in the range B4..B7.

2. Choose the **R**ange menu and select the **N**ame option.
3. Select the **L**abel Create option.

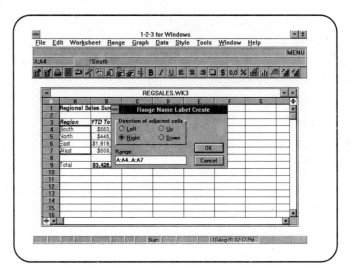

1-2-3 displays the Range Name Label Create dialog box.

In this example, you select the **R**ight option button because the range to be named is immediately to the right of the range containing the labels.

4. Select the appropriate option under Direction of adjacent labels: **L**eft, **R**ight, **U**p, or **D**own, depending on the location of the cells to be named relative to the labels you selected.

5. Select the OK button to assign the range names.

Removing Range Names

To remove a range name from a spreadsheet, you use the **R**ange **N**ame **D**elete command, and then select the name of the range to remove from the Range Name list box. If you used the range name in a formula in the worksheet, 1-2-3 automatically converts the range name to the appropriate range address in the formula without affecting the calculated results.

To remove all range names from the entire worksheet file (as may become necessary if you run low on memory and need to add data to a spreadsheet), you select the Delete **A**ll command button in the Range Name Delete dialog box.

Note: 1-2-3 for Windows doesn't require that you confirm the removal of all range names when you choose Delete **A**ll. The program deletes all range names in the current file as soon as you choose the command. The only way to restore the range names is to use the Undo function. You select Undo by pressing Alt + ◆Backspace or choosing **E**dit **U**ndo.

To leave the range name in the worksheet but detach it from the range to which it refers, select the Undefine command button in the Range Name Delete dialog box. Any formulas that use the undefined range name return ERR. As soon as you redefine the range name, however, 1-2-3 evaluates the formulas using the values in the cells referred to by the redefined range name.

Listing Range Names

You can use the F3 (Name) key to display a listing of all the range names that you defined in the current worksheet. When you press F3, 1-2-3 displays the Range Names dialog box. This dialog box contains the Range name text box that shows the current cell or range address. To replace this address with a range name, you select the range name from the list box.

The Name key is useful when you're creating a formula that uses range names and are not sure of how you spelled the name. Suppose that you are building a formula that sums the totals for the first quarter for the southern region and have forgotten what name you gave this range, you can type @SUM(in the Contents box on the Edit line and then press F3.

1-2-3 displays the Range Names dialog box containing a Range scroll box listing all the range names in the worksheet. You can scroll through this list until you find the name of the range you want to use.

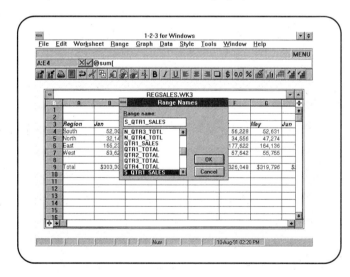

After you locate the name in the Range name list box, select it, and then choose OK.

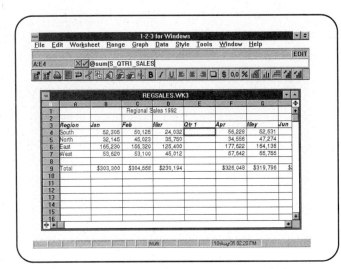

1-2-3 inserts the range name you selected into the formula on the Edit line.

After the range name is inserted into the formula, you can finish entering the formula by pressing ⟨⟩ and selecting the Confirm button on the Edit line.

Creating a Table of Range Names

If you create several range names in your worksheet, you can document their names and locations by creating a table in your worksheet file with the **Range Name Paste** Table command.

To create a table of range names, follow these steps:

1. Select the cell in which you want the upper left corner of the range name table.

2. Choose **Range Name.**

3. Select **Paste** Table

   1-2-3 displays the Range Name Paste Table dialog box.

4. Check the address of the range in the Range text box.

5. Click the OK button. If the range is incorrect, enter the correct range address or select another cell in the worksheet.

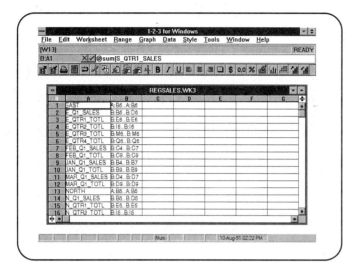

1-2-3 pastes a table showing the range names in the first column and their range address in the second column into your worksheet.

Note: When you paste a range table into a worksheet, 1-2-3 replaces any existing data with the information in the range name table. The best way to avoid this is to insert a new worksheet into the file and paste the table into the new worksheet.

Any range table that you create is static. It does not automatically reflect changes that you make to named ranges. You must re-create the table with the **R**ange **N**ame **P**aste Table command to keep it up-to-date.

Erasing a Range

1-2-3 for Windows provides two commands for erasing a range: **E**dit **C**lear (also activated by pressing the Del key) and **E**dit **C**lear Special. The **E**dit **C**lear command erases the data and any number or style formatting assigned to the selected cells. If the cell range you selected contains an entire graph, the **E**dit **C**lear command removes it from the worksheet (note that it has no effect on the graph in its own graph window).

To restore a range erased with the **E**dit **C**lear command, use the **E**dit **U**ndo command (Alt + ←Backspace).

To remove only the formatting assigned to a cell range and leave the data or to erase the data and leave the formatting intact, you use the Edit Clear Special command. The Edit Clear Special command enables you to designate which part of the information assigned to the range should be removed.

Note that Edit Clear Special, unlike Edit Clear, does not use the Clipboard. Any information copied to the Clipboard remains there. Therefore, you can still copy the contents of the Clipboard into the worksheet after erasing a range with Edit Clear Special. This procedure is not possible with Edit Clear.

You can restore the information that you remove with Edit Clear Special by selecting the Edit Undo command (or pressing Alt + ◆Backspace) before you select another 1-2-3 command.

To use the Edit Clear Special command to remove data or formatting from a range, follow these steps:

1. Select the cell range that contains the data or formatting you want to remove.

2. Choose the Edit command and select the Clear Special option.

   1-2-3 displays the Edit Clear Special dialog box, which contains four deletion options. By default, the command removes the cell contents and the number format in the range.

3. Place a check mark in each of the check box deletion options you want to use. The commands are as follows:

   • Cell contents deletes all data that has been entered into the range.

   • Number format removes all formatting created with the Range Format command.

   • Style removes all formatting created with the commands on the Style menu.

   • Graph deletes a graph from the range.

4. Make sure that the range address shown in the Range text box is correct.

5. Select the OK button to delete only the types of information you specified in the dialog box from the range.

Cutting and Pasting Ranges

In the days of manual spreadsheets, the process of moving data around on the page was called cutting and pasting because scissors and glue were used to move sections of the spreadsheet. 1-2-3 for Windows enables you to cut and paste sections of the worksheet electronically.

The program offers two methods for moving or copying data in the worksheet. As with erasing ranges, one method uses the Clipboard and the other does not. Note that you must cut or copy your worksheet data or graphs to the Clipboard if you are transferring the information to another worksheet file or to a document created with another program.

Moving and Copying Ranges with the Clipboard

When you want to move or copy all the information in a range to a new place in the worksheet or to another file, you need to use the **Edit Cut** (Shift+Del) or **Edit Copy** (Ctrl+Ins) command with the **Edit Paste** (Shift+Ins) command. Both the Cut and Copy options move the data in the selected range into the Clipboard. **Edit Cut** deletes the data and formatting from the worksheet before moving it to the Clipboard; **Edit Copy** copies the data and formatting to the Clipboard.

Once you have cut or copied data into the Clipboard, it remains there until you cut or copy some new information. To insert the contents of the Clipboard into the worksheet, you use the **Edit Paste** command. 1-2-3 inserts the formatted data into the worksheet starting at the cell pointer's position.

To cut or copy a range of cells to a new place in your worksheet or to another file, follow these steps:

1. Select the range that you want to cut or copy.
2. Choose the **Edit Cut** (⇧Shift + Del) or **Edit Copy** (Ctrl + Ins) command.

   Remember that when you choose the Cut option, 1-2-3 removes the range from the worksheet.
3. Select the cell in the upper left corner of the new range location. You can paste the range in the Clipboard into the same worksheet, into a new worksheet in the same file, or into a different worksheet file.
4. Choose the **Edit Paste** (⇧Shift + Ins) command to paste the range into its new location.

Note: If you are using the mouse, you can cut selected data by clicking the scissors SmartIcon on the Icon palette. To copy the data you selected, click the copy icon. To page data you have cut or copied to the Clipboard, click the paste bottle icon.

5

Moving Ranges with the Move Cells Command

The Edit Move Cells command enables you to move a range with or without its formatting to a new location in the same worksheet file. Remember that you cannot use this command to move a range to a new file: use Edit Cut and Edit Paste instead.

To move a range in your worksheet with the Edit Move Cells command, follow these steps:

1. Select the range you want to move.

2. Choose Edit Move Cells.

1-2-3 displays the Edit Move Cells dialog box showing the address of the selected range in the From text box and the address of the current cell in the To text box.

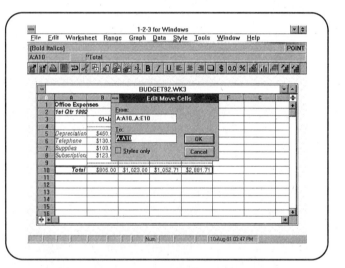

3. To change the address of the range you want moved, enter the new range address or modify its highlighting in the worksheet (remember that you can move the dialog box if it's in your way).

   If you change the range with the mouse or keyboard, the Edit Move Cells dialog box disappears temporarily. The dialog box returns as soon as you signal you are finished modifying the range, either by releasing the mouse button or pressing ⏎Enter if you are using the keyboard.

4. Press Tab⇥ to select the To text box.

5. Enter the address of the cell in the upper left corner of the new range location or select the cell in the worksheet.

188

If you select the cell with the mouse or keyboard, the Edit Move Cells dialog box disappears again. It returns as soon as you select a cell, either by clicking the mouse on a new cell or by pressing ⏎Enter after moving the cell pointer.

1-2-3 displays the Edit Move Cells dialog box showing the address of the range to be moved in the From text box and the address of the cell in the upper left corner of the new location in the To text box.

6. Place a check mark in the Styles only check box to have 1-2-3 move all formatting selected with the Style commands without moving the contents of the range.

7. Select the OK button to move the range (or the formatting in the range if you selected the Styles only option).

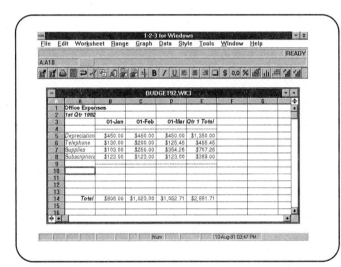

1-2-3 moves the range to the new location you specified.

Copying Ranges with the Quick Copy Command

The Edit Quick Copy command works just like the Edit Move Cells command. Edit Quick Copy does not use the Clipboard. You also can use this command to copy just the formatting without the data in the range by selecting the Styles only check box. Note that you can use this command only when you copy ranges to new locations in the same worksheet file.

To see how Edit Quick Copy works, follow these steps to copy a range of column titles from the first worksheet to the second and third worksheets in the file:

189

1. Select the range to copy.

2. Choose **E**dit **Q**uick Copy.

1-2-3 displays the
Edit Quick Copy
dialog box in
which you see the
range A:E4..A:E4
in the **F**rom text
box.

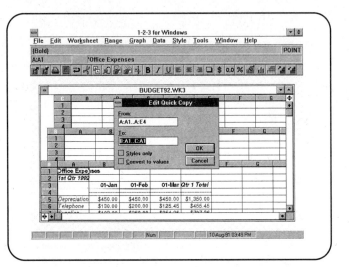

3. Press `Tab⇥` to select the **T**o text box.

4. Click the mouse in the first cell of the second worksheet (B:A1), and
   then press the Next Sheet key combination (`Ctrl` + `PgUp`) and `⏎Enter`
   to extend the range to the first cells in worksheets B and C.

   1-2-3 displays the range address B:A1..C:A1 in the **T**o text box.

5. Select the OK button.

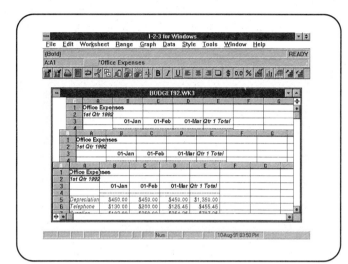

1-2-3 copies the selected range to worksheets B and C.

Remember that 1-2-3 replaces any existing data in the To range when you use the Edit Quick Copy command. You can recover from this mistake by selecting Edit Undo (Alt + ◆Backspace) to restore the data that has been deleted.

Copying or Moving Data with SmartIcons

The 1-2-3 for Windows Icon palette contains two SmartIcons that greatly simplify the procedure for copying or moving ranges to new places in the same worksheet file or even to new files open in the work area. You use the Select Range to Copy SmartIcon to copy the selected range to a new place. You use the Select Range to Move SmartIcon to move the range.

To copy or move a selected range of data with the Icon palette, follow these steps:

1. Select the range of cells you want to copy or move.

2. Click the Select Range to Copy SmartIcon to copy the range, or click the Select Range to Move SmartIcon to move it.

    The mouse pointer changes shape from an arrowhead to a hand with the forefinger pointing to the right.

3. Position the hand icon in the cell in the upper left corner of the range in which the selected data is to be copied or moved, and click the mouse button. 1-2-3 copies or moves the data (including all formatting) to the new range.

5

Note: When using the SmartIcons to copy or move ranges between worksheet files, the first time you click a cell in the new Worksheet window, 1-2-3 makes the Worksheet window current instead of completing the copy or move operation. You must position the hand icon in the first cell of the range to which you want to move or copy before you click the left mouse button a second time. If you prefer, you can make the new file current by pressing Ctrl + F6 or selecting the file name on the Window pull-down menu before clicking the hand icon to complete the copy or move operation.

Copying Formulas

Many spreadsheets are set up in such a way that you can create a single master formula, and then copy that formula to adjacent cells that need to perform the same type of calculation. 1-2-3 can do this because it uses *relative cell addresses* in a formula.

When you copy the formula, 1-2-3 automatically adjusts the cell references in the copied formulas to suit their new location. Suppose, for example, that you create the master formula @SUM(B5..B8) in cell B10 and you need to copy the formula to range C10..E10.

When you copy this formula using the Edit Copy or Edit Quick Copy commands, 1-2-3 enters the formula @SUM(C5..C8) into cell C10, @SUM(D5..D8) into cell D10, and @SUM(E5..E8) into cell E10.

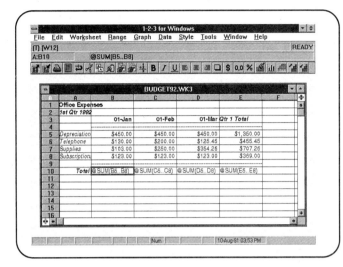

In this example, you can see the contents of each copied formula (rather than the resulting values) because the values are formatted with the text format.

5

When you copy a formula across columns in the worksheet, 1-2-3 adjusts only the column letters of the relative addresses. When you copy a formula down the rows of a worksheet, 1-2-3 adjusts only the row numbers in the cell addresses. When you copy a formula both across and down, 1-2-3 adjusts both the column letters and the row numbers in the copies.

Using Absolute and Mixed Cell References

You may not want some cell references in a master formula to be adjusted when you make copies of it. To prevent this adjustment, you can convert the cell address from relative to *absolute reference*. As the name implies, the cell reference remains constant in each copy of the formula.

In 1-2-3, you designate absolute references by prefacing the worksheet or column letter or row number in the cell address with a $ (dollar sign)—+A:B12/$A:$E$12, for example. In this formula, the cell address A:B12 is adjusted according to the direction in which the copy is made, but the address A:E12 remains unchanged.

In some formulas, you may want 1-2-3 to adjust just one part of the cell reference in the copies you make, such as the column letter but not the row number. Such a cell address is referred to as a *mixed reference*. A mixed reference is indicated by preceding just the absolute part of the cell reference with a dollar sign—+A:C$14/$A:$D$2, for example. In the address C$14, the column letter adjusts, but the row number remains constant.

To indicate an absolute or mixed address in a formula, you can either type the $ or, if you are highlighting the range, you can press the F4 (Absolute) key. When you press F4 in POINT or EDIT mode, 1-2-3 changes the cell address to absolute. When you press F4 a second time, the address changes to a mixed address. The Absolute key acts like an eight-way toggle that cycles through every possible mixed address combination.

Suppose, for example, that you wanted to know what percent of the quarterly sales total each month's sales represents.

Because you want the formula in cell B11 to continue to reference cell E9 when you copy the formula to range C11..D11, you enter the formula as +B9/$E$9.

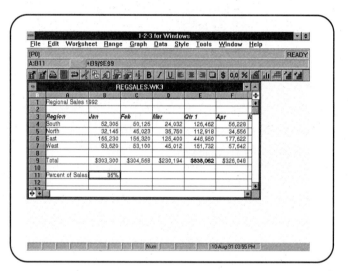

To enter this formula using the Absolute key, follow these steps:

1. Select cell B11.
2. Press + to start the formula.
3. Select cell B9.
4. Press /.
5. Select cell E9.
6. Press F4 once to change the formula reference to $A:$E$9.
7. Press ↵Enter to enter the formula +B9/$E$9 into cell B11.

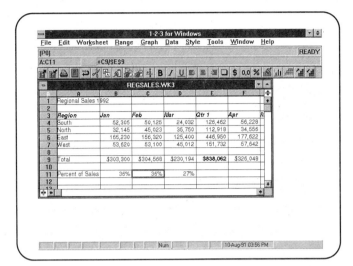

When you copy this formula to the range C11..D11, 1-2-3 adjusts only the first cell reference: The value in cell E9 remains constant in both copies of the formula.

Copying Formulas as Values

Formulas remain fluid in a worksheet. If you enter new values into the cells that a formula refers to, 1-2-3 automatically recalculates the formula to reflect the new values. Most of the time, this arrangement is preferred, but in some situations you may want to freeze calculated values so that they cannot be changed.

To do this procedure, you use the **Edit Quick Copy** command and place a check mark in the **Convert to values** check box before you select OK. If you want to keep one copy of the range with formulas and one without, use different ranges in the **From** and **To** text boxes. If you want only the calculated values, use the same range in both the **From** and **To** text boxes.

Transposing Rows and Columns

Sometimes you set up a table in your worksheet only to find that you wished that it went "the other way," in other words, that you had switched the axis and placed the information running across the columns down the rows instead. You can accomplish this action with the **Range Transpose** command.

When you use this command on a table containing formulas with relative or mixed addresses, you must be careful so that the data doesn't become corrupted in the transposition. If this problem should happen, you can use the **E**dit **U**ndo (Alt + ◆Backspace) command to remove the transposed table. The best way to avoid this problem is first to make a copy (using **E**dit **Q**uick Copy) of the table containing values only, and then use the **R**ange **T**ranspose command.

To transpose a table of data, follow these steps:

1. Select the cells in the table you want to transpose.
2. From the **R**ange menu, select the **T**ranspose option.

1-2-3 displays the Range Transpose dialog box with the address of the currently selected range shown in the **F**rom text box.

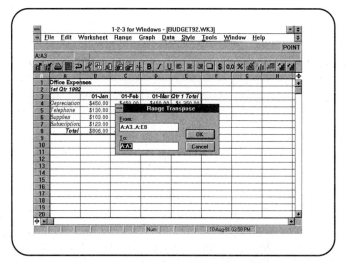

3. Press Tab↹ to select the **T**o text box.
4. Select the upper left corner of the location for the new transposed table or type the address in this box.
5. Select the OK button.

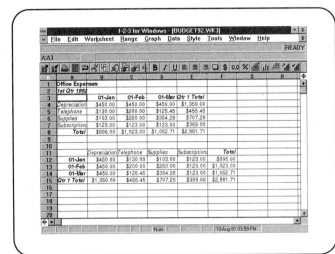

1-2-3 copies the table and transposes its columns and rows into the new location.

Note: As with any other copy or move operation in 1-2-3, be sure that the new location of the transposed table does not overlay any existing data because 1-2-3 will replace its data.

Searching a Range

Looking for a word or string of characters in a large worksheet can be time-consuming and tedious. 1-2-3 offers a feature that enables you to search for text easily. If necessary, you can replace a specified string of characters with other text everywhere the string occurs. Search and replace can be particularly useful for changing all occurrences of a particular misspelling to the correct spelling or updating a value in several formulas.

Whether you want to find the first occurrence of a string or you want to replace one string with another, you use the same command, **Edit Find**. 1-2-3 performs the search column-by-column in the defined search range. You then either can find the next occurrence or quit the search.

Searching for a String

To search a specified range for a particular string in labels or formulas, follow these steps:

1. Select the range of cells that you want searched.

   By confining your search to a specific range, you can accelerate the search operation.

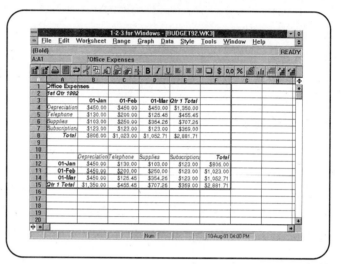

5

In this example, the range A1..F15 is selected to search both the original table and the transposed copy.

2. Choose Edit Find.

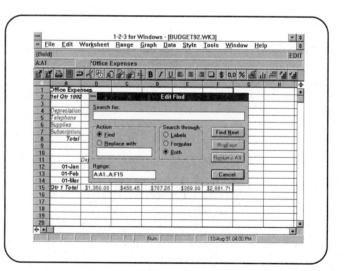

1-2-3 displays the Edit Find dialog box, which contains the range you selected in the Range text box.

3. Type the string you want 1-2-3 to find in the Search for text box. The search string is not case sensitive; you can enter the string in upper- or lowercase characters.

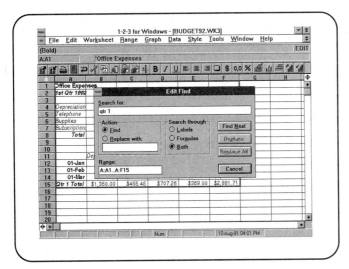

In this example, to search for all occurrences of *Qtr 1* in the selected range, you type **qtr 1**.

4. Indicate whether to search formulas, labels, or both formulas and labels by selecting the Labels, Formulas or Both option button under Search through.

5. Check under Action to make sure that the Find button is selected, and then select the Find Next command button.

   1-2-3 searches for the first occurrence of the string you entered. When 1-2-3 finds the string, it displays the cell address and the contents of the cell that contains the string in the Edit line of the Control panel.

5

In this example, the first occurrence of *Qtr 1* in the search range is cell A15, whose contents are displayed in the Control panel. 1-2-3 displays this cell because the search string Qtr 1 is contained in the label 1st Qtr 1991.

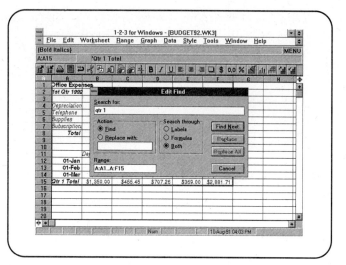

6. To find the next appearance of the string, select the Find Next command button.

   The second occurrence of the string, if present, is highlighted by the cell pointer.

7. Continue to select the Find Next option until you have located the cell you want to find or 1-2-3 finds the last occurrence of your string in the range. If you want to end the search before all occurrences of the string have been found, select the Cancel button.

When 1-2-3 cannot locate another string, a message dialog box is displayed.

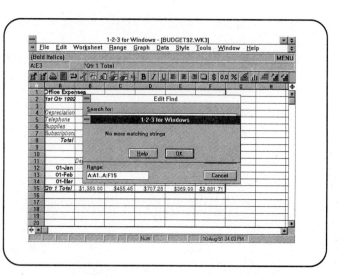

8. Select the OK button in the No more matching strings dialog box to return to READY mode.

Replacing One String with Another

To replace a string in the range with another string, you follow a procedure similar to finding a string within a range. You must, however, also supply the string of characters to replace the existing string.

To search a range for a particular string and replace that string with another, follow these steps:

1. Select the range of cells that you want to search and replace.

2. Choose the Edit menu, and then select the Find option.

3. Type the string you want to locate and replace in the Search for text box.

4. Indicate whether to search formulas, labels, or both by selecting the Labels, Formulas, or Both option button under Search through.

5. Select the Replace with option button under Action.

6. Type the replace string in the Replace with text box exactly as you want it to appear in the worksheet.

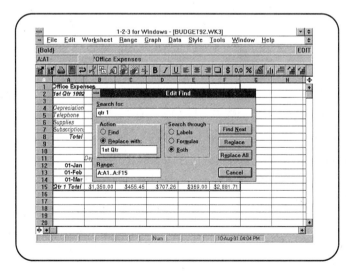

In this example, you type 1st Qtr in the Replace with text box.

7. Select the Find **N**ext command button.

   1-2-3 searches for the first occurrence of the string you entered. As before, the program displays the cell address and contents of the first cell containing the search string in the Control panel.

8. Select the Replace command button to replace the current string or select the **R**eplace All option to replace this and all subsequent matching strings.

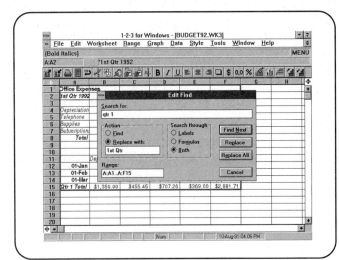

In this example, you select the Find **N**ext button to find the next occurrence of the search string.

You select the Find **N**ext option to avoid replacing the `Qtr 1` string in the label in cell A2 which would change it to `1st 1st Qtr992`. Next, you use the **R**eplace option to replace the two other occurrences of `Qtr 1` in the selected range.

9. When 1-2-3 cannot locate another appearance of the string after you select Find **N**ext, it displays the No more matching strings dialog box. Select the OK button in this dialog box to return to READY mode. If you want to abandon the search-and-replace operation, select the Cancel button in the Edit Find dialog box.

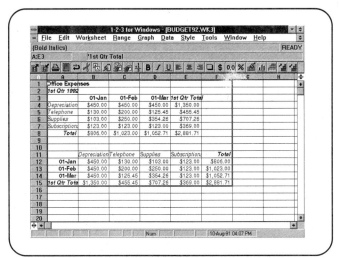

In this worksheet, 1-2-3 has replaced the labels in cells A15 and E3.

5

Summary

In this chapter, you learned how to work with ranges of cells in your worksheet. First, you learned the methods for designating cell ranges. Remember that in 1-2-3 for Windows, you usually select a range before you select the command you want to apply. You can preselect a range with either the mouse or the keyboard. After learning how to designate a range in 1-2-3, you learned some of the key commands that work with ranges, including the following:

- The Range Name command is used to assign descriptive names to ranges up to 15 characters long. You use the Create option to name multicell ranges or single-cell ranges without adjacent labels; you use the Label Create option to name several single-cell ranges with adjacent labels in one operation.

- The Edit Clear (Alt + Backspace) and Edit Clear Special commands are used to erase the contents of ranges. The Edit Clear command erases both the contents and formatting in the range. Use the Edit Clear Special command when you want to designate what type of information to remove from the selected range.

- The Edit Cut or Edit Copy and Edit Paste commands are used to move or copy ranges to and from the Clipboard. You can use Edit Cut or Edit Copy to transfer ranges to new locations within the same worksheet file or to a different worksheet file.

- The Edit Move Cells and Edit Quick Copy commands are used solely to move and copy ranges in the same worksheet file. Remember that neither command makes use of the Clipboard: any information you have copied to the Clipboard remains intact after using these commands.

- The Range Transpose command is used to reverse the orientation of columns and rows in a range of data.

- The Edit Find command searches for a string of characters in a range. By selecting the Replace with option and designating a replacement string, you can have the program replace all or some of the occurrences of the search string within the selected range.

In the next chapter, you learn about the 1-2-3 commands for controlling the worksheet environment. You learn how to add and delete columns, rows, or worksheets in a file, modify the worksheet view, and freeze information on the screen. In addition to commands for controlling the display of information, you learn how to control when your worksheet is recalculated and protect data from changes or deletion.

5

Managing the Worksheet Environment

6

As the size of the worksheets you build increases, you will find that you must manipulate the worksheet environment to work comfortably with the limited worksheet display.

In this chapter, you learn commands that give you control over the display of information in the Worksheet window. You learn how to change column widths and row heights; insert and delete columns, rows, and worksheets; freeze the display of columns and rows in the window; hide columns and worksheets; customize the 1-2-3 window; protect certain areas of your worksheet; and control when and how the Worksheet window is recalculated.

Manipulating columns, rows, and worksheets

Hiding columns and worksheets

Working in GROUP mode

Freezing columns and rows

Using perspective view

Suppressing the display of zeros

Controlling worksheet recalculation

Protecting a worksheet

Finding the status of 1-2-3

Key Terms in This Chapter

Grid lines	The lines that separate the columns and rows in the Worksheet window, outlining the cells.
Worksheet frame	The horizontal bar at the top of the Worksheet window that displays the worksheet and column letters, and the vertical bar on the left side of the window that displays the row numbers.
Global protection	Protects all cells in the current worksheet from changes. After global protection is turned on, you cannot edit, move, or copy data in the worksheet.
Automatic recalculation	1-2-3's default mode in which 1-2-3 recalculates the formulas in the worksheet each time a cell's content changes.

Manipulating Columns, Rows, and Worksheets

In Chapter 4, you learned that 1-2-3 for Windows uses certain global default settings in each new worksheet that you begin. Among these defaults are equal column width of 9 characters and equal row heights (12 points when the default font is 10 points).

When you build a new worksheet, you may have to increase the width of some columns to display the labels or values they contain. Some columns may not require the default width, especially if you use a smaller than normal font. In such cases, you can decrease the width of the columns to accommodate more data in the window view and your printed reports. Because 1-2-3 automatically adjusts the height of a row to accommodate the largest font in the row, you have to adjust the height of the rows in your worksheet less frequently.

1-2-3 also enables you to insert or delete columns and rows. You must be careful as you insert or delete columns because these operations affect the entire worksheet. If you use these commands without knowing what unseen ranges of data exist in the selected columns or rows, you can damage your spreadsheet without even being aware of it.

In addition to inserting new columns and rows, the program enables you to insert new worksheets into a file. By adding new worksheets to a file, you can organize your work as you would pages in a written report, thus enabling you to work in smaller areas of each worksheet. You can segregate different parts of the spreadsheet and arrange them in order of importance.

Adjusting Column Widths

You can set the worksheet's column widths to accommodate data entries that are too wide for the default column width. You also can reduce column widths to give the worksheet a better appearance when a column contains narrow entries. 1-2-3 offers the following options for setting column widths:

- You can set one column at a time with the mouse or keyboard.
- You can set a range of adjacent columns.
- You can set widths for all the columns in the worksheet at once.

The easiest way to change the width of a single column is with the mouse, as follows:

1. Position the mouse pointer on the right border of the column you want to adjust so that the mouse pointer changes to a double-headed arrow pointing left and right.

2. Click and hold down the left mouse button.

3. Drag the mouse to the right to increase the column width or to the left to decrease its width.

    As you drag the mouse, you see a thin vertical line beneath the double-headed arrow indicating the boundary of the new column.

4. Release the mouse button when you reach the desired column width.

You also can set the width of a single column with the Worksheet Column Width command as follows:

1. Position the cell pointer in the column whose width you want to change.

2. From the Worksheet menu, select the Column Width option.

3. Enter the new column width (1 to 240).

6

The Worksheet
Column Width
dialog box
appears.

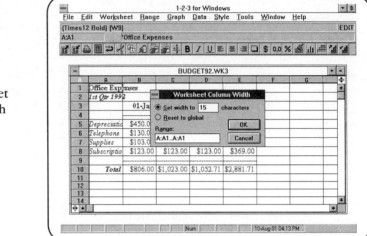

4. Select the **S**et width to option button.

5. Select the OK button.

To return the width of a single column to the default width of 9 characters, select the **R**eset to global option button in the Worksheet Column Width dialog box.

To set the width of a range of columns, simply select the range of columns with the mouse or keyboard before you select the Wor**k**sheet **C**olumn Width command. Enter the new column width in the Set width to text box and select OK.

If you forget to preselect the columns, you can do so after you display the Wor**k**sheet **C**olumn Width dialog box. Press ⌷Tab⌷ until the range in the Range text box is selected, and then point out the columns you want to change.

If you preselect a range of cells, that range address determines which columns the Wor**k**sheet **C**olumn Width command affects. This range is displayed in the Range text box of the dialog box.

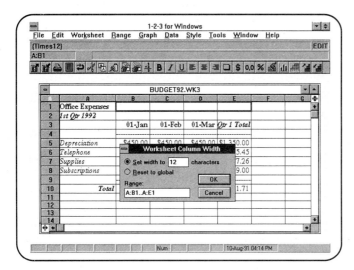

In this example, the range B1..E1 was selected before the Worksheet Column Width command was selected.

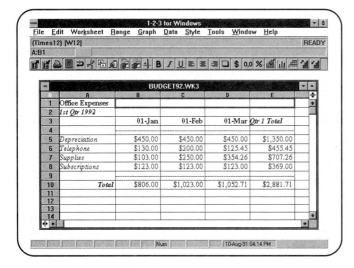

The width of columns B through E has increased to 12 characters.

Setting the Widths of All Columns at Once

You can set all the column widths in the worksheet at one time with the Column width option in the Worksheet Global Settings dialog box. This option usually is used in the early stages of worksheet creation.

To change the widths of all columns in the worksheet at one time, follow these steps:

1. From the Worksheet menu, select the Global Settings option.

   1-2-3 displays the Worksheet Global Settings dialog box.

2. Select the Column width text box and enter the new default column width setting (1 to 240).

3. Select the OK button.

Note: The Worksheet Global Setting Column width command does not alter the width of columns already set with the mouse or with the Worksheet Column Width command.

Setting Row Heights

1-2-3 for Windows makes it possible for you to view a variety of fonts on-screen. Many fonts, however, are too large to fit into a normal-size cell (with a default height of 12 points when the default font is 10 points). Although 1-2-3 automatically adjusts the height of the row to accommodate the largest font in the row, the program also enables you to adjust the row height manually.

You can use the mouse to set the height of a single row. To adjust the height of a range of rows (as well as a single row), you use the Worksheet Row Height command.

To adjust the height of a single row with the mouse, follow these steps:

1. Position the mouse pointer within the frame of the worksheet and point to the horizontal line that marks the bottom of the row you want to size.

   A double-headed arrow pointing up and down appears in the frame.

2. Press and hold down the left mouse button.

3. To increase the height of the row, move the mouse down. To decrease the height of the row, move the mouse up.

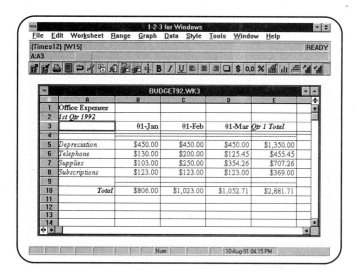

A thin horizontal line appears to the right of the double-headed arrow, marking the boundary of the row.

4. Release the left mouse button when you reach the desired row height.

To adjust the height of a range of rows (or a single row) with the keyboard, follow these steps:

1. Select a cell in the row you want to resize. If you want to change the height of a range of rows, select a range of cells in a column that includes all the rows to be sized.

2. From the Worksheet menu, select the Row Height option.

3. Select the Set height to option button,

   Enter a new row height (1 to 255) in the Set height to text box.

4. Check the Range text box to be sure that its range address includes the row or rows you want to change.

5. Select the OK button.

6

In this example, rows 5 through 8 were selected before choosing the Worksheet Row Height command.

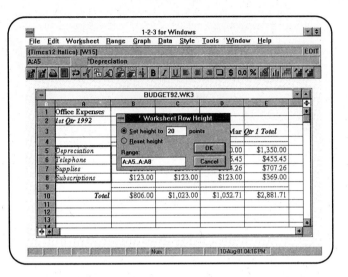

In this example, you enter 20 as the new value in the Set height to text box of the Worksheet Row Height dialog box.

In rows 5 through 8, the row height is increased to 20 points.

After you set the height of a row or rows by using this command, the height does not adjust when you change the font size in that row. To make the row sizes adjust again, select the range of rows, and then select the Reset height option button in the Worksheet Row Height dialog box before you choose OK.

Inserting Columns, Rows, and Worksheets

Suppose that you are finished creating a worksheet, but you want to enhance its general appearance. You can improve the appearance by inserting blank columns and rows in strategic places to highlight headings and other important items. Whether you want to insert additional data or add blank rows or columns to separate sections of your worksheet, you can use the Worksheet Insert command to insert columns or rows. You can insert multiple adjacent columns and rows each time you invoke this command. Later in this section, you learn how to use Worksheet Insert to add worksheets to a multiple-worksheet application.

To insert a new column or row into the worksheet, follow these steps:

1. Select the cell in which you want to insert the new column or row.

2. From the Worksheet menu, select the Insert option.

    1-2-3 displays the Worksheet Insert dialog box.

3. Select the Column or Row option button.

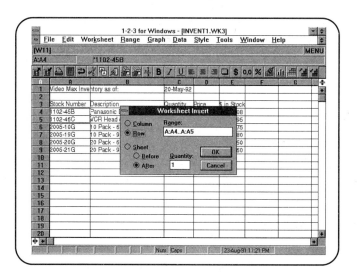

In this example, the range A4..A5 was selected before the Row option button was chosen in the Worksheet Insert dialog box.

4. Check the address of the range listed in the Range text box. If necessary, modify this range to include all the columns or rows you want to insert.

5. Select the OK button.

You see two
blank rows
inserted starting
at row 4 after you
select OK.

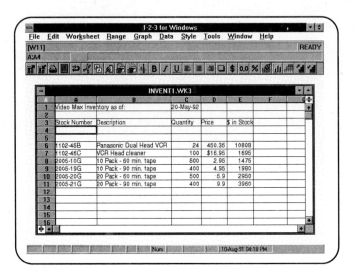

When you insert columns, 1-2-3 automatically shifts all data to the right of the
new column or columns and modifies all the cell formulas to reflect their new
locations. If you insert rows, 1-2-3 inserts a blank row or rows, all data located
is automatically shifted down, and any formulas are modified. 1-2-3 for
Windows does not have the capability of inserting or deleting partial columns
and rows.

To create a multiple-worksheet application, you can insert worksheets with
the Worksheet Insert command. You can insert up to 255 worksheets into a
file for a total of 256. 1-2-3 enables you to insert the new worksheet or worksheets either before or after the current worksheet.

To add one or more worksheets to the current file, follow these steps:

1. From the Worksheet menu, select the Insert option.

2. Select the Sheet option button.

3. Select the Before or After option button to indicate whether you want
   the new worksheet(s) inserted before or after the current worksheet.

4. Select the Quantity text box, and then type a number from 1 to 255 to
   indicate how many worksheets are to be inserted.

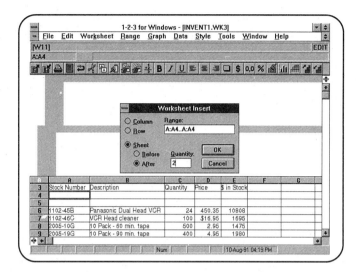

In this example, select the **After** option button and type **2** in the **Q**uantity text box to add two new worksheets to the file.

5. Select the OK button.

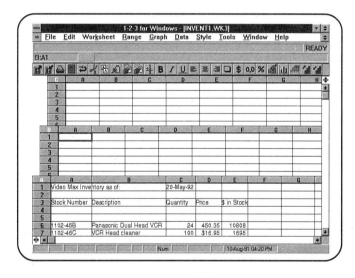

1-2-3 adds two blank worksheets (shown in perspective view) after the original worksheet.

6

215

Note: After adding worksheets to a file, you can move quickly between them by clicking the Go to the next worksheet SmartIcon or the Go to the previous worksheet SmartIcon.

Deleting Columns, Rows, or Worksheets

You can delete columns, rows, or worksheets with the Worksheet Delete command. After you select this command, you choose the Column, Row, or Sheet option button in the Worksheet Delete dialog box.

To delete existing columns or rows from the worksheet or existing worksheets from the current file, follow these steps:

1. Select the range of columns, rows, or worksheets to be deleted.

   For example, select the range A6..A7 to delete rows 6 and 7 in the worksheet.

2. From the Worksheet menu, select the Delete option.

3. Select the Column, Row, or Sheet option button.

In this example, you leave the Row option button selected to delete rows you previously selected in the worksheet.

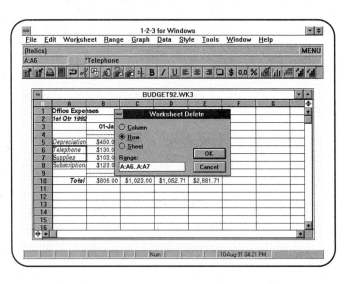

4. Check the address of the range listed in the Range text box. If necessary, modify this range to include a part of all the columns, rows, or worksheets you want to delete. To select the range, press Tab until the Range text box is selected, and then select the range with the mouse or keyboard.

216

5. Select the OK button.

The original data in rows 6 and 7 is removed from the worksheet, and the data that originally appeared below these rows moves up.

If you plan to use Worksheet Delete to delete a column, row, or worksheet containing values, keep in mind that all formulas that refer to the deleted cells will result in ERR. Also remember that when you use the Worksheet Delete command, it deletes entire columns, rows, or worksheets, not just the range of cells you specify in those columns, rows, or sheets.

When you delete worksheets at beginning or middle of a file, 1-2-3 moves up the remaining worksheets to fill in the gap and updates the worksheet letters to reflect their new position in the file. You cannot delete all the worksheets in a file: you must keep at least one worksheet open. If you want to abandon an entire worksheet file, use File Close instead.

If you have deleted columns, rows, or worksheets in error, select the Edit Undo command or press Alt + ◆Backspace before executing another command.

Hiding Columns and Worksheets

With the Worksheet Hide command, you can suppress the display of one or more columns or worksheets in the current file. One important use of this command is to suppress the display of unwanted columns when you are printing reports. When you hide intervening columns, a report can sometimes display data from two or more separated columns on a single page without being compressed.

Other uses of these commands include suppressing the display of sensitive information (such as financial statements), hiding the display of cells that have a numeric value of zero, and fitting noncontiguous columns on-screen. The procedures that follow describe how to hide and redisplay columns, and how to hide and redisplay worksheets.

To hide one or more columns, follow these steps:

1. Select the column or range of columns you want to hide.

Columns B through D are selected by pointing out the cell range B3..D3.

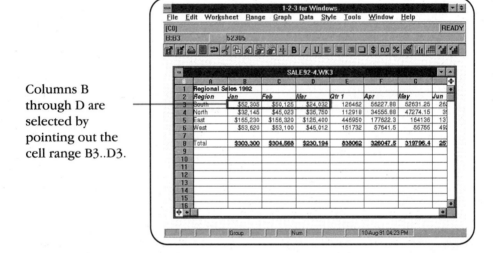

2. From the Worksheet menu, select the Hide option.

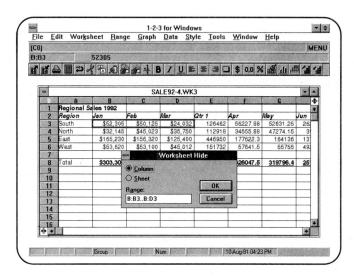

1-2-3 displays the
Worksheet Hide
dialog box.

6

3. Check to make sure that the Column option button is selected and
   that the column range in the Range text box is correct, and then
   select OK.

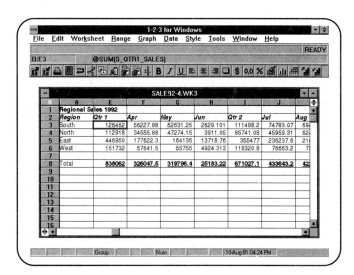

Columns B
through D are
hidden.

Although the hidden columns do not appear in the worksheet display, numbers and formulas in hidden columns are still present, and cell references to cells in hidden columns continue to work properly. You can tell which columns are missing only by noting the break in column letters at the top of the frame. The hidden columns are temporarily redisplayed, however, when you select cells or use certain commands, such as Edit Move Cells or Edit Quick Copy. The hidden columns are marked with an asterisk (such as C*) during this temporary display.

This screen shows how hidden columns are temporarily displayed when you select a range of cells in an adjacent column.

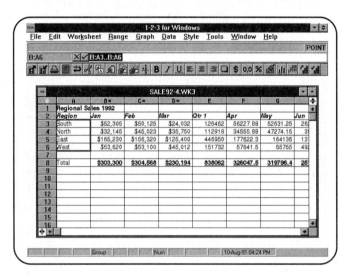

Note: When you use the Worksheet Hide Column command, 1-2-3 hides all of the data in that column (from row 1 through 8,192). If you only want to hide the display of a range of data in a column, select the range, and then choose the Hidden format in the Format list box of the Range Format dialog box.

To redisplay hidden columns, follow these steps:

1. From the Worksheet menu, select the Unhide option.

    1-2-3 displays the Worksheet Unhide dialog box.

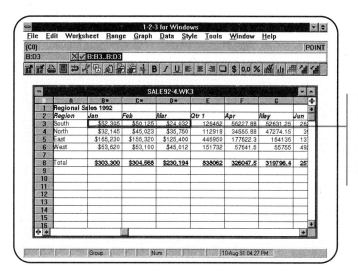

Specify the columns B through D by pointing out the cell range B3..D3 with the → key.

2. With the **C**olumn option button selected, press `Tab⇥` until you select the **R**ange text box. Enter or point out the range of columns to redisplay.

   1-2-3 temporarily redisplays hidden columns in the Worksheet window as you highlight them.

   1-2-3 enters the selected range into the Range text box.

3. Select the OK button.

In multiple-worksheet applications, you can hide entire worksheets with the **W**orksheet **H**ide command. You can use this feature to hide worksheets containing formulas, macros, and sensitive data (such as salary information). To hide one or more worksheets in a multiple-worksheet file, follow these steps:

1. Select a cell in the worksheet you want to hide. To hide more than one adjacent worksheet, select a 3D range by anchoring the cell with the Abs (`F4`) key and pressing the Next Sheet (`Ctrl` + `PgUp`) or Prev Sheet (`Ctrl` + `PgDn`) key.

221

Worksheet B is specified by selecting cell B:A1.

2. From the Worksheet menu, select the **H**ide option.

3. Select the **S**heet option button in the Worksheet Hide dialog box.

4. Verify that the range listed in the **R**ange text box includes the worksheet(s) you want to hide, and then select **OK**.

Worksheet B is hidden.

6

Although hidden worksheets do not appear in the Worksheet window, numbers and formulas in hidden worksheets are still present, and references to cells in hidden worksheets continue to work properly. You can tell which worksheets are missing only by noting the break in worksheet letters on the left side of the worksheet frames when viewing multiple sheets in perspective view. Like hidden columns, hidden worksheets are temporarily redisplayed, however, when you use certain commands, such as Edit Quick Copy or Edit Move Cells; the hidden worksheet letters are marked with an asterisk (such as B*) during this temporary display.

To redisplay hidden worksheets in the current file, follow these steps:

1. From the Worksheet menu, select the Unhide option.

2. Select the Sheet option button in the Worksheet Unhide dialog box.

3. Press Tab⇥ to select the Range text box, and then enter or highlight the range of worksheets to redisplay.

   1-2-3 temporarily redisplays hidden worksheets in the Worksheet window as you highlight them.

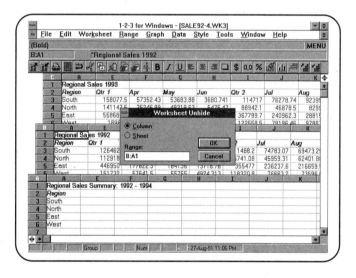

Press the Prev Sheet key (Ctrl + PgDn) to select cell B:A1 and redisplay worksheet B.

   1-2-3 enters the selected range in the Range text box.

4. Select the OK button.

   1-2-3 redisplays worksheet B in the Worksheet window.

Working in GROUP Mode

1-2-3 for Windows has a GROUP mode that helps you create a multiple-worksheet application where each worksheet in the file uses the same formatting. GROUP mode is useful, for example, when you are consolidating financial reports from different regions, and each report has its own worksheet that uses the same layout and formatting.

GROUP mode also offers an alternative to using three-dimensional ranges by having certain commands affect the same range on all worksheets in the current file. The following 1-2-3 commands affect every worksheet in the current file:

- On the Worksheet menu, all the commands including Global Settings, Insert, Delete, Hide, Unhide, Column Width, Row Height, Titles, and Page Break.
- On the Range menu, the Format, Protect, and Unprotect commands.
- On the Style menu, the Alignment command.

To turn on Group mode, follow these steps:

1. From the Worksheet menu, select the Global Settings option.
2. Place a check mark in the Group mode check box.
3. Select the OK button.

1-2-3 displays the GROUP indicator on the Status line.

When you need to make formatting changes to just one worksheet in the file, you need to turn off GROUP mode. Remove the check mark in the GROUP mode check box in the Worksheet Global Settings dialog box.

Note: Formatting changes made to all of the worksheets in the file when GROUP mode is turned on are not reversed when you turn off GROUP mode.

Controlling the Worksheet Window Display

Sometimes the size of a 1-2-3 worksheet can be unwieldy given the limited view of the worksheet afforded by the size of the screen. To make it easier to work with larger worksheets, 1-2-3 for Windows includes commands designed to control the screen view.

You can split the 1-2-3 Worksheet window into two panes, either horizontally or vertically. To keep column headings or row headings in view, you can set worksheet titles that stay visible in the window as you scroll to distant parts of the worksheet. If you're working with a file that contains multiple worksheets, you can switch to perspective view so that you can see a small part of three adjacent worksheets in the Worksheet window. All these features help you to overcome some of the inconvenience of not being able to see all of your work at one time.

Splitting the Worksheet Window

You can split the current worksheet into two panes either with the mouse or the Window Split command. By splitting the Worksheet window into panes, you can make the changes in one area of the worksheet and immediately see their effects in the other.

Because each Scroll bar in the worksheet is equipped with a split box (the button with two arrow heads pointing opposite that you drag to the place where you want the window to be split, using the mouse is by far the easiest way to divide the window into panes.

6

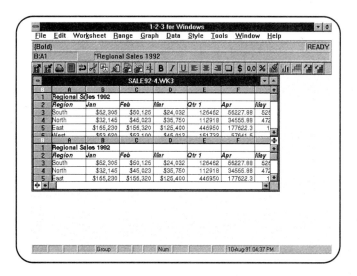

The window is divided into upper and lower panes by dragging the split box down to row 5.

To clear the panes in the current Worksheet window, you simply scroll the appropriate split box back to the left or top frame of the 1-2-3 window before releasing the left mouse button.

The Horizontal and Vertical options in the Window Split dialog box split the Worksheet window in the manner indicated by their names. The window is divided where the cell pointer is positioned when you select the **W**indow **S**plit command.

To split the window into two horizontal or two vertical panes with the keyboard, follow these steps:

1. Place the cell pointer where you want to split the window.

   Place the cell pointer in any column of row E to split the window vertically.

2. From the **W**indow menu, select the **S**plit option.

3. Select either the **H**orizontal or **V**ertical option buttons to split the window.

To compare two columns that cannot be seen together in the Worksheet window, select the **V**ertical option button.

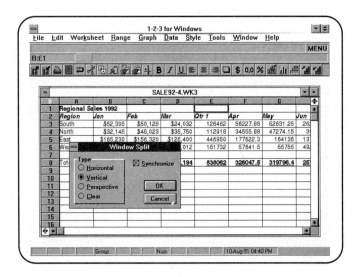

4. Select the OK button.

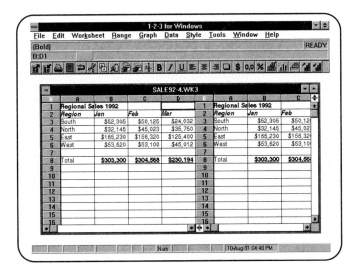

1-2-3 splits the Worksheet window vertically into left and right panes.

After you use the Horizontal option button to split the window, the cell pointer appears in the top pane. When you specify a Vertical division, the cell pointer appears in the left pane. To jump back and forth between different panes in the window, you use the F6 function key, or click the left mouse button in a cell in the opposite pane.

After the window splits, you can change the window display so that the panes scroll independently rather than together (the default mode). To scroll the panes independently, unmark the Synchronize check box in the Window Split dialog box. If you later want to scroll the panes together again, return to the Window Split dialog box and check the Synchronize option.

Using Perspective View

You can use the Perspective option button in the Window Split dialog box to display up to three adjacent worksheets in the Worksheet window at a time. You cannot add horizontal or vertical panes to the Worksheet window when perspective view is in use.

To return to the single-pane or single-Worksheet window after selecting the Horizontal, Vertical, or Perspective options in the Window Split dialog box, select the Clear option button. When you select Clear, the single Worksheet window takes on the settings of the top or left pane, depending on how the screen was split.

227

Note: If you use the mouse, you can turn on and off perspective view by clicking the Perspective SmartIcon. Click the icon once to turn on perspective view, and click it a second time to turn off perspective view.

Freezing Titles on the Screen

To freeze rows or columns along the top and left edges of the worksheet so that they remain in view as you scroll to different parts of the worksheet, use the Worksheet Titles command. The Worksheet Titles command freezes all the cells to the left or above (or both to the left and above) the cell pointer's position so that those cells don't move off the screen.

Suppose that you want to keep on-screen the date headings in rows 1 and 2, and the regional headings in column A.

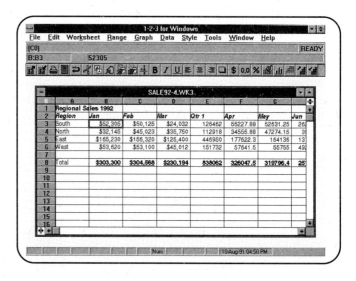

To freeze worksheet titles on the screen, follow these steps:

1. Select the cell that is located one cell below and to the right of the rows or columns you want to freeze.

   In this example, you select cell B3 to freeze column A and rows 1 and 2.

2. From the Worksheet menu, select the Titles option.

3. Select the Horizontal, Vertical, or Both option button. The Both option freezes both rows and columns above and to the left of the cell pointer.

228

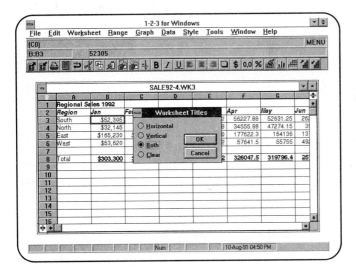

In this example, select the **B**oth option button.

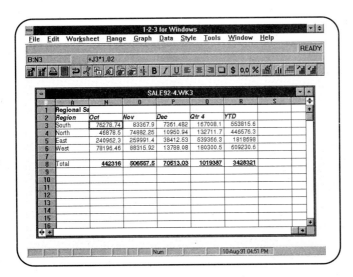

When the titles are frozen, no matter how you scroll the worksheet, rows 1 and 2 and column A are always displayed in the Worksheet window.

When you freeze columns or rows, you cannot move the cell pointer into the frozen area nor can you select any of its cells. Press Home to move the pointer to the upper left cell in the unfrozen area. (Usually Home moves the cell pointer to cell A1.)

229

The **W**orksheet **T**itles **H**orizontal command freezes rows above the cell pointer. Rows 1 to 3 remain at the top of the screen when you scroll up and down.

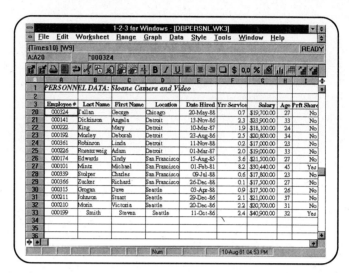

To unlock the frozen worksheet titles, you select the **C**lear option button in the Worksheet Titles dialog box. After you select the **C**lear command, you can move the cell pointer freely in your worksheet.

Suppressing the Display of Zeros

The Zero Display options in the Worksheet Global Settings dialog box enable you to suppress the display of all cells in the current worksheet file that contain the value of 0 (zero). This feature is useful for preparing reports in which cells showing $0.00 would look odd. As an alternative, you may choose to have a label (such as Not Available), instead of a blank, displayed in zero-value cells.

You can enter formulas and values for all the items in the report, including the zero items, and then display the results with all the zeros removed or replaced by a label. When the cell pointer highlights a cell that contains a zero or a formula that evaluates to zero, the actual formula or value is displayed in the control panel.

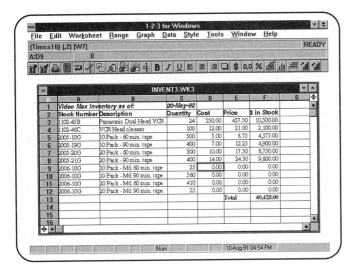

Suppose that you have an inventory worksheet that lists product codes and their associated costs. In some cases, the costs are 0.00.

To suppress the display of zeros or to substitute a label for zero entries, follow these steps:

1. From the Worksheet menu, select the Global Settings option.

2. To suppress the display of zeros with blanks, select the Leave zeros blank option button under Zero display. To substitute a label for zeros, select the Use label option button, and then enter the label to be used in the Use label text box.

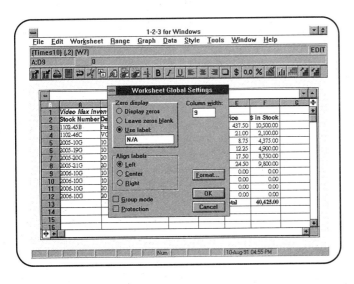

Select the Use Label option button and enter N/A (for not available) in the text box.

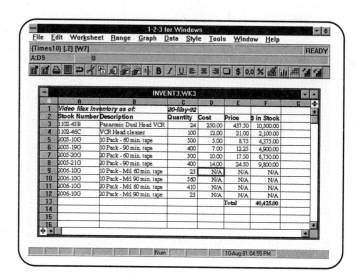

All zero values in the worksheet are replaced with the label N/A.

If you want to display the zeros again, select the Display zeros option button in the Worksheet Global Settings dialog box. Unlike earlier versions of 1-2-3, in 1-2-3 for Windows, the zero suppression or label substitution are saved as part of the worksheet and are, therefore, present when you next open the file.

Note: When you suppress the display of zeros or substitute a label for zeros, all cells in the worksheet with a zero value are affected by the substitution. This feature does not affect cases such as when a cell with the value .004 is displayed as 0.00 using a two-decimal place format. Because the value is not truly zero, it is displayed in the worksheet as before.

Controlling the 1-2-3 Window Display

1-2-3 for Windows gives you a great deal of freedom in determining the way the 1-2-3 window appears on your screen with the Window Display Options command. If you have a color monitor, you can use this command to change the colors used to display the worksheet frame, cell background, cell contents, negative values, drop shadows, grid lines, range borders, selected ranges, and unprotected cells. If you're using a monochrome monitor, you set the display to monochrome.

You also can use this command to switch to draft mode, change the display size of cells in the worksheet, suppress or customize the display of the frame, and suppress the display of page breaks and grid lines.

Note: Any new display settings that you select in the Window Display Options dialog box for the current worksheet are applied to all the other worksheets in a file.

Changing the Display Colors

You can use the Window Display Options dialog box to customize colors for the 1-2-3 window display and apply them to various parts of the window. 1-2-3 for Windows uses a default palette of eight colors. You can assign new colors to this palette from a larger palette of 256 colors.

To change the colors on the palette, follow these steps:

1. Choose the Window menu, and then select Display Options.

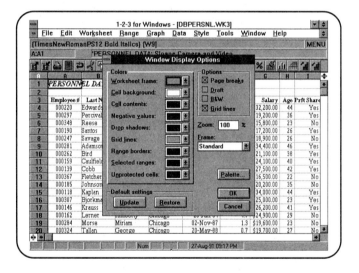

1-2-3 displays the Window Display Options dialog box that contains a number of options for customizing the 1-2-3 window display.

2. Select the Palette command button.

6

1-2-3 displays the
Window Display
Options Palette
dialog box in
which you can
assign new colors
to the palette.

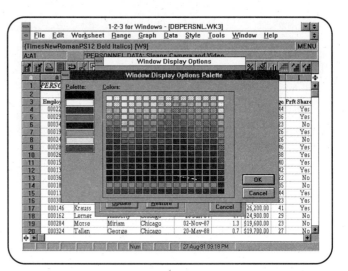

3. To select a new color for the palette, select the color bar under **P**alette
   that you want to modify, and then select the color square under
   Colors that you want to replace it with.

4. Repeat Step 3 for every color in the palette that you want to change.

5. After you make all your changes to the palette, select the OK button to
   return to the Window Display Options dialog box.

You can assign colors on the palette to many parts of the window display
using the drop-down list boxes under **C**olors. Select the color option that you
want to change, and then click the drop-down button and select the new color
from the palette in the drop-down list box. Table 6.1 describes the options
found under **C**olors in the Window Display Options dialog box.

Table 6.1
The Window Display Color Options

Option	Sets the color for
Worksheet Frame	Worksheet frame.
Cell background	Background in cells.
Cell contents	Values and labels displayed in the cells.
Negative values	Negative values in the worksheet.
Drop shadows	Drop shadows in the worksheet.

Option	Sets the color for
Grid lines	Grid lines that separate the columns and rows of the worksheet.
Range borders	Lines surrounding the cell borders in a selected range.
Selected ranges	The cell pointer's heavy outline that expands to indicate the extent of the range.
Unprotected cells	Unprotected cells in the worksheet (see "Turning Off Protection in a Range" later in this chapter).

Note: To restore the default color scheme, select the Restore command button. If you want the colors you have assigned to the palette and to the parts of the 1-2-3 window to become the program's new default color settings, select the Update command button under Default Settings.

Setting Other Window Display Options

Colors aren't the only display options you can change in the Window Display Options dialog box. You can turn on or off the following screen attributes listed under Options by inserting or removing a check mark in its check box:

- Select the Page breaks check box to display the page breaks (shown as dotted lines) inserted by the program when a print range is selected or the page breaks you insert with the Worksheet Page Break command. Deselect this option to suppress display of page breaks in the worksheet.

- Select the Draft check box to switch to draft mode in which 1-2-3 displays all data in a monospaced font and eliminates the display of borders and formatting assigned to the worksheet. Deselect this option to return to the default graphics mode, which shows the worksheet more-or-less as it will print.

- Select B & W if you're using a monochrome monitor. You also can use this option if you have a color monitor but use a black and white printer so that you can see how the colors you have selected will appear in the printout. Deselect this option to return to color display.

- Select the Grid lines check box to display the grid lines that outline the cells in the worksheet. Deselect this option to turn off grid lines display.

6

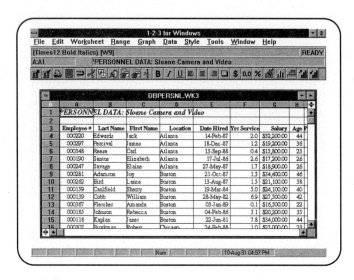

You see the worksheet in standard graphics mode in which formatting is displayed as it will print.

1-2-3 performs all screen operations faster in draft mode than graphics mode (especially if you aren't running 1-2-3 for Windows on the latest hardware) because the program doesn't have to take time to redraw all the fonts and borders assigned to the data as you move around and work in the worksheet.

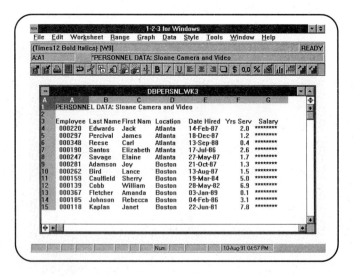

You see the worksheet after selecting the **D**raft option in the Window Display Options dialog box.

You can use draft mode to speed up data entry in a new spreadsheet, and then switch back to graphics modes when you're ready to format the worksheet. If you don't switch back to graphics mode before you format your data, you must rely on the style abbreviations shown in the format line of the control panel to keep track of the formatting assigned to a cell. You have no way, however, to judge how wide to make the columns or how high to adjust the rows to suit the fonts you have selected. Draft mode shows the worksheet data in only a single monospaced font.

The Zoom option in the Window Display Options dialog box enables you to adjust the size of the cell display in the Worksheet window. To change the size of the display, you select the Zoom text box, and then enter a value between 25 and 400, representing the percentage of the default display size (100% is the default). When you increase the size of the cells, the number of columns and rows displayed in the Worksheet window decreases. When you decrease the size of the cells, the number of columns and rows displayed increases.

6

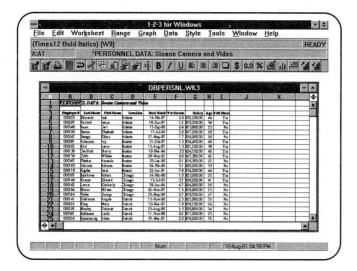

In this example, the Zoom option reduces the cell display to 65 percent of normal.

In this example, the Zoom option increases the cell display to 150 percent of normal.

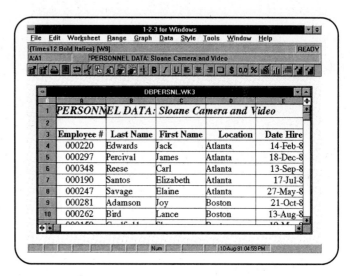

The Frame option enables you to select a new frame display for the Worksheet window. To change the frame, select the Frame drop-down button to open the drop-down list box, and then choose one of the following options:

- Standard returns to the default frame display.
- Characters replaces the standard frame with a horizontal and vertical ruler showing tick marks based on 10-point characters.
- Inches replaces the standard frame with a horizontal and vertical ruler showing tick marks based on inches.
- Metric replaces the standard frame with a horizontal and vertical ruler showing tick marks based on centimeters.
- Points/Picas replaces the standard frame with a horizontal and vertical ruler showing tick marks based on picas.
- None removes the frame display entirely from the Worksheet window.

You might, for example, change the Frame option to Inches so that you can see how much of the worksheet can be printed on a page given the size of the font you're using.

6

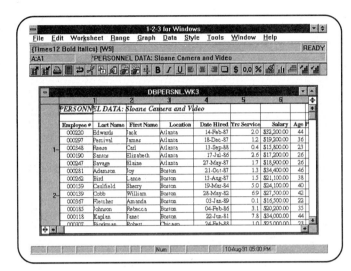

In this example, the Frame option is set for Inches.

You can use the Zoom and Frame options together when doing detail work in the Worksheet window. If you choose one of the ruler-based Frame options and then increase cell display with Zoom, 1-2-3 increases the number of tick marks on the rulers to suit the new scale. Although you might not have much call for these options when entering and formatting regular labels and values in a spreadsheet, these options can be invaluable when creating, annotating, sizing, and placing graphs in your worksheet (see Chapter 10 for information on creating graphs).

After you finish making changes to the display settings in the Window Display Options dialog box, select the OK button to put them into effect in the current worksheet file. To return to the defaults created by Lotus, return to the Window Display Options dialog box and select the Restore command button. If you want to save your changes and make them the new program defaults, select the Update command button under Default Settings.

Controlling Recalculation in the Worksheet

One of the primary functions of a spreadsheet program is to recalculate cells with formulas when a value or formula changes. 1-2-3 provides two basic recalculation methods: automatic and manual. Using automatic recalculation,

239

the default, 1-2-3 recalculates the formulas that are affected whenever a cell in the worksheet changes. In manual recalculation, the worksheet is recalculated only when the user requests it, either from the keyboard using the F9 (Calc) key or from a macro.

1-2-3 also provides three orders of recalculation: natural order and two linear orders—columnwise or rowwise. Natural order is the default. You also can choose the number of times (iterations) that worksheets are recalculated.

You select the recalculation options in the Tools User Setup Recalculation dialog box. Settings specified in this dialog box affect all active worksheets and files. The recalculation options are described in table 6.2.

Table 6.2
Options on the Tools User Setup Recalculation Dialog Box

Selection	Description
Order of Recalculation	
Natural	1-2-3 does not recalculate any cell until the cells that it depends on have been recalculated. This is the default setting.
Columnwise	Recalculation begins at cell A:A1 of the first active file and continues down column A, and then goes to cell A:B1 and down column B, and so forth—through all worksheets of all active files.
Rowwise	Recalculation begins at cell A:A1 of the first active file and proceeds across row 1, and then goes across row 2, and so forth—through all worksheets of all active files.
Method of Recalculation	
Automatic	The worksheet is recalculated whenever a cell changes. This is the default setting.
Manual	The worksheet is recalculated only when you press F9 (Calc).
Number of Recalculations	
Iterations	The worksheet is recalculated a specified number of times when you change cell contents in automatic recalculation or press F9 (Calc) in manual recalculation. The default is one iteration per recalculation.

As a new 1-2-3 user, you may not need to change the recalculation settings at all. 1-2-3's default settings are Automatic recalculation (meaning that each time a cell's content changes, the program automatically recalculates any formulas that are affected), and Natural order (meaning that 1-2-3 does not recalculate a cell until after the cells that it depends on have been recalculated). To save processing time, you can switch to Manual recalculation so that 1-2-3 recalculates the worksheet only when you press F9.

Note: If you open a spreadsheet and see the CALC indicator in the Status line, be sure that you press F9 to recalculate the worksheet before you print a report from it.

Protecting the Worksheet

6

1-2-3 has special features that protect areas of a worksheet from possible destruction. These features enable you to set up ranges of cells that cannot be changed or deleted from the worksheet without special effort. These commands are particularly beneficial when you are setting up worksheets in which data will be entered by people who are not familiar with 1-2-3.

Protecting the Entire Worksheet

When you first create a worksheet, the global protection feature is not active, enabling you to make changes and add data anywhere in the worksheet. To turn on global protection, you place a check mark in the Protection check box in the Worksheet Global Settings dialog box.

Think of this protection system as a series of barriers set up around all the cells in the worksheet. The barriers go down when the worksheet is first loaded, and all the cells in the worksheet can be modified. This arrangement is appropriate because you want to have access to everything in the worksheet when you first begin entering data.

After you finish making entries in the worksheet, you may want to make sure that certain areas are not modified or inadvertently erased. To do this, you turn on global protection by selecting the Protection option in the Worksheet Global Settings dialog box. After you select this option, all the cells in the worksheet are protected—this command restores all the barriers in the worksheet.

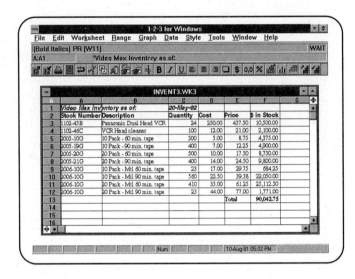

To save the
completed
inventory spread-
sheet from further
changes, you turn
on global protec-
tion.

All cells in the worksheet are protected as indicated by the PR cell indicator in
the format line of the control panel.

Turning Off Protection in a Range

You can selectively unprotect certain cells or ranges with the Range Unprotect
command. In effect, you "tear down the barriers" that surround these individual cells or ranges of cells. You can reprotect these cells at any time by
selecting Range Protect.

To turn off protection for a cell or range of cells in your worksheet, follow these steps:

1. Select the range of cells that you want to unprotect.

2. Choose the Range menu, and then select the Unprotect option.

3. Check the range address in the Range text box. If it's correct, select the OK button.

   Unprotected cells are identified by a U in the format line of the control panel. They are also displayed in a different color on a color monitor.

Finding the Status of 1-2-3

If you select the Help menu and then select the About 1-2-3 option, the program displays a dialog box that contains the 1-2-3 for Windows copyright notice along with information on the location of any circular references.

6

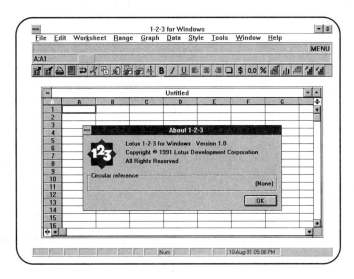

The About 1-2-3 dialog box indicates the cell location of any circular reference.

When the CIRC indicator appears in the Status line, you can use the **Help About 1-2-3** command to locate the formula containing the circular reference in the worksheet. A circular reference in a formula is one that depends in some way on its own value. A circular reference is almost always entered by mistake and should be corrected as soon as the CIRC indicator appears.

Summary

In this chapter you learned techniques for controlling the worksheet display and environment. Most of these techniques are designed to help you work with worksheets larger than the screen display. You also learned how to control recalculation, and protect your worksheets from unwanted changes.

You learned the following 1-2-3 commands and techniques:

- The **Worksheet Column Width Set** width to command changes the width the range of columns that you select. To reset the columns to the global default, select the **Reset** to global option button in the Worksheet Column Width dialog box.

- The **Worksheet Global Settings Column** width command changes the column width of all columns in the worksheet, except for those already changed.

- The **Worksheet Row Height Set** height to command enables you to change the height of rows you select. Select the **Reset** height option button in the Worksheet Row Height box to reset columns to their default height.

- You can use the mouse to set individual column widths and row heights. Position the mouse pointer on the right column boundary or the bottom row boundary in the worksheet frame, press and hold the left mouse button, and move the mouse pointer in the direction of the desired column width or row height. Then release the mouse button.

- The **Window Split** command splits the Worksheet window into separate panes so that two different parts of the same or a different worksheet in the file can be viewed at the same time. Worksheet windows can be split with the **Horizontal** or **Vertical** option buttons. Use the **Perspective** option button to display three worksheets at a time in the Worksheet window. Select the **Clear** option button in the Window Split dialog box to remove the panes from the Worksheet window or clear the perspective view. You also can use a mouse to split the screen horizontally or vertically by dragging the split box at the top and far left of the Scroll bars.

- The Worksheet Titles command freezes titles along the top and left borders of the worksheet so that the titles remain in view when scrolling the worksheet. Select the Clear option button in the Worksheet Titles dialog box to unfreeze the titles.

- The Worksheet Insert command can insert one or more columns, rows, or worksheets into the current file. To delete one or more columns, rows, worksheets, use Worksheet Delete.

- The Worksheet Hide command temporarily removes columns or worksheets from the Worksheet window. Hidden columns also do not print when included in a print range. Hidden columns or worksheets can be restored with the Worksheet Unhide command.

- The Worksheet Global Settings Leave zeros blank command suppresses the display of all zero values in the worksheet. To substitute a label for zeros, select the Use label option button in the Worksheet Global Settings dialog box and enter the new label in the text box. To redisplay zeros in the worksheet, select the Display zeros option button.

- The Tools User Setup Recalculation command changes the method, order, and number of iterations used in worksheet recalculation.

- The Worksheet Global Settings Protection command enables you to turn protection on or off in a worksheet. You then can use the Range Unprotect command to unprotect individual cells or ranges in the worksheet to allow entry in those cells.

- The Help About 1-2-3 command displays a dialog box that indicates the location of any circular reference. Use this command whenever the CIRC indicator appears in the Status line of the 1-2-3 window.

The next chapter covers using 1-2-3's built-in functions. 1-2-3 offers eight differ types of functions designed to perform specialized and complex operations. Using functions to build your formulas can save valuable time when you are designing complicated spreadsheet models.

6

245

Using
Functions

7

In addition to creating formulas, you can use a variety of ready-made formulas provided by 1-2-3. These built-in formulas or functions enable you to take advantage of 1-2-3's analytical capability. Functions are helpful when used with business, engineering, scientific, and statistical applications. You can use many of these powerful functions even in the simplest of worksheets. You can use functions by themselves, in your own formulas, or in macros and advanced macro-command programs to calculate results and solve problems.

1-2-3 provides the following types of functions:

- Mathematical and trigonometric
- Date and time
- Financial
- Statistical
- Database
- Logical
- String
- Special

> ### Key Terms in This Chapter
>
> *Functions*   1-2-3's built-in formulas that perform many different types of calculations.
>
> *Arguments*   Inputs needed by most functions to perform their calculations.
>
> *Syntax*   The format of a specific function.

This chapter first describes the basic steps for using 1-2-3 functions and then covers each of these groups in more detail. Several tables briefly describe all 1-2-3 functions, and separate sections expand on the most commonly used 1-2-3 functions. Refer to Que's *Using 1-2-3 for Windows* for comprehensive coverage of each of 1-2-3's functions.

7

Entering a 1-2-3 Function

This chapter does not include numbered steps for entering each function because you use the following four-step process when entering any function in your worksheet:

1. Type @, the character that identifies a function.

2. Type the function name or press the F3 (Name) key to display a list of functions, then select the one you want to use by double-clicking the function name or pressing ⏎Enter.

3. Enter any input values, or *arguments*, that the function requires enclosed in parentheses. If the function uses a cell range as an argument (as many do), you can select the range by clicking the function name.

4. Press ⏎Enter or the appropriate direction key (such as ↓ or ↑) to enter the function in the current cell.

Note that you can use upper- or lowercase letters in the function name as long as you spell the name correctly. This book uses the standard practice of showing function names in uppercase letters. Do not use spaces when you enter any part of a function. The only time you can use spaces is when you enter text enclosed in quotation marks as one of the arguments. For example, in

   @IF(B5>90,"Account Overdue"," ")

the text Account Overdue is the first argument of the IF function and is enclosed in quotes.

In functions that use multiple arguments, separate each argument with a comma (,)—although 1-2-3 accepts a semi-colon (;) as well.

Using Mathematical and Trigonometric Functions

1-2-3's mathematical and trigonometric functions are useful in engineering and scientific applications. In addition, these functions are convenient tools that you can use to perform a variety of standard arithmetic operations (such as rounding values or calculating square roots).

Table 7.1 lists the mathematical and trigonometric functions, their arguments, and the operations they perform. The sections that follow cover the INT and ROUND mathematical functions in detail.

7

Table 7.1
Mathematical and Trigonometric Functions

Function	Description
@ABS(*number* or *cell_reference*)	Computes the absolute value of the argument.
@ACOS(*angle*)	Calculates the arccosine, given an angle in radians.
@ASIN(*angle*)	Calculates the arcsine, given an angle in radians.
@ATAN(*angle*)	Calculates the arctangent, given an angle in radians.
@ATAN2 (*number1*, *number2*)	Calculates the four-quadrant arctangent.
@COS(*angle*)	Calculates the cosine, given an angle in radians.
@EXP(*number* or *cell_reference*)	Computes the number e raised to the power of the argument.
@INT(*number* or *cell_reference*)	Returns the integer portion of a number.

continued

Table 7.1 *(continued)*

Function	Description
@LN(*number* or *cell_reference*)	Calculates the natural logarithm of a number.
@LOG(*number* or *cell_reference*)	Calculates the common, or base 10, logarithm of a number.
@MOD(*number*, *divisor*)	Computes the remainder of a division operation.
@PI	Returns the value of π.
@RAND	Generates a random number between 0 and 1.
@ROUND(*number* or *cell_reference*, *precision*)	Rounds a number to a specified precision.
@SIN(*angle*)	Calculates the sine, given an angle in radians.
@SQRT(*number* or *cell_reference*)	Computes the positive square root of a number.
@TAN(*angle*)	Calculates the tangent, given an angle in radians.

Computing Integers with INT

The INT function converts a decimal number into an integer, that is, a whole number. INT creates an integer by truncating, or removing, the decimal portion of a number (without rounding). INT uses the following syntax:

@INT(*number* or *cell_reference*)

INT has one argument, which can be a numeric value or a cell reference to a numeric value. Applying INT to the values 3.1, 4.5, and 5.9 yields integer values of 3, 4, and 5, respectively.

INT is useful for computations in which the decimal portion of a number is irrelevant or insignificant. Suppose, for example, that you have $1,000 to invest in a publicly traded company and that its shares sell for $17 each. You divide 1,000 by 17 to compute the total number of shares that you can buy. Because you cannot buy a fractional share, you can use INT to truncate the decimal portion.

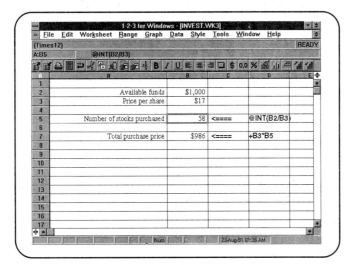

The INT function calculates the number of shares that you can buy.

Rounding Numbers with ROUND

The ROUND function rounds a value to the precision you specify. The function uses two arguments: the value you want to round, and the precision you want to use in the rounding. ROUND uses the following syntax:

@**ROUND**(*number* or *cell_reference,precision*)

The first argument can be a numeric value or a cell reference to a numeric value. The precision argument determines the number of decimal places and can be an integer between –100 and +100. Positive precision values specify positions to the right of the decimal place; negative values specify positions to the left. A precision value of 0 rounds decimal values to the nearest integer.

Note: The ROUND function and the Range Format command perform differently. ROUND actually changes the contents of a cell; Range Format alters only how 1-2-3 displays the cell's contents.

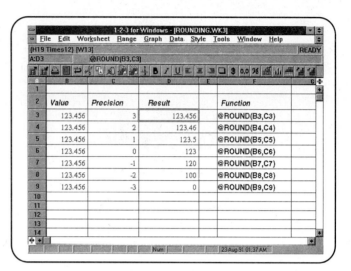

The ROUND function rounds values to a specified precision.

7 Using Date and Time Functions

The date and time functions enable you to convert dates (such as November 26, 1991) and times (such as 6:00 p.m.) to serial numbers and time fractions, respectively. You then can use the values these functions return to perform date and time arithmetic. These functions are valuable tools when dates and times affect calculations and logic in your worksheets.

1-2-3's internal calendar begins with the serial number 1, which represents January 1, 1900. The calendar ends with the serial number 73050, which represents December 31, 2099. 1-2-3 represents a single day with an increment of 1; therefore, 1-2-3 represents January 2, 1900, as 2. To display that serial number as a text date, select (in the Format list box of the Range Format dialog box) the date format (a number between 1 and 5) that you want to use.

Table 7.2 summarizes 1-2-3's date and time functions. The sections that follow review examples of the DATE, DATEVALUE, and NOW functions.

Table 7.2
Date and Time Functions

Function	Description
@DATE(*year,month,day*)	Calculates the serial number of the specified date.
@DATEVALUE(*date_string*)	Converts a date expressed as a string into a serial number.

Function	Description
@DAY(*date_number*)	Extracts the day number from a serial number.
@D360(*date1,date2*)	Calculates the number of days between two serial dates, based on a 360-day year.
@HOUR(*time_number*)	Extracts the hour number from a time fraction.
@MINUTE(*time_number*)	Extracts the minute number from a time fraction.
@MONTH(*date_number*)	Extracts the month number from a serial number.
@NOW	Calculates the serial date and time from the current system date and time.
@SECOND(*time_number*)	Extracts the seconds from a time fraction.
@TIME(*hour,minutes,seconds*)	Calculates the time fraction of the specified time.
@TIMEVALUE(*time_string*)	Converts a time expressed as a string into a time fraction.
@TODAY	Calculates the serial number for the current system date.
@YEAR(*date_number*)	Extracts the year number from a serial number.

7

Converting Date Values to Serial Numbers with DATE

To use dates in arithmetic operations, first convert the dates to serial numbers. You then can use those serial numbers in arithmetic operations and sorting. The most frequently used date function is DATE, which converts any date into a serial number. You can use the resulting number in calculations or display it as a date in 1-2-3. DATE uses the following syntax:

@DATE(*year,month,day*)

You use numbers to identify the year, month, and day. For example, you enter the date November 26, 1992, into the DATE function as @DATE(92,11,26). The resulting serial number is 33934. For dates in the Twenty-first century, you must specify three digits for the year argument. The year argument for the year 2000 is entered as 100, for 2001 as 101, and so on. For example, to enter the date January 11, 2010, into the worksheet with DATE, you enter

> @DATE(110,1,11)

and 1-2-3 returns the serial number 40189 to the cell.

The DATE function calculates the number of days a bill is overdue as of July 31, 1992.

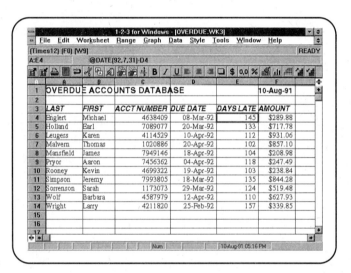

Note: The numbers you enter to represent the year, month, and day must create a valid date. If the date is not valid, 1-2-3 returns ERR. For example, 1-2-3 enables you to specify February 29 during leap years only. You never can specify February 30.

Converting Date Strings to Serial Numbers with DATEVALUE

DATEVALUE calculates the serial number for the date that is expressed as a text string in the referenced cell. The text string must use one of the date formats recognized by 1-2-3. DATEVALUE uses the following syntax:

> @DATEVALUE(*date_string*)

7

If 1-2-3 cannot recognize the format used for the argument, the function returns ERR. After you enter the function, select (in the Format list box of the Range Format dialog box) the date format you want to use to display the serial date number as a text date.

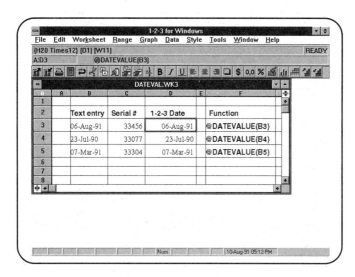

The DATEVALUE function converts a date string into a serial number that you can format as a date.

Entering the Current Date and Time with NOW

The NOW function calculates the serial number and time fraction using the current system date and time and displays this value in the cell. The integer part of the number (the part to the left of the decimal point) specifies the date, and the fractional part of the number (the part to the right of the decimal point) defines the time.

After you enter the NOW function, select (in the Format list box of the Range Format dialog box) the date format (1 through 5) or time format (6 through 9) that you want to use to display the value in the worksheet as a date or time.

This function, which requires no arguments, provides a convenient tool for adding dates to worksheets and reports. Be aware, however, that the date or time you enter with the NOW (or TODAY) function is not static in the worksheet. Each time you open the worksheet file (or press the Calc key), 1-2-3 recalculates this function and returns a new (current) date or time. Therefore, do not use this function in any cell whose purpose is to store a historical (static) date, such as the date you hire a new worker or the date a customer orders your product, even when the historical date and the current date coincide. To enter the date in such cells, enter the date as text according to one of 1-2-3's date formats or use the DATE function instead.

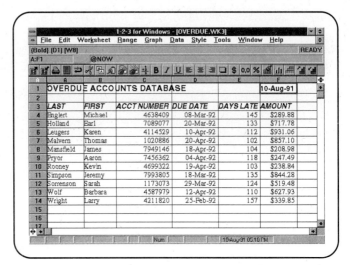

The NOW function, formatted as a date, inserts the current date in a worksheet.

Using Financial Functions

The financial functions enable you to perform a variety of complex business-related calculations. These calculations include discounting cash flows, computing loan amortization, calculating depreciation, and analyzing the return on investments. This set of functions helps you perform investment analysis and accounting or budgeting for depreciable assets. Table 7.3 summarizes the financial functions available in 1-2-3. The sections that follow describe the PMT, PV, and FV functions in greater detail.

Table 7.3
Financial Functions

Function	Description
@CTERM(*interest, future_value,present _value*)	Calculates the number of periods required for a present-value amount to grow to a future-value amount, given a periodic interest rate.
@DDB(*cost,salvage, life,period*)	Calculates depreciation, using the double-declining-balance method.
@FV(*payments,interest, term*)	Calculates the future value of a series of equal payments compounded at the periodic interest rate.

Function	Description
@IRR(*estimate,range*)	Calculates the internal rate of return on an investment.
@NPV(*interest,range*)	Calculates the present value of a series of future cash flows at equal intervals when payments are discounted by the interest rate.
@PMT(*principal, interest,term*)	Calculates the loan payment amount.
@PV(*payments,interest, term*)	Calculates the present value of a series of future cash flows of equal payments discounted by the periodic interest rate.
@RATE(*future_value, present_value,term*)	Calculates the periodic rate required to increase the present-value amount to the future-value amount in a specified length of time.
@SLN(*cost,salvage,life*)	Calculates straight-line depreciation for one period.
@SYD(*cost,salvage, life,period*)	Calculates sum-of-the-years' digits depreciation for a specified period.
@TERM(*payments, interest,future_value*)	Calculates the number of payment periods necessary to accumulate the future value when payments compound at the periodic interest rate.
@VDB(*cost,salvage,life, start_period,end_period, depreciation,switch*)	Calculates the depreciation, using the variable-rate declining balance method.

Calculating Loan Payment Amounts with PMT

You use the PMT function to calculate the periodic payments necessary to pay the principal on a loan with a given interest rate and length of time. To use PMT, you need to know the total loan amount (principal), periodic interest rate, and term, as shown in the following syntax:

> **@PMT(*principal,interest,term*)**

Express the interest rate and the term in the same units of time. For example, if you make monthly payments, you should use the annual interest rate

257

divided by 12. The term should be the number of months you will make payments. PMT operates on the assumption that payments are made at the end of each period.

To calculate the monthly car payment on a $12,000 car loan, you can use the PMT function. You repay the loan over 48 months, and the interest rate is 1% (12% divided by 12 periods per year).

7

The PMT function calculates loan payments.

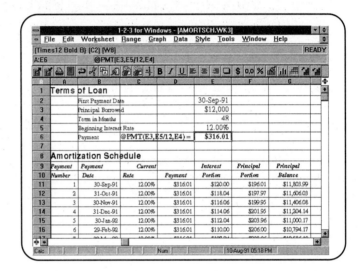

Calculating Present and Future Values with PV and FV

PV calculates the present value of a series of future cash flows of equal amounts discounted by the periodic interest rate. Express the interest rate and the term in the same units of time. The PV function uses the following syntax:

> @PV(*payments,interest,term*)

The FV function calculates the future value to which a current amount will grow, based on the specified interest rate and the length of time. Again, express the interest rate and the term in the same units of time. FV uses the following syntax:

> @FV(*payments,interest,term*)

You can use FV to calculate the future value of a savings account to which you make equal automatic deposits on a monthly basis. Simply specify the amount of the monthly deposit (payments), the monthly interest rate, and the specified number of months (term).

258

Using Statistical Functions

The statistical functions enable you to perform all the standard statistical calculations on data in your worksheet or in a 1-2-3 database. SUM, the most commonly used 1-2-3 function for computing totals, is a statistical function. Other statistical functions enable you to find minimum and maximum values, calculate averages, and compute standard deviations and variances.

All statistical functions use the same types of argument, a list consisting of value(s), cell reference(s), range(s), or formula(s). If the argument list contains more than one item, separate the items with commas, as in the following example:

> **@SUM(B5..B20,B30..B40,B55,10%*B80,1000)**

Table 7.4 lists the statistical functions, their arguments, and the operations they perform. The sections that follow cover the AVG, COUNT, MAX, and MIN statistical functions.

7

Table 7.4
Statistical Functions

Function	Description
@AVG(*list*)	Calculates the arithmetic mean of a list of values.
@COUNT(*list*)	Counts the number of cells that contain entries.
@MAX(*list*)	Returns the maximum value in a list of values.
@MIN(*list*)	Returns the minimum value in a list of values.
@STD(*list*)	Calculates the population standard deviation of a list of values.
@STDS(*list*)	Calculates the sample population standard deviation of a list of values.
@SUM(*list*)	Sums a list of values.
@SUMPRODUCT (*range1,range2*)	Multiplies range1 by range2 and sums the values.
@VAR(*list*)	Calculates the population variance of a list of values.
@VARS(*list*)	Calculates the sample population variance of a list of values.

Note: The statistical functions perform differently when you specify cells as ranges rather than individually. When you specify a range of cells, 1-2-3 ignores empty cells within the specified range. When you specify cells individually, however, 1-2-3 performs the function using empty cells. Also, when you specify cells, keep in mind that 1-2-3 treats cells containing labels as zeros. For this reason, always erase cells with the Del key; do not try to erase cells by pressing the space bar and Enter key.

Computing the Arithmetic Mean with AVG

To calculate the average of a set of values, you add all the values and then divide the sum by the number of values. Essentially, the AVG function produces the same result as if you had divided SUM(*list*) by COUNT(*list*). The AVG function is a helpful tool for calculating the commonly used arithmetic mean, or average. The AVG function uses the following syntax:

> **@AVG(*list*)**

The list argument can contain any combination of values, cell addresses, single and multiple ranges, and range names.

For example, the AVG function can calculate the mean price-per-share of a company's stock. The function's argument is a range that includes the list of stock prices. 1-2-3 ignores any empty cells in the range when calculating the average.

The AVG function calculates the average price-per-share of stock.

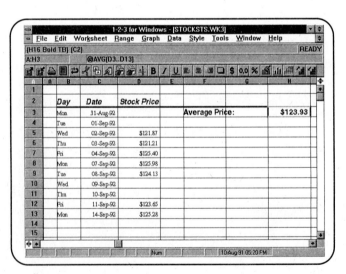

260

Counting Cell Entries with COUNT

The COUNT function totals the number of cells that contain entries of any kind, including labels, label-prefix characters, and the special values ERR and NA (not available). Use the following syntax for COUNT:

> **@COUNT(*list*)**

The list argument can contain any combination of values, cell addresses, single and multiple ranges, and range names. For example, you can use COUNT to show the number of share prices included in the AVG calculation of the prior example.

The COUNT function calculates the number of prices per share used in the average calculation.

Finding Maximum and Minimum Values with MAX and MIN

The MAX function finds the largest value included in the argument list. The MIN function finds the smallest value included in the argument list. These functions use the following syntax:

> **@MAX(*list*)**

> **@MIN(*list*)**

The MAX and MIN functions can help you find the highest and the lowest prices in the stock prices example. Although the example shows only seven values, the true power of these functions is clear when your list consists of several hundred items.

The highlighted MAX function shows the highest price-per-share. The MIN function shows the lowest price in the list.

[Screenshot of 1-2-3 for Windows - [STOCKSTS.WK3] spreadsheet]

Menu bar: File Edit Worksheet Range Graph Data Style Tools Window Help

{H16 Bold}   READY

A:H7   @MAX[D3..D13]

	A	B	C	D	E	F	G	H
1								
2	Day	Date	Stock Price					
3	Mon	31-Aug-92				Average Price:		$123.93
4	Tue	01-Sep-92						
5	Wed	02-Sep-92	$121.87			Number of Prices		7
6	Thu	03-Sep-92	$121.21					
7	Fri	04-Sep-92	$125.40			Maximum Price		125.98
8	Mon	07-Sep-92	$125.98			Minimum Price		121.21
9	Tue	08-Sep-92	$124.13					
10	Wed	09-Sep-92						
11	Thu	10-Sep-92						
12	Fri	11-Sep-92	$123.65					
13	Mon	14-Sep-92	$125.28					
14								
15								

Num   10-Aug-91 05.21 PM

7

Using Database Functions

1-2-3's database functions are similar to the statistical functions, but require different arguments in order to work with database ranges (see Chapter 11 for information on creating database tables). Like other functions, the database functions perform in one operation calculations that otherwise require several different steps. Their efficiency and ease of use make these functions excellent tools for manipulating 1-2-3 databases. Table 7.5 describes the database functions. Each of these functions (except DQUERY) uses the following general syntax:

@D*function*(*input_range*,*field*,*criteria_range*)

The input range and criteria range entered in the Data Query dialog box (see Chapter 11) usually correspond to the input_range and criteria_range arguments, respectively. The input_ range argument specifies the database to search. The criteria_range argument specifies the records to select, and the field argument specifies the database field to use in the function calculation. When specifying the field argument with the field name used in the database table, you must enclose it in quotes, as in the following example:

@DSUM(REVENUE,"AMOUNT",CRITERIA)

In this example, REVENUE is the range name assigned to the database table, and CRITERIA is the range name assigned to the criteria range.

Table 7.5
Database Functions

Function	Description
@DAVG(*input_range*,*field*, *criteria_range*)	Calculates the arithmetic mean of items in a list.
@DCOUNT(*input_range*, *field*,*criteria_range*)	Counts the number of entries in a list.
@DGET(*input_range*,*field*, *criteria_range*)	Extracts a value or label from a field in a database that matches the selected criteria.
@DMAX(*input_range*,*field*, *criteria_range*)	Returns the maximum value among items in a list.
@DMIN(*input_range*,*field*, *criteria_range*)	Returns the minimum value among items in a list.
@DQUERY(*external_fn*, *arguments*)	Sends a command to an external data management program.
@DSTD(*input_range*,*field*, *criteria_range*)	Calculates the standard deviation of items in a list.
@DSTDS(*input_range*,*field*, *criteria_range*)	Calculates the sample standard deviation of items in a list.
@DSUM(*input_range*,*field*, *criteria_range*)	Sums the values of items in a list.
@DVAR(*input_range*,*field*, *criteria_range*)	Computes the variance of items in a list.
@DVARS(*input_range*,*field*, *criteria_range*)	Computes the sample variance of items in a list.

7

Suppose that you need some statistical information about the products you have in your inventory. You want to know the total value of all the items that each cost $50.00 or more, the average price of the items for which you charge more than $100.00, and the number of such items on-hand.

To find the answers to these questions and others like them, you can use the database functions. First, you set up a range that contains the criteria that determines which data is used in the calculation, such as items that cost

263

$50.00 or more (the formula +A:C3>=50 in cell C:B4) or items that are priced at more than $100.00 (the formula +A:D3>100 in cell C:C4). Then you set up the formula using the appropriate database function (such as @DSUM, @DAVG, or @DCOUNT).

When evaluating each database function, 1-2-3 uses the criteria (specified by the criteria_range argument) to determine which data in the field (specified by the field argument) of the database (specified by the input_range argument) to use in the calculation.

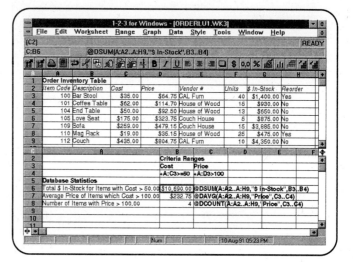

Using Logical Functions

Each of 1-2-3's logical functions enables you to test whether a condition is true or false. These functions operate in a similar manner—by returning a 1 if the test is true or a 0 if the test is false. Logical tests are important for creating decision-making functions; the results of these functions depend on conditions elsewhere in the worksheet.

Table 7.6 summarizes the nine logical functions that 1-2-3 provides. The text that follows describes the IF and ISERR logical functions in more detail.

264

Table 7.6
Logical Functions

Function	Description
@FALSE	Returns the logical value 0, for false.
@IF(condition,true,false)	Tests a condition and returns one result if the condition is true, but another result if the condition is false.
@ISERR(cell_reference)	Tests whether the argument results in ERR.
@ISNA(cell_reference)	Tests whether the argument results in NA.
@ISNUMBER(cell_reference)	Tests whether the argument is a number.
@ISRANGE(cell_reference)	Tests whether the argument is a defined range.
@ISSTRING(cell_reference)	Tests whether the argument is a string.
@TRUE	Returns the logical value 1, for true.

7

Creating Conditional Tests with IF

The IF function represents a powerful tool—one you can use to manipulate text within your worksheets and to affect calculations. For example, you can use an IF statement to test the following condition: is the inventory on-hand below 1,000 units? You can return one value or label if the answer to the question is true or another value or label if the answer is false. The IF function uses the following syntax:

> **@IF(*condition,true,false*)**

The IF function uses the logical operators when testing conditions. For a review of these operators, refer to "Other Types of Formulas" in Chapter 4.

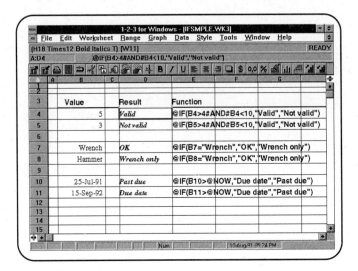

Examples of the IF function test for specified values or labels.

In the example, the IF functions check whether a specified cell's content is between 4 and 10, whether a cell contains a specified text string, and whether a 1-2-3 date falls before or after the current date. The results of these tests depend on whether 1-2-3 evaluates the condition as true or false.

Trapping Errors with ISERR

You use the ISERR function to prevent the spread of ERR values in the worksheet (a technique referred to as *error trapping*). By inserting (*nesting*) the ISERR function inside an IF function, you can have 1-2-3 return 0 (the IF true argument) to a cell any time the formula would return ERR or otherwise perform the intended calculation (the IF false argument).

For example, suppose that you have a worksheet that contains a formula for calculating what percentage of the total annual sales the total sales for the first quarter represents. If B9 holds the total first quarter sales and E9 holds the total annual sales, you enter the following formula in cell B11:

+B9/$E$9

Suppose further that you use this percentage in cell F50 of the worksheet. To bring the calculated value forward to this new part of the worksheet, you enter the following formula in cell F50:

+B11

7

This formula links the percent of sales value calculated in cell B11 directly to cell F50.

The formula in B11 is fine as long as the first quarter total stored in cell B9 contains a value other than zero (because division by zero in a formula results in ERR). Zero, however, is precisely the value in cell B9 until you obtain the sales figures for the first quarter and enter them in this cell. During the time cell B9 contains 0, both the formula in B11 and F50 return ERR (because they are linked by formula).

To trap the ERR value in cell B11 and stop it from spreading to cell F50 (and beyond, if this cell is referenced to by other formulas in the worksheet), you enter the following formula in cell F50:

@IF(@ISERR(B11),0,B11)

In essence, this formula says, "If cell B11 returns ERR, put the value 0 in the cell instead; otherwise, go ahead and use the value stored in cell B11." This technique prevents the spread of the ERR value beyond its original location (B11 in this example), but still enables 1-2-3 to use non-ERR values in other parts of the worksheet.

7

Using String Functions

Another set of 1-2-3 functions is the group of string functions that manipulate text. You can use string functions to repeat text characters, convert letters in a string to uppercase or lowercase, change strings into numbers, and change numbers into strings. String functions also are important when you prepare 1-2-3 data for use in other programs, such as word processing programs.

Included with the string functions are a few special functions for working with the Lotus International Character Set (LMBCS). The complete set of LMBCS characters, listed in the 1-2-3 documentation, includes everything from the copyright sign (©) to the lowercase é with the grave accent.

Table 7.7 summarizes the string functions available in 1-2-3. The sections that follow discuss the LOWER, UPPER, PROPER, and REPEAT string functions in more detail.

Table 7.7
String Functions

Function	Description
@CHAR(number)	Converts a code number into the corresponding LMBCS character.
@CLEAN(string)	Removes nonprintable characters from the specified string.
@CODE(string)	Returns the LMBCS code that corresponds to the first character of the specified string.
@EXACT(string1,string2)	Returns 1 (true) if arguments are exact matches; otherwise, returns 0 (false).
@FIND(search_string, string,start_number)	Locates the start position of one string within another string.
@LEFT(string,number)	Returns the specified number of characters from the left side of the string.
@LENGTH(string)	Returns the number of characters in the string.
@LOWER(string)	Converts all characters in the string to lowercase.
@MID(string, start_number,number)	Returns a specified number of characters from the middle of another string, beginning at the specified starting position.
@N(range)	Returns as a value the contents of the cell in the upper left corner of a range.
@PROPER(string)	Converts the first character in each word of the string to uppercase, and the remaining characters in each word to lowercase.
@REPEAT(string,number)	Duplicates the string the specified number of times in a cell.
@REPLACE(original_string, start_number,number, new_string)	Replaces a number of characters in the original string with new string characters, starting at the character identified by the start position.

7

Function	Description
@RIGHT(string,number)	Returns the specified number of characters from the right side of the string.
@S(range)	Returns as a label the contents of the cell in the upper left corner of a range.
@STRING(number, decimal_places)	Converts a value to a string with the specified number of decimal places.
@TRIM(string)	Removes blank spaces from the string.
@UPPER(string)	Converts all characters in the string to uppercase.
@VALUE(string)	Converts the string to a value.

Strings are labels or portions of labels. Strings used within functions consist of characters enclosed in quotation marks (such as "Total"). Some 1-2-3 functions produce strings, but other functions produce numeric results. If a function's result is not of the data type you need, use STRING to convert a numeric value to a string, or VALUE to convert a string to a numeric value.

Converting the Case of Strings with LOWER, UPPER, and PROPER

1-2-3 offers three different string functions for converting the case of a string argument. The LOWER and UPPER functions convert all characters in the referenced string to lowercase or uppercase, respectively. The PROPER function converts characters in the string to proper capitalization—with the first letter of each word in uppercase and all remaining letters in lowercase. These functions use the following syntax:

@LOWER(*string*)

@UPPER(*string*)

@PROPER(*string*)

These three functions work with strings or references to strings. If a cell contains a number or is empty, 1-2-3 returns ERR for these functions.

The LOWER, UPPER, and PROPER functions convert the case of alphanumeric strings. The text versions of the formulas appear in column A, and the formulas and their results are in column B.

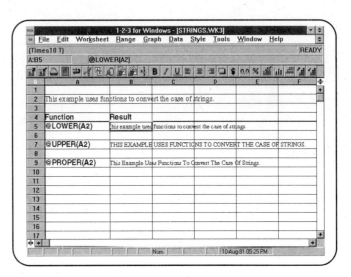

You can use LOWER, UPPER, or PROPER to modify the contents of a database table so that all entries in a field appear with the same capitalization. This technique produces reports with a consistent appearance. To be sure that 1-2-3 sorts data with different capitalizations correctly, create a column that uses one of these functions and references the original data, then sort the new column.

Repeating Strings with REPEAT

The REPEAT function repeats a string a specified number of times, much as the backslash (\) repeats strings to fill a single cell. The REPEAT function, however, has some distinct advantages over the backslash. With REPEAT, you can repeat the string a precise number of times. If the result is wider than the cell width, the result displays in empty adjacent cells to the right. REPEAT uses the following syntax:

@**REPEAT**(*string,number*)

The number argument specifies the number of times you want to repeat the string in a cell. For example, if you want to repeat the string -**- four times, you can enter the following function:

@**REPEAT**("-**-",4)

The resulting string appears as follows:

-**- -**- -**- -**-

270

Using Special Functions

The set of special functions performs a variety of tasks. For example, two special functions return up to 10 characteristics of a cell. Other special functions count the number of rows, columns, or worksheets in a range. Special functions also enable you to identify worksheet errors and use specified keys in the functions' arguments to look up values in tables or lists.

Table 7.8 lists 1-2-3's special functions. The sections that follow discuss the ERR, NA, HLOOKUP, and VLOOKUP functions in more detail.

Table 7.8
Special Functions

Function	Description
@@(location)	Returns the contents of the cell referenced in the specified location.
@CELL(attribute,range)	Returns an attribute of the cell in the upper left corner of the range.
@CELLPOINTER(attribute)	Returns an attribute of the current cell.
@CHOOSE(offset,list)	Locates in a list the entry specified by the offset number.
@COLS(range)	Counts the number of columns in a range.
@COORD(worksheet, column,row,cell_absolute)	Constructs a cell address from values corresponding to rows, columns, and worksheets.
@ERR	Enters ERR value in the cell.
@HLOOKUP(key,range, row_offset)	Locates the number in a table and returns a value from that row of the range.
@INDEX(range, column_offset,row_offset)	Returns the contents of a cell specified by the intersection of a row and column within a range.
@INFO(attribute)	Retrieves system information.
@NA	Enters NA value in the cell.
@ROWS(range)	Counts the number of rows in a range.

continued

7

271

Table 7.8 *(continued)*

Function	Description
@SHEETS(range)	Calculates the number of worksheets in a range.
@VLOOKUP(key,range, column_offset)	Locates the number in a lookup table and returns a value from that column of the range.

Identifying Errors with ERR and NA

When you create 1-2-3 applications, you can use ERR or NA to identify certain cell entries. Formulas that depend on cells with NA or ERR return NA or ERR. Suppose, for example, that you are creating a worksheet for balancing your checkbook in which checks with dollar amounts less than or equal to zero are unacceptable. One way to show that these checks are unacceptable is to use ERR to signal that fact. You can use the following version of the IF function:

@IF(B9<=0,@ERR,B9)

This statement says, "If the amount in cell B9 is less than or equal to zero, then display ERR in that cell; otherwise, display the amount."

In an inventory database, you can place the NA function in cells to show uncounted inventory items. You also can use IF and NA together, as in the following example:

@IF(C4=0,@NA,C4)

This statement says, "If the value in cell C4 is equal to zero, display NA in that cell, otherwise display the value."

Finding Table Entries with HLOOKUP and VLOOKUP

The HLOOKUP and VLOOKUP functions retrieve a string or value from a table, based on a specified key used to find the information. The operation and format of the two functions are essentially the same except that HLOOKUP searches horizontal tables and VLOOKUP searches vertical tables. These functions use the following syntax:

@**HLOOKUP(***key,range,row_offset***)**

@**VLOOKUP(***key,range,column_offset***)**

The key argument is the string or value that tells 1-2-3 which column (HLOOKUP) or row (VLOOKUP) to search. The corresponding key strings or values must be located in the first column or row of the lookup table. Numeric keys must be in ascending order for the functions to work properly. The range argument is the area that contains the entire lookup table. The offset argument specifies from which row (HLOOKUP) or column (VLOOKUP) to retrieve data. The offset argument is always a number, ranging from 0 to the highest number (minus one) of columns or rows in the lookup table.

The HLOOKUP and VLOOKUP functions are useful for finding any type of value you otherwise would need to look up manually in a table. For example, suppose that you set up an inventory database table that contains all of the latest price information about the products you sell. To eliminate the risk of entering incorrect prices and facilitate order entry, you can then use the VLOOKUP function to take the price information directly from the inventory table into the customer order table.

The VLOOKUP function looks up the prices in the order inventory table (range A:A3..A:H9) based on the code number entered in the Item Code field of the customer order table.

To accomplish this, the VLOOKUP function compares the item code number that you enter in the customer order table's Item Code field (cell C3 in the example) with the item codes in the first (key) column of the order inventory table (range A:A3..A:H9). When the program finds a match in the Item Code (key) column of the order inventory table, it then moves over to the Price column (because that column is located 3 columns to the right of the key column and the column_offset argument is 3) and copies the entry it finds there to the Price field in the customer order table that contains the VLOOKUP function.

Notice that the VLOOKUP function returns ERR values in the rows of the customer order table where you have not yet entered item codes. If 1-2-3 can't find a match for the key argument in the key column of the order inventory table, it returns ERR to that cell.

Summary

This chapter described the functions that 1-2-3 provides to make formula and worksheet construction easier and more error-free. Use the tables of this chapter as a reference for the available functions, their syntax, and the types of arguments they require. Specifically, you learned the following key information about 1-2-3 functions:

- 1-2-3 provides eight types of functions. These functions perform a variety of powerful calculations that can save you much time when building worksheets.

- Enter 1-2-3 functions by typing the @ symbol, followed by the function name and any required arguments within parentheses. Press Enter or an arrow key to complete the process.

- The mathematical and trigonometric functions perform standard arithmetic operations, such as computing the integer with INT and rounding numbers with ROUND.

- The date and time functions convert dates and times to serial numbers and time fractions. You then can format the numbers as dates and use them in sorting and arithmetic calculations. Examples include NOW, DATE, and DATEVALUE. You also can use NOW to stamp the date on a worksheet or report.

- The financial functions calculate cash flows, loans, annuities, and asset depreciation. The PMT function calculates loan payments, and the PV and FV functions calculate present and future values, respectively.

- The statistical functions perform standard statistical calculations on lists. For example, AVG calculates the average of values in a list, COUNT counts the total number of entries in a list, and MAX and MIN find the maximum and minimum values in a list.

- The database functions are similar to the statistical functions, but perform their calculations on database tables.

- The logical functions test whether a condition is true or false. The IF function returns a different value or label depending on the outcome of the specified condition.

■ The string functions manipulate text. The LOWER, UPPER, and PROPER functions convert the case of a specified label. The REPEAT function repeats a string a specified number of times.

■ The special functions perform a variety of worksheet tasks. The ERR and NA functions identify errors or distinguish certain cell entries. The HLOOKUP and VLOOKUP functions return values from the specified row or column of a table.

In the next chapter, you learn how to print reports created in 1-2-3 for Windows. This chapter also discusses various options available for enhancing reports.

7

Printing Reports

8

1-2-3 for Windows makes it easy to produce professional-looking reports from your worksheets. The reports that you create can include graphs as well as specific ranges of worksheet data. Multiple-page reports can include a header and footer that indicate the nature of the report, the page numbers, and the date of printing.

This chapter covers all the basics of printing, including how to select a printer, specify the range of data to be printed, change the page layout settings, use the print preview feature, and control page breaks. For information on how to create and place graphs in your worksheets so that you can include them in printed reports, see Chapter 10.

Key Terms in This Chapter

Print defaults	Preset, standard specifications for a 1-2-3 print job.
Borders	One or more rows or columns of data or labels that 1-2-3 repeats on a multiple-page report.
Header	Information 1-2-3 displays on one line at the top of a page. A header can include a date and a page number.
Footer	Information 1-2-3 displays on one line at the bottom of a page. A footer can include a date and a page number.

Selecting a Printer

With Windows, you can install more than one printer. When you first install the program, you can install printers with the Microsoft Windows Setup program. Later you can install printers with the Windows Control Panel. When you install your printers, you designate one of the printers as the default printer. When you print reports in 1-2-3 for Windows, the program uses the default printer listed in the Printers dialog box unless you tell 1-2-3 otherwise.

In this example, the HP LaserJet is the default printer in Windows. 1-2-3 uses this printer to print all of your reports.

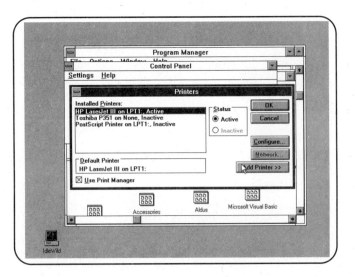

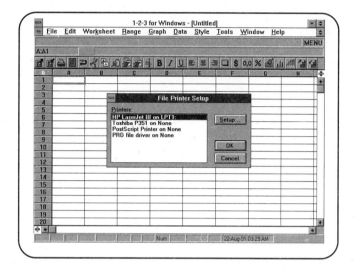

The File Printer
Setup dialog box
shows you all of
the printers
installed in
Windows.

To select a new printer, follow these steps:

1. From the **F**ile menu, select the Printer Setup option.
2. In the **P**rinters list box, select the name of the printer you want to use.
3. Click the OK button.

Depending on the printer you select, you can change some of the settings at
this time. These printer settings can include the paper size, the orientation of
the page, the source of the paper, and the print quality of the text or graphics.

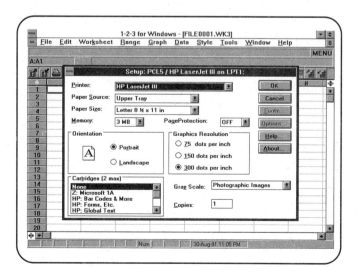

A dialog box
similar to the one
pictured here
appears when you
select one of the
HP laser printers.

8

If you select an
Epson dot-matrix
printer, this
dialog box
appears.

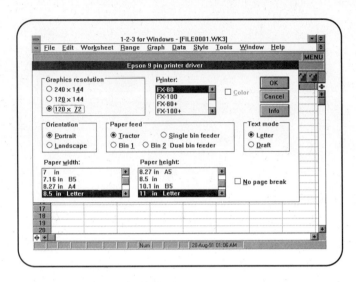

If you select a
PostScript printer
such as the Apple
LaserWriter Plus,
this dialog box
appears.

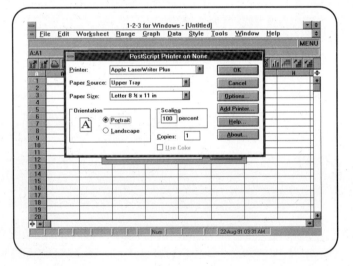

To change the settings for the printer you selected, choose the Setup command button in the File Printer Setup dialog box.

The particular printer settings available in the File Printer Setup dialog box
vary according to the capabilities of the printer you selected. Table 8.1 describes the printer settings options you may encounter.

Table 8.1
Printer Settings Options

Option	Function
Printer	Changes the model of the printer within a family of printers (such as the HP LaserJet) that share a group of print settings. Use this option to select the particular model you use.
Paper Source	Changes the tray or bin that supplies the paper during printing. Use this option to tell 1-2-3 to supply paper from a different bin.
Memory	Indicates the amount of RAM memory installed in your laser printer. If your printer has more than the minimum RAM, use this option to increase the amount of RAM available.
Paper Size	Changes the paper size from letter (8 1/2 x 11) to another standard size. Select this option to use another paper size. Note that in some dialog boxes you must select both Paper width and Paper height options to specify a new paper size.
Cartridges	Indicates the font cartridges you are using with your laser printer.
Orientation	Changes the orientation of the printing on the page from Portrait to Landscape or vice versa. In Portrait mode, the printing aligns with the short edge of the paper; in Landscape mode, the printing aligns with the long edge of the paper.
Paper feed	Indicates (for some dot-matrix printers) whether the paper is fed by a tractor feed or a single- or dual-bin feeder.
Graphics resolution	Changes the print quality of the graphics printed in your reports (this option has no effect on text quality). Graphics resolution is rated in dots per inch. The higher the number of dots, the sharper the resolution of the graphic elements in your report. The lower the number of dots, the faster the printing.

continued

8

281

Table 8.1 *(continued)*

Option	Function
Text mode	Changes the quality of text printing (for dot-matrix printers) from Letter (quality) to Draft (quality) and vice versa. Letter quality has higher resolution, but draft quality prints substantially faster.
No page break	Removes the white space that some dot-matrix printers leave at the top and bottom of the page even when the top and bottom margins of the report are set to zero.
Scaling	Increases or reduces the size of the printout by the percentage you enter (100% is full size) in the Scaling text box. This option is available only for laser printers using PostScript.
Copies	Changes the number of copies produced each time you print a report with that printer. Note that multiple copies of a report are not collated during printing.

8

Printing Simple Reports

Printing simple reports with 1-2-3 for Windows is an easy task. You can print quick reports using the program's printing defaults by designating the range to print and then selecting the **File Print** command as follows:

1. Select the range of data you want to print.

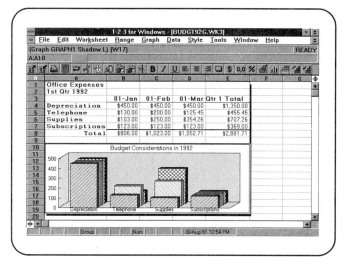

If the data you
want to print
includes a graph,
make sure that
you include the
entire graph in
the selected print
range.

8

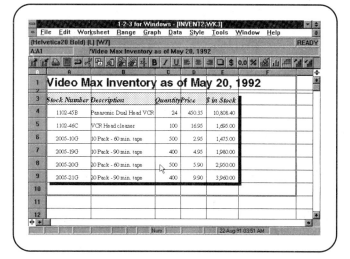

If the data you
want to print
includes any long
labels, make sure
that the print
range includes all
of the cells that
labels overhang.

2. From the **F**ile menu, select the **P**rint option.

1-2-3 displays the File Print dialog box.

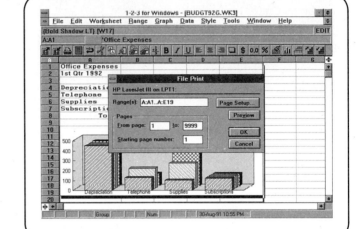

8

Note: If you use the mouse, you can display the File Print dialog box by clicking the print icon in the icon palette.

3. Click the OK button to print one copy of the report.

1-2-3 prints the selected range using the program's printing defaults.

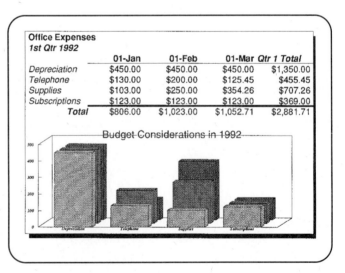

1-2-3 displays the Cancel Printing dialog box while the program prepares to send the report to the printer. The dialog box disappears as soon as 1-2-3 sends the report. To cancel printing after you select the OK button in the File Print dialog box, you must select the Cancel command button in the Cancel Printing dialog box before the box disappears.

Specifying Multiple Print Ranges

Sometimes you need to print more than one range of data in a single report. To designate multiple ranges for printing, you indicate the address or range name for each range separated by the argument separator (by default, the comma). For example, to print the ranges A:A1..A:H100 and B:C40..B:J50 (located in the same worksheet file), you enter

> A:A1..A:H100, B:C40..B:J50

in the Range(s) text box of the File Print dialog box. If you named these ranges Income_92 and Expenses_92, however, you enter

> Income_92,Expenses_92

in the Range(s) text box.

Remember that you can use the same techniques to select the print range that you use to designate any other cell range in 1-2-3. To highlight the range, you can use the mouse or keyboard. To use the assigned range name, type the name or press the Name key (F3) and then select the name from the list that appears in the Range dialog box.

8

Specifying the Pages To Print

With 1-2-3 for Windows, you can modify the number of copies that are printed, the range of pages printed, and the starting page number.

The Pages options in the File Print dialog box enable you to modify these settings.

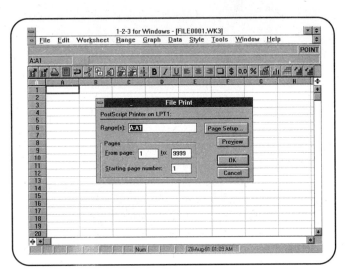

To print more than one copy of the report, enter the number in the Number of Copies text box. If you are printing a multiple-page report, 1-2-3 does collate the pages when you use this option.

Some reports require more than one page; by default, 1-2-3 prints all pages of the report when you select OK in the File Print dialog box. If you need to print only a specific range of pages, enter the number of the first page you want to print in the From page text box and the number of the last page you want to print in the to text box.

Sometimes the range of data you want to print represents only a portion of the complete report. If you added page numbers in the header or footer of the report (see "Creating a Header or Footer" later in this chapter) and you want the first page to have a number other than one (1), enter the correct beginning page number in the Starting page number dialog box.

Modifying the Page Setup

Although the default print settings are fine when you need to generate a quick report from your worksheet data, you often need to refine the page layout before printing. You use the options in File Page Setup dialog box to change the page settings for your report.

1-2-3 enables you to choose the Page Setup command in two ways: you can select the Page Setup option from the File menu or you can select the Page Setup command button in the File Print dialog box.

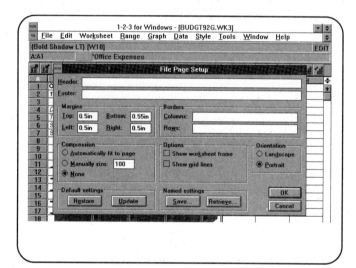

1-2-3 displays the File Page Setup dialog box.

8

Creating a Header or Footer

A header is a line of text that prints at the top of every page of the report. A footer is a line that prints at the bottom of every page. You can use both a header and a footer to describe the contents of a multiple-page report.

For example, you can print the name of report and the page number in the header and print a warning that the report is confidential and the current date in the footer.

8

Regional Income Report and Analysis				Page 1
REGIONAL INCOME REPORT				
	Qtr 1	*Qtr 2*	*Qtr 3*	*Qtr 4*
Sales				
Northeast	$30,336	$33,370	$36,707	$40,377
Southeast	20,572	22,629	24,892	27,381
Central	131,685	144,854	159,339	175,273
Northwest	94,473	103,920	114,312	125,744
Southwest	126,739	139,413	153,354	168,690
Total Sales	$403,805	$444,186	$488,604	$537,464
Cost of Goods Sold				
Northeast	10,341	11,272	12,286	13,392
Southeast	6,546	7,135	7,777	8,477
Central	65,843	71,769	78,228	85,269
Northwest	63,967	69,724	75,999	82,839
Southwest	72,314	78,822	85,916	93,649
Total Cost of Goods Sold	$219,011	$238,722	$260,207	$283,626
Operating Expenses				
Northeast	$21,529	$23,036	$24,649	$26,374
Southeast	15,946	17,062	18,257	19,535
Central	27,554	29,483	31,547	33,755
Northwest	16,130	17,259	18,467	19,760
Southwest	32,361	34,626	37,050	39,644
Total Operating Expenses	$113,520	$121,466	$129,969	$139,067

Confidential				17-Jun-91

The text of your header or footer can contain up to 512 bytes (usually one byte per character), but its text must fit within one line of your printed report; the size of the paper and the font you are using limit the number of characters. If you specify more characters for the header or footer than can fit on the page, 1-2-3 does not print the excess characters. You also can position the header and footer at the left, right, or center of the page.

1-2-3 leaves two blank lines (whose measure is based on the font size) between the header and the body of the report and two blank lines between the body and the footer.

To add a header or footer, follow these steps:

1. From the File menu, select the Page Setup option

   or

From the File menu, select the Print option and then select the Page Setup command button in the File Print dialog box.

2. Type the header text in the Header text box. Type the footer text in the Footer text box.

3. Select the OK button in the File Page Setup dialog box.

4. Select OK in the File Print dialog box if you want to print the report with the new header and footer now. If you want to print the report later, select Cancel to return to the worksheet.

1-2-3 uses special characters to control page numbers, the current date, positioning of text within a header or footer, and formatting of the header or footer with attributes such as boldfaced type and italics. To place the page number, current date, or the contents of a cell in a header or footer, use the following symbols:

Symbol	Action
#	Prints consecutive page numbers on each page of the report, starting with the number specified in the Starting page number text box in the File Print dialog box (by default, 1).
@	Prints the current date on each page of the report. The date uses the format set by the Date option in the Tools User Setup International dialog box.
\	When followed by a cell address or range name, fills the header or footer with the contents of the indicated cell. If you specify a multicell range, 1-2-3 uses the contents of the cell in its upper left corner only.

To align text in a header or footer, insert | (the vertical bar entered by pressing Shift+\). 1-2-3 left-aligns all text entered before one vertical bar, centers all text entered after one vertical bar, and right-aligns all text entered after a second vertical bar. For example, to center the page number in a footer, enter

|Page #

in the Footer text box. To right-align the page number, you enter

||Page #

in the Footer text box.

To print the header

Preliminary   BUDGET 1992   Page 1

289

you enter

> **Preliminary|BUDGET 1992|Page #**

in the Header text box.

Changing the Margins

1-2-3 for Windows measures all margins from the edge of the page. By default, 1-2-3 sets the left, right, and top margin to 0.50 inches from the left, right, and top edges of the page, and sets the bottom margin to 0.55 inches from the bottom edge of the page.

To change the margin settings, select the appropriate text box (**T**op, **L**eft, **B**ottom, or **R**ight) under Margins in the File Page Setup dialog box and enter the new measurement. You can set new margins in millimeters or centimeters (rather than in the default units of inches) by adding **mm** (for millimeters) or **cm** (for centimeters) after the new values you type in the Margins text boxes.

In this example, the top and bottom margin are being increased to 1 inch and the left and right margins are being reduced to 0.25 inch.

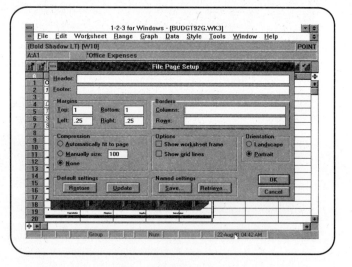

Using Borders in Multiple Page Reports

When printing multiple-page reports, you can use the Borders options (Columns and Rows) to print on every page the titles and headings that you entered in specified columns and rows of the print range. If you specify a range of columns, 1-2-3 prints the information in these columns on the left side of each page of the report. If you specify a range of rows, the program prints the information in these rows at the top of each page.

You can specify a range of columns and a range of rows for the borders of your report. In such cases, 1-2-3 prints the column information on the left side and the row information at the top of each page. Note that the program prints borders only within the columns and rows in the print range.

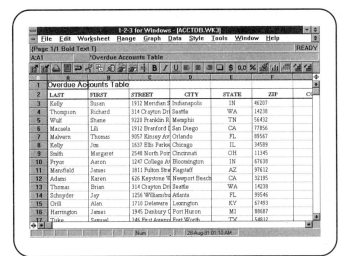

For example, if you specify the range A3..H50 as the print range and specify A1..A2 as the border in the **Rows** text box, 1-2-3 prints information in the range A1..H2 at the top of each page of the report.

If you are using a border with a three-dimensional print range, keep in mind that 1-2-3 takes the border columns and rows from each worksheet in the print range. For example, if you designate the 3-D range, A:A3..C:F35 as the print range and the range A1..A2 as the row border for this report, 1-2-3 prints A:A1..A:F2 as the border for the range A:A3..A:F35, B:A1..B:F2 as the border for the range B:A3..B:F35, C:A1..C:F2 for the range C:A3..C:F35, and so on.

To specify borders for a report, follow these steps:

1. From the File menu, select the Page Setup option (or select the Print option, and then select Page Setup in the File Print dialog box).

2. To use columns as borders, select the Columns option under Borders, and then select the range of columns you want to include.

   When designating the range of columns, you must include only one cell from each column. For example, you can select the range A1..B1 to specify columns A and B as the left borders of the report.

8

3. To use rows as borders, select the Rows option under Borders, then select the range of rows you want to include.

   When designating the range of rows, you need to include only one cell from each row. For example, you can select the range A1..A4 to specify rows 1 through 4 in the print range as the top borders of the report.

4. Select the OK option.

To set up the borders for a report, do not include the columns and rows specified as borders in the print range. If you do, 1-2-3 prints the information in the borders area twice on the first page: once as the border(s) and a second time as report data.

In this example, the contents of A1 are designated as the header and the contents of row A2 (the column headings) as the border row, for the report.

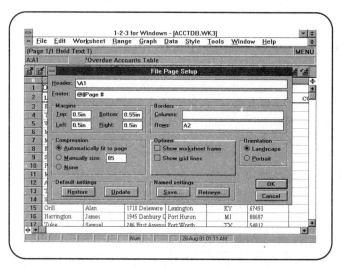

8

292

Overdue Accounts Table

LAST	FIRST	STREET	CITY	STATE
Kelly	Susan	1912 Meridian Street	Indianapolis	IN
Thompson	Richard	314 Crayton Drive	Seattle	WA
Wulf	Shane	9220 Franklin Road	Memphis	TN
Macaela	Lili	1912 Branford Drive	San Diego	CA
Malvern	Thomas	9057 Kinsey Avenue	Orlando	FL
Kelly	Jim	1637 Ellis Parkway	Chicago	IL
Smith	Margaret	2548 North Point	Cincinnati	OH
Pryor	Aaron	1247 College Avenue	Bloomington	IN
Mansfield	James	1811 Fulton Street	Flagstaff	AZ
Adams	Karen	626 Keystone Way	Newport Beach	CA
Thomas	Brian	314 Crayton Drive	Seattle	WA
Schnyder	Jay	1256 Williamsburg	Atlanta	FL
Grill	Alan	1710 Delaware	Lexington	KY
Harrington	James	1945 Danbury Court	Port Huron	MI
Tuke	Samuel	246 First Avenue	Fort Worth	TX
Wright	Amy	6327 Arlington	Des Moines	IA
Holland	Mark	316 Atwood Terrace	Miami	FL
Englert	Michael	397 Drexel Boulevard	Boston	MA
Kelly	Susan	1912 Meridian Street	Indianapolis	IN
Thompson	Richard	314 Crayton Drive	Seattle	WA
Wulf	Shane	9220 Franklin Road	Memphis	TN
Macaela	Lili	1912 Branford Drive	San Diego	CA
Malvern	Thomas	9057 Kinsey Avenue	Orlando	FL
Kelly	Jim	1637 Ellis Parkway	Chicago	IL
Smith	Margaret	2548 North Point	Cincinnati	OH
Pryor	Aaron	1247 College Avenue	Bloomington	IN
Mansfield	James	1811 Fulton Street	Flagstaff	AZ
Adams	Karen	626 Keystone Way	Newport Beach	CA
Thomas	Brian	314 Crayton Drive	Seattle	WA
Schnyder	Jay	1256 Williamsburg	Atlanta	FL
Grill	Alan	1710 Delaware	Lexington	KY
Harrington	James	1945 Danbury Court	Port Huron	MI
Tuke	Samuel	246 First Avenue	Fort Worth	TX
Wright	Amy	6327 Arlington	Des Moines	IA
Holland	Mark	316 Atwood Terrace	Miami	FL
Englert	Michael	397 Drexel Boulevard	Boston	MA
Kelly	Susan	1912 Meridian Street	Indianapolis	IN
Thompson	Richard	314 Crayton Drive	Seattle	WA
Wulf	Shane	9220 Franklin Road	Memphis	TN
Macaela	Lili	1912 Branford Drive	San Diego	CA
Malvern	Thomas	9057 Kinsey Avenue	Orlando	FL

14-Jun-91   Page 1

As a result, 1-2-3 prints the worksheet title (as the header) and the column headings in row 2 of the worksheet (as the border) at the top of both pages of the report.

Compressing the Print Range to Fit the Page

The **A**utomatically fit to page option under Compression in the File Page Setup dialog box takes the guess work out of fitting the entire print range on a single page. If your printer supports font scaling (as do many laser printers), you can use this option or the **M**anually size option to modify the size of the printed text and graphics in a report.

If you select the **A**utomatically fit to page option button, 1-2-3 determines how much to compress the data in the print range (up to a factor of 7) so that the entire print range prints on a single page.

When you use the Automatically fit to page option, this report that normally requires two pages appears on a single page.

Overdue Accounts Table

Kelly	Susan	1912 Meridian Street	Indianapolis	IN
Thompson	Richard	314 Crayton Drive	Seattle	WA
Wulf	Shane	9220 Franklin Road	Memphis	TN
Macaela	Lili	1912 Branford Drive	San Diego	CA
Malvern	Thomas	9057 Kinsey Avenue	Orlando	FL
Kelly	Jim	1637 Ellis Parkway	Chicago	IL
Smith	Margaret	2548 North Point	Cincinnati	OH
Pryor	Aaron	1247 College Avenue	Bloomington	IN
Mansfield	James	1811 Fulton Street	Flagstaff	AZ
Adams	Karen	626 Keystone Way	Newport Beach	CA
Thomas	Brian	314 Crayton Drive	Seattle	WA
Schnyder	Jay	1256 Williamsburg	Atlanta	FL
Grill	Alan	1710 Delaware	Lexington	KY
Harrington	James	1945 Danbury Court	Port Huron	MI
Tuke	Samuel	246 First Avenue	Fort Worth	TX
Wright	Amy	6327 Arlington	Des Moines	IA
Holland	Mark	316 Atwood Terrace	Miami	FL
Englert	Michael	397 Drexel Boulevard	Boston	MA
Kelly	Susan	1912 Meridian Street	Indianapolis	IN
Thompson	Richard	314 Crayton Drive	Seattle	WA
Wulf	Shane	9220 Franklin Road	Memphis	TN
Macaela	Lili	1912 Branford Drive	San Diego	CA
Malvern	Thomas	9057 Kinsey Avenue	Orlando	FL
Kelly	Jim	1637 Ellis Parkway	Chicago	IL
Smith	Margaret	2548 North Point	Cincinnati	OH
Pryor	Aaron	1247 College Avenue	Bloomington	IN
Mansfield	James	1811 Fulton Street	Flagstaff	AZ
Adams	Karen	626 Keystone Way	Newport Beach	CA
Thomas	Brian	314 Crayton Drive	Seattle	WA
Schnyder	Jay	1256 Williamsburg	Atlanta	FL
Grill	Alan	1710 Delaware	Lexington	KY
Harrington	James	1945 Danbury Court	Port Huron	MI
Tuke	Samuel	246 First Avenue	Fort Worth	TX
Wright	Amy	6327 Arlington	Des Moines	IA
Holland	Mark	316 Atwood Terrace	Miami	FL
Englert	Michael	397 Drexel Boulevard	Boston	MA
Kelly	Susan	1912 Meridian Street	Indianapolis	IN
Thompson	Richard	314 Crayton Drive	Seattle	WA
Wulf	Shane	9220 Franklin Road	Memphis	TN
Macaela	Lili	1912 Branford Drive	San Diego	CA
Malvern	Thomas	9057 Kinsey Avenue	Orlando	FL
Kelly	Jim	1637 Ellis Parkway	Chicago	IL
Smith	Margaret	2548 North Point	Cincinnati	OH
Pryor	Aaron	1247 College Avenue	Bloomington	IN
Mansfield	James	1811 Fulton Street	Flagstaff	AZ
Adams	Karen	626 Keystone Way	Newport Beach	CA
Thomas	Brian	314 Crayton Drive	Seattle	WA
Schnyder	Jay	1256 Williamsburg	Atlanta	FL
Grill	Alan	1710 Delaware	Lexington	KY
Harrington	James	1945 Danbury Court	Port Huron	MI
Tuke	Samuel	246 First Avenue	Fort Worth	TX
Wright	Amy	6327 Arlington	Des Moines	IA
Holland	Mark	316 Atwood Terrace	Miami	FL
Englert	Michael	397 Drexel Boulevard	Boston	MA

14-Jun-91   Page 1

If you want to specify how much to compress or expand the print range, select the Manually size option, then enter the percentage of compression in its text box. To compress the print range, enter a percentage between 15 and 99 (100 represents actual size) in the text box. To expand the print range, enter a percentage between 101 and 1000 in the text box.

To remove any compression or expansion settings you applied to a print range, select the None option under Compression.

Note that 1-2-3 clears the printer and returns it to normal print as soon as the program finishes the print job.

8

Changing the Orientation

Some dot matrix and all laser printers are capable of printing in Portrait (vertical) or Landscape (horizontal) mode. A wide report enables you to fit more columns on the page by changing the Orientation option in the File Page Setup dialog box from Portrait to Landscape.

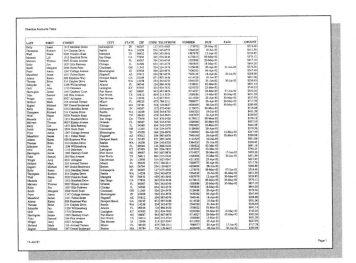

In this example, the Landscape and Automatically fit to page options were used to print the wide report on a single page.

Specifying Other Print Options

The options in the File Page Setup dialog box enable you to print the worksheet frame (the worksheet and the column letters and row numbers) or the worksheet grid lines in a report. Select each Options check box that you want to use.

8

To print the column and worksheet letters and row numbers along with the worksheet grid lines, select both the Show worksheet frame and the Show grid lines check boxes.

	A	A	B	C	D	E
1		REGIONAL INCOME REPORT				
2			Qtr 1	Qtr 2	Qtr 3	Qtr 4
3		**Sales**				
4		Northeast	$30,336	$33,370	$36,707	$40,377
5		Southeast	20,572	22,629	24,892	27,381
6		Central	131,685	144,854	159,339	175,273
7		Northwest	94,473	103,920	114,312	125,744
8		Southwest	126,739	139,413	153,354	168,690
9		**Total Sales**	$403,805	$444,186	$488,604	$537,464
10						
11		**Cost of Goods Sold**				
12		Northeast	10,341	11,272	12,286	13,392
13		Southeast	6,546	7,135	7,777	8,477
14		Central	65,843	71,769	78,228	85,269
15		Northwest	63,967	69,724	75,999	82,839
16		Southwest	72,314	78,822	85,916	93,649
17		**Total Cost of Goods Sold**	$219,011	$238,722	$260,207	$283,626
18						
19		**Operating Expenses**				
20		Northeast	$21,529	$23,036	$24,649	$26,374
21		Southeast	15,946	17,062	18,257	19,535
22		Central	27,554	29,483	31,547	33,755
23		Northwest	16,130	17,259	18,467	19,760
24		Southwest	32,361	34,626	37,050	39,644
25		**Total Operating Expenses**	$113,520	$121,466	$129,969	$139,067
26						
27		**Net Income**				
28		Northeast	($1,534)	($938)	($228)	$611
29		Southeast	(1,920)	(1,568)	(1,142)	(630)
30		Central	38,289	43,602	49,564	56,249
31		Northwest	14,376	16,937	19,846	23,144
32		Southwest	22,064	25,964	30,388	35,397
33		**Total Net Income**	$71,275	$83,997	$98,428	$114,772

8

Naming and Saving Print Settings

If you have a large worksheet, you may want to print different areas of the worksheet with different print options. Rather than resetting the options for each range or creating complex print macros, you can save your print settings in a page layout library file. Then to reuse these settings for printing a different range, you simply retrieve the file containing the proper print settings before sending the job to the printer.

To name and save print settings, follow these steps:

1. From the File menu, select the Page Setup option (or select the Print option, then select the Page Setup command button in the File Print dialog box).

2. Modify the print settings in the File Page Setup dialog box so that they are the way you want to save them in the page layout library file.

3. Select the Save command button under Named settings in the File Page Setup dialog box.

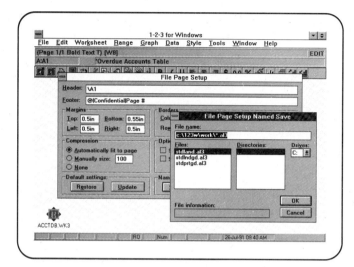

1-2-3 displays the File Page Setup Named Saved dialog box.

4. Type a name (up to eight characters) for the page layout library file in the File name text box.

   1-2-3 appends the extension AL3 to the file name you assign in the File Page Setup Named Saved dialog box.

5. Select the OK button.

To use a page layout library file in a worksheet, select the Retrieve command button in the File Page Setup dialog box. Then select the name of the library file that holds the settings you want to use in the File Page Setup Named Retrieve dialog box and select OK.

Restoring or Changing Default Settings

To return to the default print settings after making various changes in the File Page Setup dialog box, select the Restore command button under Default settings.

If you find that you always change certain page layout settings (such as the margins or the orientation) and you want to make your changes part of the program's default print settings, simply modify the settings in the File Page Layout dialog box and then select the Update command button under Default settings before you select OK.

8

Previewing Reports

Nothing is quite as disappointing as printing a long report, then discovering that something is not quite right and that you must reprint the entire thing. To avoid wasting paper and valuable time, you can use the 1-2-3 for Windows print preview feature to see how each page of the report will appear after it is printed. Print preview shows on-screen where page breaks will occur in the report, as well as any header or footer that you created.

To use print preview before printing a report, follow these steps:

1. From the File menu, select the Preview option (or select the Print option, then select the Preview command button in the File Print dialog box).

1-2-3 displays the File Preview dialog box. The print range you selected appears in the Range(s) text box.

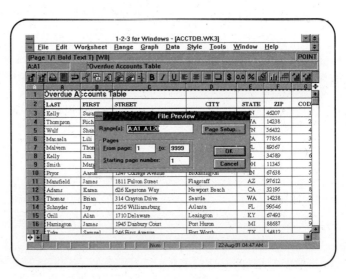

2. Select the OK button.

    1-2-3 shows you the first page of the report.

8

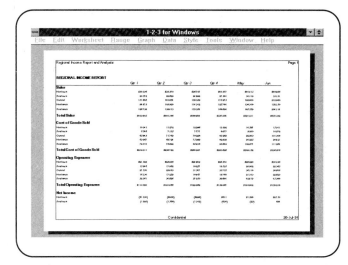

In this example, you see the preview of the first page of a four-page report.

3. To see the preview of the next page in the report, press `PgDn`.

8

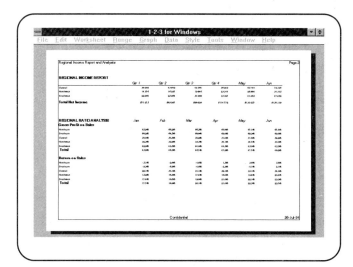

When you press `PgDn`, 1-2-3 shows you how the next page will appear after it is printed.

4. Continue to press `PgDn` to see succeeding pages of the report. To return to the normal Worksheet window, press `Esc`.

299

After previewing a report, you can print the document with the **File Print** command (if everything is okay) or you can make the necessary changes before you print.

Note: If you use the mouse, you can preview the print range that is selected by clicking the Preview the print range SmartIcon.

Inserting Page Breaks

Sometimes as you preview a report, you find that some of the page breaks 1-2-3 inserted into the report are in inappropriate places. Suppose that you find a table of data that has been split across two pages so that the headings for the table are at the bottom of the first page and the columns of data appear at the top of the following page.

You can correct paging problems by inserting your own page breaks with the **Worksheet Page Break** command. Before you try to modify the page breaks in a report, however, you need to make sure that 1-2-3 is displaying page breaks in the worksheet window.

8

To display page breaks in the window, select the Page breaks check box in the Window Display Options dialog box.

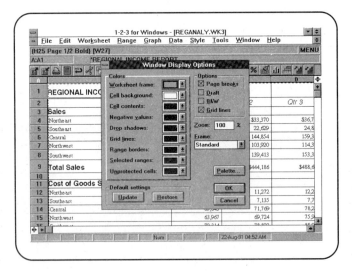

1-2-3 displays page breaks in the Worksheet window as dotted lines. The top and bottom edges of each page appear as horizontal dotted lines, and the left and right edges of each page appear as vertical dotted lines. You can see page breaks in the worksheet window if you temporarily remove the grid lines (by deselecting the Grid lines option in the Window Display Options dialog box).

After you preview or print a report, 1-2-3 displays a page cell indicator in the format line of the control panel whenever the cell pointer is in the upper left corner of a page. This indicator shows the current page number and the total number of pages in the report. For example, if your report has four pages, you see the indicator

    {Page 1/4}

If you insert your own page breaks with the Worksheet Page Break command, 1-2-3 displays a

    {MPage}

indicator (for manual page) in the format line when the cell pointer is in the upper left corner of a page.

To enter a manual page break in a worksheet, follow these steps:

1. Position the cell pointer in the cell you want to be in the leftmost column of the new page, in the topmost row of the new page, or in the upper left corner of the new page.

2. From the Worksheet menu, select the Page Break option.

   1-2-3 displays the Worksheet Page Break dialog box.

3. Select the appropriate page break option:

   Horizontal inserts a page break in the print range with the top edge of the selected cell as the top edge of the new page.

   Vertical inserts a page break in the print range with the left edge of the selected cell as the left edge of the new page.

   Both inserts a page break in the print range with the left and top edges of the selected cell determining the left and top edges of the new page.

4. Select the OK button to insert the page break.

   1-2-3 displays the page break in the worksheet window and inserts the {MPage} indicator in the format line of the control panel.

8

301

To prevent 1-2-3 from splitting the net income data on two pages, add a horizontal manual page break in row 27 of the worksheet.

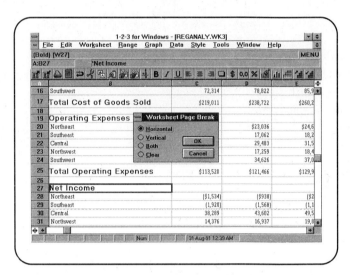

8

1-2-3 inserts a horizontal page break at row 27. The Net income data is printed together on the second page of the report.

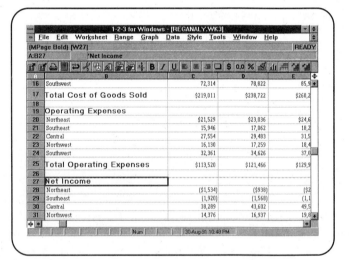

The biggest problem with manual page breaks is that you often have to keep adjusting them. As soon as you add or delete data in the print range, the manual page break that worked so well for one version of the report becomes inappropriate for the current version. To remove a manual page from your report, follow these steps:

1. Position the cell pointer in a cell that contains the {MPage} cell indicator (displayed in the format line of the control panel)

   To clear a vertical page break, select any cell in the print range in the leftmost column of the page. To clear a horizontal page break, select any cell in the print range in the top row of the page. To clear both a horizontal and a vertical page break, select the cell you used to create the page break.

2. From the Worksheet menu, select the Page Break option.

3. Select the Clear option button.

4. Select the OK button.

   1-2-3 removes the page break from the worksheet window. Note that you may have to redraw the screen by pressing `PgDn` and then `PgUp` to get the page break display to disappear.

Excluding Columns, Rows, and Worksheets within the Print Range

For some reports, you do not need to print all the columns or rows within the print range you selected. 1-2-3 for Windows enables you to suppress the printing of specific columns and rows in the print range. If you are using a three-dimensional print range, the program even enables you to suppress the printing of specific worksheets within the range.

To suppress the printing of columns or worksheets in the print range, suppress their display before you print the report. As you learned in Chapter 5, you can suppress the display of a specific column or range of columns with the Worksheet Hide Column command. You also can suppress the display of a particular worksheet or range of worksheets in a file with the Worksheet Hide Sheet command.

To suppress the printing of specific rows of the worksheet, you must mark the rows with a symbol for nonprinting. You enter two vertical bars (||) in the first column of each row of the print range you want to exclude. Although you type two vertical bars, only one appears in the cell display in the worksheet window, and neither appears on the printout.

8

If the row you want to exclude contains data in the first column of the print range, you must insert a new column for the vertical bars and redefine the print range to include the new column. Keep in mind that the column with the vertical bars must be the first column of the print range. To avoid alignment problems after inserting this new column, use the Worksheet Hide Column command to suppress printing of the column.

In this example, you insert a new column A, then enter two vertical bars (||) in cell A9 (although only one is displayed), and redefine the print range to include this new column in order to suppress the display of Total Sales information in the printed report.

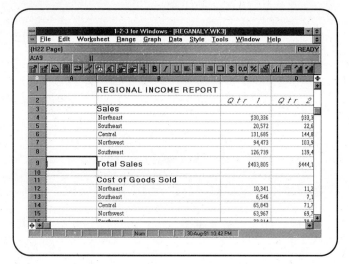

After you preview the printing of the first page of the report, row 9 with the Total Sales data no longer appears.

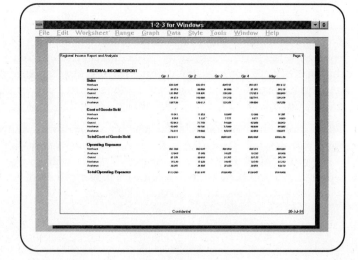

To restore the worksheet after you finish printing, delete the vertical bars from the leftmost cells of the nonprinting rows. If you inserted a column for the vertical bars, display the column again (if necessary) with the Worksheet Unhide Column command, then delete the column with the Worksheet Delete Column command.

Summary

This chapter showed you how to print reports with the File Print command. You learned how to print simple reports using a single print range and the program's printing defaults. You also learned how to specify more than one range and to produce a multiple-page report from a worksheet.

The chapter showed you many ways to enhance printed reports. You can add headers and footers that can include the date and a page number. You also can change the layout of a page by adjusting the margins, changing the orientation, and compressing or expanding the data to fit the page.

Specifically, you learned the following key information about 1-2-3:

8

- ■ To select a new printer, choose the File Printer Setup command.
- ■ To print a simple report using the printing defaults, select the range to be printed, then select the File Print command, and then select OK.
- ■ To change the page layout settings, select the File Page Setup command (or select the File Print command, then select the Page Setup command button in the File Print dialog box).
- ■ To print the date in a header or footer, enter the @ symbol. To print the page number, enter the # symbol.
- ■ To preview your report on-screen before you print it, select the File Preview command (or select the File Print command, then select the Preview command button in the File Print dialog box).
- ■ To display page breaks on-screen, select the Page breaks check box in the Window Display Options dialog box.
- ■ To insert a manual page break, use the Worksheet Page Break command.

The next chapter discusses file management. Chapter 9 teaches you how to password-protect your files, save part of a worksheet in a separate file, consolidate worksheet files, and dynamically link your files.

Managing Files

9

You already have learned some of 1-2-3's basic file management tasks such as naming, saving, and opening files. This chapter covers some of the other valuable procedures for managing and securing your worksheet files. As part of this discussion, you learn how to specify a new directory in which to work and how to protect files with passwords so unauthorized users cannot access the files.

You also learn how to save and retrieve parts of files. You learn how to extract a section of data from one worksheet and save it in a separate file. In addition, you learn how to combine parts of several files into one master file. This capability is useful for consolidating data from similar worksheets.

As an alternative to file consolidation, you can link worksheet files. You link files by building formulas in an active worksheet that reference information in another worksheet on disk. After you establish the links, 1-2-3 automatically updates the linked cells when you retrieve a file containing the links.

Finally, this chapter teaches you how to import certain types of data from other programs into a 1-2-3 worksheet file.

Changing the current directory

Protecting files with passwords

Saving and retrieving partial files

Managing multiple worksheet files

Linking files with formulas

Importing files to 1-2-3

Key Terms in This Chapter

Password	A string of up to 15 characters used to limit worksheet file access to those who know the password.
Template	An empty master file with labels and formulas, but without data. You use a template to create new worksheets or to combine data from multiple files.
File linking	A feature that enables you to build formulas in the current worksheet that are dynamically linked to the values to which they refer in other worksheets.
ASCII file	A standardized text file format that many programs can create, and which 1-2-3 can import into a worksheet with the File Import From Text command.

Changing the Current Directory

Whenever you start 1-2-3 for Windows, the directory listed in the Worksheet directory text box in the Tools User Setup dialog box becomes the current directory. When you choose a command that uses files, such as the File Open or File Save As command, 1-2-3 automatically displays the files in that directory in the associated dialog box. The directory appears in the path name in the File name text box and the files appear in the current directory in the Files list box.

In this example, the current directory is a 123W subdirectory called WORK; its files appear in the File Open dialog box.

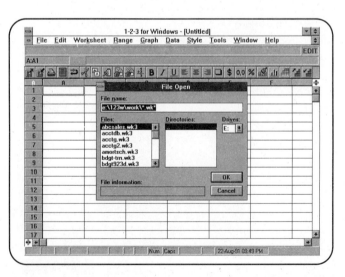

Often you may want to work and save files in a directory other than the one that is current. To make a new directory current so that you don't have to change the path name each time you want to open or save a worksheet file, change the current directory by following these steps:

1. From the Tools menu, select the User Setup option.

2. Select the Worksheet directory option in the Tools User Setup dialog box by pressing Tab⁵, and type a new path name or use the pointer to select the part of the path name you want to change and re-enter that part.

   As you enter the path name, remember to add a colon (:) after the drive letter, and a backslash (\) between each directory name in the path.

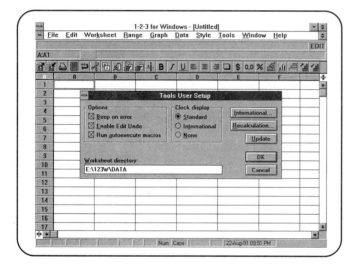

In this example, select WORK and type DATA to make C:\123W\DATA the current worksheet directory.

3. To make the new directory the default directory (so that it will become the current directory each time you start 1-2-3), select the Update command button. To make the new directory the current directory only until you exit 1-2-3, select OK.

When C:\123W\DATA is the worksheet directory, 1-2-3 displays all the subdirectories of C:\123\DATA in the Directories list box and all the files within the directory in the Files list box of the dialog box that appears when you select a File menu option such as Open or Save As.

Protecting Files with Passwords

When you protect your files by using 1-2-3's password-protection system, you prevent access to the files by unauthorized users. The only people who can retrieve a protected file are those who know the password. This feature is particularly useful for worksheets that contain confidential information, such as sales and payroll worksheets.

Assigning a Password

You password-protect a file by selecting the **P**assword protect check box in the File Save As dialog box. To assign a password to a worksheet, follow these steps:

1. From the **F**ile menu, select the Save **A**s option.
2. Specify the name and path of the file in the File **n**ame text box.
3. Select the **P**assword protect check box and place a check mark in the box.
4. Select the OK button.

1-2-3 displays a second File Save As box in which you enter and verify password.

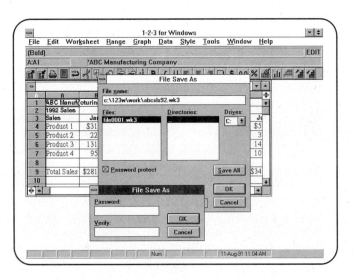

5. Type a password of up to 15 characters in the Password text box exactly. Remember that passwords are case-sensitive: you must remember the precise sequence of upper- and lowercase letters.

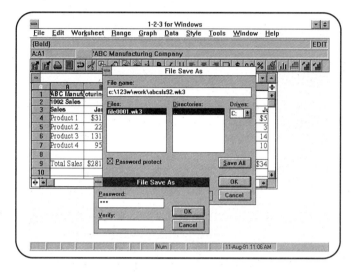

The password never appears on-screen in the second File Save As dialog box. As you type, 1-2-3 displays asterisks to hide the characters.

6. Select the Verify text box and type the same password in the second text box, making certain that you enter it precisely as you did earlier.

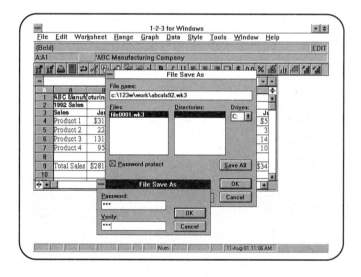

9

The password entered in the Verify text box must match the one in the Password text box (including case); otherwise, you must start the procedure again.

7. Select the OK button to save the file with the new password. Now, only those who know the password can open the worksheet file. If you previously saved the file you are password protecting under the same name, 1-2-3 displays a File Save As dialog box that tells you that the file already exists.

Note: Be very careful with passwords; you cannot open a file to remove or change the password unless you can accurately reproduce the password.

Retrieving a Password-Protected File

To open a worksheet file protected with a password follow these steps:

1. From the File menu, select the Open option.
2. Select the password-protected file in the File name list box.
3. Select the OK button.

1-2-3 displays a second File Open dialog box containing a Password text box.

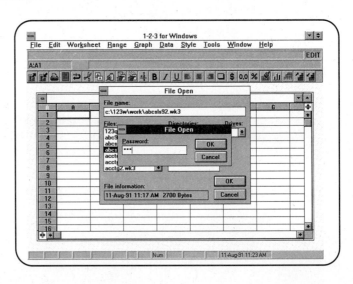

4. Type the password in the Password text box.
5. Select the OK button.

   If you enter the password correctly, the worksheet appears.

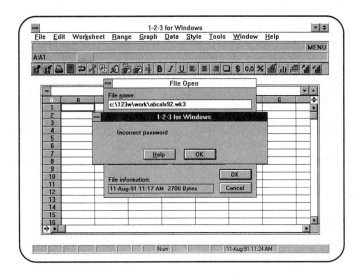

If you enter the wrong password, however, this dialog box appears.

If the Incorrect password dialog box appears, select the OK button and try the entire procedure again.

Deleting or Changing a Password

The only way to delete a password is open it with the File Open command (which requires that you successfully reproduce the password), and deselect the Password protect option by removing its check mark. When you complete the file saving procedure by selecting the OK button, 1-2-3 saves the file without the password.

To change a password, you first must delete the existing password. Then, you must save the file again with the File Save As command and assign a new password as outlined in the preceding section.

Saving and Retrieving Partial Files

Sometimes you want to store a part of a worksheet, such as a particular table or schedule, in a separate file on disk. For example, you may want to extract a table of customer order information for the current month and save it into its own file. You also can use extracting to break a huge worksheet file into smaller files if the original file becomes too large to back up on a single floppy disk.

Conversely, you may have several individual worksheet files whose data you want to use combine into one file. For example, you may have your sales-people prepare their own monthly expense worksheets and then combine the data from each into one worksheet file from which you prepare an expense report.

When combining data from separate 1-2-3 worksheet files, you can consolidate data from different files as well as simply copying the information into a new part of the worksheet. When the files share the same layout (as do budgets, income statements, and the like), you can have 1-2-3 add or subtract the data in the specified range of each file as you combine the file.

Note: Usually, the term *extract* means to remove something from its place of origin, as in extracting ore from a mine. When you perform an extraction with 1-2-3's File Extract To command, however, you are essentially performing a copying operation between files (in which a specific range of data in a larger worksheet file is copied into its own disk file).

Extracting Data

When you use the File Extract To command, you can save the selected range in the current worksheet file with its formulas, with the calculated values of formulas, or strictly as text. The Formulas and Values options create separate worksheet files that you can open in 1-2-3 with the File Open command. The Text option creates a separate text file that other software applications (such as word processors) can use. You cannot, however, open such a text file with the File Open command in 1-2-3; rather, you must use the File Import From Text command.

The File Extract To command requires that you specify the portion of the worksheet you want to save. To use this command to copy a part of your worksheet to a separate file, follow these steps:

1. Select the range of cells you want to copy into the new file you are creating.
2. From the File menu, then select the Extract To option.

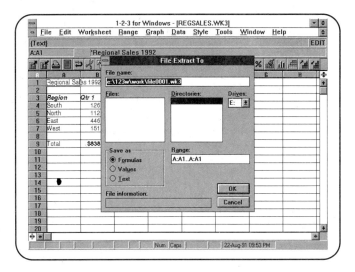

1-2-3 displays the File Extract To dialog box.

3. Enter a new file name in the File name text box. If necessary, change the drive letter with the Drives drop-down list box and the directory path with the Directories list box.

4. Select the appropriate option button under Save as:

   Select Formulas (the default) to save all of the formulas in the selected cell range. Be sure that the selected range includes all the cells to which the formulas refer (in order to avoid ERR values in the new worksheet file).

   Select Values to save only the current values calculated by the formulas. If the CALC indicator appears on the Status line, press F9 to recalculate the formulas before using this option.

   Select Text to save the range in an ASCII text file.

5. Check that the range in the Range text box is correct, and select OK to create the new worksheet or text file.

Suppose that you want to save the first quarter budget figures stored in worksheet B of your file in a separate worksheet. You select the range B:A3..B:E9, and choose the File Extract To command.

In this example, you enter **QTR1BDGT** as the file name and select Values as the Save as option. The Range box lists B:A3..B:E9 because this is the range you selected before choosing the **File Extract To** command.

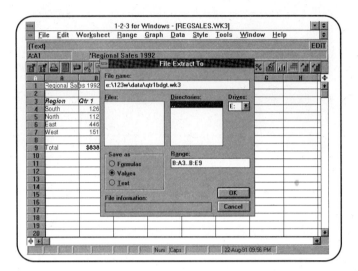

When you select the OK button, 1-2-3 creates a new worksheet (named QTR1BDGT.WK3) in the current directory. When 1-2-3 extracts the range, it always places its upper left corner cell in cell A1 of the new worksheet file.

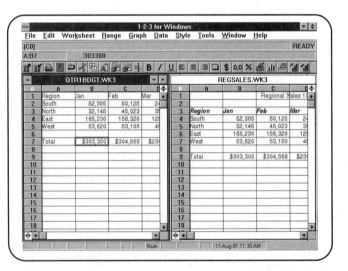

The QTR1BDGT.WK3 file contains none of the original formulas, only the calculated values. Also, notice that the extracted data occupies a range that starts in cell A1 in the new file.

If you perform the same operation, but selected the Text option button in the File Extract To dialog box, 1-2-3 creates a new file called QTR1BDGT.PRN. 1-2-3 uses the PRN extension to distinguish ASCII text files created from

9

worksheet files with the File Extract To Text command. You also can use the extension TXT to differentiate text files from worksheet files (some programs are set up to look for text files in a listing that use the TXT extension).

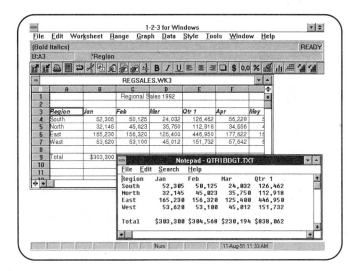

Other programs can read these text files. Here, you see the QTR1BDGT.TXT file (created in 1-2-3) opened with Notepad, a Windows 3.0 accessory program.

Remember that 1-2-3 cannot read text files directly. To open a text file, you must use the File Import From Text command (covered later in this chapter).

9

Combining Files

Another task you may need to perform is copying ranges of cells from other worksheets and placing them in strategic spots in your current worksheet. For example, if you work in a large firm, you may want to combine quarterly sales information by region into one consolidated worksheet.

You use the File Combine From command to combine data from different files. The Copy option of this command copies the selected worksheet or range into the current worksheet, replacing any existing data in the cells it occupies. The Add option adds the values from the selected worksheet or range to the values in the current worksheet. The Subtract option subtracts the values in the selected worksheet or range from the values in the current worksheet.

317

A simple technique for this kind of consolidation is to start with a copy of an empty master file, or template. A *template* contains exactly the same labels and formulas as the combined worksheets, but all ranges that usually contain specific data values are left blank or contain zero.

To begin a consolidation, you open the template worksheet file. Next, you copy the range containing the sales for each quarter from each file into the same place in the blank template using the File Combine From Add command. This action totals the sales for all quarters in the template file, which then you save under a new file name with the File Save As command.

To combine data from different worksheet files, follow these steps:

1. Select the cell in the upper left corner of the range in the current worksheet where you want to copy the data from the worksheet file on disk.

   Be sure that you are in an area of the worksheet where the data combined from the disk cannot wipe out any existing data.

In this example, select cell B4 to copy the first quarter sales figures for 1992 into the range B4..D7. Because all cells in this range are blank, all the formulas in row 9 return 0 (zero).

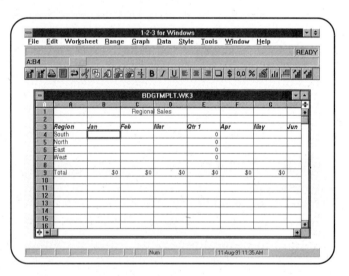

2. From the File menu, select the Combine From option.
3. In the File name text box, select the name of the file that contains the data you want to combine. If necessary, change the drive in the Drives drop-down list box and the directory path in the Directories list box.
4. To copy a worksheet or range from another file to the existing worksheet, select the Copy option button (the default). Otherwise, select the Add option button to add the incoming values to the values

in the current worksheet or the **S**ubtract option button to decrease them.

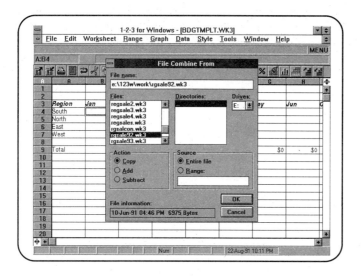

In this example, to bring the quarterly sales figures into a blank range of the worksheet template, select the RGSALE92.WK3 file and leave the **C**opy option button selected.

5. To copy all data from the selected file into the current worksheet file, select the **E**ntire file option button (the default) under Source. Otherwise, select the **R**ange option button and indicate the range of data in the **R**ange text box.

   To specify a range, you can enter the range address or the range name.
6. Select the OK button.

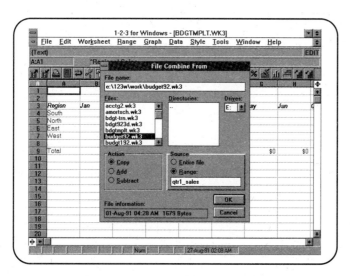

In this example, select the **R**ange option and enter **QTR1_SALES** as the range name.

9

319

The first quarter data is now in the range B4..D7. 1-2-3 automatically updates the formula in range B9..E9.

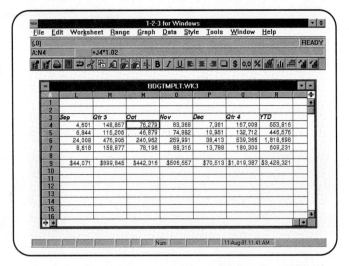

After you repeat this command to combine data for all quarters, the template is filled and all formulas in row 9 display values.

The Copy option in the File Combine From dialog box copies in an entire worksheet or named range and writes the new data over the corresponding data in the current worksheet. If you want to add or subtract corresponding values, you need to select the Add or Subtract option instead.

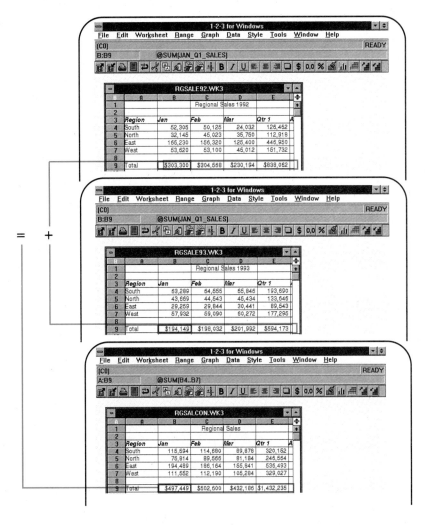

In this example, you selected the Add option. 1-2-3 added the values in the center worksheet (the worksheet you combined) to the values in the corresponding cells of the top worksheet to create this consolidated worksheet.

9

The Add and Subtract options affect only blank worksheet cells or cells containing numeric values. Any cells in the current worksheet that contain formulas or labels do not change.

Managing Multiple Worksheet Files

Instead of extracting and combining information in different worksheet files with the File Extract To and File Combine From commands, you can open multiple worksheet files in their own windows. You then can transfer information between them with the Cut, Copy, Paste, Move Cells, and Quick Copy options on the Edit menu.

You can open as many files as your computer's memory can hold. To retrieve an existing worksheet file, you choose the File Open command. To open a new worksheet file, you choose the File New command. 1-2-3 opens each file in its own Worksheet window and makes that window current, placing it on top of the work area.

In this example, two worksheet files are open. The last file opened becomes the current file and appears on top.

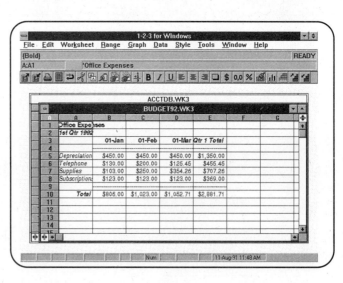

As you open more files, 1-2-3 for Windows adds their file names at the bottom of the Window menu.

322

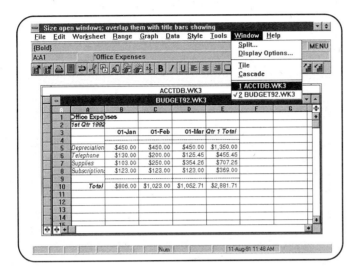

To make another worksheet file current, select its name on the Window menu.

You also can make a new window current by pressing the Next Window (Ctrl + F6) function key or by clicking somewhere on the window (provided that some part of the window is visible in the work area).

To close a worksheet file when you no longer need to work with it, you have several alternatives:

- You make that Worksheet window current, then choose the File menu and select the Close option.

- You can click that Worksheet's Control menu box, and select the Close option on the Control menu.

- You can double-click the Worksheet's Control menu box or press Ctrl + F4

No matter which method you use, 1-2-3 prompts you to save the file.

Viewing More than One Worksheet Window at a Time

When working with several worksheet files in the 1-2-3 window, you may want to rearrange their Worksheet windows so that you can see part of each window in the work area. 1-2-3 provides two Window menu options that you can use to rearrange the active files.

9

323

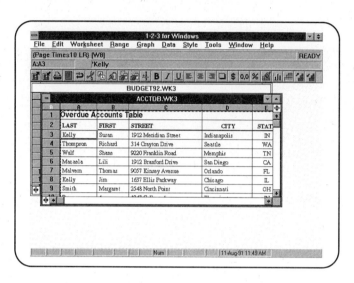

Select the **C**ascade option on the **W**indow menu to overlap the windows.

9

Select the **T**ile option on the **W**indow menu to place the windows side-by-side.

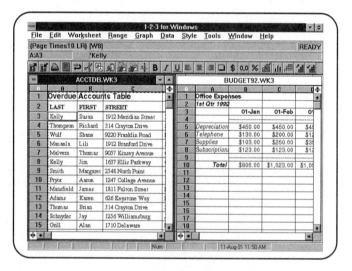

Copying a Range from One File to Another

Cutting and pasting a range from one worksheet file into another is as easy as copying a range from one part of a single worksheet to another. The easiest way to copy a range from one file to another is through the Clipboard:

1. Use the **File Open** command to open the worksheet file that contains the data you want to copy and the worksheet file to which you want to copy data. For example, open the QTR1BDGT.WK3 worksheet file and a new worksheet file.

2. Make current the worksheet window that contains the range you want to cut or copy.

3. Select the range of data you want to cut or copy.

4. From the **Edit** menu, select the **Cut** option (Shift + Del) to move the data or select the **Copy** option (Ctrl + Ins) to copy the data.

    1-2-3 cuts or copies the selected data into the Clipboard.

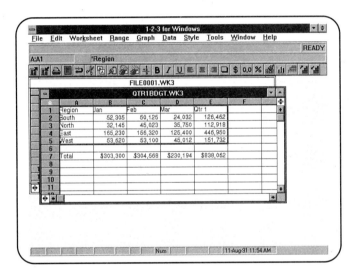

In this example, select the range A1..E5 in the QTR1BDGT.WK3 worksheet, and then copy it to the Clipboard with the **Edit Copy** command (Ctrl + Ins).

9

5. Select the window that contains the worksheet where you want to move or copy the selected range.

6. Select the cell in the upper left corner of the range where you want the selected range of data to appear.

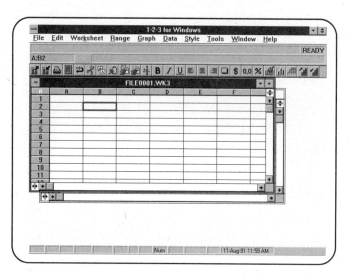

In this example, select cell B2 in the FILE0001.WK3 Worksheet window as the cell in the upper left corner of the range where you want to place the copied data.

7. From the **Edit** menu, then select the **Paste** option (⇧Shift + Ins) to copy the data from the Clipboard into the worksheet.

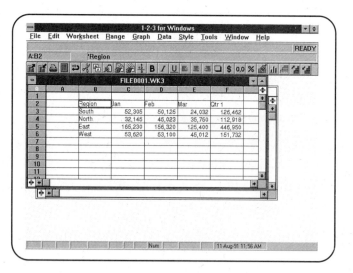

Here, you see the range of data in the FILE0001.WK3 Worksheet window after you copy it from the Clipboard with the **Edit Paste** command (⇧Shift + Ins).

Note that when you cut or copy data into a new worksheet file, 1-2-3 displays the data within the default columns widths of the new file, but retains the fonts and attributes assigned in the original file.

Linking Files with Formulas

Instead of combining data from several worksheet files with the **F**ile **C**ombine **F**rom command, 1-2-3 offers the alternative of linking the files by formula. Linking enables you to draw data from several different files without opening the files in the work area. Thus, linking provides great flexibility in consolidating data from various sources while saving valuable computer memory and recalculation time. After you link values in two files, 1-2-3 reflects any change made to the source cell in the target cell as soon as you open the target cell's worksheet. Note that linking is quite unlike copying values from one file to another (in which changes in one file are not reflected in the other).

In 1-2-3 for Windows, you establish the links between files by building formulas in the current worksheet that contain an *external reference* (a reference that refers to a cell or cell range in another file). The cell that contains the formula with the external reference and receives the information is the *target cell*. The cell that sends the information is the *source cell*. 1-2-3 automatically updates the linked formulas when you open the worksheet file that contains them.

Creating the Linking Formula

A formula with an external reference that links two worksheet files must contain the file reference and the range address or range name. The file reference consists of the name of the worksheet enclosed in a pair of angle brackets (<< and >>), as in the following example:

    +<<TAXES92>>A:D53

If the file listed in the file reference is not located in the same directory as the current worksheet, you need to add the directory path as in this example:

    +<<C:\123W\ACCOUNTS\TAXES92>>A:D53

Note that you don't have to include the file extension if the file uses the standard WK3 extension. If you are establishing a link with a worksheet file that uses another extension, you do need to include the extension.

To create a linking formula, follow these steps:

1. Use the **F**ile **O**pen command to open the worksheet file that contains the source cell or range.
2. With the **F**ile **O**pen command, open the worksheet file that you want to contain the target cell with the linking formula.

3. From the Window menu, select the Tile option.

In this example, cell B11 of the LA92.WK3 file (the value of the total operating expenses) is the source cell. You will link this cell's value to the IS92CON.WK3 file by a formula in the target cell, B8.

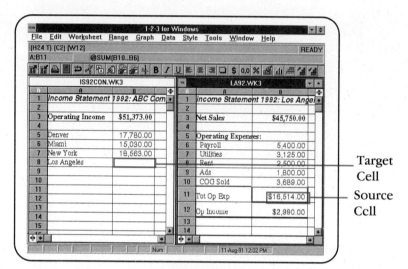

4. Select the target cell in which you want the linking formula to be.

5. Type ⊞ (plus sign) to begin the linking formula and place 1-2-3 in VALUE mode.

6. Select the source cell in the other worksheet file that contains the value you want in the file containing the target cell.

   You can select the source cell by clicking it with the mouse or by pressing the direction keys to move the cell pointer to this cell. If you are using the keyboard, start pointing by pressing Ctrl+End or Ctrl+F6 before you press the other direction keys.

7. After you select the source cell, press ⏎Enter to enter the linking formula in the target cell.

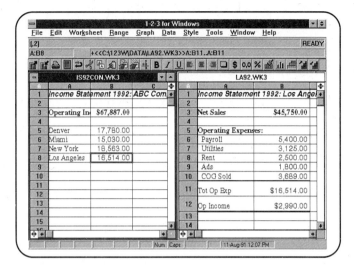

The linked
formula appears
in the target cell
after you press
↵Enter

When you alter the values in a source range, 1-2-3 does not immediately
recalculate the linked formula in the target cell. In fact, you can change a
source range and save the file many times without the target cell reflecting any
of these interim values. 1-2-3 does, however, update the target cell whenever
you open the worksheet file that contains the linking formula.

9

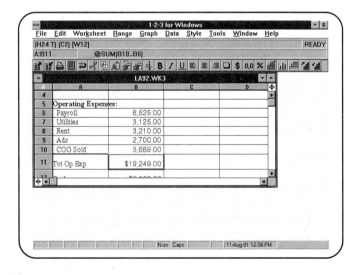

In this example,
the total operat-
ing expenses
in the source
cell B11 have
increased to
$19,249.00

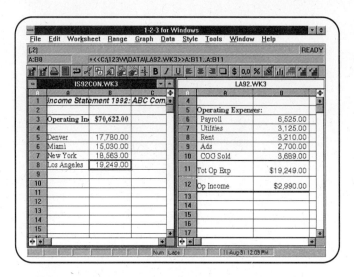

1-2-3 updates the target cell (B8) in the consolidation worksheet file as soon as you open the file.

If you are using 1-2-3 for Windows on a network, someone else may modify the worksheet files containing the values linked to the worksheet you are working on. In this case, you can use the File Administration Update Links command periodically to update all the linked formulas.

You also can link a range of values in one worksheet file to another worksheet file by creating a linking formula that uses one of 1-2-3's built-in functions. For example, you can create a linking formula that calculates total expenses in the range B6..B10 of the LA92 worksheet file with the SUM function. To have the linking formula in the target cell calculate the total expenses in source range in the LA92 worksheet file, enter

@SUM(<<LA92>>B6..B10)

in cell B11 of the IS92CON file.

Listing Linked Files

To learn which files are linked to the current file, you can create a *linked file table*. As when you create a table of range names, you may want to place the table of linked files in its own worksheet (so that the table doesn't replace any existing data). Also, like a range name table, a linked file table is static. If you add or delete linking formulas during a work session, you must recreate the table if you want it to reflect the changes.

To create a linked file table, follow these steps:

1. Select the cell in the upper left corner of the range in which you want the linked file table to appear.

2. From the File menu, select the Administration option.

    1-2-3 displays a cascade menu of Administration options.

3. Select the Paste Table option.

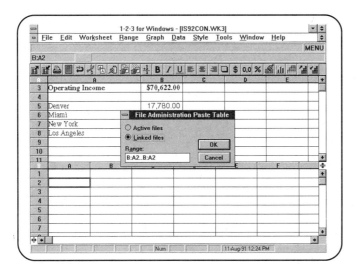

1-2-3 displays the File Administration Paste Table dialog box.

4. Select the Linked files option button in the File Administration Paste Table dialog box.

5. Select the OK button.

9

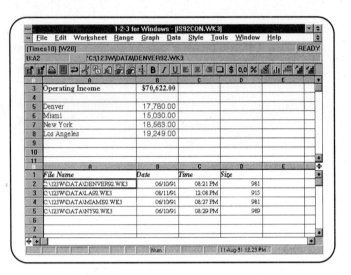

In this example, the linked file table indicates that four files are linked to the current file.

The linked file table shows you the name of each file containing a source range, the date and time of that file's last revision, and the size of that file in bytes.

Note: 1-2-3 merely reads the serial numbers and time fractions of the dates and times, so you must format these cells with the Range Format command.

9

Importing Files into 1-2-3

As you already know, 1-2-3 for Windows enables you to transfer data between different programs via the Clipboard. Cutting and pasting information through the Clipboard is sufficient as long as you are transferring a limited amount of data. For situations in which you need to import a large amount of data into 1-2-3, you may be able to use the File Import From command instead.

Importing ASCII Text Files

The File Import From command enables you to import ASCII text files directly into the current worksheet file. For example, 1-2-3 creates standard ASCII text files from the selected data in your worksheet when you select the Text option of the File Extract To command. Other standard ASCII files include files produced by different word processing and text editors (such as the Notepad accessory). Many programs, such as database and word processing programs, also produce ASCII files that you can import into 1-2-3.

332

In addition to enabling you to import ASCII data, the File Import From command contains a Styles option that enables you to import formatting information from format files used by previous versions of 1-2-3. You can import the formats, font set, named styles, or graphics used in an FM3 format file created by WYSIWYG in Release 3.1 or by 1-2-3 for Windows, an FMT format file created by Impress in Release 2.3, or an ALL format file created by Allways in Release 2.2.

To import an ASCII text file into the current 1-2-3 worksheet, follow these steps:

1. Select the cell in the upper left corner of the range where you want the imported ASCII data to appear.

2. From the File menu, select the Import From option.

   1-2-3 displays a cascade menu of import options.

3. Select the Text or Numbers option.

   Use the Text option for importing an ASCII file created by your word processor. Use the Numbers option to import delimited files (ASCII files that contain separator characters to distinguish items of data).

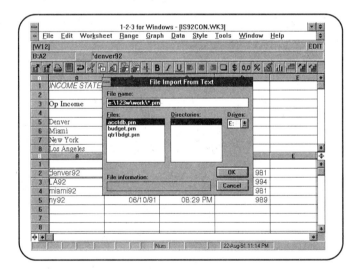

When you select the Text or Numbers option, 1-2-3 lists all PRN files in the current directory.

4. To display files in a different path, select the appropriate drive in the Drives drop-down list box and the appropriate directory in Directories list box. To display files with a different extension, edit the PRN extension in the File name text box.

5. In the Files list box, select the name of the text file you want to import.

6. Select the OK button.

When you import data using the Text option, 1-2-3 imports each line of data in the text file as long label in the current worksheet. If the text file uses a proportionally-spaced font, the data is not aligned in the worksheet. To separate the data in long labels into columns, you use the Data Parse command (see Que's *Using 1-2-3 for Windows* for detailed information on using this command). If you select the File Import From Numbers command, 1-2-3 places numbers—separated by commas, colons, semicolons, or spaces—into separate columns. Keep in mind that if you import a file with the Numbers option, 1-2-3 imports only text that is enclosed in quotation marks.

Importing Styles

To import the styles, fonts, or information about graphs used in another worksheet and saved in an FM3, FMT, or ALL file, follow these steps:

1. From the File menu, select the Import From option.

2. Select the Styles options in the cascade menu.

   1-2-3 displays the File Import From Styles dialog box.

1-2-3 displays in the Files list box all files in the current directory that use the FM3 or FMT extension.

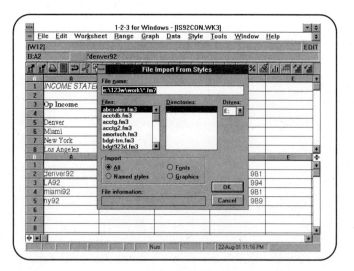

3. To display files in a different path, select the appropriate drive in the Drives drop-down list box and the appropriate directory in Directories list box. To display files with a different extension (such as ALL), edit the .fm? extension in the File name text box.

4. In the Files list box, select the name of the text file you want to import.

5. Select the appropriate Import option:

   Select All (the default) to replace all formats, fonts, named styles, and graphs in the current file with those in the format file you selected.

   Select Named Styles to replace only the named styles in the current file with those in the format file you selected.

   Select Fonts to replace only the font set in the current file with the one used in the format file you selected.

   Select Graphics to import only graphic information (including the location of graphs in the file as well as all graphic enhancements) into the current file from the format file you selected. Note that this option does not import the graph itself into the current worksheet file.

6. Select the OK button.

The formats you import with this command appear in the same location in the current worksheet file as they do in the original worksheet file. Therefore, choose this command to speed up the formatting of a new worksheet only when you are creating a worksheet that uses the same layout and formatting as the original file.

9

Summary

Knowing how to manage files is essential for the efficient use of 1-2-3. In addition to the basic tasks of naming, saving, and opening files you learned in Chapter 3, you need to perform other file-management tasks. This chapter showed you how to change the current directory, to protect files with passwords, and to save partial files when you want to extract or combine portions of a worksheet. You even can link worksheet files so that 1-2-3 automatically updates values in the linked file whenever you open it. You also learned how to import text files directly into a 1-2-3 worksheet file.

Specifically, you learned the following key information about managing files in 1-2-3 for Windows:

■ You can use the Directory text box in the Tools User Setup dialog box to change the current drive and directory used by 1-2-3. You select the Update command button to make the current directory the new default.

■ You can add passwords to your files by selecting the Password protect check box in the File Save As dialog box so that only those who know the exact password can open your files.

■ You can save part of the worksheet file with the File Extract To command. You can save the formulas existing in a range of cells or the current values of the formulas in the range. You also can use this command to create ASCII text files to use with programs that can't read 1-2-3 worksheet files.

■ You can combine data from different files with the File Combine From command. You can copy the source worksheet or range on top of the current worksheet. You also can add or subtract the values in the current worksheet to or from the values in the combined worksheet or range.

■ You can use the File Administration Paste Table command to create a table in the worksheet that lists all active files or all files linked to the current worksheet.

■ You can update all target cells in the current worksheet to reflect the current contents of the source cells with the File Administration Update Links command. This command is particularly helpful for users on a network.

■ You can use the File Import From command to import ASCII text files into a 1-2-3 worksheet or to import styles, fonts, or information about graphs saved in format files used by various versions of 1-2-3.

The next chapter shows you how to create graphs within 1-2-3. You learn about the graph creation process and how to select graph types and data ranges. The chapter also includes steps to enhance the appearance of a graph and to place and size a graph in the worksheet.

9

Creating
Graphs

1-2-3 for Windows provides powerful and versatile graphing capabilities. You can choose from seven two-dimensional and four three-dimensional basic graph types. You can enhance your basic graphs with headings and legends and with text and line drawings that direct attention to various facets of the graphs.

With the information in this chapter, you learn how to create graphs from spreadsheet data. The procedure involves selecting the range of data you want to graph and choosing a graph type. You then learn how to enhance a basic graph by annotating it with such elements as headings, legends, free-floating text, and line drawings. You then learn how to save a graph and place it in your worksheet so that it can be printed.

Understanding
1-2-3 graphs

Creating a new
graph

Selecting a graph
type

Specifying data
ranges

Enhancing the
appearance of a
graph

Working with
graphic objects

Selecting fonts
for a graph

Assigning colors
and patterns to a
graph

Saving a graph

Adding a graph to
a worksheet

Key Terms in This Chapter

Graph type	The manner in which 1-2-3 graphically represents data.
X-axis	The bottom horizontal edge of a graph, including tick marks that indicate the scale of the graph (usually the time period of each data point).
Y-axis	The left vertical edge of a graph, including tick marks that indicate the scale of the graph (usually the value of each data point). 1-2-3 also enables you to create graphs with a second y-axis on the right vertical edge of the graph.
Legend	The description of the shading, color, or symbols assigned to data ranges in a line or bar graph. The legend appears across the bottom of the graph.
Tick marks	The small marks on the axes of a graph that indicate the increments between the minimum and maximum graph values.

Understanding 1-2-3 Graphs

10

You create 1-2-3 for Windows graphs from data in the current worksheet. After you select the data you want to graph, choose the Graph New command and assign a graph name. 1-2-3 for Windows displays the new graph in a separate Graph window that has its own Menu bar and Icon palette. To enhance the basic graph, use the Graph window commands. After you are satisfied with the graph, you embed it in the worksheet. Then you can print the graph alone or as part of a report that includes the graph's supporting worksheet data.

Table 10.1 lists the options on the Graph window's Menu bar. Table 10.2 lists the tasks performed by the SmartIcons that appear on the Graph window's Icon palette.

Table 10.1
The Graph Window Menus

Command	Description
File	Enables you to close the current Graph window and exit the 1-2-3 program.
Edit	Enables you to select, copy, move, or delete objects in the current Graph window.
Chart	Enables you to set the data ranges you want to graph; change the graph type; and add titles, a legend, and other formatting in the current Graph window.
Draw	Enables you to add text, arrows, lines, various closed shapes, and freehand drawings in the current Graph window.
Layout	Moves selected objects in front of or behind others or prevents changes to the objects in the current Graph window.
Rearrange	Changes the rotation, orientation, and size of selected objects in the current Graph window.
Style	Controls the fonts, colors, line styles, and alignment of text graphic objects and controls the way 1-2-3 displays graphs when you add them to a worksheet.
Tools	Enables you to change the position or hide the display of the Icon palette in the work area.
Window	Enables you to change the size of the display in the current Graph window and to tile or cascade all the windows open in the work area.
Help	Enables you to access 1-2-3 for Windows' on-line help.

10

Table 10.2
The Graph Window Icon Palette

SmartIcon	Function
	Add an arrow
	Add a line
	Add an ellipse
	Add a polygon
	Add a rectangle
	Add text
	Draw freehand
	Line graph
	Bar graph
	Horizontal bar graph
	Mixed graph
	Pie graph
	Area graph
	HLCO graph
	Three-dimensional line graph
	Three-dimensional bar graph
	Three-dimensional pie graph
	Three-dimensional area graph
	Select a graph type
	Delete permenently
	Duplicate
	Rotate
	Flip backwards
	Flip upside down
	Place in front of all other objects
	Place behind all other objects

10

Creating a New Graph

The process for creating a new graph in 1-2-3 for Windows is simple. You select the data you want to graph, and then select the **Graph New** command and assign a name for the graph.

Suppose that you created a summary worksheet that consolidates the year-to-date totals for four regional offices, and you want to plot a chart that shows their relationship. To graph the data range containing these totals, follow these steps:

1. Select the data you want to graph.

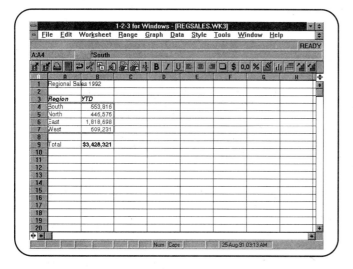

In this example, select the range A4..B7, which contains the column of region names and the column of year-to-date totals.

10

2. From the **Graph** menu, select the **New** option.

    1-2-3 displays the Graph New dialog box. You can specify a name for the graph in the **Graph** name text box.

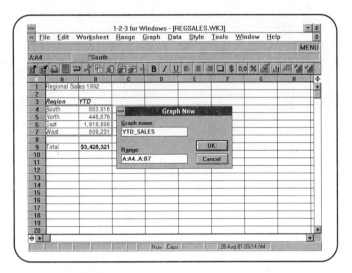

In this example,
enter **YTD_SALES**
in the Graph
name text box.

If you don't enter a graph name, 1-2-3 assigns a default graph name by
appending the next available number to GRAPH (such as GRAPH1,
GRAPH2, and so on).

3. Check that the graph range in the Range text box is correct and select
the OK button.

1-2-3 draws a line graph in a separate Graph window.

10

The Title bar of
the Graph win-
dow contains the
name of the
worksheet file to
which the graph
is linked followed
by the graph
name.

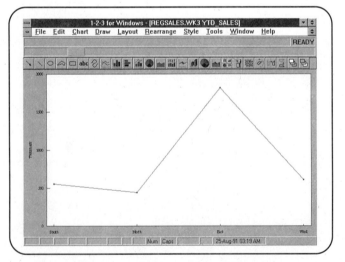

Note: If you are using the mouse, you can create a new graph with the default graph name simply by clicking the Graph SmartIcon in the Icon palette, which appears in the Worksheet window.

1-2-3 automatically uses the labels in the first column of the selected range for the x-axis labels at the bottom of the graph. The values in subsequent columns of the selected range are then used to construct the scale for the graph and to place the data points. 1-2-3 uses the lowest and highest values in the selected range to determine the lowest and highest values of the y-axis scale and the increment of the y-axis tick marks. Then 1-2-3 graphically represents the values in the range with individual data points (which are connected by lines).

Naming Graphs

As you assign graph names, keep the following guidelines in mind:

- A graph name can include up to 15 characters. 1-2-3 does not distinguish between upper- and lowercase letters in a graph name.

- Within a file, each graph name must be unique. If you reuse a graph name, 1-2-3 replaces the existing graph with the new graph you create.

- Do not assign a graph name that duplicates a cell address, range name, @function, or any other 1-2-3 command. Do not assign a graph name that begins with a number.

- Do not include spaces or any of the following characters in a graph name:

    + – * / & > < @ # { ?

- To link the graph you are creating with an active file other than the current active file, include the file reference as part of the graph name. For example, to link the YTD_SALES graph to the BUDGT92.WK3 file, use

    <<BUDGT92.WK3>>PYTD_SALES

    as the graph name (assuming that the BUDGT92 file is open in the work area, but does not contain the data you want to graph).

10

343

Using the Graph Menu Commands

You use some of the options on the Graph menu (such as New or View) every time you create a graph. Other options, such as Add to Sheet, Go To, Size, or Refresh, you use less frequently. Table 10.3 describes all the options that apear on the Graph menu.

Table 10.3
Graph Menu Options

Options	Description
New	Creates a graph using the data selected in the work-sheet and enables you to name the graph.
View	Enables you to select the graph you want to display in the Graph window.
Add to Sheet	Enables you to select the graph you want to add to the selected range in the current worksheet.
Name	Enables you to delete graphs or to list all graphs in the current file.
Import	Enables you to copy a PIC or CGM graph file from a disk to the selected range in the current worksheet.
Size	Enables you to change the size of a graph you added to the current worksheet by modifying the size of the range that contains the graph.
Refresh	Updates all graphs in the current file to reflect any changes made to values or labels in the graphed worksheet.
Go To	Enables you to move the cell pointer directly to the upper left cell in the range that contains the graph you select.

Selecting a Graph Type

By default, when you use the Graph New command, 1-2-3 for Windows represents the selected data as a line graph in the Graph window. You easily can change the type of graph with the Chart Type command (from the Graph window's Menu bar).

10

The Chart Type dialog box is a special dialog box that contains not only option buttons for choosing from the 11 basic graph types, but also a *graph gallery* that shows you the variations available within each type.

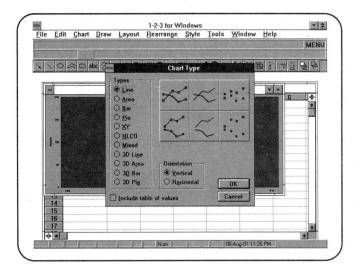

When you select the Line option button in the Chart Type dialog box, 1-2-3 displays six line graph variations in the graph gallery.

To choose one of the graph type variations displayed in the graph gallery, click that variation. 1-2-3 outlines the graph type variation you select so that it appears more three-dimensional than the other variations.

The number and kind of variations differ with each graph type. Graph types, such as the Area, Pie, HLCO, and 3D Pie, provide only one choice. Other basic types (Line, Bar, XY, Mixed, 3D Area, and 3D Bar) provide two or more variations.

Graph type variations encompass differences in the way data points or data ranges are represented in the graph. In many cases, you can choose between stacked (also called clustered) and unstacked versions of the graph. When you use a stacked version, 1-2-3 for Windows draws each data range on top of the other. The exact way this is accomplished varies from graph type to graph type. In the stacked versions of a line graph, the lines representing each data range often cross each other. In the stacked version of a bar graph, each data range is represented by its own color or pattern in a single bar.

10

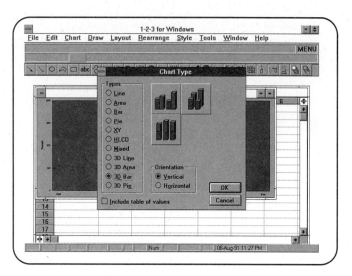

When you select the 3-**D** Bar option button in the Chart Type dialog box, 1-2-3 displays three 3-D Bar graph variations in the graph gallery.

To change the graph type, select the basic graph type (under Types), click the variation you want to use (in the graph gallery), then click the OK button.

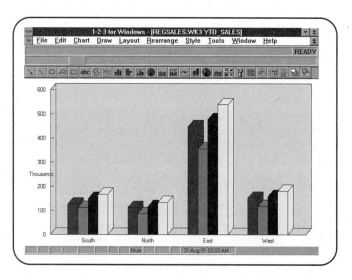

10

In this example, you see the YTD_SALES data in a 3-**D** Bar graph, using the first variation in the graph gallery.

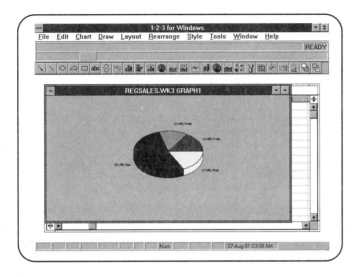

In this example,
you see the
YTD_SALES data
as a 3-D pie chart.

Guidelines for Selecting a Graph Type

As you select a graph type, consider which basic graph type best represents
your data. Keep in mind the following guidelines:

- Line and area graphs usually plot changes in data over time.
- Bar graphs usually plot data at a specific point in time.
- Pie graphs show the relation of each part to the whole. A pie graph uses only one set of data and each value must be positive.
- XY graphs (also called *scatter graphs*) show correlations between two types of numeric data.
- HLCO graphs (also known as *stock market graphs*) track fluctuations in data. These graphs are ideal for tracking stock prices.
- Mixed graphs combine bar and line graphs. These graphs are useful for plotting different types of data in the same graph.

Table 10.4 describes each of these graph types.

Table 10.4
Graph Types in 1-2-3 for Windows

Type	Description
	Line graphs plot up to six sets of data as stacked or unstacked lines, points, or lines.
	Area graphs plot up to six sets of data as lines with the area beneath each line filled in.
	Bar graphs plot up to six sets of data as clustered or stacked bars.
	Pie graphs plot a single set of data as wedges of a circle.
	XY graphs plot up to six sets of data as stacked or unstacked points, lines, or points and lines, using a scaled x-axis.
	HLCO graphs plot up to four sets of data as high-low-close-open lines, a fifth set as 2-D or 3-D bars, and a sixth set as a line.
	Mixed graphs plot up to three sets of data as clustered or stacked bars and up to three sets of data as lines or as lines with the area beneath each line filled in.
	3D **Li**ne graphs plot up to six sets of data as stacked or unstacked three-dimensional lines.
	3D **A**rea graphs plot up to six sets of data as three-dimensional lines with the area beneath each line filled in.
	3**D** Bar graphs plot up to six sets of data as clustered or stacked three-dimensional bars.
	3D **Pie** graphs plot a single set of data as wedges of a three-dimensional disk.

10

Changing the Orientation of the Graph

Of the eleven graph types in 1-2-3 for Windows, all but the pie graphs display both x- and y-axes. Line, area, bar, HLCO, and mixed graphs display numbers (centered on the tick marks) along the y-axis only. The XY graph displays numbers on both axes.

By default, 1-2-3 draws the x-axis along the bottom of the graph and the y-axis along the left side of the graph. If the graph has a second y-axis, as is often used when drawing an HLCO or mixed graph, the program draws this axis along the right side. You can select this normal orientation (*portrait* mode) with the Vertical option button under Orientation in the Chart Type dialog box.

You also can change the orientation to *landscape* mode by selecting the Horizontal option button under Orientation in the Chart Type dialog box. In this case, 1-2-3 draws the x-axis along the left side of the graph, the y-axis along the top of the graph, and the second y-axis (if the graph has one) along the bottom of the graph.

Including a Table of Values

If you select a line, area, bar, or mixed graph type (in 2-D or 3-D form), you can include a table that shows the data point values at the tick marks along the x-axis (beneath the x-axis labels).

To create such a table, select the Include table of values check box, which appears at the bottom of the dialog box only when you select a graph type that supports this feature, before you select the OK button.

10

In this example, you see the YTD_SALES data in a graph drawn by selecting the 3-D Line and Include table of values options in the Chart Type dialog box.

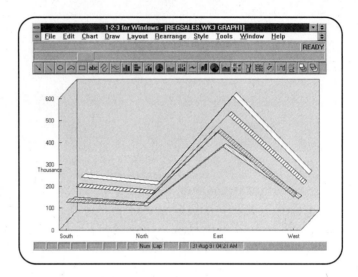

Specifying Data Ranges

All graph types, with the exception of pie graphs, can represent more than one set of data. You can graph up to six different sets of values, for example, when you create a line, area, or bar graph. 1-2-3 assigns a letter (from A through F) to each set of data in the graph.

If each set of data in the graph is in an adjacent column with the labels for the x-axis in the first column, you can specify all the data ranges in one operation by selecting the range in the worksheet before choosing the **G**raph **N**ew command. Suppose that you have a worksheet that contains a table with sales figures for all four quarters. You can plot the numbers for every quarter by selecting the entire range of values before choosing the **G**raph **N**ew command.

10

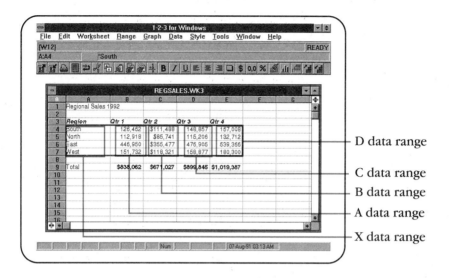

D data range

C data range

B data range

A data range

X data range

1-2-3 for Windows assigns the data in each column of the range you select to a new data range in the graph.

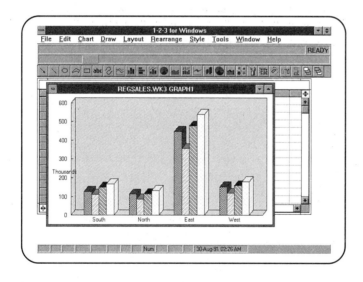

The graph generated from the selected range is visible after you change the graph type from Line to 3-D Bar. Each bar represents sales in a different quarter.

10

To check or change the data ranges that 1-2-3 assigns when you choose the Graph New command, choose the Chart Ranges command from the Graph window's Menu bar.

The Chart Ranges dialog box displays the X, A, B, C, and D data ranges that 1-2-3 assigned.

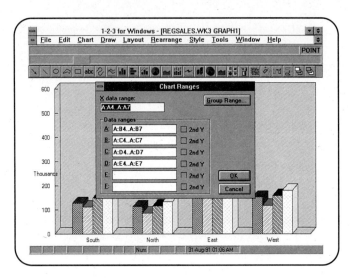

Defining One Data Range at a Time

Many times the sets of data you want to graph do not appear in the worksheet in such a way that you can define them correctly by selecting a range in the worksheet and choosing the Graph New command. For example, if the ranges you want to plot are located in various parts of the worksheet, you must define one range at a time.

To define each data range individually, follow these steps:

1. Position the cell pointer on the first cell of the range that contains the x-axis labels.

2. From the Graph menu, select the New option.

3. Enter a name for your graph in the Graph name text box, and select the OK button.

    1-2-3 opens a new Graph window that contains only a graph frame.

4. From the Window menu, select the Tile option.

5. From the Chart menu, select the Ranges option.

6. With the range in the **X** data range text box selected, designate the new range in the worksheet that contains the x-axis data (you can highlight the range by clicking the worksheet). Then drag the mouse pointer or type the range address.

7. Press ⟨Tab⟩ to select the **A** text box under Data ranges, and then designate the range in the worksheet that contains the A data. To assign this data range to the second y-axis, select the 2nd Y check box to the right of the text box.

8. Repeat step 7, selecting **B**, **C**, **D**, **E**, and **F** (as needed) to define the other data ranges in your graph.

9. Select the OK button.

Defining a Group Range

If the ranges are adjacent to one another, but the data in each one runs across the rows rather than down the columns, you must use the Chart Ranges dialog box to redefine the data ranges. In this case, however, you can select the **G**roup Range command button and define all the data ranges in a single operation.

For example, assume that you want to graph the quarterly sales data by region rather than by quarter. In this case, the X and the A through D data ranges extend across each row of the table rather than down each column so that the x-axis labels are in the range B2..E2, the A data range is in B3..E3, the B data range is in B4..E4, and so on.

To modify all the data ranges at one time, follow these steps:

1. Select the Graph window that contains the graph whose data ranges you want to modify, then choose the **C**hart menu and select the **R**anges option.

2. Select the **G**roup Range command button in the Chart Ranges dialog box.

   1-2-3 displays the Chart Ranges Group Range dialog box.

3. Select the **R**owwise option button under Divide into data ranges.

4. Select the **R**ange text box, then designate the range that contains all the data sets for the graph.

10

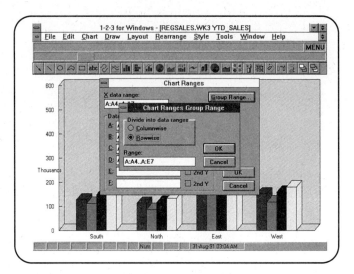

In this example, select the range A4..E7 to designate the data sets.

5. Select the OK button in the Chart Ranges Group Range dialog box.

   1-2-3 updates all the data ranges in the Chart Ranges dialog box to suit the new orientation.

6. Select the OK button in the Chart Ranges dialog box.

   1-2-3 redraws the graph in the Graph window.

10

In this example, you see the 3-D bar graph plotted by regions after you specify a Rowwise orientation and a new group range. Notice that the quarters appear as the x-axis labels. Each bar represents sales in a different region.

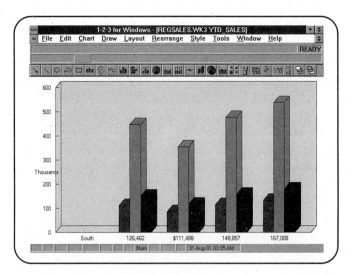

Enhancing the Appearance of a Graph

1-2-3 for Windows provides a host of features designed to enhance the appearance of a basic graph. This section examines the most used features for augmenting a graph, including how to add headings, a legend, data labels, and background grids and how to modify and format the scales of the axes. The next section describes techniques for annotating a graph with graphic objects such as boxes and arrow callouts, as well as how to select fonts and assign colors or shading patterns to the graph. You make all enhancements in the Graph window with the Graph window commands.

1-2-3 for Windows refers to the different parts of a graph as *objects*. The graph itself (including the x- and y-axes, grid, headings, and data points) is a single object. Each line, rectangle, arrow, or other shape you then add to the graph is considered a separate object. Likewise, each unit of text you add to the graph (outside of headings) is a separate object. 1-2-3 enables you to manipulate these objects individually or as a group.

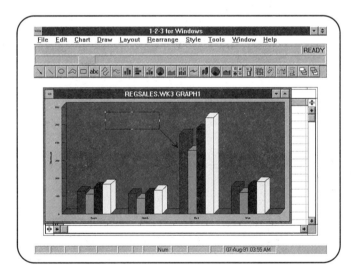

You can select an object in a graph by clicking it with the mouse. *Selection indicators* (small squares) appear within the object or around its sides.

10

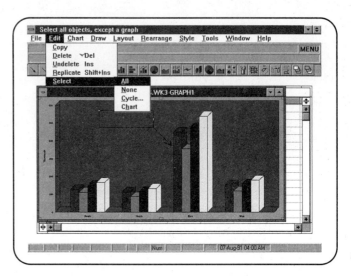

You also can select an object by choosing the **Edit Select** command, then choosing the appropriate option in the cascade menu.

You can select an individual object in a graph by clicking it with the mouse or choosing the **Edit Select** command, then selecting the appropriate option in the cascade menu. To select every object in the graph, use the **Edit Select All** command. To select just the graph (including its headings and legend), choose the **Edit Select Chart** command. To deselect all selected objects, choose the **Edit Select None** command.

10

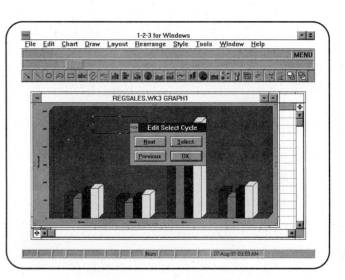

You can use the **Next** or **Previous** buttons in the Edit Select Cycle dialog box to select an object in the graph, then click the **Select** and OK buttons.

You can select a group of objects by dragging the mouse to draw a rectangle that encloses the objects. As you drag the mouse, the pointer changes shape from an arrowhead to a hand pointing to the left. You also can select a group of objects by holding the Shift key as you click each object you want to include. You can deselect an object simply by clicking the mouse somewhere outside that object. The only exception is the graph itself: to deselect the graph, you must click somewhere inside its borders (but not on one of the squares).

To help you enhance a graph, you can use the **W**indow options to change the size of the graph as you work:

- **En**large (+) incrementally enlarges the size of the graph.
- **Re**duce (–) incrementally reduces the size of the graph.
- **F**ull (*) returns the graph to its original size.
- **Z**oom (@) enlarges a particular portion of the graph. To use this option, use the cross-hair pointer to draw a box around the area of the graph you want to enlarge.

The shortcut keys (especially + and –) make it easy to experiment with various graph sizes as you add enhancements.

Adding Headings to a Graph

You can use the **Chart H**eadings command to add a centered title or subtitle to a graph. You also can use this command to add up to two lines of footnotes at the bottom of a graph. By default, 1-2-3 centers the title and subtitle at the top of the graph and prints the title in a larger font than the subtitle. The text of the notes appears in the lower left corner of the graph in a much smaller font.

When entering headings in the Chart Headings dialog box, you can type the text of the heading or enter a backslash (\) followed by the address of the cell that contains the label you want to use as the heading (such as \C15).

To add titles or footnotes to a graph, follow these steps:

1. Select the Graph window that contains the graph to which you want to add headings by clicking the window or by pressing ⌨Ctrl + ⌨F6.
2. Choose the **C**hart menu, then select the **H**eadings option.

   1-2-3 displays the Chart Headings dialog box containing four text boxes: **T**itle, **S**ubtitle, **N**ote, and **2**nd Note.

10

357

3. Select the Title text box, then type the text for the title of your graph or enter a backslash (\) followed by the address of the cell that contains the label you want to use as a title.

4. To use a subtitle, select the Subtitle text box and enter the text or cell address.

5. To add a footnote to the graph, select the Note text box and enter the text or cell address of the first note.

6. To add a second footnote to the graph, select the 2nd Note text box and enter the text or cell address of the second note.

7. Select the OK button.

You can enter a title, subtitle, and footnotes for the graph in the Chart Headings dialog box.

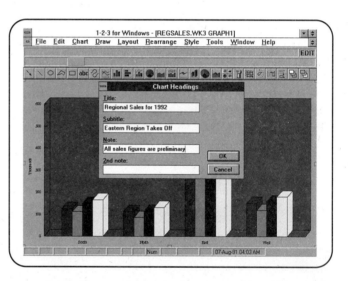

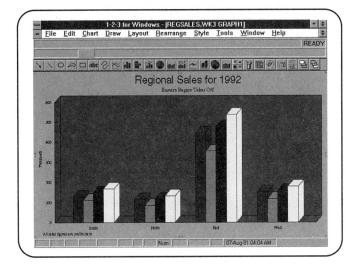

Here, the headings added in the Chart Headings dialog box appear in the graph.

Adding a Legend to a Graph

Whenever a graph plots more than one set of data, you need to distinguish one data set from another. To distinguish the sets of data, you can create a *legend* that indicates the color, pattern, or symbol assigned to each data set. As with headings for the graph, you can enter the legend text in the appropriate text box by typing the text or by entering a backslash (\) followed by the address of the cell that contains a label you want to use (such as \B10).

To add a legend to your graph, follow these steps:

1. Select the Graph window that contains the graph to which you want to add the legend.

2. Choose the Chart menu, then select the Legend option.

   1-2-3 displays the Chart Legend dialog box containing six text boxes: A through F.

3. In the A text box, type the text of the legend for the A data range or enter a backslash (\) followed by the address of the cell that contains the text.

4. Press Tab ⇄ to select the next Legend text box. Repeat step 3 to enter legend text for all the data sets in your graph, then select the OK button.

10

359

Enter legend text for all the data sets in your graph, then select the OK button.

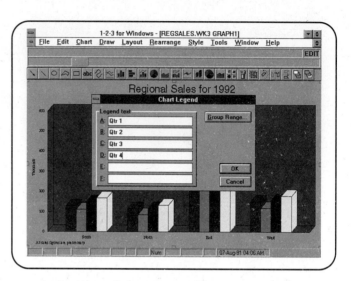

1-2-3 displays the legend for the graph at the bottom of the x-axis.

10

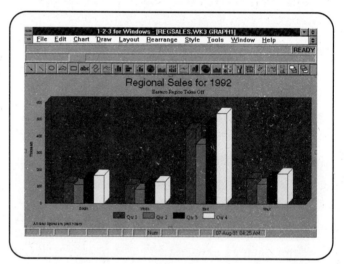

To edit a legend, return to the Chart Legend dialog box and edit the legend text, cell reference, or range name for the appropriate data range, then select the OK button.

Note: If your worksheet contains a range of labels in a single column or row that appear in the same order as the data sets appear in the graph, you can create the legend with the **G**roup Range option in the Chart Legend dialog box. Designate the range containing the labels for the legend in the Chart Legend Group Range dialog box, then select the OK option to return to the Chart Legend dialog box, then select the OK option again to return to the Graph window.

Adding Data Labels to a Graph

After you have graphed a data series, you can enter values or labels to explain each point plotted on a bar, line, or XY graph. For example, on a line graph illustrating sales figures, you can label points with the specific values for each point.

To add data labels to a graph, you use the **C**hart **D**ata Labels command. You then designate the range that contains the labels or values you want to display in the graph and the position (in relation to the data points) you want them to have.

To add labels to a graph, follow these steps:

1. Select the Graph window that contains the graph to which you want to add the data labels.

2. Choose the **C**hart menu, then select the **D**ata Labels option.

   1-2-3 displays the Chart Data Labels dialog box containing six text boxes: **A** through **F**. Each text box has a drop-down list box.

3. In the **A** text box, designate the range that contains the data labels for the A data range.

4. To place the labels for a data set in a position other than centered on each data point, select the data set's drop-down list box and select a different option: Above, Below, Left, or Right.

10

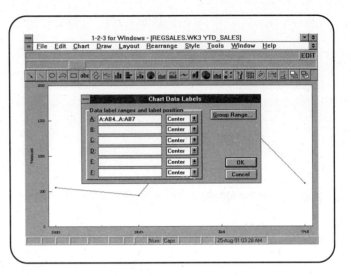

In this example, designate A:B4..A:B7 as the **A** data label range and select Center as the label position.

5. Repeat steps 3 and 4 for all the other data ranges (**B** through **F**) used in the graph, then select the OK button.

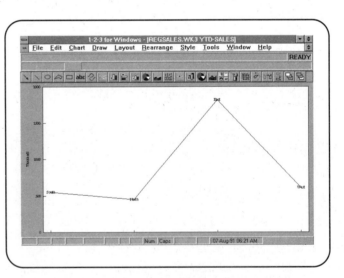

Here, 1-2-3 displays the YTD_SALES graph with data labels centered above each data point.

Note: If your worksheet contains a range of values that appear in the same order as the data sets appear in the graph, you can add the labels with the **Group Range** option in the Chart Data Labels dialog box. Designate the range containing the data labels in the **Range** text box of the Chart Data Labels

10

Group Range dialog box, then select the appropriate position in the **Label** position drop-down list box, then select the **Columnwise** or **Rowwise** option button. Finally, select the OK option to return to the Chart Data Labels dialog box, then select the OK option again to return to the Graph window.

Adding a Background Grid

As the default background for all graph types that use x- and y-axes, 1-2-3 draws a frame (borders) that encloses the data points and tick marks on each axis. Sometimes you may want to add grid lines to the background so that the data points are easier to read. You also may want to remove part or all of the borders that form the graph frame.

To add a grid to your graph or alter the borders, follow these steps:

1. Select the Graph window that contains the graph you want to modify.

2. Choose the **Chart** menu, then select the **Borders/Grids** option.

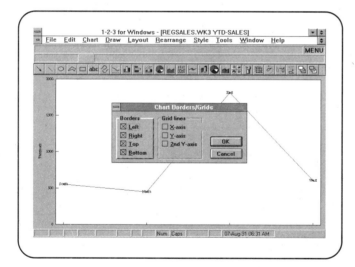

1-2-3 displays the Chart Borders/ Grids dialog box.

3. To add grid lines, select the appropriate check box(es) under Grid lines:

   X-axis draws vertical grid lines from each tick mark on the x-axis.

   Y-axis draws horizontal grid lines from each tick mark on the y-axis.

   2nd Y-axis draws horizontal grid lines from each tick mark on the second y-axis.

4. To remove part or all of the frame around the graph, deselect the appropriate check box(es) under Borders: **Left, Right, Top,** or **Bottom.**

5. Select the OK button.

In this example, the YTD_SALES graph includes grid lines added to the x- and y-axes with the **Chart Borders/ Grids** command.

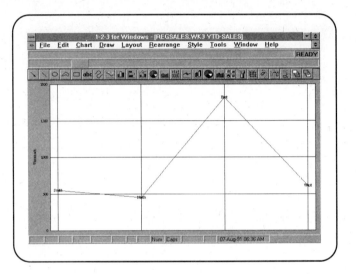

Changing Axis Scale Settings

You can use the **Chart Axis** command to alter various attribute and format settings for the x-axis, y-axis, or second y-axis.

To change axis settings, select an axis option from the **Chart Axis** cascade menu.

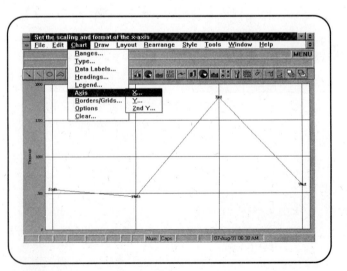

When you choose an axis option (**X**, **Y**, or **2**nd Y) from the **Chart Axis** cascade menu, 1-2-3 displays a dialog box that enables you to change axis attribute and format settings. These settings include the upper and lower limits of the scale, the axis units, the type of scale, the format of the axis values, the title of the axis, and the name of the scale indicator. For the x-axis, you also can change the number of labels.

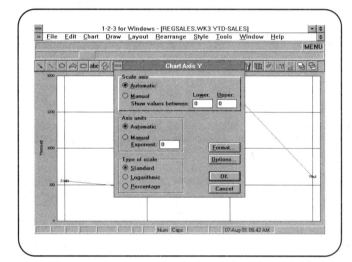

Here, you see the options and default settings in the Chart Axis Y dialog box. The same options appear when you select the **X** or 2nd Y Chart Axis options.

Changing the Upper and Lower Limits of the Scale

When you create a line, XY, bar, or stacked-bar graph, 1-2-3 automatically sets scale limits for the y-axis, taking into account the smallest and largest numbers in the plotted data ranges. (For XY graphs only, 1-2-3 also establishes x-axis scale values.)

You can change the upper and lower limits of the scale, but you cannot determine the increment (indicated by the tick marks) of the scale between the maximum and minimum values you set.

To change the scale for one of the axes of a graph, follow these steps:

1. Select the Graph window that contains the graph whose scale you want to modify.

2. Choose the Chart menu, then select the Axis option.

   1-2-3 displays a cascade menu of axis options.

10

3. Select the X, Y, or 2nd Y option on the cascade menu to set the scale of the corresponding axis.

   1-2-3 displays the Chart Axis (X, Y, or 2nd Y) dialog box.

4. Select the Manual option button under Scale axis, then enter the lower limit for the scale in the Lower text box and the upper limit in the Upper text box.

   In establishing manual limits, remember two basic rules:

   You must specify both upper and lower settings.

   The upper limit must be larger than the lower limit. You can use negative figures for scale values in line and XY graphs only: the lower limit in a bar, stacked-bar, or mixed graph is 0 (zero).

5. Select the OK button.

   1-2-3 redraws the graph using the new limits for the selected scale.

To reestablish 1-2-3's automatic scale, select the Automatic option button under Scale axis in the appropriate Chart Axis dialog box, then select the OK button.

Formatting the Axis Values

1-2-3 automatically sets the format of the scale values to General. 1-2-3 does not automatically display dollar signs, commas, and decimal points along the y-axis. To change the format of the values on the y-axis, second y-axis, or x-axis (for XY graphs only), follow these steps:

1. Select the Graph window that contains the graph whose scale you want to format.

2. Choose the Chart menu, then select the Axis option.

3. Select the X, Y, or 2nd Y option on the cascade menu to format the scale of the corresponding axis.

4. Select the Format command button in the Chart Axis (X, Y, or 2nd Y) dialog box.

5. In the Format list box, choose a new format for the selected scale.

6. In the Decimal places text box, enter the number of decimal places you want to use in the format (0 is standard, although 2 is the default).

10

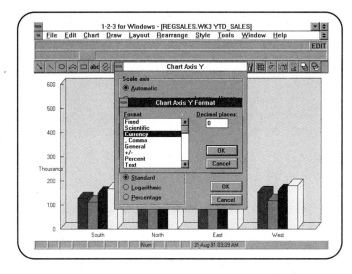

In this example, select the Currency format with 0 decimal places as the new format for the y-axis scale.

7. Select the OK button to return to the Chart Axis (X, Y, or 2nd Y) dialog box.

8. Select the OK button again to return to the Graph window and put the new scale format into effect.

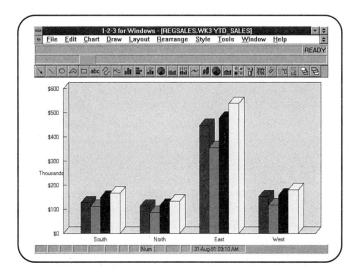

Here, you see the YTD_SALES graph after selecting the Currency format with 0 decimal places for the y-axis scale.

10

Note: Assigning a new format to the scale values has no effect on numbers displayed in the graph as data labels. Format these values in the worksheet.

Modifying the Scale Indicator or Adding an Axis Title

The *scale indicator* indicates the magnitude of the scale values displayed along the y-axis (and the 2nd y-axis, if used) when you create a graph. On an XY graph, a scale indicator also appears along the x-axis.

You can use the **M**anual option in the Chart Axis (X, Y, or 2nd Y) Options dialog box to change the scale indicator or to suppress its display. You also can use the A**x**is title option in this dialog box to add a title for the selected axis. 1-2-3 displays this x-, y-, or 2nd y-axis title in the same orientation as the scale indicator.

To understand why you might want to change the indicator or suppress its display, imagine a worksheet that contains data where you did not enter trailing zeros (for example, you entered sales figures such as 94,008,000 into the worksheet as 94,008). Graphing such figures produces the y-axis indicator Thousands, but you need the indicator Millions. In this case, you modify the indicator to display the appropriate text.

To modify the axis scale indicator or add an axis title, follow these steps:

1. Select the Graph window that contains the graph whose scale indicator you want to modify.
2. Choose the **C**hart menu, then select the A**x**is option.
3. Select the **X**, **Y**, or **2**nd Y option on the cascade menu to set the scale of the corresponding axis.
4. Select the **O**ptions command button in the Chart Axis (X, Y, or 2nd Y) dialog box.

    1-2-3 displays the Chart Axis (X, Y, or 2nd Y) Options dialog box.
5. To add an axis title, select the A**x**is title option, then type the text of the title or enter a backslash followed by the address of the cell or name of the range that contains the title.
6. To change the scale indicator, select the **M**anual option button under Name of units, then enter the new scale indicator in the text box. To suppress the display of the default scale indicator, select the **M**anual option, but leave the text box empty (or delete its contents).

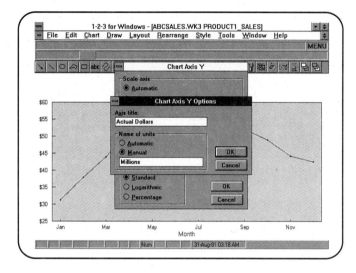

In this example, enter **Actual Dollars** as the y-axis title and **Millions** as the y-axis scale indicator (replacing Thousands).

7. Select the OK button.

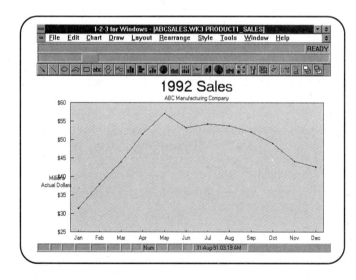

Here, you see a graph after adding Actual Dollars as the y-axis title and replacing Thousands with Millions as the y-axis scale indicator.

10

Spacing the Display of X-Axis Labels

Sometimes, when graphing data sets that contain many values, you find that the x-axis labels are so crowded that 1-2-3 truncates or overlaps their text (especially when you use a large font). To avoid overcrowding and improve the appearance of this part of the graph, you can suppress the display of every other or every third x-axis label.

369

To suppress the display of some labels, you select the **Chart Axis X O**ptions command, then enter a *skip factor* in the **D**isplay label every ___ ticks text box. For example, to display every other x-axis label, you enter a skip factor of 2 in this text box. You seldom need to set the skip factor higher than 3 or 4.

In this example, enter **Month** as the x-axis title and **2** as the skip factor.

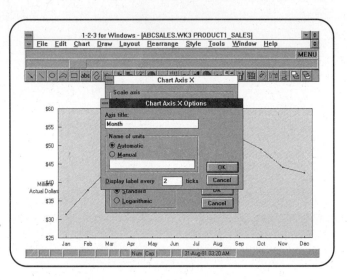

10

Here, you see the graph after using a skip factor of 2 to display every other month as the x-axis labels.

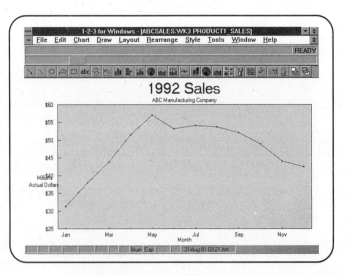

Specifying Connecting Lines or Symbols

By default, 1-2-3 line graphs include lines connecting the symbols that represent each data point. You can use the **Chart Options Lines** command to add or suppress the connecting lines or the symbols, and you can fill in the area of any line-type graph (including line, XY, and mixed graphs).

To specify the use of connectors, symbols, or area fill in a line-type graph, follow these steps:

1. Select the Graph window that contains the line-type graph whose data point symbols you want to modify.

2. Choose the Chart menu, then select Options.

   1-2-3 displays a cascade menu of Chart Options.

3. Select the Lines option.

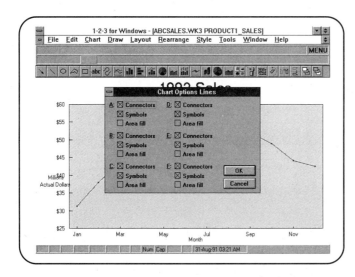

1-2-3 displays the Chart Options Lines dialog box with Connectors, Symbols, and Area fill check boxes for every possible data set (**A** through **F**).

10

4. Select the appropriate check boxes for the first data set you want to modify:

   To display the connecting lines between data points, select the Connectors check box.

   To display the symbols for each data point, select the Symbols check box.

   To have 1-2-3 fill the area beneath the data points, select the Area fill check box.

To suppress the display of any of these elements, deselect that check box.

5. Repeat step 4 for every data set you want to modify.

6. Select the OK button.

Working with Graphic Objects

1-2-3 for Windows provides a number of drawing tools that enable you to add to your graph such graphic objects as text, lines, arrows, polygons, rectangles, and ellipses. You also can draw graphic objects freehand.

You can use graphic objects to help you annotate your graphs. For example, you can add a brief explanation about why a data point is unusually high or low. The following example demonstrates how text, an arrow, and a rectangle can point out a value on a graph.

This graph is annotated with text enclosed in a rectangle and an arrow that points out an unusual value in the graph.

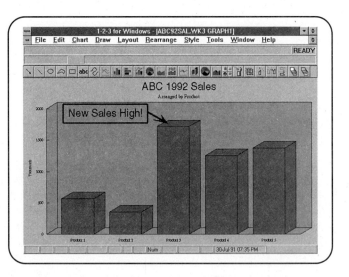

Adding Text to a Graph

You do not type text directly into the graph. Instead, you add the text in two steps. First, you type the phrase in the text box of the Draw Text dialog box. Second, you position the text in the graph. The text can include up to 512 characters.

To add text to a graph, follow these steps:

1. Choose the Draw menu, then select the Text option.

    1-2-3 displays the Draw Text dialog box.

2. In the text box, type the text you want to add to the graph or enter a backslash (\) followed by the address of the cell or name of the range that contains the text (such as \A5).

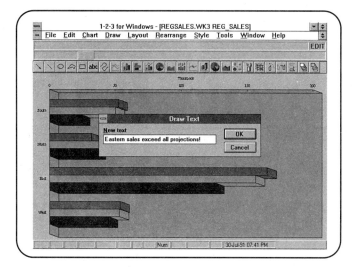

In this example, enter the phrase **Eastern sales exceed all projections!** in the text box.

3. Click the OK button.

    The text appears in the graph and remains selected (the selection indicators appear in the text).

4. With the mouse, move the cross-hair pointer to position the text in the appropriate location in the graph. Click the mouse to fix the text's position (the selection indicators appear around the text).

5. Click the mouse a second time outside of the text to deselect the text.

10

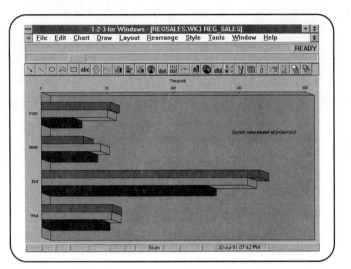

In this example, you see the text you entered in the Draw Text dialog box positioned and fixed in the graph.

To add text quickly with the mouse, click the Draw Text SmartIcon in the Icon palette, which appears in the Worksheet window.

Adding Lines and Arrows

The process of drawing lines and arrows involves indicating the beginning and end point of the line or arrow. Note that the only difference between a line and arrow is that the arrow has an arrowhead at the end point of the line.

To draw a line or arrow, follow these steps:

1. Choose the Draw menu, then select the Line or Arrow option.

10

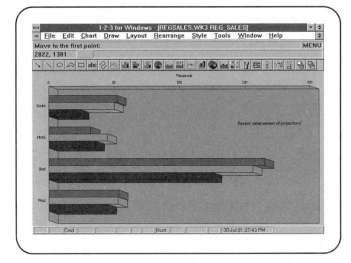

The pointer
changes shape
from an arrow-
head to a cross-
hair. The prompt
`Move to the`
`first point`
appears in the
Format line of the
control panel.

2. Click the first point of the line or arrow.

   The prompt `Stretch the line to the next point` appears in the
   Format line of the control panel.

3. Drag the cross-hair pointer to the end point of the line, then double-
   click the mouse or press ⏎Enter to complete the line.

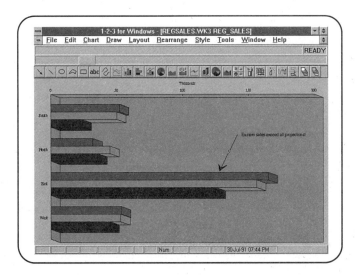

1-2-3 completes
the line.

10

375

If you don't use a mouse to draw your lines or arrows (by far the easiest method), you use the arrow keys to move the cross-hair pointer to the first point and press the space bar to anchor that point. Then, you use the arrow keys to move the pointer to the second point and press Enter to complete the line or arrow.

The line or arrow appears on-screen and the selection indicator appears in the center of the line. If you are adding an arrow, the arrowhead appears at the second point you indicated. To reverse the direction of the arrow, use the **Start of line** option in the Style Lines dialog box. To change the style or line width of the line or arrow, use the **Style** or **Width** option in the Style Lines dialog box.

You can connect several lines by pressing the space bar or clicking the left mouse button for each line-ending. When you finish drawing connected lines, double-click or press ⏎Enter

You may find that drawing straight horizontal, vertical, or diagonal lines is difficult; the lines look somewhat jagged. To prevent jagged lines, press and hold the Shift key before you stretch a line to its last point. The line segment then snaps to the nearest 45-degree angle, enabling you to draw a perfectly straight line.

Adding Polygons to a Graph

A polygon is a closed graphic figure with more than one side. The figure can have as many line segments as you want to include. When you use the **Draw Polygon** command, 1-2-3 automatically draws the last line segment, connecting the last point selected to the first point.

The steps for creating a polygon are similar to the steps for creating lines and arrows:

1. Choose the **D**raw menu, then select the **P**olygon option.

   The Format line prompts you to Move to the first point.

2. Use the mouse or arrow keys to move the cross-hair pointer to one end of the line.

3. Click the mouse or press the space bar to anchor this point.

   The Format line prompts you to Stretch the line to the next point.

10

4. Use the mouse or arrow keys to move the cross-hair pointer to the end of the first line segment.

5. Click the mouse or press the **space bar** to anchor this point.

6. Repeat steps 4 and 5 to draw every side except the last side of the polygon.

7. Double-click the mouse or press ⏎Enter when you reach the beginning point for the last side of the polygon.

   1-2-3 automatically connects the last point to the first point in the polygon, drawing the last side of the figure.

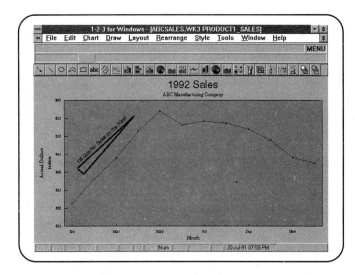

In this example, you see a triangle created with the **D**raw **P**olygon command.

Adding Rectangles and Ellipses

You can use the **D**raw **R**ectangle and **D**raw **E**llipse commands to enclose text and other objects on a graph. For example, you can annotate a part of a graph by drawing a rectangle around graphic text and then drawing an arrow to the part of the graph.

To draw rectangles and ellipses, follow these steps:

1. Choose the **D**raw menu, then select the **R**ectangle or **E**llipse option.

377

2. Position the cross-hair pointer in the upper left corner of the rectangle or ellipse.

3. Drag the mouse diagonally until the rectangle or ellipse has the size and shape you want, then release the mouse button.

The middle of each side of a rectangle or ellipse has selection indicators. To change the type of line (solid, dashed, or dotted) used in the rectangle or ellipse, use the **Style** option in the Style Lines dialog box. To change the width of the line, use the **Width** option in this dialog box.

To create a circle (when you choose **Ellipse**) or a square (when you choose **Rectangle**), press and hold the Shift key before you set the object's size. The object may not appear perfectly circular or square on-screen, but it does print accurately.

Adding Freehand Drawing

When you use the **Draw Freehand** command, the effect is like drawing in the Graph window with a pencil. Unless you have artistic ability, freehand drawing looks like freehand scribbling. To add free-floating text that annotates your graph, you may want to use the **Draw Text** command rather than the **Draw Freehand** command.

For freehand drawing, you must use a mouse. To draw freehand, follow these steps:

1. Choose the **Draw** menu, then select the **Freehand** option.

2. Position the cross-hair pointer at the place where you want to begin drawing.

3. Click and hold the left mouse button.

   The pointer changes shape from the cross-hair to a pencil.

4. Drag the mouse to draw the freehand shape or text you want to add.

5. Release the mouse button when you finish drawing the last part of the freehand graphic or text.

Each segment of the freehand drawing displays a selection indicator.

To change the type of line (solid, dash, or dotted), use the Style option in the Style Lines dialog box. To change the width of the line, use the **Width** option in this dialog box.

10

Manipulating and Transforming Objects in a Graph

1-2-3 for Windows provides a wide variety of commands for manipulating the objects you place in a graph. You can copy a selected object with the **Edit Replicate** command or by pressing Shift+Ins. You can delete objects with the **Edit Delete** command or by pressing Del. You can undelete objects with the **Edit Undelete** command or by pressing Ins.

You can rotate, flip, or adjust the size of a selected graphic object with the following options on the Graph window's **Rearrange** menu:

- **Flip** has two options: **Horizontal** and **Vertical**. Use the Horizontal option to flip the object over so that the upper left corner of the object becomes the upper right corner. Use the **Vertical** option to flip the object upside down so that the upper left corner of the object becomes the lower left corner. To restore an object to its original position, select the same **Flip** option or SmartIcon.

- **Quarter-Turn** rotates the selected object counterclockwise in 90-degree increments.

- **Turn** rotates the selected object clockwise or counterclockwise in any increment. When you select this option, 1-2-3 displays an axis line with the cross-hair pointer at its end. Drag the pointer in either direction to rotate the object. Double-click the object or press Enter when the object has the orientation you want.

- **Adjust Size** enables you to change the size of the object. When you select this option, 1-2-3 encloses the object in a dotted rectangle with the cross-hair pointer in its lower right corner. Move this pointer to increase or decrease the size of the object, then double-click the mouse or press Enter to set the new size.

- **Clear** returns the selected object to its original size and orientation.

You can move objects in front of or behind other objects or lock objects in the graph (so that no further changes can be made to them) with the following options on the Graph window's **Layout** menu:

- **Send Forward** places the selected object in front of any other objects that overlay it. Use this command when an object (such as text) is obscured by another (such as a filled shape).

10

- **Fall Back** places the selected object in back of any other objects that it overlays. Use this command when an object (such as a filled shape) obscures another (such as text).
- **Lock** prevents you from changing the selected object in any way. When you lock an object, you can no longer move, delete, or transform it (you can, however, still replicate it). 1-2-3 indicates that an object is locked by changing the shape of the selection indicators from squares to diamonds.
- **Unlock** removes the protection from the selected locked object.

Note: Remember that before using any of these commands, you must first select the object(s) you want to affect. The easiest way to select an object is to click it with the mouse. To select more than one object, drag the mouse to draw a boundary that encloses all the objects or press the Shift key as you click each object. You also can select all the objects in a graph by choosing the **Edit Select All** command.

Moving Objects in a Graph

To move an object in a graph, you simply click the object and drag it to its new position. While you drag the object, a rectangle of dotted lines appears around it (until you release the mouse button). When you are satisfied with the position of the object, click outside the object to deselect it.

10

Selecting Fonts for Graphs

1-2-3 for Windows enables you to select different fonts for the graph headings and text graphic objects in your chart. To select new fonts for the titles and headings, you use the **Chart Options Fonts** command as follows:

1. Choose the **Chart** menu, then select **Options**.

   1-2-3 displays a cascade menu of chart options.

2. Select the **Fonts** option from the cascade menu.

   1-2-3 displays the Chart Options Fonts dialog box.

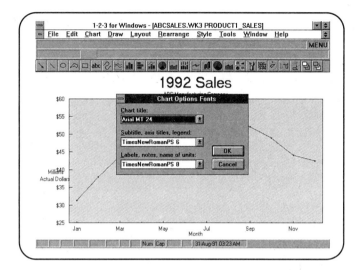

In the Chart
Options Fonts
dialog box, you
can change the
font used for the
graph title; for the
subtitle, axis
titles, and legend;
or for the data
labels, footnotes,
and the x-axis and
y-axis labels.

3. To change the font for the graph's title, select a new font in the Chart
   title drop-down list box.

4. To change the font used for the subtitle, axis titles, and legend, press
   Tab⁺ to select the Subtitle, axis title, and legend drop-down list box,
   then select a new font.

5. To change the font used for data labels, footnotes, and the x-axis and
   y-axis labels, select the Labels, notes, name of units drop-down list
   box, then select a new font.

6. Select the OK button.

To select a font for the text you entered as graphic objects with the Draw Text
command, use the Style Font command rather than the Chart Options Fonts
command.

10

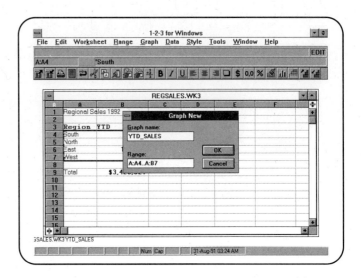

When you select the **S**tyle **F**ont command, 1-2-3 displays the Style Font dialog box.

In the Style Font dialog box, select a new font in the **F**onts list box. To decrease or increase the size of the font by a particular percentage, select the **M**agnify all fonts text box and enter a percentage between 1 and 1000 (100 percent represents the actual size of the selected font).

Assigning Colors and Patterns to Graphs

10

When you create a new graph, 1-2-3 automatically assigns colors to the parts of the graph (on a monochrome monitor, the colors appear as shades of gray). You can change the colors used to represent any of the data sets, any of the headings, or any of the graphic objects you created.

To change the color of the graph's headings or data points, you use the **Chart Options Colors** command as follows:

1. Choose the **C**hart menu, then select **O**ptions.
2. Select the **C**olors option from the Chart Options cascade menu.

   1-2-3 displays the Chart Options Colors dialog box.

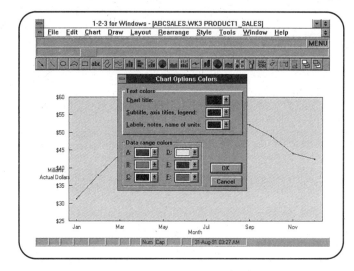

In the Chart Options Colors dialog box, you can change the color of the headings or of any data range in the graph.

3. Select the drop-down box for the text or data range colors you want to change:

   Select **Ch**art title to change the color of the graph title.

   Select **S**ubtitle, axis titles, legend to assign a new color to the subtitle, axis titles, or legend in the graph.

   Select **L**abels, notes, name of units to assign a new color to any data labels or footnotes in the graph and to the x-axis and y-axis labels.

   Select **A**, **B**, **C**, **D**, **E**, or **F** to change the color of the data points representing any of the data sets used in your graph.

4. After selecting new colors for all the parts of the graph you want to modify, select the OK button.

To change the colors of the graphic objects in a graph (including text added with **Draw Text**), you use the **Style Color** command rather than the **Chart Options Colors** command. To change the colors of graphic objects, follow these steps:

1. Choose the **Style** menu, then select the **Color** option.

   1-2-3 displays the Style Color dialog box.

10

In the Style Color dialog box, the Text and Line drop-down list boxes each display a list of nine color choices. The Interior fill and Background drop-down list boxes each display a palette of 256 colors and patterns.

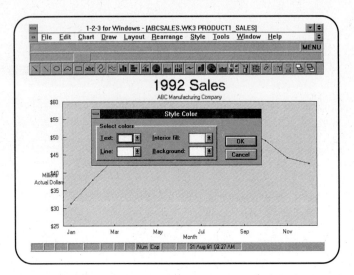

2. Select the drop-down list box of one of the Select colors options:

Select Text to set a new color for text added with the Draw Text command.

Select Line to set the color for the selected line or arrow or for the outline of the selected rectangle, ellipse, polygon, or freehand drawing.

Select Interior fill to set the color for the inside of the selected rectangle, ellipse, polygon, or freehand drawing. If an arrow is selected, 1-2-3 assigns the color to the interior of the arrowhead.

Select Background to set a new color for the background of the entire graph.

Assigning Hatch Patterns

In addition to assigning new colors, you also can assign hatch patterns to the data sets. To assign hatch patterns, follow these steps:

1. Choose the Chart menu, then select Options.
2. Select the Hatches option from the Chart Options cascade menu.

1-2-3 displays the Chart Options Hatches dialog box.

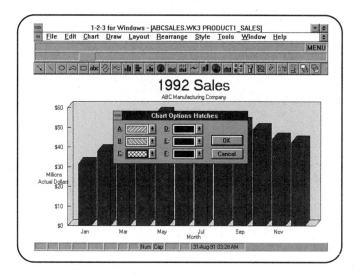

In the Chart Options Hatches dialog box, you can assign patterns to any data range in your graph (**A** through **F**).

3. Select the drop-down box of the data set to which you want to assign a hatch pattern, then select the new pattern.

4. After assigning hatch patterns to all the data ranges you want to modify, select the OK button.

Assigning Colors to Pie Charts

Pie charts plot values in a single (A) data range. Therefore, you can't use the Data range colors options in the Chart Options Colors dialog box to assign different colors to a pie chart's slices. To assign colors to individual slices of the pie, you must enter code numbers that indicate the color you want to use. You enter the code numbers in a range of the worksheet that is the same size as the A data range used to generate the pie chart. Then, you assign these code numbers to the pie chart as the B data range using the **Chart R**anges command.

To assign a color for each pie slice, you choose a color, then enter its code number (between 0 and 7) in the corresponding cell of the worksheet range designated as the pie chart's B data range. The colors represented by the numbers from 1 to 7 correspond to the colors assigned to the color palette in the Window Display Options Palette dialog box. In other words, if green is the second color on this palette, you enter the code number 2 to make a

10

particular slice of the pie chart green. You enter this code number in the same position in the B data range that the value used to draw this slice has in the A data range. To suppress the display of a particular slice of the pie chart, you enter 0 as the color code number.

For example, assume that you created a pie chart with five slices using the range A8..A12 as the X data range and B8..B12 as the A data range of the graph.

To assign colors to this chart, you enter the color code numbers in the range C8..C12 of the worksheet and then designate C8..C12 as the B data range in the Chart Ranges dialog box.

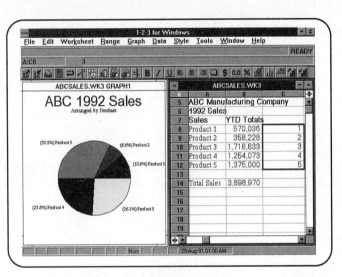

To explode a slice of the pie chart (that is, to emphasize a slice by drawing it apart from the rest of the pie), add 100 to the color code number you enter in the worksheet.

10

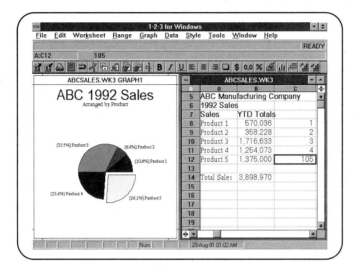

For example, if yellow is the third color and you want to make a slice yellow and explode it at the same time, you enter 103 as the code number.

Note: You can suppress the display of percentages in front of the labels in a pie chart by entering 0 for each slice, then assigning this range of 0 values as the C data range in the Chart Ranges dialog box. Leave blank any cell in the C data range whose corresponding slice you want to continue to display the percentage.

Saving Graphs

1-2-3 automatically links the graphs you create to the worksheet files that are current when you create the graphs (unless you add a file reference for another active file to the graph name). Therefore, 1-2-3 saves your graphs with their worksheets whenever you choose the **File Save** command on the Worksheet window Menu bar. Remember that to use this command, you must switch from the graph to the Worksheet window by clicking part of the Worksheet window (if that window is visible) or by pressing Ctrl+F6 (if it is not visible).

10

1-2-3 saves all changes made to the graph under the graph name you assigned to the graph when you first created it with the **Graph New** command. If you want to save two versions of the worksheet file—one without graphs and another with graphs—use the **File Save As** command to save your graphs and give the worksheet a new name.

Selecting a Graph to Work On

You can create and save as many graphs as you want in any worksheet file. To display a graph so that you can modify it, you use the **Graph View** command on the Worksheet window Menu bar. When you choose this command, 1-2-3 displays the Graph View dialog box.

To view a new graph, select its name in the Graph name list box, then select the OK button.

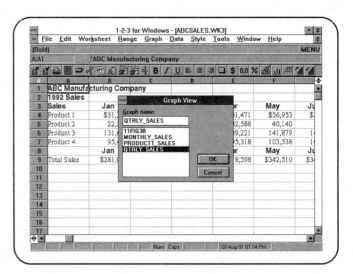

1-2-3 opens a graph window containing the graph you selected and cascades this window in front of the Worksheet window that was current (and in front of any other open windows). To save any changes you make to this graph, remember to select the Worksheet window to which the graph is linked, then select the **File Save** command in the Worksheet window Menu bar.

Clearing Graph Settings

When you enhance a graph, 1-2-3 always saves the changes you make to the default settings. If you are creating a series of graphs during the same work session, you may want to clear some or all of the preceding graph's settings before you create a new graph.

To clear a graph's settings after you create the graph with the **Graph New** command, follow these steps:

1. Choose the **C**hart menu, then select the **C**lear option.

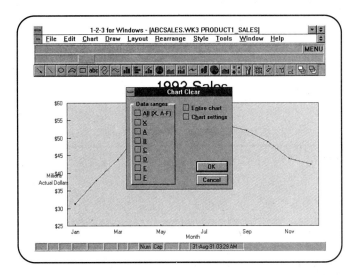

1-2-3 displays the Chart Clear dialog box.

2. Select the check boxes of all options you want to clear:

   Select **A**ll (X, A-F) to clear current x-axis and A through F data-range and data-label settings.

   Select **X, A, B, C, D, E,** or **F** to delete the data range and data labels for the data set(s) you select.

   Select **E**ntire chart to clear all the graph's settings.

   Select **C**hart settings to clear the data-label, headings, legend, axis, color, hatch, font, and line settings.

3. Select the OK button.

Deleting Graphs from a File

As your worksheet file grows, you may find that you need to get rid of older graphs to make room for more data. To delete a graph you no longer need or want in a worksheet file, follow these steps:

1. Choose the **G**raph menu, then select the **N**ame option.

10

1-2-3 displays a cascade menu of Graph Name options.

2. Select the **D**elete option.

   1-2-3 displays the Graph Delete dialog box.

3. To delete a particular graph, select its name in the **G**raph name list box, then select the **D**elete command button. To delete all graphs in the file, select the Delete **A**ll command button instead.

4. Select the OK button.

Note: You can use the **G**raph Na**m**e **P**aste Table command to create a worksheet table that lists all the graphs linked to the current worksheet file. This command works just like the **R**ange **N**ame **P**aste Table command.

Adding Graphs to a Worksheet

To print a graph, you must first add it to the current worksheet file. To print the graph alone, you can place it in a new area of the worksheet or in its own worksheet. To print a graph with its supporting worksheet data, you must place the graph in a blank cell range that is above, below, or to the side of the data you want to print with the graph.

To add a graph to a worksheet, follow these steps:

1. Select the Graph window that contains the graph you want to add to the worksheet.

2. Choose the **S**tyle menu, then select **D**isplay Options.

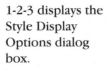

1-2-3 displays the Style Display Options dialog box.

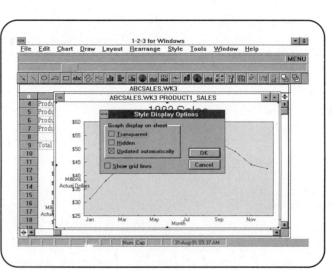

390

3. Select one or more of the following check boxes:

Select Transparent to change the display from opaque (the default), which hides worksheet data under the graph, to transparent, which enables you to see worksheet data under the graph.

Select Hidden to turn off the display of the graph in the worksheet. The program shows only a shaded rectangle in the range where you place the graph; however, even when you hide a graph in the worksheet, 1-2-3 prints the graph when you include its range in the print range.

Select Updated automatically to make 1-2-3 update the graph in the worksheet as soon as you make changes to the graph's supporting data.

Select Show grid lines to include in the worksheet display any x-axis or y-axis grid lines you added to the graph in the Graph window.

4. Select the OK button.

5. Select the Worksheet window where you want to add the graph by clicking the window or by pressing Ctrl + F6.

6. In the worksheet, select the cell range that you want to contain the graph. Remember that the size and shape of the range you select determine the size and shape of the graph: make sure that the range is large enough to display the graph without distorting it.

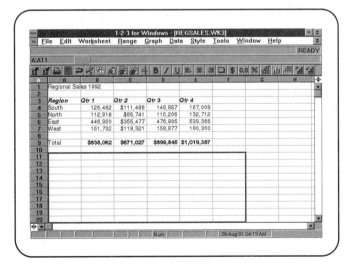

10

Select the cell range you want to contain the graph.

7. Choose the **Graph** menu, then select the **A**dd to Sheet option.

   1-2-3 displays the Graph Add to Sheet dialog box.

8. In the **Graph** name list box, select the name of the graph you want to add to the worksheet.

Select the name of the graph you want to add to the worksheet.

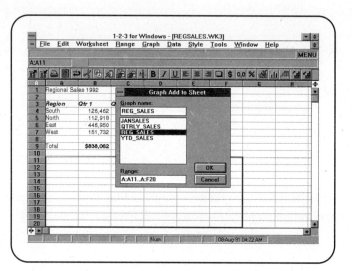

9. Check that the range in the **R**ange list box is correct, then select the OK button.

10

1-2-3 draws the graph in the selected cell range.

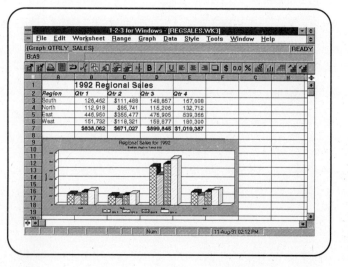

After you embed a graph in a worksheet, you can print the graph by designating its cell range as the print range in the File Print dialog box. To print the graph with other data in the worksheet, include the graph's cell range as part of the print range in the File Print dialog box.

To delete a graph from a worksheet, position the cell pointer in any cell in the range containing the graph and choose the **Edit Delete** command or press the Del key. To restore a graph you deleted in error, choose the **Edit Undo** command or press Alt+Backspace.

If you use the **Graph Name Delete** command to delete the graph from the file, 1-2-3 clears the graph from the range in the worksheet but does not restore the worksheet grid. To enter data in this range of the worksheet again, you must use the **Edit Delete** command or press Del to restore this cell range.

When a graph is embedded in a worksheet, any changes you make to the widths of the columns or heights of the rows in the range containing the graph affect that part of the graph.

To move a graph to a new place in the worksheet file, you can use the **Edit Cut** (Shift+Del) and **Edit Paste** (Shift+Ins) commands or the **Edit Move Cells** command (just as you would move any other range of data in the worksheet).

If you selected the **Updated automatically** check box in the Style Display Options dialog box, 1-2-3 automatically redraws the embedded graph to reflect any changes to its supporting values. If you did not select this check box, you must use the **Graph Refresh** command to update the graph after you make changes to its supporting values.

Note: 1-2-3 does not automatically update the embedded graph to reflect changes to worksheet labels used as graph headings or x-axis labels, even when the Updated automatically option is on; to update these labels, you must use the **Graph Refresh** command.

10

To change the size of a graph after you add it to a worksheet, use the **Graph Size** command as follows:

1. Position the cell pointer somewhere in the range that contains the graph.

2. Select a larger or smaller cell range to increase or decrease the size of the graph.

To decrease the size of an embedded graph, select a smaller cell range.

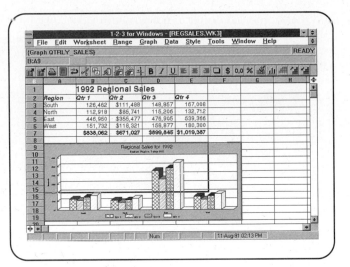

3. Choose the Graph menu, then select the Size option.

   1-2-3 displays the Graph Size dialog box with no names in the Graph name list box.

4. Check the range listed in the Range text box. If the new range is correct, select the OK button.

1-2-3 redraws the graph to fit within the new selected cell range.

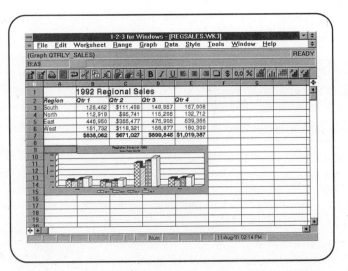

Note: Use the **G**raph Go To command to position the cell pointer in the upper left corner of a range that contains the embedded graph you want to view.

Summary

In this chapter, you learned how to create and print graphs. You learned the basic steps for creating a graph and how to select any one of 1-2-3's seven basic graph types: line, XY, bar, area, pie, HLCO, and mixed. You learned, too, how to improve the appearance of graphs by adding titles, data labels, legends, grids, and formatting; assigning connecting lines and symbols; and altering the scaling of the x- and y-axes. You also learned how to add and manipulate graphic objects, including text, lines, arrows, rectangles, ellipses, polygons, and freehand drawings.

Specifically, you learned the following information about creating and printing graphs in 1-2-3:

- To create a new graph, you select its data in the worksheet, then choose the **G**raph **N**ew command.

- To enhance a graph, you work in a Graph window that has its own Menu bar and Icon palette.

- To choose a new graph type, you use the Chart **T**ype command in the Graph window. You can choose from seven basic graph types, many with several variations.

- To define the ranges for the data sets in your graph, you use the Chart **R**anges command in the Graph window.

- To enhance your graph, you use the other options on the Chart menu. You use **H**eadings to add titles; **D**ata Labels to add labels to each data point; **L**egend to add a legend; **A**xis to modify or format the x-, y-, or 2nd y-axis scales; **B**orders/Grids to draw grid lines for the x- or y-axis; or **O**ptions to set colors, hatch patterns, fonts, or line styles for your graph.

- To add graphic objects to your graph (including text, lines, arrows, polygons, rectangles, ellipses, or freehand drawings), you use the **D**raw menu options.

- To make enhancements to selected graphic options (including selecting new colors and line styles and changing the font or alignment of graphic text), you use the **S**tyle menu options.

10

- To save your graph as part of the worksheet file, you use the **File Save** command in the Worksheet window Menu bar.
- To embed the graph in your worksheet so that you can print it with the **File Print** command, you use the **Graph Add to Sheet** command.
- To remove a graph from a worksheet file, you use the **Graph Name Delete** command.

In the next chapter, you will learn about the third major aspect of 1-2-3: creating and maintaining databases. As part of this process, you learn how to plan, develop, and build a database as well as how to sort and search for specific data.

10

Managing Data

11

In addition to the electronic spreadsheet and business graphics, 1-2-3 provides a third element: database management. 1-2-3's database feature is fast, easy to access, and relatively simple to use. The ease of use is a result of integrating data management with the program's spreadsheet and graphics functions. The procedures for adding and editing items in a database table are the same as those for manipulating cells within a worksheet. On top of that, graphing data in a database table is no different from graphing any other worksheet data.

Planning and building a database

Sorting database records

Searching for records

Copying records

Performing other query operations

11

Key Terms in This Chapter

Database	A collection of data organized into fields and records so that you can list, sort, or search its contents.
Field	One information item, such as an address or a name.
Field names	Labels in the first row of a database that identify the contents of each field or column.
Record	A collection of associated fields. In 1-2-3, a record is a row of cells within a database.
Key field	A column (or field) that determines sorting order for rows in a database.
Input range	The range of the database on which 1-2-3 performs query operations.
Output range	The range to which 1-2-3 copies data when extracted from the database.
Criteria range	The range of the database in which you enter range search criteria.

Understanding a 1-2-3 Database

A *database* is a collection of data organized so that you can easily list, sort, or search its contents. The data stored in a database may contain any kind of information, from a list of addresses to overdue accounts. A Rolodex is one form of a database. Other examples of databases include address books and a file cabinet of employee records.

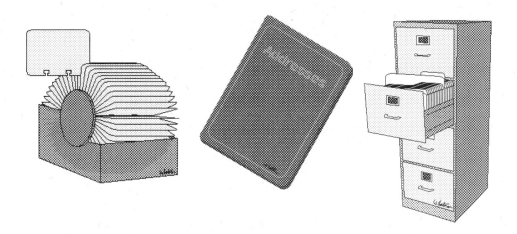

In 1-2-3, you create the database table in a worksheet just as you would create any other schedule or table of data. What distinguishes a database from other tables in the worksheet is the way you organize the data. After you establish the structure of your database table, all the data you enter into the table must follow this structure.

The smallest unit in the structure of a database table is a *field*, or single data item. For example, if you were to develop a database table that contains customer accounts, you might include the following fields of information:

Customer last name
Customer first name
Street
City
State
ZIP code
Area code
Telephone number
Account number
Credit limit

A database *record* is a collection of associated fields. For example, the fields that pertain to one customer form a record in the customer database table. In 1-2-3, a record is a row of cells within the database table just as a field is a single column.

11

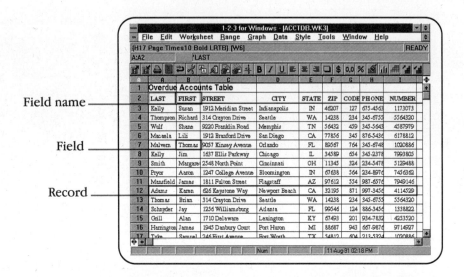

Field name

Field

Record

Always arrange the records in a database table so that you can access the information the table contains. Organizing records on key fields helps you to retrieve information. A *key field* is any field (or column) on which you sort the records in the database table. For example, you might use the ZIP code as a key field to sort the data in a customer accounts database to assign contact representatives to specific geographic areas.

After you build the database table, you can perform a variety of operations. You can sort its data with one or more keys, in ascending or descending order. You can perform various statistical analyses on a field of data over a specified range of records. For example, you can count the number of items in a database that match a set of criteria, or you can compute a mean, variance, or standard deviation. In addition, you can search the database table for specific information using the database commands found in the Data Query dialog box.

Planning and Building a Database

Before you can create a database in 1-2-3, you must determine the categories (fields) of information to include. You can determine these fields by planning what kind of output you expect to produce from your data. Next, decide which area of the worksheet to use. Then create a database by specifying field names in the first row. Finally, enter data in cells beneath these names, as you would for a standard worksheet application.

Entering database contents is simple. The most critical step in creating a database is choosing your fields accurately.

Determining Required Output

1-2-3's data-retrieval techniques rely on finding data by field names. Before you begin typing the kinds of data items you think you may need, write down the output you expect from the database. You also need to consider any source documents already in use that can provide input to the file.

Before you set up the items in your database, consider how you might look for data in each field. For example, consider how you will look for a particular item. Will you search by date? By last name? Knowing beforehand how you will use your database will save time that you would lose if you have to redesign the database.

After you decide on the fields, select the appropriate column width (which you can later modify) and determine whether you will enter the data as a number, label, or date.

	Overdue Accounts Database	
Item	Column Width	Type of Entry
1. Customer Last Name	15	Label
2. Customer First Name	10	Label
3. Street Address	25	Label
4. City	15	Label
5. State	7	Label
6. ZIP Code	6	Label
7. Area Code	6	Number
8. Telephone Number	11	Label
9. Account Number	10	Number
10. Payment Due Date	11	Date
11. Date Paid	11	Date
12. Amount Due	12	Number

Use the following tips for planning various types of fields (columns) in your database:

- For ease in sorting, put last and first names in separate columns. Optionally, put both names in the same cell and separate the last and first names with a comma.

401

11

- Some ZIP codes begin with zero, which would not appear in the cell if you entered it as a value. Enter zip codes as labels by preceding them with a label prefix.

- Set up a separate area code in a different field than your telephone number. This method helps if you want to search, sort, or extract records by area code.

Plan your database carefully before you type field names, set column widths and range formats, and enter data. Although you can make changes after you set up the database, planning helps to reduce the time required for making those changes.

Positioning the Database

You can create a database table in a new worksheet file or as part of an existing one. If you decide to build a database as part of an existing file, choose an area where inserting or deleting rows won't affect the worksheet or another database.

The best way to safeguard your worksheet is to place the database in its own worksheet in the file. That way, you can maintain the database without worrying about corrupting any worksheet data or macros that you use.

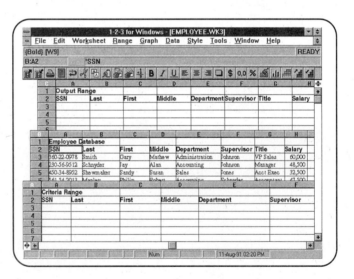

Entering Records

After you plan your database and decide which area of the worksheet to use, you can start entering data. Build a database by specifying field names as labels in the first row of the database table.

402

Make sure that each field name is unique and in a separate column. You can use one or more rows for field names, but 1-2-3 processes only the bottom row. Each field name in the bottom row, therefore, must be unique.

After you enter the field names, enter data for each record as you would for any other 1-2-3 application. Remember that some fields such as ZIP codes, which can be entered as values, should be entered as labels with the use of a label prefix (', ^, or "). Other fields such as address and telephone fields can only be entered as labels and, therefore, always require the use of a label prefix. Because it's easy to forget to add an apostrophe, you can preformat a range of cells in the appropriate column with the Label format. That way, 1-2-3 will enter all data in those cells as labels without requiring any sort of label prefix.

To enter the first record, move the cell pointer to the row directly below the field-names row. Then enter the data across the row in each applicable column (field). As you enter new records, don't skip rows in the database. Don't be overly concerned about the order in which you initially enter the records. Remember that 1-2-3 can sort the database at any time.

After you add your first set of records to the database, change the column widths to fit the information. Either drag the column border with the mouse or use the Worksheet Column Width command.

When you need to add more records to the database later, always add them to the blank rows at the bottom of the table. After you finish adding these records, you can use the Data Sort command to sort the records into the desired order.

Editing the contents of fields in a database is the same as altering the contents of cells in any standard worksheet application. You change the contents by retyping the entry or by using the Edit (F2) key and editing the entry.

Understanding the Data Menu

You use the Data menu for a wide variety of 1-2-3's data management tasks. All other options from the 1-2-3 Main menu work as well on databases as they do on worksheets.

11

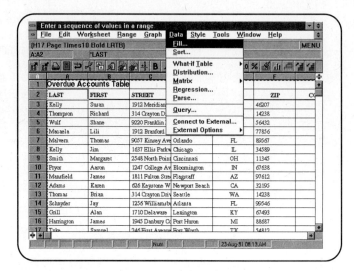

When you choose
the Data menu,
this pull-down
menu of options
appears.

Table 11.1 describes each of the Data menu options.

Table 11.1
The Data Menu Options

Selection	Description
Fill	Fills a specified range with values. You can choose the increment by which 1-2-3 increases or decreases successive numbers or dates.
Sort	Organizes the database in ascending or descending order based on one or two specified key fields.
What-if Table	Substitutes different values for a variable used in a formula; often used to perform extended "what-if" analyses.
Distribution	Finds how often data within a specific range occurs in a database.
Matrix	Enables you to solve systems of simultaneous linear equations and manipulate the resulting solutions.
Regression	Performs multiple regression analysis on X and Y values.

11

Selection	Description
Parse	Separates long labels resulting from the use of the File Import From Text command into discrete text and numeric cell entries.
Query	Offers different options for performing search operations and manipulating the found data items.
Connect to External	Connects you to an external database file. The file may have been created with a database management program such as Paradox or dBASE.
External Options	Lets you work with data from the external database you're connected to.

In the Data menu, the Sort and Query (search) options are true database management operations. Sort enables you to specify the order in which you want the records of the database organized. You can, for example, sort by number, by name, or by date. With Query, you can perform many search operations, enabling you quickly to display a specific record without having to scan a multitude of records.

Sorting Database Records

Storing data in a database is meaningless if you cannot alphabetize the data or sort it numerically. Sorting is an important function of any database. 1-2-3's data management capability enables you to change the order of records by sorting them according to the contents of the fields.

11

In this example, the records in the database (range A1..L20) will be sorted alphabetically by name.

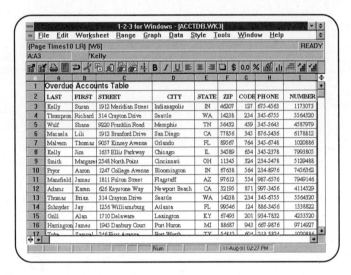

To sort data in a worksheet or a database table, use the Data Sort command as follows:

1. Select the range of data you want sorted.

   If you are sorting a database, don't include the row of field names with the other records in the sort range. Otherwise, 1-2-3 will sort them in with the other records.

1-2-3 displays the Data Sort dialog box. The Data range text box shows the currently selected range. The **P**rimary key text box shows the current cell.

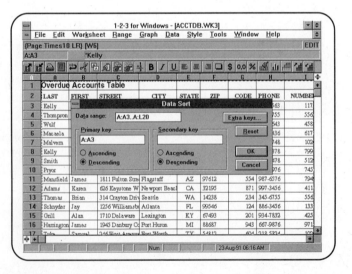

11

2. From the **D**ata menu, select the **S**ort option.

3. Press [Tab ⇄] or use the mouse to select the **P**rimary key text box. Then select a cell in the first column that should be used in sorting the data range.

4. Leave the Desc ending option button (the default) selected to sort on the primary key in the order Z to A and largest to smallest value. Otherwise, select the Asc ending option to sort on this key in order of A to Z and smallest to largest values.

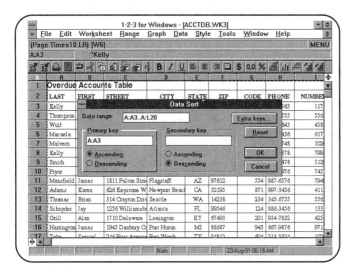

In this example, the Asc ending option button is selected to sort alphabetically by last name.

5. If the column used as the primary key contains duplicates and you want to sort them on a second key, press [Tab ⇄] or use the mouse to select the **S**econdary key text box. Then select a cell in the second column that should be used in sorting the data range.

6. Leave the Desc ending option button (the default) selected to sort on the secondary key in the order Z to A and largest to smallest value. Otherwise, select the Asc ending option to sort this key in order of A to Z and smallest to largest values.

11

In this example, B3 is selected as the secondary key and the Ascending option button is selected to sort alphabetically by first name in the case of duplicate last names (such as the Kellys).

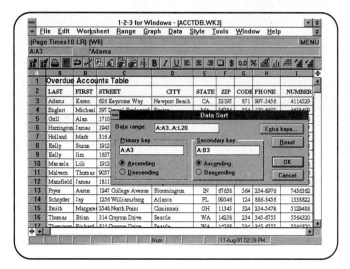

7. If you need more than two keys for sorting, select the Extra keys command button (see next section for details) and define these keys.

8. Select the OK button to sort the selected data range.

Here, you see the database after it was sorted alphabetically in first name, last name order.

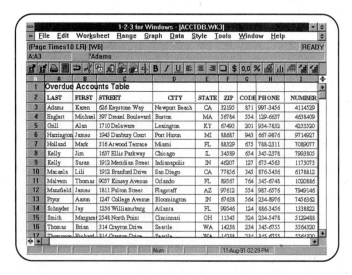

Note: By default, 1-2-3 uses the Numbers First Sort order, which means that the program sorts data in ascending order using the following sequence:

1. Blank cells
2. Labels that begin with a space
3. Labels beginning with a number in numerical order
4. Labels beginning with letters in alphabetical order with lowercase letters preceding uppercase
5. Labels beginning with other characters in order of code in the Lotus Multibyte Character Set (LMBCS)
6. Values in numerical order

If you select the Descending option, 1-2-3 reverses this order. To select a new sorting order (also called the collating sequence), you must use the 1-2-3 Install program (see the Appendix for more information).

Sorting on More Than Two Keys

Some database tables require more than two keys to obtain the desired record arrangement. Assume, for example, that you're working with a personnel database that tracks information on each employee and contains the following fields:

> Social security number
> Last name
> First name
> Middle name
> Department
> Supervisor
> Job title
> Salary

To sort this table by employee's department, supervisor, and name requires at least three keys: department, supervisor, and last name. However, if two employees in the same department share not only the same supervisor, but the same last name, you need to define at least four keys total.

11

In this example, you see the Employee database that needs to be sorted alphabetically by department, supervisor, and employee name.

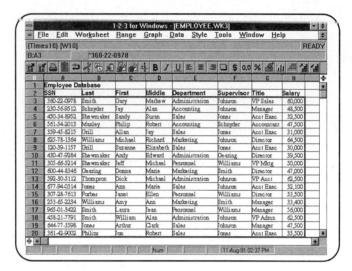

To see how this is done, follow along with the steps for sorting this database with four keys (department, supervisor, last name, and first name):

1. Select the data to be sorted (the range A3..H20 in this example).

2. From the Data menu, select the Sort option.

3. Select E3 in the Primary key text box and the Ascending option to first sort alphabetically by department.

4. Select F3 in the Secondary key text box and the Ascending option to next sort alphabetically by supervisor.

First, you set up the department field (E3) as the primary key and the supervisor field (F3) as the secondary key.

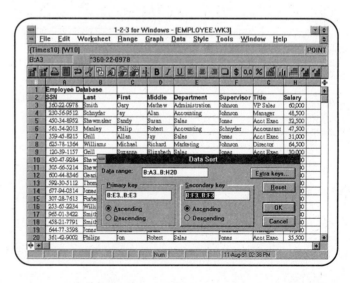

11

5. Select the Extra keys button.

   1-2-3 displays the Data Sort Extra Keys dialog box. The number 1 is already entered in the Key text box. 1-2-3 automatically numbers the extra keys for you as you add each one.

6. Select the Key range text box and select the column you want to use by designating one of its cells in the data range.

7. Select the Ascending or Descending option button under Sort direction.

8. Select the Accept command button and the OK button to add this new key to the Key range list box.

9. Repeat steps 5 through 8 to add as many extra keys (up to 253 total) as you need to perform the sort.

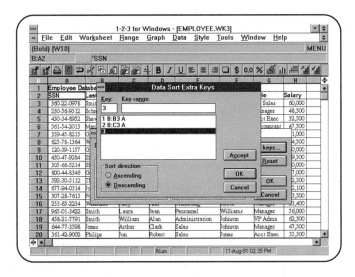

In this example, the Last name field (B3) is designated as the first extra key and the First name field (C3) as the second extra key.

10. Select the OK button in the Data Sort dialog box to sort the data range.

11

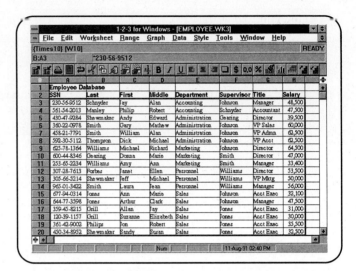

Here, you see the employee database after it has been sorted alphabetically by department, supervisor, last name, and first name.

Removing or Resetting Sort Keys

1-2-3 remembers the data sort range and sort keys that you define in the Data Sort dialog box. If you need to sort a different data table or database in the same worksheet, you may want to use the **R**eset button to clear the data range as well as all the keys that you defined.

If you only need to redefine the sort keys without changing the Data range, you simply select the appropriate key and replace it. To remove a primary or secondary key that you no longer need, simply select the key in the appropriate text box and press `Del`.

To remove an extra sort key, you must redefine it with a key range and sort order used by one of the other extra sort keys. If you want to remove the second extra sort key, for example, select the number 2 in the **K**ey list box of the Data Sort Extra Keys dialog box. Select the Key range text box and enter the same key range used by the first extra key as well as the same sort order option button (**A**scending or **D**escending). Then select the OK button to remove the extra key from the **K**ey list box.

Using Data Fill To Add Record Numbers

After you sort the original contents of the database on any field, you cannot restore the records to their original order unless you use the **E**dit **U**ndo command (Alt+BkSp) before you select another 1-2-3 command. To avoid mistakes and retain the ability to restore the records to the original order at any time, you can add a record number field to the database before sorting. Then, if you need to restore the original order, you simply include the record number field in the data sort range and use this column as the primary key in ascending order.

The quickest way to add sequential numbers in a worksheet or database table is with the Data Fill command. You can use Data Fill to add any sequence of numbers either in ascending or descending order. You also can select the increment to be used to fill in the range with values. For example, you can use Data Fill to increase a range by fives (5, 10, 15, and so on) by using 5 as the step value, or decrease a range by twos (10, 8, 6, and so on) by using –2 as the step value.

To create a record number field and fill it with the Data Fill command, follow these steps:

1. Insert a blank column with the Worksheet Insert Column command. Then reduce the column width with the mouse or use the Worksheet Column Width command.

2. Select the range of cells you want to fill with sequential values.

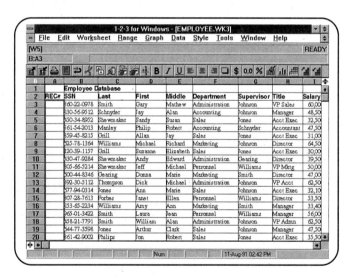

In this example, the range A3..A20 is selected as the data fill range to add record numbers to the employee database.

3. From the Data menu, select the Fill option.

    1-2-3 displays the Data Fill dialog box.

4. To specify a beginning value other than 1, select the Start option and enter the new start value in this text box.

11

5. To specify a step value other than 1, select the Step option and enter the new step value in this text box.

6. To specify a stop value less than 8191, select the Stop option and enter the new stop value in this text box.

In this example, the default values are displayed in the Data Fill dialog box.

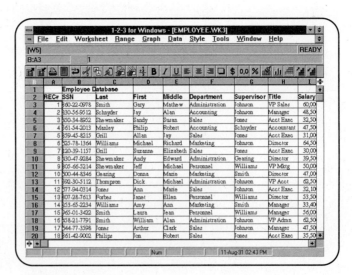

Note: Although the default Stop value of 8191 is larger than it needs to be, 1-2-3 uses only the numbers necessary to fill the specified range.

7. Select the OK button to add the numbers.

1-2-3 fills the range with consecutive numbers beginning with 1 and ending with the number of the last row in the data fill range.

11

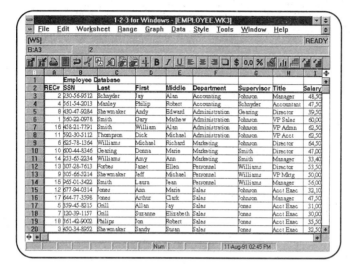

When you sort the database, include the record number field in your data sort range. To restore the table to its original order, use the record number field as the primary key.

Understanding Query Operations

The process of searching for information in a database is called a query operation from the Latin *quaero* (I seek). 1-2-3 enables you to perform several different kinds of query operations.

Finding records that meet your criteria is the simplest form of querying a 1-2-3 database table. You can use the Find operation to edit records. For example, if you're working with a personnel database and you need to update the salary for a particular employee, you can find the record by searching for the person's last and first name and then edit the Salary field.

Extracting records that meet your criteria is one of the most commonly used query operations. You can use the Extract operation any time to compile a special report from the database that includes certain information. In a sales database, for example, you can compile a report that includes only those customers who have ordered more than $500 in merchandise in the last six months. You then can print a report using this group of records or even save them in their own file that you then pass on to the marketing department.

With 1-2-3's query operations, you also have the option of deleting records that meet your criteria or editing them. You then can replace or add the records to the database.

You perform all query operations with the options in the Data Query dialog box.

415

11

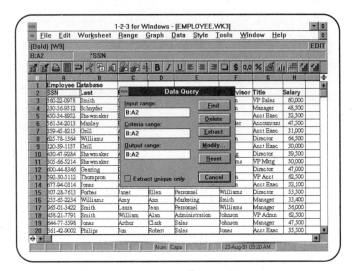

When you select the **Data Query** command, the Data Query dialog box containing these options appears on screen.

Table 11.2 describes the options in the Data Query dialog box. You must create an *input range* and a *criteria range* before you use any of the **Data** Query commands. You also must specify an *output range* if you want to use the Extract or Modify commands.

Table 11.2
Options in the Data Query Dialog Box

Selection	Description
Input range	Specifies the range or ranges that contain(s) the database table.
Criteria range	Specifies the range that contains the criteria for selecting records in the input range.
Output range	Specifies the range where you want the program to copy selected records from the input range.
Extract unique only	Eliminates duplicate records in the output range when you select the Extract command button.
Find	Searches the input range for records based on the criteria.
Delete	Removes selected records from the input range.

416

Selection	Description
Extract	Copies from the input range the records matching the specified criteria and places them in the output range.
Modify	Inserts or replaces records in the input range with records from the output range.
Reset	Resets the input, criteria, and output ranges.

Searching for Specific Records

If you want to search for one or several records that meet certain criteria, you must specify the input and criteria range in the Data Query dialog box, and select the Find command button. Suppose, for example, that you want to search a database table containing a list of all employees to find a specific worker. The following sections describe the procedure.

Defining the Input Range

The input range in the Data Query dialog box indicates the range of records you want to search. The specified area does not have to include the entire database. Whether you search all or only part of a database, you must include the field-names row in the input range. (In contrast, remember that you do not include the field names in a sort operation.) If field names occupy space on more than one row, specify only the bottom row to start the input range. Do not use a blank row or a dashed line to separate the field names from the database records. If you want to separate the field names from the database records, use the Style Border command to place a border on the bottom edge of the range that contains the field names.

Specify the input range and then select the Input range option in the Data Query dialog box. You do not have to specify the range again in later query operations unless the search area changes.

417

11

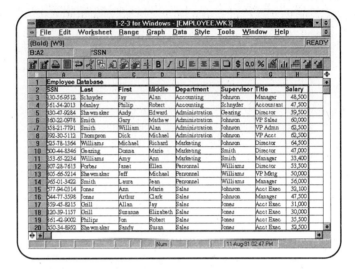

The input range
for the employee
database includes
all the records as
well as the field
names in the
range A2..H20.

Setting Up the Criteria Range

To search for data that meets certain conditions, or criteria, you must set up a special range called a *criteria range*. In the first row of this range, copy all the field names or just the names of the fields you plan to search. Then enter the criteria in one or more rows of the criteria range beneath the field names to be searched. For example, if you want to find all the records in which the supervisor is Jones, enter **Jones** under the field name Last in the criteria range. If you want to find all the records in which the salary is $50,000, enter **50000** under the field name Salary in the criteria range.

Note: The field names of the input range and the criteria range must match exactly.

To keep the criteria range separate from the input range, locate your criteria range on a different worksheet. This technique protects both ranges from the accidental erasing of rows or columns. To add a worksheet, use the Worksheet Insert Sheet command.

Suppose that you want to locate and edit Arthur Jones's record in the employee database. First, insert a new worksheet in the file and then copy all of the field names into the worksheet.

11

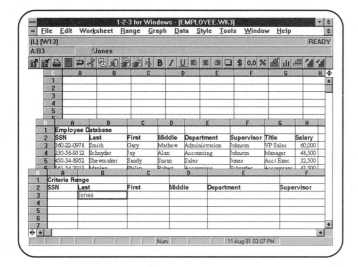

Then, enter the criteria **Jones** under the field name Last in the criteria range.

Finding Records That Meet the Criteria

After you identify the input range and set up the criteria range, you are ready to define them in the Data Query dialog box and select the query operation you want to perform.

To search for records that meet the criteria you have specified, follow these steps:

1. Select the input range (B:A2..B:H20 in this example).

2. From the **D**ata menu, select the **Q**uery command.

    The range you selected appears in the **I**nput range text box.

3. Select the **C**riteria range option, then select the criteria range.

    When designating this range, be sure that you include the row of field names and the row (or rows) beneath the range that contain search criteria.

419

11

In this example, the range A:A2..A:H3 is selected as the criteria range.

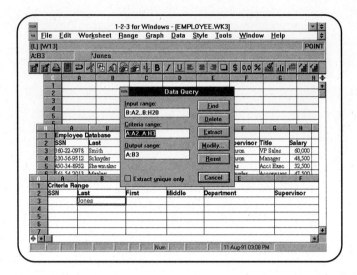

4. Select the **Find** command button.

1-2-3 outlines the first record in the input range that meets the conditions specified in the criteria range. Notice that the mode indicator changes to Find during the search.

In this example, the program selects the first record that includes Jones in the Last field. The record is of Ann Marie Jones in row 14 of worksheet B.

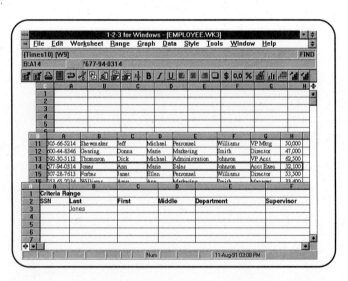

5. Press ↓ to find the next record that meets the specified criteria. You can continue pressing ↓ until 1-2-3 outlines the last record that meets the search conditions.

11

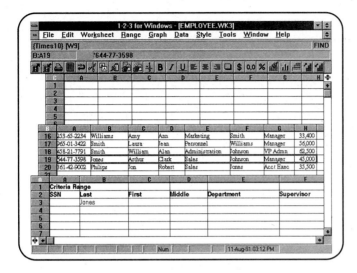

This time 1-2-3 outlines Arthur Jones's record in row 19 of the worksheet, the next occurrence of Jones in the Last name field of the input range.

6. When you want to end the search, press Esc to return to the Data Query dialog box.

7. To return to READY mode, double-click the control menu button in the Data Query dialog box or select the Cancel button.

While 1-2-3 is in Find mode, you can use several keys to navigate the input range. Table 11.3 shows you these keys and describes their functions.

Table 11.3
Editing and Movement Keys in Find Mode

Key	Function
↓	Outlines the next record in the input range that matches the criteria.
↑	Outlines the previous record in the input range that matches the criteria.
→	Selects the next field to the right in the outlined record.
←	Selects the next field to the left in the outlined record.
Home	Outlines the first record in the input range that matches the criteria.

continued

Table 11.3 *(continued)*

Key	*Function*
End	Outlines the last record in the input range that matches the criteria.
F2	Places 1-2-3 in EDIT mode so that you can edit the selected field in the outlined record.
F7	Returns you to READY mode from Find mode, leaving the cell pointer in the currently selected record. Press F7 again to resume the Find operation.
Esc or ↵Enter	Quits the Find operation and returns you to the Data Query dialog box.

Editing Records During a Search

As you can see in table 11.3, in FIND mode you use the right- and left-arrow keys to move to different fields in the currently selected record. Then you can enter new values or use the Edit (F2) key to update the current values in the field. After you finish editing the record, you can continue searching for other records that meet your criteria by using the up- and down-arrow keys.

Suppose, for example, that you want to update the salary for Arthur Jones from $45,000 to $47,500 now that you have located his record. To make this edit, follow these steps:

1. Press → seven times until you see the value 45000 in Contents box in the Edit line.
2. Press F2 or select the value with the I-beam pointer if you're using the mouse.

   1-2-3 changes from Find to Edit mode.
3. Type in the new salary 47500, then press ↵Enter

11

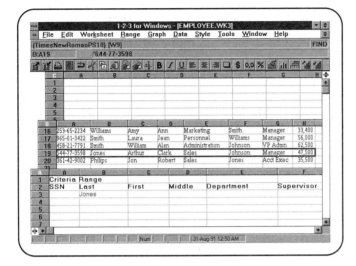

The program enters the new value in the salary field and returns to FIND mode.

4. To find another record with the last name Jones, press ↓. Otherwise, press Esc to exit FIND mode and return to READY mode.

Copying Selected Records

The Find command in the Data Query dialog box has limited use, especially in a large database. The command must scroll through the entire file to find each record that meets the specified criteria. For an alternative to the Find command, you can use the Extract command. This command copies to a blank area of the worksheet only those records that meet specified conditions.

Before you select this option, you must define the blank area of the worksheet as an output range. You can view a list of all the extracted records, or you can print the range of the newly extracted records. You can even use the File Extract To command to copy only the extracted record range to a new file on disk (see Chapter 9 for information on using this command).

Setting Up the Output Range

Choose a blank area in the worksheet as the output range to receive records copied in an extract operation. In the first row of the output range, type the names of only those fields whose contents you want to extract. You do not have to type these names in the same order as they appear in the database. If

11

you want to rearrange or limit the number of fields that appear in the output range, you can do so. Just make sure that the field names in the output range match exactly the corresponding field names in the input range. If you enter a database field name incorrectly in the output range, an extract operation based on that field name does not work.

You can create an open-ended output range by entering only the field-name row as the range. The output range, in this case, can be any size, according to how many records meet the criteria. Or, you can set the exact size of the extract area so that no data located below the area is accidentally overwritten.

An open-ended output range does not limit the number of incoming records. To create an open-ended range, specify only the row containing the output field names as the output range. Keep in mind that an extract operation first removes all existing data from the output range. To limit the size of the output range, select a range that includes a range of empty rows beneath the field names. If you do not allow enough room in the fixed-length output area, 1-2-3 fills the output range and then aborts the extract operation and displays the error message Too many records. Select OK, then designate a larger output range and perform the extract operation again.

To keep the output range separate from the criteria range and input ranges, put your output range on a different worksheet. This protects all ranges from the accidental erasing of rows or columns.

Defining the Output Range

After you enter the names of the fields you want to use in the order you want to see them in the output range, you are ready to define the output range.

To define the output range, follow these steps:

1. From the Data menu, select the Query option.
2. Press Tab ⇄ until the Output range option is selected or select the option with the mouse.
3. To create an open-ended output range, designate just the range that contains the output field names in the Output range text box. To create a fixed-length output range, designate a range that includes the number of blank rows you want to use beneath the output field names.

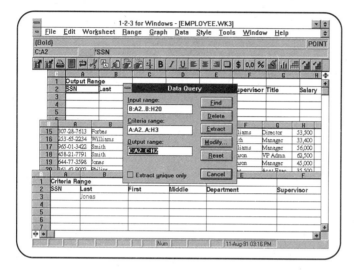

In this example, an open-ended output range is created by selecting the range of output field names in C:A2..C:H2. Note that output field names don't include all of the fields in the input range and don't follow exactly their order.

Using the Extract Command

Before you can use the Extract command, you need to make sure that you have entered the correct search conditions in the criteria range of the worksheet. Then to extract (or copy) to the output range records that meet the specified criteria, select the Extract command button in the Data Query dialog box.

1-2-3 copies all records that meet the criteria specified in the criteria range to the output area. 1-2-3 keeps the same order as in the input range.

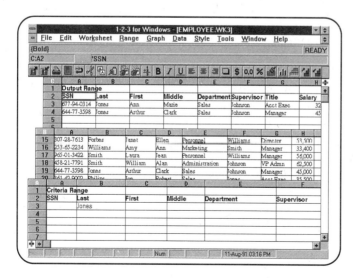

In this example, 1-2-3 copied to the output range all records in which the last name is Jones.

425

11

After 1-2-3 returns to READY mode, you can press the Query (F7) key to repeat the most recent query operation (Extract would repeat in this example, Find would repeat in the previous example). This technique eliminates the need to select the Extract command button again in the Data Query dialog box after changing the search criteria in the criteria range. Use the shortcut method when you don't need to change the locations of the input, criteria, and output ranges.

Setting Up More Complex Criteria

In addition to searching for an exact match of a specified entry within a field, 1-2-3 offers a wide variety of other more complex searches. For example, you can set up search criteria that only partially match the contents of specified fields. Or you can include formulas in your search criteria that match values that are exact or fit within a range of values. You can also use multiple criteria that involve searching for specified conditions in more than one field.

Using Wild Cards in the Criteria Range

Depending on the complexity of your database operations, you may need to be a bit more creative when you are specifying criteria ranges in 1-2-3. For that reason, 1-2-3 enables you to use wild cards and formulas in your criteria range. The following examples show how you can use wild cards in search operations:

Enter	To find
N?	NC, NJ, and NY
BO?L?	BOWLE, but not BOWL
BO?L*	BOWLE, BOWL, BOLLESON, and BOELING
SAN*	SANTA BARBARA and SAN FRANCISCO
SAN *	SAN FRANCISCO and SAN DIEGO, but not SANTA BARBARA
~N*	Strings (in specified fields) that do *not* begin with the letter N

426

You can use 1-2-3's wild cards to match labels in database operations. The characters ?, *, and ~ have special meanings when used in the criteria range. The ? character instructs 1-2-3 to accept any single character in that specific position. Only use ? to find fields of the same length. Use the * character to tell 1-2-3 to accept any and all characters that follow. You can use * on field contents of unequal length. Use the ? and * wild-card characters when you are unsure of the spelling used in field contents. By placing a tilde (~) at the beginning of a search condition, you tell 1-2-3 to accept all values *except* those that follow.

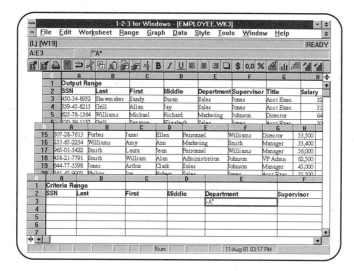

Here, you see the use of wild cards in the ~A* criteria under Department in the criteria range. The output range on worksheet C after an **Extract** includes all records in which the department does not start with the letter A.

Entering Formulas in Criteria Ranges

To set up formulas that query numeric fields in the database, set up logical formulas using the following operators:

>	Greater than
<	Less than
=	Equal to
>=	Greater than or equal to
<=	Less than or equal to
<>	Not equal to

11

Be sure to start the formula with a + (plus sign) and enter the formula under the correct field.

In this example, the logical formula >=60000 was entered in the Salary field of the criteria range. The output range after an extraction includes all records with an amount due greater than or equal to $60,000.

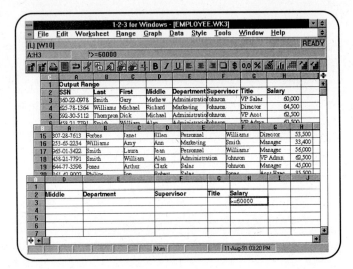

Specifying Multiple Criteria

So far, you have seen how to base a Find or Extract operation on only one criterion. Many times, you will need to use multiple criteria for your queries. When you maintain a criteria range that includes all (or many) field names, you can quickly extract records based on alternative conditions. You also can continue to add more conditions.

You can set up multiple criteria that contain AND conditions or OR conditions. If you want to extract all of the records where the supervisor is Johnson *and* the salary is greater than $45,000, you set up an AND condition. If you want to extract all of the records where the department is Accounting, Marketing, *or* Sales, you set up an OR condition.

To set up an AND condition in the criteria range, you enter the criteria for each field in the same row of the criteria range. When you create an AND specification in the criteria range, 1-2-3 will select the record during the query operation only if each specification is met.

11

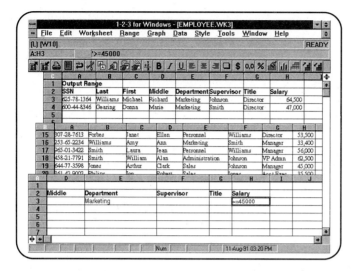

Here is an example of an AND condition. Only records where the department is Marketing and the salary is greater than $45,000 are selected in the output range

To set up an OR condition in the criteria range, enter the criteria for each field on different rows of the criteria range. When you use an OR condition, if any specification is met, 1-2-3 will select the record during the query operation.

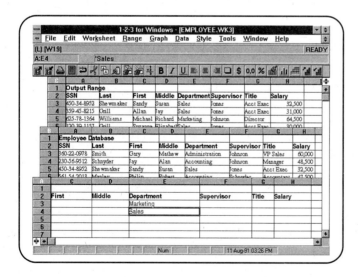

Here is an example of an OR condition. Records where the department is either Marketing or Sales are selected.

When setting up an OR condition that uses several rows in the criteria range, don't forget to increase the size of the Criteria range in the Data Query dialog box. The criteria range should include all of the rows with OR specifications before you perform your query operation.

11

If you are careful when you specify conditions, you can mix both multiple fields and multiple rows within the criteria range. Place all criteria to meet at once in the AND condition in a single row immediately below the criteria field-names row. To find records that match this or that criteria in an OR condition, place criteria specifications in separate rows. Because using multiple criteria may sometimes get confusing, test the logic of your criteria on a small sample of records and verify the results. Then proceed to search all your records according to the multiple criteria.

In this example, 1-2-3 extracts records in which the department is Marketing AND the supervisor is Smith OR the department is Accounting AND the supervisor is Schnyder.

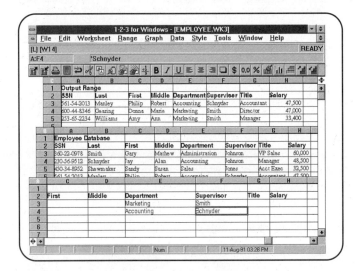

Using Logical Operators in Criteria Formulas

To combine search conditions within a single field, use the logical operators #AND# and #OR#. Use the special operator #NOT# to negate a search condition. Use #AND# or #OR# to search on two or more conditions within the same field. Suppose, for example, that you want to extract all records for the employees in the Personnel and Sales departments in the company. Use the #AND#, #OR#, and #NOT# operators to enter in one field conditions that you could enter another way (usually in at least two fields). You can enter, for example, the following in a single cell in the criteria range:

+Department="Personnel"#OR#Department="Sales"

The reference to Department in the formula shows that you are searching the Department field located in column E.

11

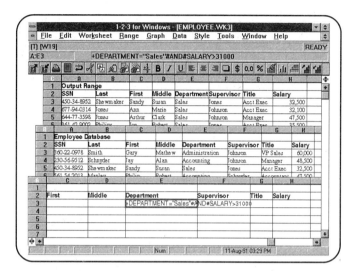

In this example, the criteria formula extracts records where the department is Sales and the salary is greater than $31,000.

Logical formulas normally return 1 when the condition is true and 0 when the condition is false. When entering a logical formula in the criteria range, however, you may find that 1-2-3 returns ERR in the cell instead. This does not mean that the formula cannot be used in the query operation. The error occurs because the 1-2-3 formula refers to the cell containing the field name, and the program can't successfully evaluate a label in a logical formula (the criteria formula works fine when it uses the data in the actual records below).

When working with criteria formulas, select the Text format in the Range Format dialog box for the cells in the criteria range. The Text format lets you plainly see the contents of the formulas in the criteria range. The contents of a criteria formula beneath a field name tells you a lot more about the query operation you're undertaking than 0, 1, or ERR.

Note: Because criteria formulas always contain the field name to which they refer, the field name under which you place them in the criteria range is not critical. Remember though, you must repeat the field name in each part of a compound formula as in this example:

> +Salary>=20000#AND#Salary<=50000

In the following example, 1-2-3 can't evaluate the formula because the field name isn't repeated in each part:

> +Salary>=20000#AND#<=50000

431

11

Performing Other Query Operations

In addition to Find and Extract, you can use the Delete and Modify options to perform specialized query operations. By selecting the Extract unique only check box before you use the Extract option, you can copy into the output range only the first occurrence of a record that meets the specified criteria.

The Delete option enables you to update the contents of your 1-2-3 database by deleting all records that meet the specified criteria. After entering the search conditions, you need to specify only the input and criteria ranges before you issue the Delete option.

The Modify option enables you to extract data to the output range, edit the data, and put the edited records back into the input range. You can also add records to the output range. Modify adds the records to the input range.

Searching for Unique Records

If you want a list of all the departments represented in the employee database, set up an output range that includes only the Department field. To search all records in the input range, you don't enter a specification in the criteria range. Then you choose the Data Query command and place a check mark in the Extract unique only check box before you select the Extract option.

In this example, a list of each department is obtained by restricting the output range to cell C:A2 and not using any specification in the criteria range.

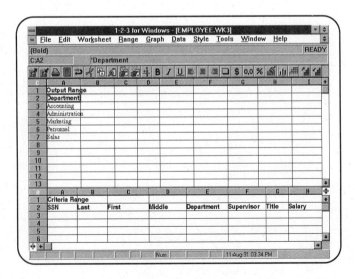

Deleting Specified Records

You can use the Delete button in the Data Query dialog box to remove records from a worksheet. When you use this option, 1-2-3 deletes all records in the input range that match the criteria entered in the criteria range. For this reason, be sure to check your criteria before selecting this button. Select the Find button and review the records that will be deleted before actually removing them with the Delete button. You should save your file with the File Save command right before you use this option.

When you select Delete, 1-2-3 displays a Data Query Delete message dialog box that contains Delete and Cancel buttons. Select Delete to remove all selected records. Select Cancel if you are unsure if you are removing the desired records and want to abort the delete operation.

When 1-2-3 deletes a record in the input range, it removes the entire record from the database table without leaving a blank row. The Delete option is somewhat like the Worksheet Delete Row command. Unlike this command, however, the Delete option does not erase any cells outside of the columns included in the input range.

Modifying Specified Records

The Modify command button in the Data Query dialog box performs a special extract operation that enables you to edit the selected records in the output range and then insert them back into their original position in the database table. This operation is useful when you need to update at one time an entire group of records in the database.

To use Modify, you must specify an output range as well as the input and criteria ranges, as you do with the Extract option. To use the Modify option to make changes in a database, follow these steps:

1. Set up in the criteria range the criteria for which you want 1-2-3 to search.
2. Set up the output range with the field names you want copied when a record is selected.
3. From the Data menu, select the Query option.
4. Check the Input range, Criteria range, and Output range in the Data Query dialog box. Modify them, if necessary.
5. Select the Modify command button.

11

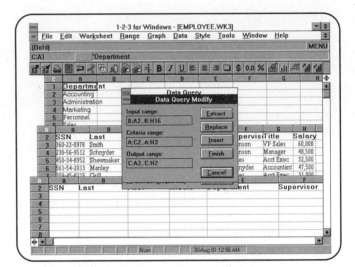

1-2-3 displays the
Data Query
Modify dialog
box.

6. Select the **E**xtract command button in the Data Query Modify dialog box.

   1-2-3 copies all records that meet your criteria to the output range.

7. Edit the records in the output range as necessary. (You can drag the Data Query Modify dialog box out the way if you need to).

8. Select the **R**eplace command button in the Data Query Modify dialog box to replace the original records in the input range with copies of the records you edited in the output range. Otherwise, select the **I**nsert command button to add the edited records as new records at the bottom of the input range.

9. Select the **F**inish command button when you are ready to exit the Data Query Modify dialog box and return to Ready mode.

Summary

In this chapter you learned how to create, maintain, and search database tables created with 1-2-3 for Windows. The options on the Data menu enable you to perform a wide range of database operations. These options include sorting data, filling a range with sequential numbers, and querying the database to find or extract records that meet specific criteria.

Sorting in 1-2-3 is fast and easy, and you can sort on up to 255 fields. When searching for and extracting records, you must create an input range that contains the field names and all records you want to search. You must also

11

create a criteria range to specify the search conditions. When extracting records from a 1-2-3 database, you must also define the output range where you want to copy the extracted data.

Specifically, you learned the following key information about 1-2-3:

■ A database consists of records and fields. In 1-2-3, a record is a row of cells in the database. A field is a column of information within the record.

■ Plan a database carefully before you create it. Determine which categories, or fields, of information you want to include. Also decide what type of output you want.

■ An ideal location for a database is on a blank worksheet. Inserting and deleting rows and columns won't affect other applications. Use the Worksheet Insert Sheet command to create a blank worksheet.

■ Data Sort enables you to change the order of records by sorting them according to the contents of specified key fields. In 1-2-3, you can sort with a primary and secondary key, and up to 253 extra keys, in ascending or descending order.

■ Use the options in the Data Query dialog box to search a database for records matching a specified criteria. Before starting a search, you must first specify an input range and a criteria range in the Input range and Criteria range text boxes, respectively. When using the Extract and Modify command buttons, you must also specify an output range in the Output range text box.

■ The Find command in the Data Query dialog box selects the records that match a given criteria. You can change records as you move the cell pointer.

■ The Extract option in the Data Query dialog box copies records (or specified portions of records) that match a given criteria to the output range. Select the Extract unique check box when you don't want 1-2-3 to copy duplicates in the output range.

■ Use the wild-card characters ?, *, and ~ for more complex search operations. You can also enter formulas in criteria ranges, as well as multiple criteria involving two or more fields.

■ The Delete command button in the Data Query dialog box erases from a database the records that match conditions specified in the criteria range. 1-2-3 asks for confirmation before deleting the records.

11

■ The Modify command button in the Data Query dialog box copies records that match a given criteria to the output range and remember their original position in the input range. You can then edit them in the output range and have 1-2-3 automatically update them or append them to the input range.

You have learned about 1-2-3's worksheet, graphics, and data management capabilities. You are now ready to learn about 1-2-3 macros in the next chapter. Macros enable you to perform simple or complex routine operations by pressing a few keys.

Using Macros

No introductory study of 1-2-3 for Windows would be complete without learning something about the creation and use of macros. Keystroke macros and the advanced macro commands enable you to automate and customize your applications and thus reduce tasks requiring multiple keystrokes to simple two-keystroke operations. Just press the key combination and 1-2-3 does the rest, whether you are formatting a range, creating a graph, or printing a worksheet. You also can control and customize worksheet applications by using 1-2-3's advanced macro commands. These built-in commands give you a greater range of control over your 1-2-3 applications.

You can think of simple keystroke macros as the building blocks of advanced macro command programs. When you add advanced macro commands to simple keystroke macros, you can control and automate many of the actions you need to build and update 1-2-3 worksheets. At the most sophisticated level, you can use 1-2-3's advanced macro commands as a full-fledged programming language for developing custom business applications.

In this chapter, you find an introduction to the concept and application of macros. You also find some simple keystroke macros that you can create and use to build your own worksheets. For more detailed information on macros and the advanced macro commands, consult Que's *Using 1-2-3 for Windows*.

Key Terms in This Chapter

Macro	A series of stored keystrokes or advanced macro commands that 1-2-3 carries out when you press a specific key combination.
Tilde (~)	The symbol used in macros to signify the ⏎Enter keystroke.
Key names	Representations used in macros to signify keyboard keys. You enclose key names in braces: {EDIT}.
Transcript window	The window in which you edit, delete, or play back recorded keystrokes and mouse actions.
Debugging	The process of identifying and fixing errors in a macro or program.

Understanding 1-2-3 Macros

A macro, in its most basic form, is a collection of stored keystrokes that you can replay at any time. These keystrokes can be simple text or numeric entries or key names or advanced macro commands. Macros provide an alternative to typing data and selecting commands with the mouse or the keyboard. Macros, therefore, can save you time by automating frequently performed tasks.

The bottom pane of the Worksheet window displays several simple keystroke macros in worksheet D. The top panel displays the data worksheet A.

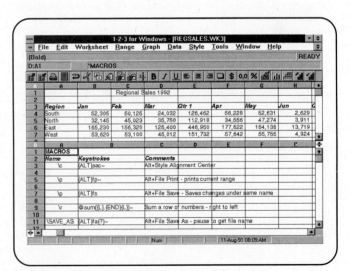

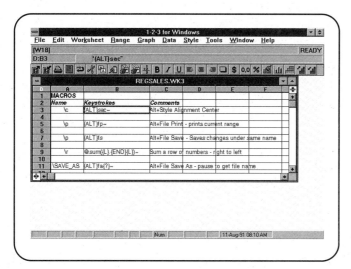

For example, a simple macro can automate the sequence of the five keystrokes needed to center a label in a cell. You can execute this macro in cell D:B3 by pressing two keys, Ctrl + C.

You can name macros in two ways. One way is to use the backslash key (\) and a single letter from A through Z. To run a Ctrl+*letter* macro, you press and hold down the Ctrl key and press the letter that identifies the macro. You also can name macros by using descriptive names of up to 15 characters. To access these macros, you choose the **Tools Macro Run** command, and then select the name of the macro in **Macro** name list box.

Note: All macros created in earlier versions of 1-2-3 work in 1-2-3 for Windows without modification. Macros containing menu commands run by accessing the / command menu in the 1-2-3 Classic Window. Although with earlier 1-2-3 versions you press the Alt key plus the letter key that identifies the macro, you now must press Ctrl plus the letter key to run the same macros in 1-2-3 for Windows.

The Elements of Macros

1-2-3 macros follow a specific format, whether they are simple keystroke macros or macros that perform complex tasks. A macro is nothing more than a specially-named text cell. You create all macros by entering the keystrokes (or representations of those keystrokes) you want to store into a worksheet cell.

You can enter the keystrokes for your macros in two ways: by performing the commands in a worksheet and then pasting the corresponding keystrokes recorded in the Transcript window by 1-2-3 in your worksheet or by typing in the keystrokes yourself.

Suppose that you want to create a simple macro that centers a label in its cell. The macro looks like this:

{ALT}sac~

The following table contains the macro elements of this formatting macro, with descriptions of the actions that result when 1-2-3 executes each element:

Macro Element	Action
{ALT}	Selects the 1-2-3 worksheet Menu bar.
s	Selects the Style menu in the Menu bar.
a	Selects the Alignment option on the Style menu.
c	Selects the Center option button in the Style Alignment dialog box.
~	Selects the OK command button in the Style Alignment dialog box (the tilde is the same as pressing ↵Enter).

If you type the keystrokes in the worksheet yourself, you enter this macro exactly the way you enter any other label. Note that the macro requires no label prefix because the { character that precedes the {ALT} key name is considered to be a label character.

When a macro starts with a non-text character (/, \, +, –, or a number), however, you must begin the macro with a label prefix. Any of the three 1-2-3 label prefixes (', ", or ^) works equally well in this situation.

The first element of the macro, {ALT}, represents the Alt key. This element activates the 1-2-3 Menu bar. The next three characters in the macro represent the menu letters you type to choose the options that select center alignment. After all, sac is simply shorthand for Style Alignment Center.

At the end of the macro is a character called a *tilde*. When used in a macro, a tilde (~) represents the Enter key. In this case, the tilde represents pressing the Enter key to select the OK command button.

Other elements used in macros include range names and cell addresses. Although you can use these two elements interchangeably, you should use range names rather than cell addresses whenever possible. Range names are preferable to cell addresses because range names adjust automatically and the macro continues to refer to the correct cells and ranges if you move data included in specified ranges, or insert or delete rows and columns. Cell references used in macros do not adjust to any changes made in the worksheet; you must change macro cell references manually.

Characters in macro commands are not case-sensitive. You can use uppercase letters wherever you want. This book uses uppercase letters in macros to indicate commands and key names.

Macro Key Names and Special Keys

To enhance the centering macro, you can add key names and special keys to select a range of column headings in a row before choosing center alignment.

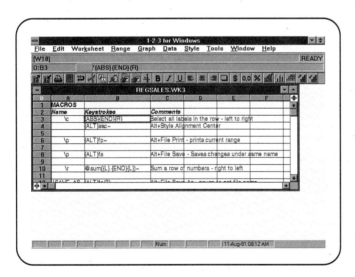

This new line in the macro anchors the range and selects all occupied cells to the right in the current row before choosing center alignment.

12

The revised macro is the same as the preceding version, except that the {ABS}{END}{R} key names anchor the cell pointer on the current cell and then select all the occupied cells to the right in the current row before choosing the center alignment command. You can use this version of the macro to center an entire row of labels rather than center just the label in the current cell.

In the line {ABS}{END}{R} of this macro, the Absolute (F4) key anchors the cell pointer on the current cell. The {END} key name represents the End key on the keyboard. The {R} key name represents the → key (you also can enter this key name as {RIGHT} in the macro). This part of the macro has the same effect as pressing these keys in sequence from the keyboard: the cell pointer moves to the right to the next boundary between blank and occupied cells in the current row.

You use representations like these to signify key names and special keys on the keyboard. In every case, enclose the key name in braces. For example, {UP} represents the ↑ key, {ESC} represents the Esc (Escape) key, and {CALC} represents the F9 function key.

Tables 12.1 through 12.4 provide lists of macro key names and special keys grouped according to their uses. They include function keys, direction keys, editing keys, and special keys.

Table 12.1
Key Names for Function Keys

Function Key	Key Name	Action
F1	{HELP}	Accesses 1-2-3's on-line help system.
F2	{EDIT}	Edits the contents of the current cell.
F3	{NAME}	Displays a dialog box containing a list of the range names in the current worksheet.

Function Key	Key Name	Action
F4	{ABS}	Anchors the cell pointer or converts a relative reference to absolute or an absolute reference to relative.
F5	{GOTO}	Moves the cell pointer directly to the specified cell address or range name.
F6	{WINDOW}	Moves the cell pointer to the other pane of a split Worksheet window.
F7	{QUERY}	Repeats the most recent Data Query operation.
F8	{TABLE}	Repeats the most recent table operation.
F9	{CALC}	Recalculates the worksheet.
F10	{ALT} or {MENU} or {MB}	Selects the Menu bar for the current window type.
Alt + F6	{ZOOM}	Enlarges or shrinks the current Worksheet window.
Alt + F7	{APP1}	Selects the add-in program assigned to keys Alt+F7.
Alt + F8	{APP2}	Selects the add-in program assigned to keys Alt+F8.
Alt + F9	{APP3}	Selects the add-in program assigned to keys Alt+F9.

12

12

Table 12.2
Key Names for Direction Keys

Direction Key	Key Name	Action
⬅	{LEFT} or {L}	Moves the cell pointer left one column.
➡	{RIGHT} or {R}	Moves the cell pointer right one column.
⬆	{UP} or {U}	Moves the cell pointer up one row.
⬇	{DOWN} or {D}	Moves the cell pointer down one row.
Ctrl + ⬅ or ⇧Shift Tab	{BIGLEFT}	Moves the cell pointer left one window-width.
Ctrl + ➡ or Tab	{BIGRIGHT}	Moves the cell pointer right one window-width.
PgUp	{PGUP}	Moves the cell pointer up one window-length.
PgDn	{PGDN}	Moves the cell pointer down one window-length.
Home	{HOME}	Moves the cell pointer to cell A1 of the current worksheet.
End	{END}	Used with {UP}, {DOWN}, {LEFT}, or {RIGHT} to move the cell pointer in the indicated direction to the next boundary between blank and occupied cells. Also used with {HOME} to move the cell pointer to the cell in the lower right corner of the active area of the worksheet.

Table 12.3
Key Names for Direction Keys in Multiple Worksheets

Direction Key	Key Name	Action
Ctrl + PgUp	{NEXTSHEET} or {NS}	Moves the cell pointer to the next worksheet in the current file (from A: to B:).
Ctrl + PgDn	{PREVSHEET} or {PS}	Moves the cell pointer to the previous worksheet in the current file (from B: to A:).
Ctrl + Home	{FIRSTCELL} or {FC}	Moves the cell pointer to cell A:A1 of the current worksheet.
End Ctrl + Home	{LASTCELL} or {LC}	Moves the cell pointer to the last cell of the current worksheet.
Ctrl + End	{FILE}	Used with Ctrl+PgUp, Ctrl+PgDn, Home, and End, to move the cell pointer to another open file.
Ctrl + End Ctrl + PgUp	{NEXTFILE} or {NS}	Moves the cell pointer to the next active worksheet file.
Ctrl + End Ctrl + PgDn	{PREVFILE} or {PF}	Moves the cell pointer to the preceding active worksheet file.
Ctrl + End Home	{FIRSTFILE} or {FF}	Moves the cell pointer to the first active worksheet file.
Ctrl + End End	{LASTFILE} or {LF}	Moves the cell pointer to the last active worksheet file.

12

445

12

Table 12.4
Macro Key Names for Editing Keys

Key	Key Name	Action
Del	{DELETE} or {DEL}	Signifies the Delete key.
Ins	{INSERT} or {INS}	Toggles between insert and overtype modes when you are editing a cell.
Esc	{ESCAPE} or {ESC}	Signifies the Esc key.
◆Backspace	{BACKSPACE} or {BS}	Signifies the Backspace key.
Ctrl + Break	{BREAK}	Clears the command and returns to READY mode.
No equivalent	{CLEARENTRY} or {CE}	Clears the entry in EDIT mode.

Table 12.5
Macro Key Names for Special Keys

Special Key	Key Name	Action
Alt	{ALT}	Activates the Menu bar.
↵Enter	~	Signifies the Enter key.
~ (Tilde)	{~}	Enters a tilde in the worksheet.
{ (Open brace)	{{}	Enters an open brace in the worksheet.
} (Close brace)	{}}	Enters a close brace in the worksheet.

12

Note: A few keys or key combinations do not have a key name to identify them. These include Shift, Caps Lock, Num Lock, Scroll Lock, Compose (Alt+F1), Step (Alt+F2), Run (Alt+F3), and Undo (Alt+Backspace). You cannot represent any of these keys or key combinations within macros.

To specify more than one use of a key name, you can include *repetition factors* inside the braces. To select a particular option in a dialog box, you can include its menu letter inside the {ALT} key name. For example, you can use the following statements in macros:

Statement	Action
{PGUP 3}	Press the PgUp key three times in a row.
{L 4}	Press the ← key four times.
{R Jump}	Press the → key the number of times indicated by the value in the cell named Jump.
{ALT "d"}	Select the option that uses the menu letter **D** in the current dialog box.

Positioning Macros in the Worksheet

You should always place macros outside the area occupied by data on your worksheet. This practice helps you to avoid accidentally overwriting or erasing part of a macro as you create your spreadsheet or graph.

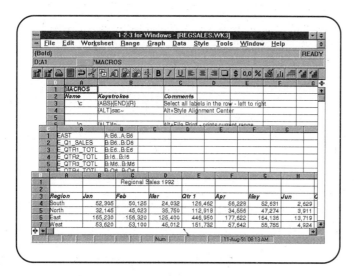

The safest place for macros is on a separate worksheet in the same file. Use the **Worksheet Insert Sheet** command to add a worksheet just for macros.

12

Positioning macros on a separate worksheet in the same file lessens the chance of accidentally including the macro's range in worksheet operations. With this technique, deleting rows or columns in the worksheet area cannot affect the cells in the macro.

1-2-3 has no rule that says you must position your macros in the same place in every worksheet or file. You may, however, want to make a habit of positioning your macros on the last worksheet of a file. You then always know where to look for the macros if you need to change them. Also, the last sheet is easy to reach with the End Ctrl+Home key combination.

You can assign the range name MACROS to the area containing the macros. Using a range name enables you to move quickly to the macro area with the Range Go To command or the GoTo (F5) key.

Documenting Macros

You can place the name of the macro to the left of the macro steps. You also can include comments in your macros that make them far easier to use. Comments are especially useful when you have created complex macros that are important to the worksheet's overall design. Suppose that you created a complex macro, but haven't looked at it for a month. Then, you decide that you want to change the macro. Without built-in comments, you may have a difficult time remembering what each step of the macro does.

Document your 1-2-3 macros by placing comments in the column to the right of the macro steps.

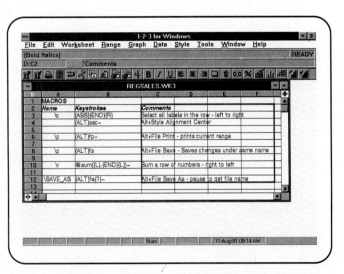

Naming Macros

Before you can execute the macro, you must give the macro a range name.

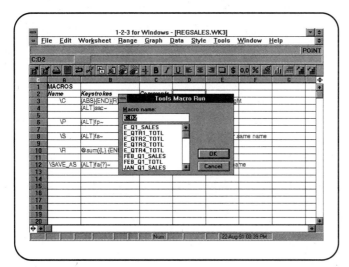

To run a macro by pressing Ctrl + *letter*, name the macro with a backslash (\) followed by the letter. You also can name a macro with a descriptive name that you can select in the Macro name list box of the Tools Macro Run dialog box.

If you choose to use the single-letter naming convention, select a character that in some way helps describe the macro. For example, use \c to name a macro that centers a label in its cell.

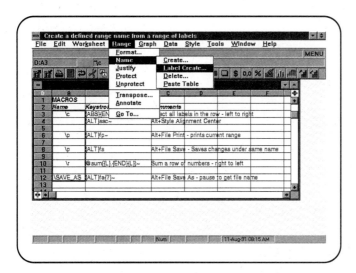

If you place the name of the macro in the cell immediately to the left of the cell that contains the macro's first command, you can use the Range Name Label Create Right command to name the macro.

449

To assign these names to the macros in the adjacent column, specify the range containing the macro names. This approach works with descriptive as well as Ctrl+*letter* macro names. Using the **Range Name Label** Create **Right** command also ensures that you include the name of the macro within the worksheet for easy identification. This command is also useful for naming several macros at one time. Otherwise, you must name the macros individually with the **Range Name** Create command.

The advantage of using a single letter for a macro name is that you can activate the macro more quickly from the keyboard. A disadvantage is that a single-letter name doesn't offer much flexibility in describing what the macro does; remembering the name and purpose of a specific macro may be difficult.

To avoid confusing macro names with other range names, you can begin descriptive macro names with the backslash (\) character. For example, this chapter includes a macro named \DROP_SHADOW, which you can use to outline a range with a drop shadow.

Note: When assigning names to a macro, avoid using a macro key name or command name as the range name.

Creating a Macro with the Transcript Window

The easiest way to create a macro is to perform the tasks you want to automate and then to copy the keystrokes from the *Transcript window* into the worksheet.

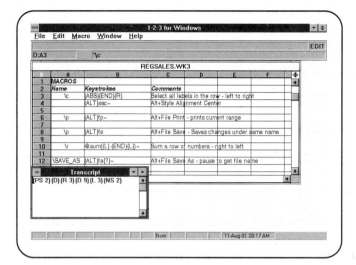

The Transcript window contains a running log of all the keystrokes you enter or mouse actions you perform. You open this window with the Tools Macro Show Transcript command.

After you open the Transcript window, you can edit, play back, or copy the recorded keystrokes or mouse actions. This window, however, can hold only 512 bytes of information at any one time (standard characters require one byte). To fit as much new information as possible in the Transcript window, 1-2-3 uses shortcuts. For example, if you select a range by pressing the Absolute (F4) key and then pressing ↓ four times, 1-2-3 places

> {ABS}{D 4}

in the Transcript window. Rather than entering {DOWN} four times, the program uses a repetition factor and the most abbreviated form of the key name—in this case, {D 4}.

The Transcript Window Menu Bar

When you make the Transcript window current, the Transcript window Menu bar replaces the standard Worksheet window Menu bar. The Transcript window Menu bar contains the five menu options described in Table 12.5.

451

12

Table 12.5
Transcript Window Menu Bar Options

Option	Action
File	This menu enables you to close the Transcript window.
Edit	This menu enables you to cut, copy, paste, and clear the contents of the Transcript window.
Macro	This menu enables you to run selected keystrokes as a macro, pause the recording in the Transcript window, or debug the keystrokes using the Tools Macro Debug dialog box.
Window	This menu enables you to tile or cascade all the windows (Transcript, Worksheet, or Graph) that are open in the work area.
Help	This menu enables you to get any kind of on-line help.

Clearing the Transcript Window

When you exceed the Transcript window's 512-byte limit, 1-2-3 removes the oldest character in the window and adds the newest keystroke or mouse action. To fit as much of your macro as possible in the Transcript window, clear the window before you perform the actions you want to record. Clearing this window also helps you find keystrokes you want copy because the window doesn't contain any keystrokes that are not part of the macro.

To clear the contents of the Transcript window, follow these steps:

1. Display the Transcript window in the work area by choosing the Tools menu, and selecting the Macro and Show Transcript options.

2. Select the Transcript window by clicking the window or pressing Ctrl + F6.

3. In the Transcript window Menu bar, choose the Edit menu, and then select the Clear All option.

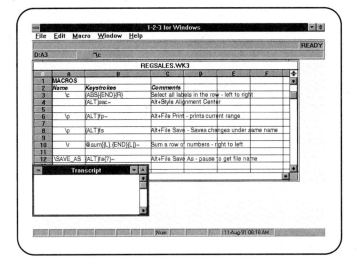

1-2-3 clears the Transcript window.

Copying Keystrokes from the Transcript Window

Suppose that you want to create a macro that sets the global worksheet format to Currency with two decimal places. To create this macro with the Transcript window, follow these steps:

1. Display the Transcript window by choosing the Tools menu, and selecting the Macro and Show Transcript options.

2. Select the Transcript window by clicking the window or pressing Ctrl + F6.

3. From the Edit menu, select the Clear All option.

4. Select the Untitled Worksheet window by clicking the window or by pressing Ctrl + F6.

   Now you can issue the commands that change the global format to Currency. You can select these commands with the mouse or the keyboard.

5. From the Worksheet menu, select the Global Settings option.

6. Select the Format command button.

453

12

7. Select the Currency option in the Format list box of the Worksheet Global Settings Format dialog box.

8. Select the OK button in the Worksheet Global Settings Format dialog box.

9. Select the OK button in the Worksheet Global Settings dialog box.

10. Select the Transcript window by clicking the window or by pressing Ctrl + F6.

1-2-3 displays the Transcript window containing the commands that change the global format to Currency with two decimal places.

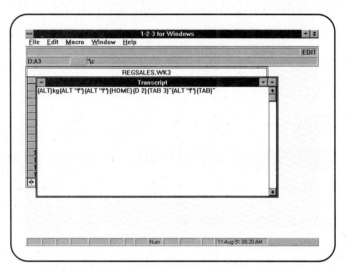

Select all the keystrokes in the Transcript window.

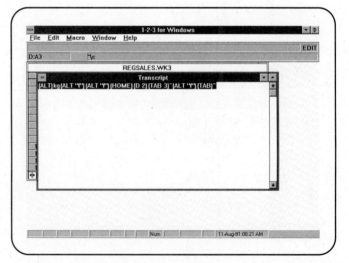

12

11. Select all the keystrokes in the Transcript window by using the I-beam pointer.

12. From the **Edit** menu, select the **Copy** option or press Ctrl + Ins.

13. Select the cell in the worksheet in which you want the macro commands to appear.

14. From the **Edit** menu, select the **Paste** option or press Shift + Ins to paste the keystrokes into the selected cell.

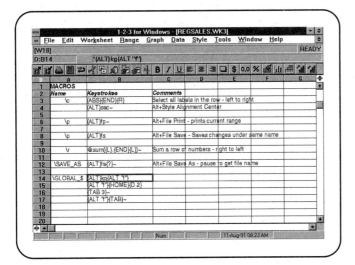

1-2-3 copies all the keystrokes from the Clipboard, using as many cells in the column as needed.

15. Enter a name for the macro in the cell to left of the first cell that contains macro commands (in this example, enter '\GLOBAL_$).

16. Document each step of the macro in the cells to the right of the cells that contain the macro commands.

12

Include com-
ments about each
step of the macro
in the cells to the
right of the cells
that contain
the macro
commands.

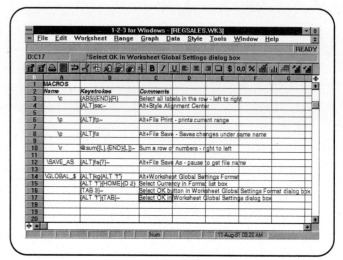

17. Select the cell that contains the macro name, and choose the **R**ange
    menu and select the **N**ame and **L**abel Create options.

18. Select the **R**ight option button in the Range Name Label Create dialog
    box, and select the OK button.

Now that you have copied the commands and named and documented the
macro, you are ready to run the macro.

Running Macros

Ctrl+*letter* macros (named with a backslash and a single letter) are the
simplest macros to run. If necessary, select the cell or range of cells that you
want the macro to affect before you run the macro. For example, when using a
format macro, you select the range you want to format before you run the
macro.

To execute a Ctrl+*letter* macro, follow these steps:

1. Press and hold down the Ctrl key.

2. Press the letter in the macro name. Release both keys.

    For example, if you named a macro \a, you invoke it by pressing
    Ctrl+A. The \ symbol represents the Ctrl key. Pressing Ctrl+A plays
    back the recorded commands in the macro.

When you name a macro with a descriptive name, running the macro takes a
few more keystrokes:

1. From the Tools menu, select the Macro and Run options or press
   Alt + F3 (Run).

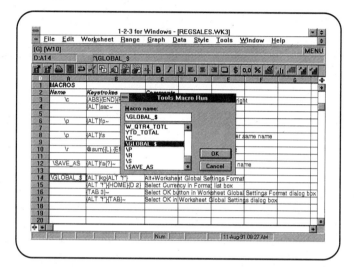

1-2-3 displays the
Tools Macro Run
dialog box.

2. Select the name of the macro you want to run in the Macro name list
   box of the Tools Macro Run dialog box.

3. Select the OK button.

As soon as you issue the command to run a macro, 1-2-3 begins playing back
commands. If the macro has no special instructions (such as a pause) and no
bugs, the macro continues to run until it is finished.

The macro executes each command much faster than you could perform
manually. You can store many macro keystrokes or commands in a single cell.
Macros that are especially long should be split into two or more cells.

When 1-2-3 runs a macro, the program begins with the first cell and continues
until it plays back all the commands in that cell. Next, 1-2-3 moves down one
cell to continue execution. If the next cell is blank or contains a value rather
than a label, the program stops. If that cell contains more macro keystrokes
and commands stored as a label, however, 1-2-3 continues reading down the
column until it finds the first blank cell or the first cell that contains a value.

To stop a macro at any time while it is running, press Ctrl + Break.

Note: You can play back keystrokes recorded in the Transcript window
without first copying them into a worksheet. To play back certain keystrokes,
select the keystrokes in the Transcript window, then choose the Macro Run
command. To reduce the Transcript window to an icon while 1-2-3 plays back

the selected keystrokes, select the **Minimize on Run** option on the **Macro** menu before you select its **Run** option.

Using an Auto-Execute Macro

12

1-2-3 enables you to create an *auto-execute macro* that runs automatically when you load the worksheet. You create this type of macro just like any other macro; the only difference is its name. A macro you want to execute automatically must have the name \0 (backslash zero). You can use only one auto-execute macro per worksheet file.

For example, you can use an auto-execute macro to redefine a range name assigned to a database each time you open its worksheet file. The macro redefines the range name by positioning the cell pointer at the upper left corner of a range named DATABASE before selecting all its records and then redefining the range name.

1-2-3 executes an auto-execute (\0) macro when you open the worksheet file that contains the macro.

You do not press the Ctrl key to start this auto-execute macro. 1-2-3 executes the macro as soon as you open the worksheet file that contains the database and this macro.

Note that you cannot run auto-execute macros with the Ctrl-0 key combination. If you want to run the macro from the keyboard, you can do so with the **Tools Macro Run** command or you can assign the \0 macro an additional name, such as \a. You then have two identical macros on your system: one that executes automatically, and one that you can execute from the keyboard. Assigning an additional Ctrl+*letter* combination so that you can run the macro from the keyboard is especially useful when testing and debugging a new auto-execute macro.

If you do not want to run auto-execute macros, you can disable this feature. To disable the auto-execute macros, you choose the Tools menu and select the User Setup option. Then, you remove the check mark in the Run auto-execute macros check box, and select the OK button in the Tools User Setup dialog box.

Writing Macros

Rather than performing the commands you want to automate in a macro and then copying their keystrokes from the Transcript window, you can write the keystrokes for these commands directly in the worksheet. Before you write the keystrokes in the worksheet, however, you must know the names assigned to each key and the exact sequence of keys you need to press to perform the tasks.

The best way to determine the key names and sequence is to step through the series of instructions one keystroke at a time. Perform the task before you start writing the macro. Take notes about each step, using the appropriate key names, as you proceed with the commands on-screen. Stepping through an operation at the keyboard is an easy way to build simple macros. The more experience you have with 1-2-3 commands, the easier it becomes to "think through" the keystrokes you need to use in a macro.

When writing a macro in a worksheet, you can divide the instructions into several cells so that they are easier for you to read and understand. Just make sure that you enter the instructions in consecutive cells in the same column. Don't skip any cells until you have entered all the instructions.

When entering the key names, be sure that each name starts with { and ends with }. You must always enter the entire key name in a single cell. If you split a key name between two cells, the macro does not run properly.

If you create more than one macro in a worksheet, be sure you leave at least one blank cell between each macro. Otherwise, 1-2-3 plays back the keystrokes in all the contiguous macros that follow the macro you meant to run.

Debugging Macros

Almost no program works perfectly the first time. In nearly every case, errors cause programs to malfunction. Programmers call these problems *bugs*. Debugging is the process of eliminating bugs.

12

As with programs written in other programming languages, you often need to debug 1-2-3 macros before you can use them. 1-2-3 for Windows includes **Single step** and **Trace** options that help make debugging much simpler. In STEP mode, 1-2-3 executes macros one step at a time. In TRACE mode, the program indicates the macro instruction that is currently being executed. By using these options together, you can follow each step of the macro as it runs and identify the step where the macro fails.

When you discover an error, you must exit the macro and return 1-2-3 to READY mode by pressing Ctrl + Break. Then you can edit the macro.

Common Macro Errors

Macros cannot discern an error in the code. For example, *you* recognize immediately that {GOTI} is a misspelling of {GOTO}. A macro, however, cannot make this distinction. The macro tries to interpret the misspelled word and, being unable to do so, delivers an error message. The following four reminders help you avoid some of the most common macro errors:

- Save your worksheet before you execute a macro.
- Verify all syntax and spelling in your macros.
- Include all required tildes (~) to represent Enter keystrokes in your macros.
- Use range names in macros whenever possible to avoid problems with incorrect cell references. Cell references in macros are always absolute. The cell references never change when you make modifications to the worksheet.

If a macro does not work correctly, you can use the STEP and TRACE modes to help you locate and correct the macro errors. You also can use the Undo (Alt+Backspace) feature to "undo" the damage to the worksheet created by faulty execution of a macro.

Using Single Step and Trace to Debug Macros

You need to debug most macros before you use them. If you have a macro error you can't locate, enter the STEP and TRACE modes and rerun the macro one step at a time. After each step, the macro pauses and waits for you to press a key. Although you can press any key to continue, you should use the space bar to step through a macro. As you step through the macro, the Macro Trace window displays the instruction the macro is executing and the location of that instruction.

To use STEP and TRACE modes to debug a macro, follow these steps:

1. From the Tools menu, select the Macro and Debug option.

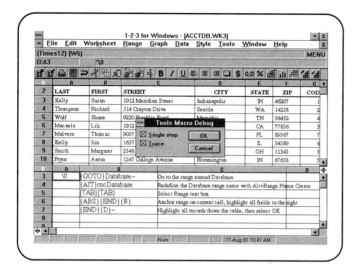

1-2-3 displays the Tools Macro Debug dialog box, containing the Single step and Trace check boxes.

2. Select the Single step and the Trace check boxes.
3. Select the OK button.

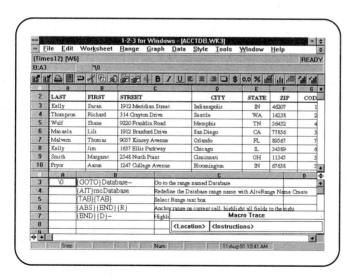

The Macro Trace dialog box appears at the bottom of the work area and the STEP Mode indicator appears in the Status line.

4. Run the macro by pressing Ctrl plus the letter of the macro name. Alternatively, select the **Tools Macro Run** command or press Alt + F3. Then select the macro in the **Macro** name list box and select the OK button.

5. Press the **space bar** to execute each keystroke and command one step at a time.

   For each keystroke or command, the Macro Trace window highlights the instruction and displays its location.

When the macro encounters an error, 1-2-3 displays an ERROR! message dialog box. In this example, the misspelled key name (AIT rather than ALT) in cell B:B4 caused the error.

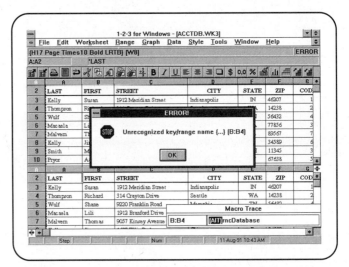

6. After you discover an error, press Ctrl + Break to make the ERROR! message box disappear and return 1-2-3 to READY mode.

7. When 1-2-3 is in READY mode, edit the macro.

8. To exit STEP and TRACE mode, choose the **Tools Macro Debug** command again; then deselect the **Single** step and **Trace** check boxes before you select OK.

Editing Macros

After you identify an error in a macro, you can correct it in the macro instructions. Fixing an error in a macro is as simple as editing the cell that contains the erroneous instruction. You don't need to rewrite the entire cell contents. You need only to change the element that is in error. Although editing a complex macro can be much more challenging than editing a simple one, the concept is exactly the same.

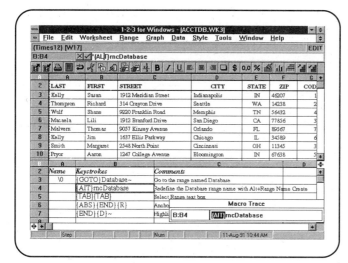

Use the Edit (F2) key to correct the cell that contains the error (indicated in the contents box), then press Enter.

Creating a Macro Library

You can create a *macro library* file that contains all the macros you usually use when building new worksheets and graphs. After you create and debug the macros in your macro library worksheet file, you can use them with any other worksheet or graph. Macro library files save the time you otherwise would need to recreate the same macros in each new spreadsheet or graph window.

After you create a macro library file, you open it with the File Open command whenever you want to use its macros. You then can run any of the macros in the library worksheet by pressing their Ctrl+*letter* keys or by selecting them with the Tools Macro Run (Alt+F3) command.

12

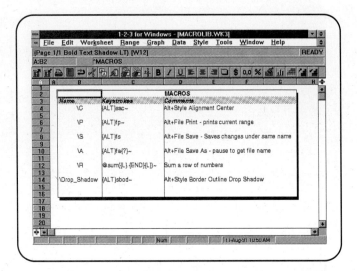

This macro library contains six simple keystroke macros.

This section introduces six simple keystroke macros that you can include in a macro library and provides a brief explanation of each macro. These macros perform common tasks that would require additional keystrokes and time to perform manually.

A Macro That Centers Labels in Their Cells

You use the \c macro in cell B4 to center labels in their cells. Select the cell range that contains the labels you want to center, and then press Ctrl+C. The macro chooses the Style Alignment Center command and then selects the OK button in the Style Alignment dialog box.

You can make a macro that right-aligns labels in their cells by copying and then modifying the \c macro as follows:

    {ALT}sar~

To create a macro that centers a label over a selected range of columns (for example, to center a title for a table), you modify the \C macro as follows:

    {ALT}saoc~

A Macro That Prints the Current Print Range

The \p macro in cell B6 prints the range specified in the File Print dialog box. When you press Ctrl+P, the macro chooses the File Print command and selects the OK button without making any changes to the print settings. Therefore, you use this macro only to reprint a range using the same settings. To modify this macro so that you can change the print range or some other setting (such as the page range), remove the tilde (~) from the macro keystrokes as follows:

```
{ALT}fp
```

This macro performs the same function as clicking the Print current range icon in the Icon palette.

If you usually print the same range in a worksheet, you can name this print range with the Range Name Create command. Then you can use this range name in the \p macro. For example, to print a range named PAGE1, use the following macro in place of the macro in cell B6:

```
{ALT}fpPAGE1~
```

If you use this print macro, remember to redefine the range named PAGE1 whenever you add new data to the print range. If you want to print multiple named ranges, you can copy this cell and change the range references. The following macro prints the ranges named PAGE1, PAGE2, and PAGE3.

```
{ALT}fpPAGE1~

{ALT}fpPAGE2~

{ALT}fpPAGE3~
```

A Macro That Saves Your Changes to a Worksheet File

The \s macro in cell B8 saves your worksheet file in the current directory on disk. To use this macro, press Ctrl+S. This macro saves all your changes under the same file name. This macro performs the same function as choosing the File Save command or clicking the File Save icon in the Icon palette.

To save a file under a new name or for the first time, use the \SAVE_AS macro described next.

A Macro That Saves a File Under a New Name

The \a macro in cell B10 selects the File Save As command and then pauses while you enter the path and file name for the worksheet file you are saving. After designating the path and file name, you press Enter to resume execution of the macro, whereupon the tilde (~) selects the OK option in the File Save As dialog box.

A Macro That Sums a Row of Values

The \r macro in cell B12 uses the @SUM function to add the values in the range of cells immediately to the left of the cell pointer. You can use this macro to create a formula that totals values at the end of each row in a table. To use this macro, select the cell at the end of the row of numbers where you want the total to appear, then press Ctrl+R.

You can modify the basic \r macro to create an \l (for coLumn) macro that totals the column of values above the cell pointer by copying the \r macro's keystrokes and changing the {L}s to {U}s as follows:

```
@sum({U}.{END}{U})~
```

Note that these macros work only when the row to the left of the cell pointer or the column above the cell pointer has no blank cells or cells that contain labels. If you are working with ranges that you must indicate manually, you can add to the \r or \l macro a pause that enables you modify the range:

```
@sum({L}.{END}{L}{?})~
```

```
@sum({U}.{END}{U}{?})~
```

To use these macros, you must remember to press the Enter key after you highlight the range of values you want to total.

A Macro That Adds a Drop Shadow

Use the \DROP_SHADOW macro in B14 to add a drop shadow and outline around the selected range. To use this macro, select all the cells you want to outline with a drop shadow, and then choose the Tools Macro Run command or press Alt+F3 and select \DROP_SHADOW from the list of range names in the Macro name list box and select the OK button.

Summary

Macros are tools you can use to save time, reduce repetition, and automate your worksheet applications. This chapter provided the basic information you need to create and use simple keystroke macros. The chapter identified each of the steps necessary to create macros, then described ways to document, name, and run macros.

You learned that the Transcript window enables you to create macros by recording your keyboard actions and then copying these keystrokes to a worksheet. You also learned about automatic (\0) macros and about methods to debug and edit your simple keystroke macros.

Specifically, you learned the following key information about macros in 1-2-3:

12

- Macros can include actual text, key names, cell addresses and range names, and the advanced macro commands.

- The tilde (~) represents the ↵Enter key.

- You enclose macro key names, which represent keyboard keys, within braces; for example, {EDIT}. Key names are available for the function keys, direction keys, editing keys, and special keys.

- You can specify more than one use for a key name by including repetition factors within the braces (separated from the key name by a space). An example is {DOWN 5}.

- You should take time to plan your macros. Consider the available input and the desired results. Use the keyboard to proceed through your tasks, while jotting down the keystrokes necessary to create simple macros. You can create more complex macros by breaking them into smaller macros that consist of simple operations.

- You should position macros outside of the main area of your worksheet. To find your macros quickly, place them on the last worksheet in your file.

- You should always document your 1-2-3 macros. An easy way to document a macro is to include comments in the cells to the right of the macro steps. You can type the macro name in the cells to the left of macro steps.

- You can name macros in two ways. You can use a backslash (\) followed by a single letter or a descriptive name of up to 15 characters. You use the Range Name Create or Range Name Label Create Right command to name your macros.

- The Transcript window enables you create macros by recording your keystrokes, and then copying and pasting them into your worksheet.

- To execute Ctrl+*letter* macros, you press and hold down the Ctrl key as you press the letter key assigned to the macro. To run macros with descriptive names, you select the Tools Macro Run command or press the Run key (Alt + F3), select the macro name in the Macro name list box, then select the OK button.

467

12

- An automatic (\0) macro executes automatically when you open the worksheet file that contains it. You can use only one auto-execute macro in each worksheet.

- You use 1-2-3's STEP and TRACE modes to debug your macros. Turn on these modes by selecting the **Single step** and **Trace** check boxes in the Tools Macro Debug dialog box. In STEP mode, you proceed through a macro one step at a time. The Macro Trace box displays the instruction being executed. When you find an error, press Ctrl+Break to terminate the macro, clear the error message, and return 1-2-3 to READY mode so that you can edit the macro's contents.

- You edit macros just like any other cell entries in the worksheet. Press Edit (F2) and correct each cell containing an error. Rewriting the entire cell is not necessary.

- A macro library is a collection of macros saved in its own worksheet file and used with several different files. You use the **File Open** command to put the library into memory.

In the next chapter, you learn how to customize the Icon palette in 1-2-3 for Windows so that it includes only the SmartIcons that you need to use. As part of this process, you learn how to add and remove SmartIcons from the Icon palette. In addition, you learn how to make custom icons to which you attach macros created using the skills and knowledge you gained in this chapter.

Customizing the Icon Palette

The Icon palette represents an important addition to 1-2-3 that is unlike anything found in the earlier releases of the program. This feature makes creating worksheets and charting data easier and more efficient for the beginner and expert alike. You now can perform routine tasks in 1-2-3 for Windows simply with a click of the mouse. In almost all situations, clicking a SmartIcon on the Icon palette is faster than selecting an equivalent command sequence from the appropriate pull-down menus. And, even in situations in which you use commonly used macros to streamline command sequences, you may find it easier to click the corresponding SmartIcon.

The assortment of SmartIcons that appear in the default Icon palettes for the Worksheet and Graph windows are by no means static. 1-2-3 for Windows includes many more standard SmartIcons than can be displayed in a single row in the work area. In this chapter, you learn how you can customize the Icon palette so that it includes only the SmartIcons you need to use to get your work done. As part of this process, you learn how to add, remove, and reorder SmartIcons on the Icon palette.

Understanding the Icon palette

Adding and removing SmartIcons

Creating custom SmartIcons

You also learn how to create custom icons for the Icon palette when none of the standard SmartIcons perform the desired task. For these situations, you create a custom icon and a macro that performs the tasks you want 1-2-3 to do when you select the icon. Then you assign the macro to the custom icon and add the icon to the Icon palette.

13

Key Terms in This Chapter

SmartIcon   An icon on the Icon palette that performs a particular 1-2-3 task or command when you click it with the mouse. You can display a description of a SmartIcon's function by positioning the mouse pointer on the icon and clicking the right mouse button.

Icon palette   A selection of SmartIcons arranged in a single bar that runs along the top of the work area just below the Control panel. 1-2-3 for Windows provides two default icon palettes: one for the Worksheet window and another for the Graph window. You can customize each of these Icon palettes.

Understanding the Icon Palette

Before you begin modifying the Icon palettes in 1-2-3 for Windows, you need to be familiar with the default palettes supplied with the program. 1-2-3 for Windows comes with two default Icon palettes that you can use as is or customize as you see fit.

13

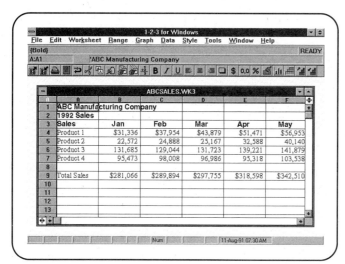

This default Icon palette performs common worksheet tasks. It appears when a Worksheet window is current.

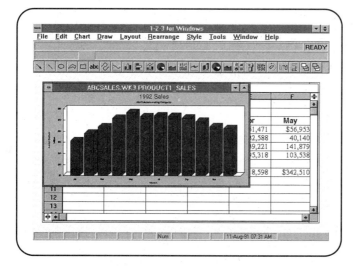

This default Icon palette performs common charting tasks. It appears whenever a Graph window is current.

13

As you experiment with the default Icon palettes, note that some of the icons select commands from the Worksheet or Graph Menu bar as though you had selected them from the pull-down menus with the mouse or the Alt+*letter* key combinations. For example, if you click the Open an existing file SmartIcon on the Worksheet window Icon palette, 1-2-3 displays the File Open dialog box just as though you chose the File menu from the Worksheet Menu bar, and then selected the Open option. Likewise, if you click the Select a graph type SmartIcon on the Graph window Icon palette, the program displays the Chart Type dialog box just as though you chose the Chart menu on the Graph Menu bar, and then selected the Type option.

Other SmartIcons do more than just select particular commands from the Worksheet or Graph menu bar. Some SmartIcons enable you to toggle on and off different attributes for the selected range or to graph objects. For example, to use boldface type for the contents of a selected range of cells in the Worksheet window, you click the Bold SmartIcon. To turn off the boldface type option and return the cells to normal text, click the Bold SmartIcon once again.

Still other SmartIcons perform tasks that supplement, but do not duplicate, commands performed with the 1-2-3 Worksheet window Menu bar. For example, to use the Select range to apply current formatting SmartIcon to copy the formatting of a particular cell to an entire range, follow these steps:

1. Select the cell that contains the formatting you want to copy (such as a new font size).

2. Click the Select range to apply current formatting SmartIcon.

   The pointer changes from an arrowhead to a paintbrush.

3. Drag the paintbrush pointer over the range of cells you want to format with the attributes of the selected cell, and then release the mouse button.

   As soon as you release the mouse button, 1-2-3 formats all the cells you outlined with the paintbrush pointer with the same format as the cell you first selected.

The Sum the nearest adjacent range SmartIcon is another example of a SmartIcon that performs a supplementary task not found on any menu. When you select an empty cell at the bottom of a column or the end of a row of numbers, 1-2-3 sums those numbers as soon as you click this SmartIcon. To automate such a task with an earlier version of 1-2-3, you must create a macro that uses the SUM function to select the range you want to sum depending on whether the cell above or to the left of the current cell position contains a number.

Note: To display a verbal description of the function of any SmartIcon on either Icon palette, position the mouse pointer on the icon and click the right mouse button. 1-2-3 then displays a short description of the icon's purpose in the upper left corner of the 1-2-3 window's Title bar.

As mentioned earlier, the SmartIcons displayed on the default Icon palettes are not the only SmartIcons available in 1-2-3 for Windows. The program offers just under 70 standard SmartIcons, each of which performs a preprogrammed command or task. Slightly more than half of these appear on the default Worksheet and Graph Icon palettes.

As you select new SmartIcons for an Icon palette, you will find that, like those on the existing palettes, some SmartIcons automate standard 1-2-3 command sequences, some toggle on and off different states in the worksheet, and others perform operations not directly available on the menus. As you select new SmartIcons in the Tools SmartIcons Customize dialog, 1-2-3 displays a description of each one. This description does not, however, indicate exactly how the SmartIcon works. To find out more about a particular SmartIcon, you can consult the SmartIcons Quick Reference included in the program's documentation. If you still can't figure out how the SmartIcon operates, you can add it to the Icon palette and then experiment with it.

Adding SmartIcons to an Icon Palette

The procedure for adding different 1-2-3 SmartIcons to an Icon palette is easy. You simply activate the Icon palette you want to modify and select the Tools SmartIcons Customize command. You select the icon you want to add in the Standard icons list box, indicate the position you want the icon to have in the Current palette list box, and select the Add command button.

Follow these steps for adding two new SmartIcons to the Worksheet Icon palette:

1. Make sure that the Icon palette you want to modify is current (the palette appears in the work area of the 1-2-3 window). If the palette you want to modify is not current, select an appropriate window (Worksheet or Graph) by clicking that window with the mouse or by pressing Ctrl + F6 until that window is current.

2. From the Tools menu, select the SmartIcons option.

   1-2-3 displays the Tools SmartIcons dialog box.

3. Select the Customize command button.

13

1-2-3 displays the Tools SmartIcons Customize dialog box.

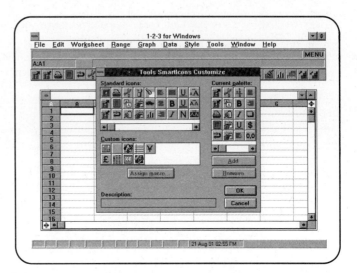

4. In the Standard icons list box, click the SmartIcon you want to add to the current palette. You can use the scroll bar at the bottom of the box to scroll other icons into view.

When you click a new SmartIcon in the Standard icons list box, 1-2-3 displays a short description of its function in the Description text box at the bottom of the dialog box.

In this example, select the Double underline SmartIcon to add to the palette.

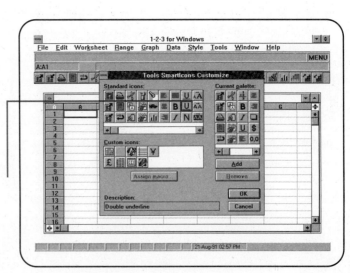

5. In the Current palette list box, indicate where you want to insert the selected SmartIcon. To add the icon at the end of the palette, click the first blank square at the end of the Current palette list box. (You may need to use the scroll bar to bring the last SmartIcon in the current palette into view.) To insert the SmartIcon elsewhere in the palette, click the icon that you want to follow the SmartIcon you are adding.

13

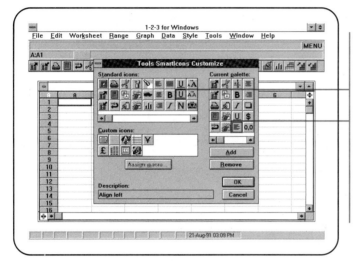

In this example, to insert the Double underline SmartIcon between the Underline SmartIcon and the Align Left SmartIcon in the current palette, click the Align Left SmartIcon.

6. Select the Add command button.

1-2-3 pastes the standard icon you selected in the current palette at the position you indicated.

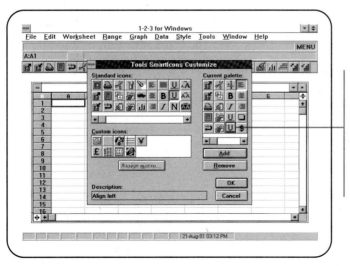

In this example, 1-2-3 places the Double underline SmartIcon just after the Underline SmartIcon in the current palette.

13

7. Repeat steps 4, 5, and 6 to add any other standard icons to the current palette.

Here, you add the Choose SmartIcons SmartIcon at the end of the current palette.

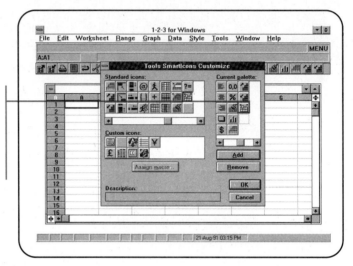

8. Select the OK button to return to the Tools SmartIcons dialog box.

9. Select the OK button in the Tools SmartIcons dialog box to return to the current Worksheet or Graph window.

1-2-3 adds the SmartIcon(s) you selected in the Standard icons list box to the current Icon palette in the position(s) you specified.

By adding the Choose SmartIcons SmartIcon to the Worksheet Icon palette, you can display the Tools SmartIcons Customize dialog box simply by clicking the icon.

Note: 1-2-3 can display no more than 27 SmartIcons on an Icon palette when the palette appears at the top or bottom of the work area and no more than 16 SmartIcons when the palette appears at the left or right of the work area. If you want your Icon palette to have more SmartIcons, you must change the palette position to Floating in the Tools SmartIcons dialog box and then arrange the size of the icons so 1-2-3 can display them all in the work area.

Removing SmartIcons from an Icon Palette

You may discover that you don't use certain SmartIcons and want to remove them from the Icon palette to make room for others. The procedure for removing SmartIcons is similar to the procedure for adding icons: make the

476

correct Icon palette current, select the SmartIcon you want to remove, then select the **R**emove command button.

To see how this procedure works, follow these steps for removing the Perspective view SmartIcon from the Worksheet Icon palette:

1. Make sure that the Icon palette you want to modify is current (the palette appears in the work area of the 1-2-3 window). If the palette you want to modify is not current, select an appropriate window (Worksheet or Graph) by clicking that window with the mouse or by pressing Ctrl + F6 until that window is current.

2. From the **T**ools menu, select the SmartIcons option.

3. Select the **C**ustomize command button.

4. In the Current **p**alette list box, click the SmartIcon you want to remove from the Icon palette. You can use the scroll bar at the bottom of the box to scroll other icons into view.

   When you click a SmartIcon in the Current **p**alette list box, 1-2-3 displays a short description of its function in the Description text box at the bottom of the dialog box.

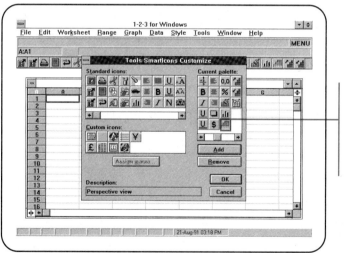

In this example, select the Perspective view SmartIcon for removal from the palette.

5. Select the **R**emove command button.

   1-2-3 deletes the selected SmartIcon from the Current **p**alette list box.

13

1-2-3 deletes the Perspective view SmartIcon from the Current palette list box

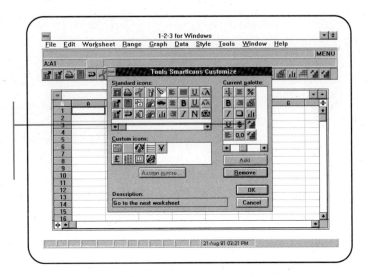

6. Repeat steps 4 and 5 to delete from the Current palette list box all the SmartIcons you no longer want on the Icon palette.

7. Select the OK button to return to the Tools SmartIcons dialog box.

8. Select the OK button in the Tools SmartIcons dialog box to return to the current Worksheet or Graph window.

   1-2-3 displays the Icon palette in the work area without the SmartIcons you removed.

Changing the Order of SmartIcons on a Palette

You may want to retain a SmartIcon, but change its position on the Icon palette. Unfortunately, 1-2-3 for Windows does not support a direct method for repositioning an icon on the palette. To change the placement of a SmartIcon, you must complete two separate operations:

- First, in the Current palette list box, delete the SmartIcon you want to reposition.

- Next, select the same SmartIcon in the Standard icons list box and then add it back to the Current palette list box in its new position.

478

To see how this procedure works, follow these steps for repositioning the Preview the print range SmartIcon so that it precedes the Print a range SmartIcon in the Worksheet Icon palette:

1. Make sure that the Icon palette you want to modify is current (the palette appears in the work area of the 1-2-3 window). If the palette you want to modify is not current, select an appropriate window (Worksheet or Graph) by clicking that window with the mouse or by pressing Ctrl + F6 until that window is current.

2. From the Tools menu, select the SmartIcons option.

3. Select the Customize command button.

4. In the Current palette list box, click the SmartIcon you want to reposition.

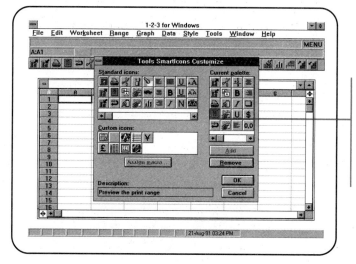

In this example, click the Preview the print range SmartIcon to remove it from the Current palette list box.

5. Select the Remove command button.

6. In the Standard icons list box, click the same SmartIcon as the icon you just deleted from the Current palette list box.

479

13

In this example, select the Preview the print range SmartIcon in the Standard icons list box so that you can add it to the current palette in a new position.

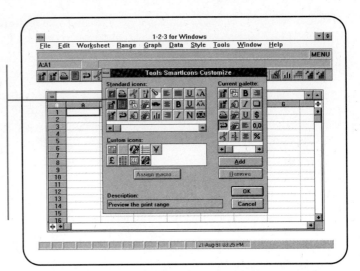

7. In the Current palette list box, click the SmartIcon that you want to follow the SmartIcon you just selected in the Standard icons list box.

8. Select the Add command button to add the SmartIcon.

In this example, you add the Preview the print range SmartIcon to the Current palette list box immediately before the Print a range SmartIcon.

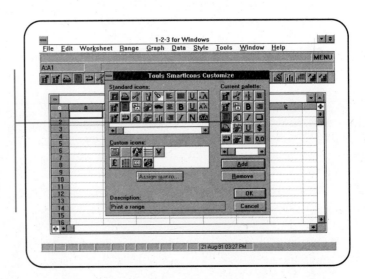

9. Repeats steps 4 through 8 for each SmartIcon that you want to reposition on the Icon palette.

480

10. Select the OK button to return to the Tools SmartIcons dialog box.

11. Select the OK button in the Tools SmartIcons dialog box to return to the current Worksheet or Graph window.

1-2-3 displays the Icon palette in the work area with the SmartIcons arranged in the new order.

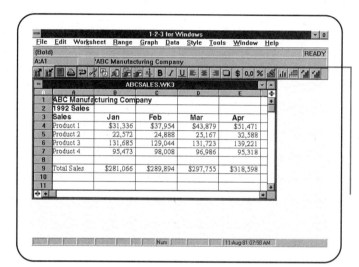

Here, you see the Worksheet Icon palette after you reposition the Preview the print range SmartIcon before the Print a range SmartIcon.

Creating Custom SmartIcons

As you discover when you begin customizing the default Icon palettes, 1-2-3 for Windows provides a good assortment of standard SmartIcons that perform the most commonly needed worksheet and charting tasks. Despite this variety, you may want to use a SmartIcon to perform an operation that 1-2-3 does not include in the collection of standard icons.

In such a situation, you can create a custom SmartIcon and add it to the Icon palette. To create a custom SmartIcon, you begin by creating a new icon in a separate Windows drawing program such as Paintbrush (an accessory program included in Windows 3.0) or CorelDRAW! (a sophisticated Windows drawing and graphics program). Then you create a macro in a 1-2-3 worksheet that performs the tasks you want your custom icon to perform. Finally, you assign this macro to the custom icon and add the icon to the Icon palette.

To demonstrate this procedure, the following sections show you how to create a custom icon in the Paintbrush program and then assign a simple macro to this icon in 1-2-3 for Windows.

481

Creating a New Custom Icon

To create a custom icon to which you can assign a macro, you must use a separate drawing program. You can use any drawing program that enables you to save your icon in a bitmap file. (Every custom icon must be saved in bitmap file format, the standard Windows 3.0 graphic file format indicated by the BMP file extension.) If you don't own a special Windows drawing program such as CorelDRAW!, you can always use the Paintbrush accessory program (bundled as part of the Windows 3.0 program) to draw your custom icon.

The icon you create must have a square shape and can include text or graphics of your choosing. Although 1-2-3 for Windows sizes the icon to fit on the Icon palette, you should limit the dimensions of the square to no more than one-and-one-half inches square (to keep the size of the bitmap file small). With these dimensions, the bitmap file remains a reasonable size, but still enables you to see your work. If you add text to an icon, choose a point size of 60 points or more (because 1-2-3 greatly reduces the text when it resizes the icon). Because you need to use such a large point size, you can fit about three characters across the width of the icon. Similarly, when you draw on the icon, you need to use very thick lines or the lines are not visible when 1-2-3 reduces the icon to its actual size.

To see how you can use Paintbrush to create a new icon, follow these steps (later in the chapter, you learn how to attach a macro that adds the current date and time to a worksheet):

1. From 1-2-3 for Windows, return to the Program Manager by reducing the 1-2-3 window to a program icon with the Minimize button or by pressing Ctrl+Esc and selecting Program Manager in the Task List.

2. Start the Paintbrush program in the Accessories group window by double-clicking its program icon or selecting its icon and pressing ↵Enter.

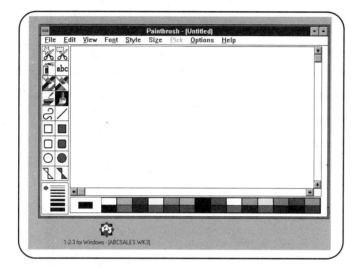

The Paintbrush program opens with it own Untitled window so that you can create your icon.

3. From the **O**ptions menu, select the **I**mage Attributes option so that you can change the size of the drawing.

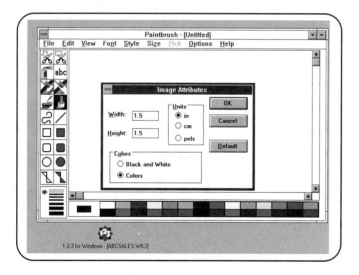

The Image Attributes dialog box appears. Here, you reduce the overall size of the drawing.

13

13

4. Select the Width text box and enter **1.5**, and then select the Height text box and enter **1.5**.

5. Make sure that the in (inches) option button under **Units** is selected and that the **Colors** option button under Colors is selected, and choose OK.

    The Paintbrush program redraws a smaller image area, representing the new drawing size, in the upper left corner of the Untitled window.

6. Draw the graphic image you want the custom icon to have (select **Help Tools** to get on-line help about using the different drawing tools).

    To add text, select a minimum point size of 60 on the Size menu, then select the Text Tool (the abc icon), click the insertion point in your icon, and begin typing.

    Before drawing lines and shapes on the custom icon, click the heaviest line thickness in the box below the Tools palette, then select the appropriate drawing tool.

Here, you see a simple drawing of a clock for the new custom icon. Note the thickness of the lines used in this drawing.

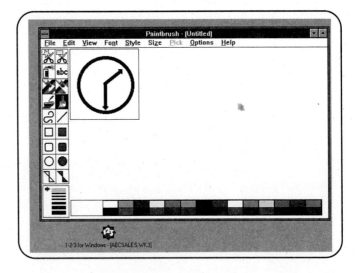

7. After you draw your icon, color the background gray (to match the other icons on the palette) by clicking the light gray sample in the color palette, then selecting the Paint Roller tool, then clicking the icon.

8. From the **File** menu, select the Save **As** option to save the icon.

9. If you are saving a custom icon for the Worksheet Icon palette, save the icon as a bitmap file in the C:\123W\SHEETICO directory. If you

are saving a custom icon for the Graph Icon palette, save the icon as a bitmap file in the C:\123W\GRAPHICO directory.

Select the appropriate directory in the Directories list box, then replace the * (asterisk) in the Filename list box with a file name up to eight characters long (make sure that you leave the BMP extension).

10. Select the **O**ptions command button to display the Save As options.

11. Make sure the **16** Color bitmap option button is selected; if not, click its option button.

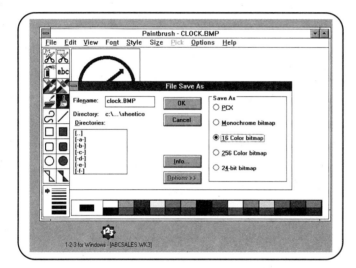

In this example, save the icon as a 16 color bitmap in the file CLOCK.BMP in the C:\123W\SHEETICO directory.

12. Select the OK button in the **F**ile Save **A**s dialog box to save the bitmap file.

13. From the **F**ile menu, select the E**x**it option to exit the Paintbrush program.

In order for 1-2-3 for Windows to recognize a bitmap file as a custom icon, the program must find a related text file that contains the macro instructions. This text file must have the same file name as the bitmap file that contains the drawing of the icon and must use the file name extension MAC. In addition, this text file must be in the same directory as the associated bitmap file (C:\123W\SHEETICO or C:\123W\GRAPHICO). For example, because you named the icon bitmap file CLOCK.BMP, you must create a text file called CLOCK.MAC that is located in the C:\123W\SHEETICO directory.

The initial contents of the MAC file that accompanies the bitmap file containing your custom icon are not important; 1-2-3 for Windows places the

13

appropriate macro instructions in this file when you assign the macro to the custom icon (a procedure explained in the next section).

The easiest way to create a MAC file is to open an existing macro text file with the Notepad accessory program. Then, use the File Save As command to save another copy of this macro text file under the same file name as the custom icon's bitmap file. Follow these steps:

1. In the Program Manager, start the Notepad program in the Accessories group window by double-clicking its program icon or by selecting its icon and pressing ⏎Enter.

2. From the File menu, select the Open option.

   The Notepad File Open dialog box appears.

3. In the Filename text box, select TXT with the I-beam pointer, and type MAC (so that this text box contains *.MAC).

4. In the Directories list box, select and open the C:\123W\SHEETICO directory by double-clicking [..], double-clicking [123W], and then double-clicking [sheetico].

Here, you see the File Open dialog box in Notepad showing all the MAC files in the C:\123W\SHEETICO directory.

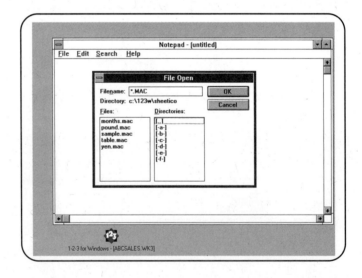

5. In the Files list box, open a MAC file by double-clicking one of the file names or by selecting a file name and then selecting the OK button. The keystrokes stored in the MAC file you selected appear in the Notepad window.

6. From the File menu, select the Save As option.

   Notepad displays the File Save As dialog box.

7. In the Filename list box, select the file name and type the same file name you assigned to the bitmap file containing your custom icon (make sure that you leave the MAC extension).

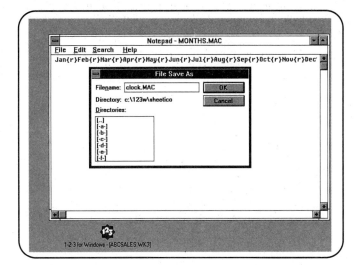

13

In this example, name the macro text file CLOCK.MAC to match the CLOCK.BMP bitmap file that contains the custom icon.

8. Select the OK button to save the text file.
9. From the File menu, select the Exit option to exit Notepad.
10. Return to 1-2-3 for Windows by clicking the 1-2-3 Window, double-clicking the 1-2-3 program icon at the bottom of the Windows desktop, or using the Task list (Ctrl + Esc).

Assigning a Macro to a Custom Icon

As part of the process of creating a custom icon for your Icon palette, you must create a macro that performs the tasks you want 1-2-3 to do when you click the icon. You create this macro the same way you create any other 1-2-3 macro: you can create the macro by performing the actions manually and then copying the keystrokes from the Transcript window or by writing the instructions directly in the worksheet. Refer to Chapter 12 for more specific information on how to create macros.

When you create a macro for a custom icon, give it a Ctrl+*letter* key range name (such as \X) so that you can test the macro before you assign it to an icon. Always make sure that the macro is thoroughly debugged and runs exactly as you intended before assigning it to a custom icon!

After creating the macro and ascertaining that it works perfectly, you are ready to assign the macro to a custom icon. Then, you simply add the custom icon to the Icon palette as you would add any standard SmartIcon.

To assign a macro to a custom icon you created and then add this icon to the Icon palette, follow these steps:

1. Create and debug the macro you want to assign to a custom icon (refer to Chapter 12 if you need more information).

   You can create this macro in a new or existing worksheet.

2. Select the range of cells that contains the macro instructions you want to assign to the custom icon.

   When designating this range, make sure that you select every cell that contains a macro instruction, not just the first cell of the range.

In this example, select the range B15..B16, the range that contains all the macro keystrokes for entering the date and time in a worksheet.

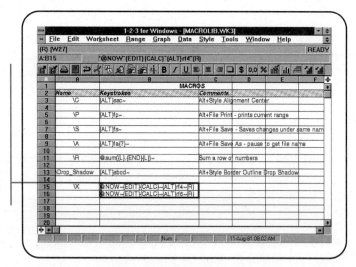

3. From the Tools menu, select the SmartIcons option.

   1-2-3 displays the Tools SmartIcon dialog box.

4. Select the Customize option.

   The custom icon you created in the Paintbrush program appears at the end of the Custom icons list. You may have to scroll the list if you have created more icons than the box can display at one time.

13

488

5. Under Custom icons, click the custom icon to which you want to assign the macro.

   When you select an icon, the Assign macro command button is no longer dimmed.

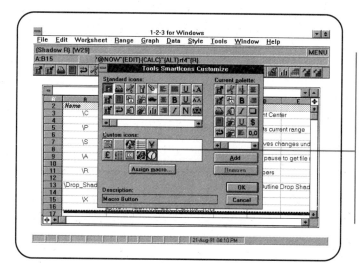

In this example, click the clock custom icon in the Custom icons list box. Notice that after you select a custom icon, the Description text box reads simply Macro Button.

13

6. Select the Assign macro command button.

   1-2-3 displays the Tools SmartIcons Customize Assign Macro. The Macro list box currently contains the keystrokes for the MAC file you copied in Notepad.

7. Make sure that the cell range in the Range text box includes all the cells that contain macro instructions. If the range is not correct, select the Range text box and specify the correct range address.

8. Select the Get Macro command button.

   1-2-3 copies the keystrokes from the designated worksheet range into the Macro list box. If necessary, edit the keystrokes and commands for the macro directly in the Macro list box.

13

When you select the Get Macro button in this example, 1-2-3 copies the keystrokes from the cell range B15..B16 into the Macro list box.

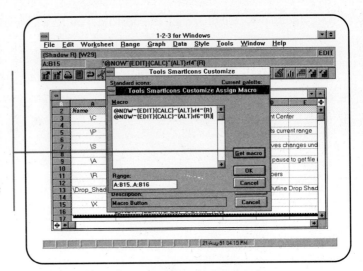

9. Select the OK button to return to the Tools SmartIcons Customize dialog box.

10. To assign the custom icon to the current Icon palette, click the icon in the Custom Icons list box, and indicate the custom icon's position in the palette by clicking the SmartIcon in the Current palette list box that you want to follow the custom icon, and then select the Add command button.

11. Select the OK button to return to Tools SmartIcons dialog box.

12. Select the OK button again to return to 1-2-3.

13. To run the macro, simply click the custom icon in the Icon palette.

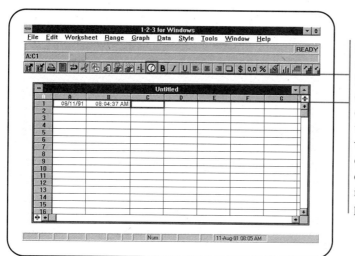

Here, you see the clock custom icon. From now on, to enter the current date and time in a worksheet, simply click the Clock custom SmartIcon in the Icon palette.

13

Summary

In this chapter, you learned how to customize the 1-2-3 for Windows default Worksheet or Graph Icon palette so that it includes only the SmartIcons that you want to use when creating worksheets or graphs. As part of this process, you learned how to add, remove, and rearrange the SmartIcons on the palette. In addition to learning how to change the standard icons on the Icon palette, you also learned how to create custom icons, assign macros to these icons, and then add the custom icons to the Icon palette.

Specifically, you learned the following key information about customizing the Icon palette:

■ To add a SmartIcon to an Icon palette, select the palette and choose the Tools SmartIcons Customize command. Then, select in the Standard icons list box the SmartIcon you want to add, indicate in the Current palette list box the position you want the icon to have, and choose the Add command button.

13

- To add a SmartIcon to the end of a palette, select in the Standard icons list box the icon you want to add, click the first blank square at the end of the icons in the Current palette list box, and then choose the Add command button. To insert an icon elsewhere in a palette, click the SmartIcon in the Current palette list box that you want to follow the icon you are adding, and then choose the Add command button.

- To remove a SmartIcon from an Icon palette, select the palette and choose the Tools SmartIcons Customize command. Then, select in the Current palette list box the SmartIcon you want to delete and choose the Remove command button.

- To change the order of a SmartIcon on an Icon palette, first delete the icon from the Current palette list box, and then add the same SmartIcon to the Current palette list box in the new position.

- To create a custom icon for the Icon palette, draw the icon within a separate drawing program such as Paintbrush and save it as a bitmap file. If you are creating a custom icon for the Worksheet Icon palette, save the bitmap file in the C:\123W\SHEETICO directory. If you are creating a custom icon for the Graph Icon palette, save the bitmap file in the C:\123W\GRAPHICO directory.

- After you create a bitmap file that holds the graphic for your icon, you must create a related macro text file that has the same file name and the MAC extension (for example, name the macro file TITLE.MAC when the bitmap file is called TITLE.BMP). The easiest way to create a macro text file is to open an existing MAC file with the Notepad accessory program, then use the File Save As command to rename the file with the same file name as the bitmap file (making sure that you retain the MAC extension).

- To assign a macro to a custom icon, first create and debug a macro that performs the tasks you want to assign to the icon. Next, select the cell range that contains these macro keystrokes. Then, choose the Tools SmartIcons Customize command and click (in the Custom icons list box) the custom icon to which you want to assign the macro. Finally, select the Assign macro command button, then click the Get macro command button and check that all the macro appear in the Macro list box, and then select the OK button.

- To place the custom icon (to which you assigned the macro) on the current Icon palette, select the icon in the Custom icons list box of the Tools SmartIcons Customize dialog box, indicate the icon's position in the Current palette list box.

- To change the graphic image on a custom SmartIcon, open its BMP file with the drawing program you used to create it, then make and save your changes there.

13

Installing 1-2-3 for Windows

Y ou must successfully install 1-2-3 for Windows before you can use the program. To install 1-2-3, run the Install program from within Windows 3.0. As you will see, the installation procedure in 1-2-3 for Windows is very straightforward. If you find that you don't understand an option in a dialog box that appears, simply select the Help button to get on-line help information.

Using the 1-2-3 Install Program

The Install program automatically copies the 1-2-3 program files from your floppy disks to your hard disk. The following steps for installing 1-2-3 for Windows assume that you are starting the Install program from a high-density B drive. If you run the Install program in a different drive, substitute its drive letter (such as A:) in the steps.

To install 1-2-3 for Windows, follow these steps:

1. Insert the 1-2-3 for Windows Install floppy disk in drive B.

2. Start Windows 3.0 by typing **win** and pressing ⏎Enter at the C:\> prompt.

3. In the Windows Program Manager, choose the File menu and then select the Run option.

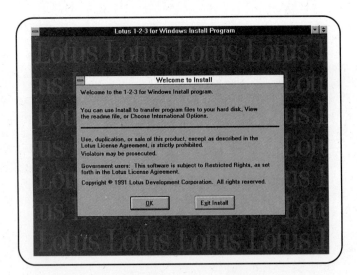

Windows displays the Run dialog box.

4. Type **b:install** in the Command Line text box of the Run dialog box.
5. Select the OK button.

   The Install program displays the following message:

   ```
   Install is copying its working files to your hard disk.
   ```

After copying the necessary work- ing files, the Install program displays the Welcome to Install dialog box.

A

6. Select the OK button to continue the installation of 1-2-3 for Windows.

   The Recording Name and Company Name dialog box appears. In this dialog box you register the software in your name.

7. Type your name in the Your name text box; then press ⟨Tab ⁎⟩ to move the cursor to the Company name text box.

8. Type the name of your company in the Company name text box.

9. Select the OK button.

   The Install program displays the Confirm Names dialog box.

10. Check your name and the name of your company. If the names are correct, select the Yes command button. Otherwise, select the No button (you return to the Recording Name and Company Name dialog box where you can make your corrections).

   The Install program displays a message telling you that it is recording your name and company name information.

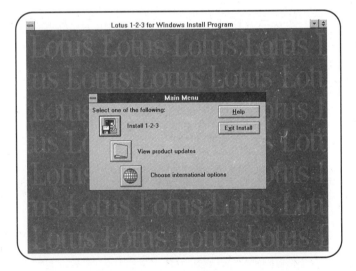

Next, the Install program displays the Main Menu dialog box.

11. Click the Install 1-2-3 button to install the program files.

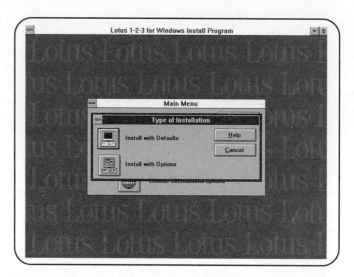

The Install program then displays the Type of Installation dialog box.

A

12. Select the Install with Defaults button to install all of the program and sample files on your hard disk. (The installation requires a minimum of 5713 kilobytes of free disk space to install only the 1-2-3 for Windows program.) Select the Install with Options button to choose which auxiliary files should be copied on the hard disk.

    The Install program then displays a message box explaining that the program is scanning the drives on your system.

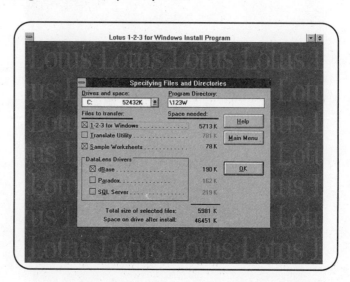

If you choose Install with Options, the Specifying Files and Directories dialog box appears. Put a check mark in the check boxes of only those items you want copied to the hard disk.

498

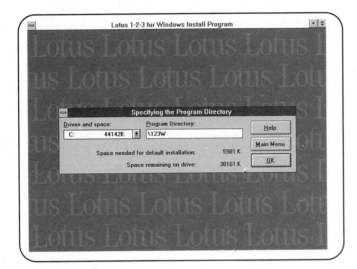

If you choose Install with Defaults, the Specifying the Program Directory dialog box appears.

A

To proceed with the program's installation, the space needed for the default files (or the files you selected, if you are installing with options) must be less than the space remaining on the drive. If this is not the case, you must exit the Install program and make sufficient room on the hard disk by removing unnecessary files.

13. Unless you indicate otherwise, the Install program copies the 1-2-3 program files onto drive C of your hard disk in a directory called \123W. To install 1-2-3 onto a different drive, select a new drive in the Drives and space drop-down list box. To install 1-2-3 into a different directory, enter the name of the directory in the Program Directory text box.

14. Select the OK command button.

If the directory you specified already exists and contains files, the Install program displays a dialog box indicating this. To continue installation in this directory, you must select the Yes command button. To return to the previous dialog box where you can change the directory, select No. If the directory doesn't exist, you see a message box indicating that 1-2-3 is creating your directory. If you elected to have the SQL Server or Paradox Datalens drivers installed (by selecting as part of Install with Options), you also see additional message boxes pertaining to these options.

15. Next, the Adding 1-2-3 Icons to a Program Manager Group dialog box appears. Select OK to add the selected program icons to the Lotus Applications group window.

A

The 1-2-3 Default
Preferences dialog
box appears.

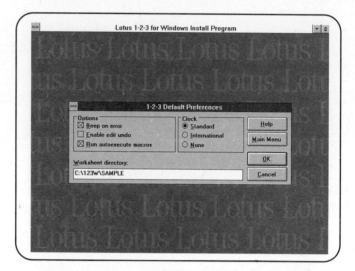

16. To enable the Undo feature, select the **E**nable edit undo check box;
    then select the **O**K command button. (**Note:** The options that appear
    in this dialog box can also be changed with the 1-2-3 for Windows
    Tools **U**ser Setup command.) Confirm the suggested directory name
    for your worksheet files by selecting **Y**es. Next, the Transferring Files
    dialog box appears. This dialog box shows you the percentage of files
    copied from the floppy disk to your hard disk as well as what percent-
    age of the total installation is complete.

When the Install
program finishes
copying all of
the files on the
current floppy
disk, you are then
prompted to
insert the next
disk.

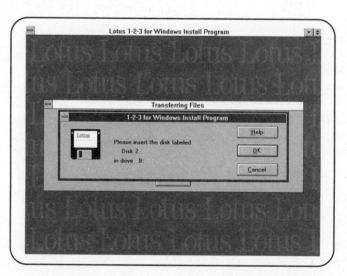

500

17. Insert the program disk listed in the 1-2-3 for Windows Install Program dialog box, and then select the **O**K button.

18. Repeat step 17, until the Install program has copied all the files from all the 1-2-3 program disks onto your hard disk.

    After Install is finished copying the program files, you see a message box indicating that the program is saving product defaults, Datalens drivers, and adding the 1-2-3 program icons.

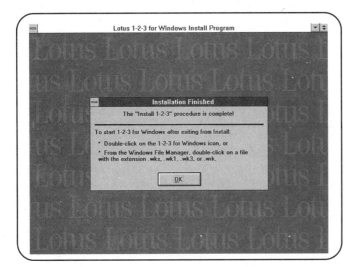

The Install program then displays this message box indicating how to start 1-2-3 for Windows.

19. Select the OK button in the message box.

    The Install program then displays the Option to Start ATM Installer dialog box, asking you if you want to install the Adobe Type Manager now.

20. To install ATM at this time, select the **Y**es command button. (For specific information on this installation process, see the following section.) To install ATM at a later time, select the **N**o button.

    As soon as you finish installing ATM or if you select the **N**o command button, the 1-2-3 Install program returns you to the Main Menu dialog box.

21. To return to the Program Manager, select the E**x**it Install command button in the Main Menu dialog box.

    When you return to the Program Manager, you will see the Lotus Applications group window containing the 1-2-3 for Windows and 1-2-3 Install program icons.

22. To arrange the Lotus Applications group window, select the **W**indow **C**ascade command (⇧Shift + F5) or the **W**indow **T**ile command (⇧Shift + F4) on the Windows menu bar.

23. Exit Windows 3.0 and save your new arrangement by choosing the **F**ile **Ex**it Windows command and selecting the OK button in the Exit Windows dialog box. Then start Windows again by typing **win** at the C:\> prompt.

    Then, to start 1-2-3 for Windows, double-click the 1-2-3 for Windows program icon (or select it and press ↵Enter). To run the Install program (to add other auxiliary files if you used Install with Defaults or to change the International Options), double-click the Install program icon (or select it and press ↵Enter).

Installing Adobe Type Manager

1-2-3 for Windows includes a version of Adobe Type Manager (ATM) that eliminates jagged screen fonts in 1-2-3 for Windows. (These jagged fonts are especially noticeable when you use larger sizes.) The ATM package includes program files, outline fonts, and metric fonts necessary to display standard screen fonts used by 1-2-3 for Windows correctly in various point sizes.

You must have at least 290K bytes of disk space free in order to copy the ATM program files along with one outline font and its metric files. Each subsequent font you add requires 40K of additional free disk space for its outline font and metric files.

To install Adobe Type Manager when you install 1-2-3 for Windows, select the **Y**es command button in the Option to Start ATM Installer dialog box. The 1-2-3 Install program then displays a dialog box asking you to insert the ATM program disk in your floppy drive. After you insert the disk in your drive, select the **O**K button in the 1-2-3 for Windows Install Program dialog box.

If you do not choose to install ATM as part of the 1-2-3 for Windows installation, you can start the ATM Installer independently in Windows by following these steps:

1. Insert the ATM floppy disk in your disk drive.
2. Start Windows 3.0 by typing **win** and pressing ↵Enter at the C:\> prompt.

3. In the Windows Program Manager, choose the File menu, and select the Run option.

   Windows displays the Run dialog box.

4. Type **b:install** in the Command Line text box of the Run dialog box.

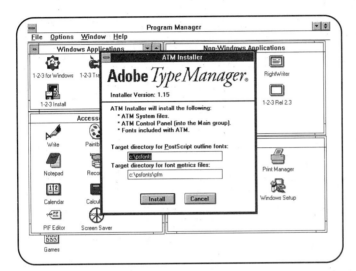

The ATM Installer dialog box appears when you enter the command to install ATM.

A

Regardless of how you start the ATM Installer, follow these steps to then install the program:

1. The ATM Installer dialog box contains text boxes showing the default directories for PostScript outline fonts (C:\PSFONTS) and metric files (C:\PSFONTS\PFM). To have these files copied in a different directory, select the text box and enter the new directory.

2. Select the Install button.

   The ATM Installer dialog box shows its progress transferring the files to your hard disk. When the installation is complete, you are given the option to install PCL bitmap fonts. If you have an HP LaserJet printer with only 512K of memory, select Install; otherwise, select Skip. Then, the Install program displays a message dialog box indicating that installation is complete and that you must restart Windows.

3. Select the OK button on the message box.

4. Select the File Exit Windows command from the Program Manager and select the OK button to return to the DOS prompt.

5. Start Windows 3.0 again by typing **win** and pressing ⏎Enter at the C:\> prompt.

   This time when you start Windows 3.0, the ATM program icon appears briefly in the lower left corner of the screen.

After installing ATM, you can change various program options from the ATM Control Panel (consult the Adobe Type Manager User Guide included in the 1-2-3 for Windows documentation for details).

To open the ATM Control Panel, follow these steps:

A

1. Select the Main group window in the Program Manager.

   If you cannot see the ATM Control Panel program icon, click the Maximize button or use the scroll bars to scroll the window until you can see this icon.

2. Open the ATM Control Panel by double-clicking the ATM Control Panel program icon or by selecting the icon and pressing ⏎Enter.

You can use the options in the ATM Control Panel dialog box to turn on and off ATM, change the size of the font cache, or install new fonts.

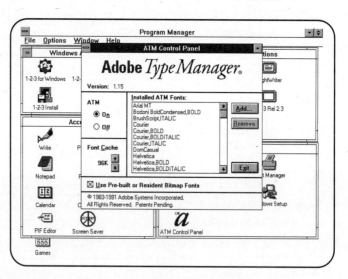

3. After making your changes to ATM, select the Exit command button to close the ATM Control Panel and return to the Program Manager.

Changing the 1-2-3 International Options

With International Options, you can change the country and the sort order that 1-2-3 for Windows follows. For example, the first three options listed in the Choose Country and Sort Order dialog box are as follows:

Option	Description
US Numbers First	Numbers are sorted before letters.
US Numbers Last	Letters are sorted before numbers.
US ASCII	Characters are sorted according to the ASCII table.

Suppose, for example, that you have four entries:

123 Main Street

Adam's Rib Plaza

4 Market Place

ADAM'S RIB PLAZA

With the US Numbers First option selected (this is the default used when you install 1-2-3), sorting the four entries in ascending order results in the following:

123 Main Street

4 Market Place

Adam's Rib Plaza

ADAM'S RIB PLAZA

Sorting the four entries with the US Numbers Last option selected results in the following:

Adam's Rib Plaza

ADAM'S RIB PLAZA

123 Main Street

4 Market Place

In an ASCII table, each character is assigned a numeric value. Numbers have lower numeric values than letters. Uppercase letters have a lower numeric value than lowercase letters. Sorting the entries with the US ASCII option selected, therefore, results in the following order:

A

505

A

123 Main Street

4 Market Place

ADAM'S RIB PLAZA

Adam's Rib Plaza

To change the collating order and select a new country in the 1-2-3 Install program, follow these steps:

1. Open the Program Manager window in Windows 3.0.

2. Double-click the 1-2-3 Install program icon, or select it and press ⏎Enter.

3. Select the OK button in the Welcome to Install dialog box.

4. Click the Choose international options button in the Main Menu dialog box.

The Choose Country and Sort Order dialog box appears.

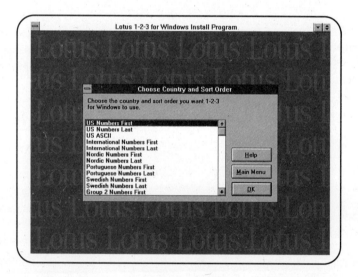

5. Select the country and sort order option you want to use in the list box.

   You may have to scroll the list of options if the one you want to use is not already visible in the list box.

6. Select the OK button.

7. Select the Exit Install command button in the Main Menu dialog box to return to the Program Manager.

Index

X-Z

Teach Yourself
With QuickStarts From Que!

The ideal tutorials for beginners, Que's QuickStart books use graphic illustrations and step-by-step instructions to get you up and running fast. Packed with examples, QuickStarts are the perfect beginner's guides to your favorite software applications.

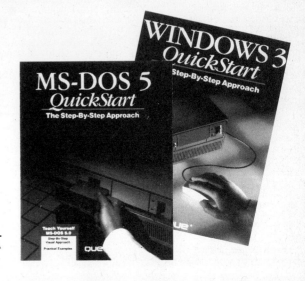

To Order, Call:
(800) 428-5331 OR (317) 573-2510

Find It Fast With Que's Quick References!

Que's Quick References are the compact, easy-to-use guides to essential application information. Written for all users, Quick References include vital command information under easy-to-find alphabetical listings. Quick References are a must for anyone who needs command information fast!

Complete Coverage From A To Z!

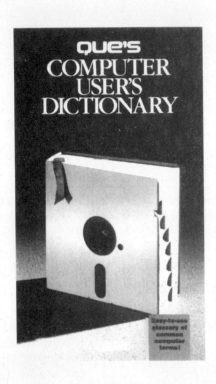

Que's Computer User's Dictionary
Que Development Group

This compact, practical reference contains hundreds of definitions, explanations, examples, and illustrations on topics from programming to desktop publishing. You can master the "language" of computers and learn how to make your personal computers more efficient and more powerful. Filled with tips and cautions, *Que's Computer User's Dictionary* is the perfect resource for anyone who uses a computer.

IBM, Macintosh, Apple, & Programming

Order #1086   **$10.95 USA**

0-88022-540-8, 500 pp., 4 3/4 x 8

The Ultimate Glossary Of Computer Terms— Over 200,000 In Print!

"Dictionary indeed. This whammer is a mini-encyclopedia...an absolute joy to use...a must for your computer library...."

Southwest Computer & Business Equipment Review

To Order, Call:
(800) 428-5331 OR (317) 573-2510

Free Catalog!

Mail us this registration form today, and we'll send you a free catalog featuring Que's complete line of best-selling books.

Name of Book _____

Name _____

Title _____

Phone (___) _____

Company _____

Address _____

City _____

State _____ ZIP _____

Please check the appropriate answers:

1. Where did you buy your Que book?
   - ☐ Bookstore (name: _____)
   - ☐ Computer store (name: _____)
   - ☐ Catalog (name: _____)
   - ☐ Direct from Que
   - ☐ Other: _____

2. How many computer books do you buy a year?
   - ☐ 1 or less
   - ☐ 2-5
   - ☐ 6-10
   - ☐ More than 10

3. How many Que books do you own?
   - ☐ 1
   - ☐ 2-5
   - ☐ 6-10
   - ☐ More than 10

4. How long have you been using this software?
   - ☐ Less than 6 months
   - ☐ 6 months to 1 year
   - ☐ 1-3 years
   - ☐ More than 3 years

5. What influenced your purchase of this Que book?
   - ☐ Personal recommendation
   - ☐ Advertisement
   - ☐ In-store display
   - ☐ Price
   - ☐ Que catalog
   - ☐ Que mailing
   - ☐ Que's reputation
   - ☐ Other: _____

6. How would you rate the overall content of the book?
   - ☐ Very good
   - ☐ Good
   - ☐ Satisfactory
   - ☐ Poor

7. What do you like *best* about this Que book?
   _____
   _____

8. What do you like *least* about this Que book?
   _____
   _____

9. Did you buy this book with your personal funds?
   - ☐ Yes   ☐ No

10. Please feel free to list any other comments you may have about this Que book.
    _____
    _____
    _____

que

Order Your Que Books Today!

Name _____

Title _____

Company _____

City _____

State _____ ZIP _____

Phone No. (___) _____

Method of Payment:

Check ☐   (Please enclose in envelope.)

Charge My: VISA ☐   MasterCard ☐

American Express ☐

Charge # _____

Expiration Date _____

Order No.	Title	Qty.	Price	Total

You can **FAX** your order to **1-317-573-2583**. Or call **1-800-428-5331, ext. ORDR** to order direct.
Please add $2.50 per title for shipping and handling.

Subtotal _____

Shipping & Handling _____

Total _____

que

BUSINESS REPLY MAIL

First Class Permit No. 9918   Indianapolis, IN

Postage will be paid by addressee

que®

11711 N. College
Carmel, IN 46032

BUSINESS REPLY MAIL

First Class Permit No. 9918   Indianapolis, IN

Postage will be paid by addressee

que®

11711 N. College
Carmel, IN 46032